Classroom Applications of Educational Measurement

Third Edition

Albert Oosterhof
Florida State University

Merrill
Prentice Hall

Upper Saddle River, New Jersey
Columbus, Ohio

Library of Congress Cataloging-in-Publication Data

Oosterhof, Albert
  Classroom applications of educational measurement / Albert Oosterhof.--3rd ed.
    p. cm.
  Includes bibliographical references and index.
  ISBN 0-13-520388-0
  1. Educational tests and measurements.   2. Examinations–Design and construction.
3. Examinations—Validity. I. Title.
  LB3051 .O57 2001
  371.26′1–dc21   00-055899

Vice President and Publisher: Jeffery W. Johnston
Executive Editor: Kevin Davis
Editorial Assistant: Christina M. Kalisch
Production Editor: Mary M. Irvin
Design Coordinator: Diane C. Lorenzo
Production Coordination and Text Design: York Production Services
Cover Design: Jeff Vanik
Cover Photo: JAM Photography
Production Manager: Laura Messerly
Director of Marketing: Kevin Flanagan
Marketing Manager: Amy June
Marketing Services Manager: Krista Groshong

This book was set in Garamond by York Graphic Services, Inc. and was printed and bound by R. R. Donnelley & Sons Company. The cover was printed by Phoenix Color Corp.

10 9 8 7 6 5 4 3 2 1
ISBN: 0-13-520388-0

For Darlene

Preface

Classroom Applications of Educational Measurement, Third Edition, is written for prospective and practicing teachers, and is designed for use as the primary text in introductory measurement courses.

This book includes but goes beyond the traditional coverage of measurement concepts. For example, four chapters are devoted to the development and use of performance assessments portfolios and informal observations and questions. Additional chapters describe how to plan and implement an overall assessment strategy, how to help students learn to take tests, and ways for using computers to facilitate assessment.

This book actively engages the reader and emphasizes the *application* of educational measurement in the classroom. Take time to page through this book to find numerous embedded queries where readers immediately apply what they are learning. To help engage the reader, the introduction to each chapter builds on familiar experiences in order to explain the relevance of concepts about to be addressed. Although the book is theoretically based, the focus is on specific implications of measurement concepts for the classroom and other instructional environments.

The book is organized into five parts. Part One introduces fundamental concepts such as validity, reliability, and criterion- and norm-referenced interpretations. A careful distinction is drawn between students' internal knowledge and the outward behaviors upon which all assessments must be based. Readers of this book learn how to distinguish between types of declarative and procedural knowledge, and how to select appropriate tasks for measurement of these distinct knowledge types. These foundational topics are introduced in Part One, and then consistently and visibly applied throughout the remainder of the book.

Part Two describes how to develop and administer written tests. Separate chapters discuss advantages and limitations of the short-answer, essay, multiple-choice, and alternate-choice formats. Checklists summarize characteristics essential to each format. Readers immediately *apply* what they are learning by finding and fixing problems within example test items rather than simply reading about qualities one should incorporate into test items.

Part Three describes alternative assessment techniques. Even though most formative evaluations in the classroom are based on informal questioning and observation, many measurement books only allude to these informal assessments. This book devotes a chapter to these assessments, using experiences common to all of us to identify their important characteristics and establish guidelines. Two chapters are devoted to performance assessments. The first addresses the characteristic of performance assessments and describes scoring options. The next chapter illustrates several performance assessments, describing how one first establishes the capability to be assessed, then selects an appropriate performance to observe, and finally designs a plan for scoring students' responses. The chapter on portfolios describes how to organize, score, and use portfolios.

Chapters in Part Four address topics that evolve from the use of measurement in the classroom. Four questions that can be used to guide the student assessment process are established. A separate chapter describes how to help students take tests. The last chapter in this section helps readers become familiar with some of the significant roles computers are beginning to play within testing.

Part Five concludes the book with a discussion of standardized tests. These chapters describe the types of tests used in schools and show how to interpret the scores most commonly used to report student performance. A unique feature of this book is a chapter that shows readers how to *evaluate* common uses of standardized tests that affect teachers, including the grouping of students, selection of students to be placed in special education, evaluating teachers and schools, and certifying teachers.

ACKNOWLEDGMENTS

I remain deeply indebted to the students, teachers, and mentors whose shared experiences have preceded the writing of this book. You will find their ideas and insights incorporated through this text. I am grateful for the thoughtful and useful suggestions provided by individuals who reviewed the third edition of this book: Susan Brookhart, Duquesne University; Stephanie Cortez, Northern Kentucky University; Frederick E. Kirschner, University of Nevada, Las Vegas; Jim Flaitz, University of Southwestern Louisiana; Carl Huberty, University of Georgia; George Maycock, Applachian State University; Stephanie Salzman, Idaho State University; Hoi K. Suen, Penn State University. The generous assistance of Kevin Davis, executive editor, and the editorial staff at Merrill/Prentice Hall are gratefully acknowledged.

Albert Oosterhof

Brief Contents

Contents

PART ONE

Foundation

CHAPTER 1

Measurement, Assessment, and Evaluation

Think for a moment of the number of tests you have taken since you entered school. If you averaged only 30 minutes of exams and quizzes per week within each of the basic subject areas, by the time you completed high school you had already answered over 1000 hours of written tests. That amounts to 40 solid 24-hour days. This does not include tests you completed in college. Nor does it include the thousands of nonwritten assessments, ranging from how you held your pencil to how you conducted a science experiment. It does not include the hundreds of papers and projects you completed, nor the notebooks or portfolios you prepared. It is estimated that more than 25% of a teacher's time is devoted to developing and using classroom assessments.

We are constantly being assessed, and we are constantly assessing others, not only in classroom settings, but also in everyday life. We assess what others say to us, their facial expressions, their choice of words, and their attitudes. We evaluate their reactions to what we say and do. We often study who and what are around us to decide what to do or where to go.

This common experience with tests and other assessments is essential to working with the material presented in this book. For example, you know that some written exams are better than others; we will use this knowledge when we try to isolate qualities that create better tests. You are aware of specific problems that occur in tests, such as questions that are ambiguous and content that does not correspond to material covered in the course. You know that essays you write, math problems you complete, and portfolios you prepare would be scored inconsistently if graded by different teachers. You also know of the many problems associated with the use of assessments. Teachers sometimes distribute results long after a test is administered; results may be reported without explanations of areas that caused difficulty, and teachers often move on to subsequent instruction before addressing difficulties identified in tests.

We know that teachers do and have to depend on informal assessments, such as casual observations and oral questions. Some teachers are more effective than others in their use of informal assessments and have a knack for knowing what is going on. Some teachers retain their initial impressions about students, whereas others are more sensitive to changes in students or errors in initial perceptions. Some teachers effectively use informal assessments to guide students' learning; other teachers seem more oblivious to what students are learning. Our common experiences with all these situations will be invaluable as we present procedures for developing written tests, preparing performance assessments, asking oral questions, and observing what students do.

SIGNIFICANCE OF MEASUREMENT

Dictionaries list a number of related definitions for the verb *measure*. The definitions most useful to our discussion include determining the characteristics of something, regulating through the use of a standard, and making comparisons to a reference such as the performance of others.

Measurement is essential in virtually every discipline. In the physical sciences, measurement is used to determine characteristics of various substances or to ascertain when a material has achieved a particular property. In engineering, such qualities as loads, torque, friction, and thermal characteristics are constantly measured. In sports, measurements are used for making decisions, such as calling a strike in baseball, designating a first down in football, or calling a personal foul in basketball. Measurement is used in politics to anticipate the outcome of an election or to evaluate another government's reaction to a policy decision. Measurement is used in the performing arts when the director selects an actor for a particular role and when critics review the performance on opening night. Business relies on data to determine the effectiveness of production techniques and to evaluate the impact of advertising.

Measurement is also critical to learning. Every theory of learning assumes the presence of feedback. Measurement, whether it originates from the teacher or the student, is a prerequisite to this feedback. Without good assessments, we cannot know whether effective learning has occurred.

In all disciplines, measurement is continuous. This is certainly true in scientific research, sports, the arts, business, and education. In each area, informal but deliberate observations are always taking place. In addition to continuous measures, planned formal observations must be used. The scientist must incorporate carefully developed measurements at selected points during and at the end of an experiment. A football coach must schedule times to analyze the progress of the team, for example, by viewing films after a game.

Teachers must also periodically develop and administer tests and other formal observations. Unlike ongoing informal observations, formal assessments are not spontaneous; they are deliberately scheduled and fully developed in advance. If teachers were to depend only on impromptu observations, the students' mastery of many crucial skills would go unexamined. The results of formal observations often guide the nature of subsequent, more frequent informal observations. Formal and informal assessments are both critical and are complementary.

Perhaps unfortunately, measurement skills are not intuitive within any discipline, and experience by itself is insufficient for ensuring these measurement skills. For instance, watching the heavens at night does not provide the measurement skills essential to being an astronomer, even though that experience provides an important base from which to learn these skills. Driving a car does not provide the skills needed by traffic-control engineers to measure traffic flow, although it provides insights essential to interpreting these measures. Your experience with classroom assessments provides a context essential to learning the concepts discussed in this book, although you will find that many of the measurement concepts introduced are new. The application of measurement, particularly in the classroom, is dynamic and highly complex. Your experience, therefore, provides not only the context for learning measurement concepts, but also a basis for adapting, applying, and evaluating the educational measurement concepts we discuss here.

DISTINCTION AMONG MEASUREMENT, ASSESSMENT, AND EVALUATION

The terms *measurement, assessment,* and *evaluation* are often used interchangeably in education. For our discussion, it will be useful to maintain a distinction, although the differences among these terms are not absolute.

The distinction between measurement and evaluation is the easiest to establish. In education, measurement is concerned with establishing characteristics of individuals or groups of individuals, usually students. Measurement does not associate value with what we see. Evaluation, however, combines our measures with other information to establish the desirability and importance of what we have observed. Evaluation is the outcome of measurement after value has been added. Here are some contrasts between measurement and evaluation:

Measurement: Performance on a test indicates that a student is unable to spell number words lower than one hundred.

Evaluation: This performance is of significant concern, because spelling number words is a prerequisite to the next unit, on writing checks.

Measurement: A teacher observes a student speaking in class without first raising her hand.

Evaluation: This behavior is encouraging because that student has never participated in class discussion.

Measurement: In education, we observe that the terms *measurement* and *evaluation* are often used interchangeably.

Evaluation: Equating measurement and evaluation is undesirable because it confuses issues discussed later in this book.

The linkage of evaluation to measurement sometimes makes it difficult to discuss measurement and evaluation separately. For example, erroneous measures lead to inappropriate evaluations. In addition, establishing what should be measured is determined by the values we expect to attach to our observations. This book focuses more on classroom applications of educational measurement than on evaluation. It will provide ideas for determining what should be measured and how to interpret student performance on these measures. Evaluation is important; however, your professional expertise in your content area is fundamental in establishing what to measure and determining the significance of what you observe. Evaluations also depend on the context of your educational measures and cannot be discussed fully in the absence of that context.

The distinction between measurement and assessment is less concise. Assessment is often used as a stylistic alternative to measurement. Some sentences sound better if you use the word *assessment* rather than *measurement*. Sometimes, measurement is perceived as quantitative, cold, and less desirable, whereas assessment is seen as qualitative and warm.

Let us clarify what is meant by measurement. Measurement is often described only in quantitative terms. Statements such as "Measurement is the process used to assign numbers to attributes or characteristics of persons" are fairly common. These statements fit well with notions of validity and reliability that are limited to statistical conceptualizations. Such statements are also consistent with the view that test scores are always numbers.

On the other hand, measurement is often given a broader meaning. Dictionary definitions such as those noted earlier do not limit measurement to quantification. Likewise, people who describe themselves as measurement specialists do more than merely associate numbers with attributes. The same can be said about books with "educational measurement" in their titles. Even the term *test score* is not necessarily a number. Messick (1989a) put it this way:

> The term "test score" is used generically here in its broadest sense to mean any observed consistency, not just on tests as ordinarily conceived but also on any means of observing or documenting consistent behaviors or attributes. This would include, for instance, any coding or summarization of observed consistencies on performance tests, questionnaires, observation procedures, or other assessment devices. This general usage also subsumes qualitative as well as quantitative summaries and applies, for example, to protocols, clinical interpretations, and computerized verbal score reports. (p. 5)

In our discussion, *educational measurement* will refer to the process of determining a quantitative or qualitative attribute of an individual or group of individuals that is of academic relevance. *Test* will refer to the vehicle used to observe that attribute, such as a written test, an observation, or an oral question. *Test score* will refer to an indication of what was observed through the test.

Assessment generally has broader connotations than does measurement. Were measurements limited to assigning numbers to attributes, assessment might be thought of as combining qualitative and quantitative attributes. Or, if measurements were limited to paper-and-pencil tests, assessment might be said to involve all techniques including observations and oral questions. In our discussion, however, measurement, not assessment, will be used to represent all these activities.

Airasian (1997) defines assessment as the "collection, synthesis, and interpretation of information to aid the teacher in decision making" (p. 4). This definition is broader than what we have defined as measurement. It is, however, unclear at what point assessment supersedes measurement. For instance, does determining a quantitative or qualitative attribute of an individual include only the collection of information, or does it include the synthesis of information, or, possibly, naming the characteristic being described? If the validation of test scores is concerned with how the scores are to be interpreted and used, then the meaning of measurement might be as broad as that of assessment.

As with many synonyms, measurement and assessment have similar meanings, yet they also have subtle differences. The subtleties are often useful, but not always applied consistently. In our discussion, assessment will be viewed as having broader connotations than measurement. Assessment will refer to a related series of measures used to determine a complex attribute of an individual or group of individuals. Portfolios, which include planned collections of student work, are an example of an assessment. Performance assessments, in which student performance on a complex task is observed, are assessments. A series of related but informal observations used to determine complex attributes of one student or a group of students is also an assessment. Each of these types of assessments involves collecting, synthesizing, and labeling information. At what point a measurement becomes an assessment, however, remains undefined.

DISTINCTION BETWEEN FORMAL AND INFORMAL ASSESSMENTS

The basic distinction between formal and informal assessments lies in their spontaneity. Formal assessments are devised in advance, whereas informal assessments happen on the spur of the moment.

Formal assessments include final exams, unit tests and quizzes, graded homework, critiques of prepared speeches, and judgments of performances in science labs. Formal assessments also include tryouts for athletic teams and roles in a school play. Details of how each of these assessments will be implemented are established prior to their occurrence.

Informal assessments, although more numerous, are less obvious. Informal assessments occur when a teacher listens to a student's questions or watches her facial expression to determine whether she understands the concept being taught. Informal assessments occur when a teacher arrives at first-day impressions of a student's ability by watching where he sits, looking at what he wears, and listening to what he says. Informal assessments include talking through a math problem to find out why the student gave a wrong answer and asking questions while teaching a concept to determine whether students are learning what is being taught.

Because formal assessments are devised in advance and informal assessments are spontaneous, they differ in a number of ways. A basic difference is that informal assessments can and do occur while instruction is being delivered, whereas formal assessments often require a pause in instruction. As a result, informal assessments can be particularly effective at redirecting instruction as it occurs. On the other hand, informal assessments are more likely to be unsystematic and more often lead to faulty conclusions about student performance.

Formal assessments are used when more controlled measures are required, whereas informal assessments are used when more frequent and responsive measures are needed. Because of their respective advantages and limitations, the use of formal versus informal assessment depends to a large extent on the role assessment is to play in the classroom.

ROLES OF ASSESSMENT IN THE CLASSROOM

Bloom, Hastings, and Madaus (1981) proposed that assessment is used to facilitate formative, summative, and diagnostic evaluations. We will add a fourth role: preliminary evaluations.

Preliminary evaluations occur during the first days of school and provide a basis for expectations throughout the school year. They are obtained mainly through a teacher's spontaneous informal observations and oral questions, and are concerned with students' skills, attitudes, and physical characteristics. These evaluations are basically the same as those you establish whenever you meet new people. They happen naturally, and they are essential to guiding our interactions with others and with students.

Formative evaluations occur during instruction. They establish whether students have achieved sufficient mastery of skills and whether further instruction in these skills is appropriate. Formative evaluations are also concerned with the attitudes students are developing. The purpose of formative evaluations is to determine what adjustments to instruction should be made. Formative evaluations are based primarily on continuous informal assessments, such as listening to what students say, using oral questions to probe comprehension, and watching students' facial expressions and other behaviors. Formative evaluations are also based on formally developed assessments such as quizzes, seatwork, and homework. Most assessments that occur in the classroom lead to formative evaluations.

Summative evaluations occur at the conclusion of instruction, such as at the end of a unit or the end of the year. Summative evaluations are used to certify student achievement and assign end-of-term grades. They serve as the basis for promoting and sometimes for grouping students. Summative evaluations also help determine whether teaching procedures should be changed before the next school year. Unlike in formative evaluations, the role that assessment plays within summative evaluations is not to establish student proficiency with each skill, but instead to provide an overview of achievement across a number of skills. Each skill might be measured by just one test item, not enough to establish with confidence proficiency with individual skills. Often, only a sampling of skills is tested. Summative evaluations are based on formal assessments.

Diagnostic evaluations occur before or, more typically, during instruction. Diagnostic evaluations are concerned with skills and other characteristics that are prerequisite to the current instruction or that enable the achievement of instructional objectives.

During instruction, diagnostic evaluations are used to establish underlying causes for a student's failing to learn a skill. When used before instruction, diagnostic evaluations try to anticipate conditions that will negatively affect learning. In both cases, the role of measurement is to assess a student's performance in specific prerequisite skills not typically taught in the present classroom setting. Diagnostic evaluations are based mostly on informal assessments, although formal measures, such as standardized tests, are sometimes used.

Figure 1.1 illustrates the relationship among the four evaluative roles of classroom assessment. Preliminary evaluations feed into formative evaluations. Formative evaluations occur during instruction and are based on frequent assessments. Diagnostic evaluations are concerned with problems that might be or, more typically, already are preventing students from learning. Summative evaluations follow instruction.

As indicated in Figure 1.1, preliminary, formative, and diagnostic evaluations depend mostly although not entirely on informal assessments. These evaluations require measures of student performance that are highly responsive to immediate situations. They require assessments that can occur without a pause in instruction. Summative evaluations, in contrast, require the more controlled measures provided by formal assessments. Summative evaluations do not depend on the spontaneous and responsive characteristics of informal assessments.

MAXIMUM VERSUS TYPICAL PERFORMANCE

Maximum performance and typical performance refer to whether students are performing at their best or at their normal level. Formal assessments such as written tests, structured performance assessments, and graded homework tend to encourage maximum performance. These assessments establish a student's ability to perform when motivated, but the performance does not necessarily generalize to other settings. Determining that a student can distinguish between statements of fact and opinion on a test, for instance, does not indicate the student will apply this skill when reading newspapers. Likewise, determining that a student has achieved knowledge in history, mathematics, or reading does not mean that she will use these skills beyond the classroom.

Typical performance is more concerned with attitudes than with academic skills. Attitudes influence students' interest in applying what they learn as well as in learning it in the first place. Typical performance is usually measured by informal assessments, particularly observation. Observations or other measures have to be unobtrusive to assess typical performance.

Whether teachers should develop and administer measures of typical performance pertinent to the content they are teaching is unclear. Certainly, values are important and can be taught. The way in which a teacher instructs affects the attitudes students develop about a subject. Whether a teacher should measure these attitudes with the intent of modifying student behavior can be argued both ways. For instance, consider the following questions:

■ Should a study of world religions include measures of students' beliefs or interests in religion?

Preliminary Evaluations

Purpose
Provide a quick but temporary determination of students' characteristics

When it occurs
During the first 10 days of school

Techniques used
Mostly informal observations and questions

Diagnostic Evaluations

Purpose
Identify problems that will prevent or are preventing a student from learning

When it occurs
When difficulties in learning new knowledge are anticipated; or more typically, after difficulties in learning have been observed

Techniques used
Typically informal observations and questions; sometimes formal assessments such as a teacher's written test or a standardized test

Formative Evaluations

Purpose
Determine what students have learned in order to plan instruction

When it occurs
Continuously, during instruction

Techniques used
Mostly informal observations and questions; also, written and oral quizzes, classroom activities and performance assessments, homework, and portfolios

Summative Evaluations

Purpose
Certify what students have learned in order to assign grades, promote students, and refine instruction for next year

When it occurs
At the conclusion of a unit of instruction

Techniques used
Mostly formal assessments, including written tests, performance assessments, projects, and portfolios

Figure 1.1
Four roles of classroom assessment

- Should a study of political history include measures of political preferences or interests in politics?

- Is it appropriate for a teacher of meteorology to measure students' attitudes toward meteorology or interest in weather systems?

Because we often are uncertain whether measuring typical performance is appropriate, particularly if the intent is to modify undesired attitudes, we might answer in the affirmative to all, part, or possibly none of these questions.

Typical performance can be measured only to a degree. To be valid, observations of typical performance may need to be conducted without students' being aware that they are being assessed. Often, obtaining unobtrusive measures of attitude is not possible, and, as a result, students fake typical responses.

SUMMARY

It is quite appropriate to examine closely the issues related to educational measurement. Measurement is germane to everything that goes on in the classroom. Students do not learn effectively unless they receive feedback, which is obtained through educational measures. Teachers similarly cannot be effective without information gained through measurement of student performance.

Each of us has already had an extensive amount of experience with educational measures, gained from years of involvement with written tests and other assessments. Our experience with measurement is also obtained through informal interactions with others. We can recognize the considerable differences in the quality of assessments and in the effectiveness with which they are used. This experience will be invaluable as we discuss the development and use of classroom assessments.

Several terms were defined in this chapter. *Educational measurement* refers to the process of determining a quantitative or qualitative attribute of an individual or group that is of academic relevance. *Assessment* refers to a related series of measures used to determine a complex attribute of an individual or group. A *test* is any vehicle used to observe that attribute. A *test score* is an indication of what is observed through the test and can be quantitative or qualitative in nature. *Evaluation* combines measures and assessments with other information to establish the desirability and importance of what we have observed.

Four types of evaluation have been identified. Preliminary evaluations occur during the first two weeks of school and provide a quick determination of students' characteristics. Formative evaluations occur continuously during instruction to determine what students are learning and to enable instruction to be adjusted accordingly. Diagnostic evaluations identify problems that are preventing students from learning. Summative evaluations occur at the conclusion of a unit of instruction and are used for tasks such as certifying what students have learned, assigning grades, and refining instruction for the next year. Preliminary, formative, and diagnostic evaluations rely more heavily on informal assessments. Summative evaluations involve formal assessments.

In the remaining chapters of Part 1, we will look first at how one provides a context to interpret student performance. We will focus on criterion-referenced and norm-referenced interpretations. Chapters 3 through 5 then address three related topics that represent the most critical issues in educational measurement. The first concerns the establishment of measurable objectives. As you realize, a person's knowledge is internal to the mind and is invisible. A major task in educational measurement is deciding what outward behaviors or *performance* will be used to indicate the presence of students' internal knowledge or *capabilities*. Chapter 4 discusses validity. There is no issue in measurement as fundamental as validity. Validity is the degree to which a test measures what it is supposed to measure. If a test lacks validity, it is of no use. The validity of a test is strongly influenced by the performances we use to represent students' internal capabilities. Validity relates also to the interpretation *and* uses of test scores, and to the consequences of interpreting and using these scores. Chapter 5 is concerned with the consistency of test scores. We will show that validity is heavily influenced by reliability.

Parts 2 and 3 describe how to develop various kinds of measures. In Part 2, we focus on written tests, including the familiar short-answer, essay, and multiple-choice formats. Part 3 discusses observations, oral questions, performance assessments, and portfolios. Part 4 then looks at the assessment process in the classroom. We will discuss the development of an assessment strategy, the teaching of test-taking skills, the use of computers in classroom assessment, and the reporting of student performance through grades and other procedures. Part 5 is concerned with standardized tests. We will look at the characteristics of standardized tests and types of scores commonly used to report performance on these tests. Of particular importance, we will evaluate uses of these tests that directly affect teachers and their classrooms.

CHAPTER 2

Criterion- and Norm-Referenced Interpretations

A teacher hands back your test. All that is written on it is a number. You got a 37. What is the first question you are probably going to ask? Most likely it will be something like, "What does 37 mean?" or, "Is this a high score or a low score?" Basically, you need a frame of reference to interpret that score. Any measure of performance needs a reference in order to be interpreted.

Any of several references can be used for interpreting performance. You probably thought of at least one of these references when you were pondering how to interpret the score of 37. Some examples of references are

If I got 37, how did others do?

Is 37 high or low with respect to what I can do?

Does 37 mean I have improved?

What does 37 mean I can and cannot do?

Each question is asking for a frame of reference. Although a frame of reference is essential to interpreting test performance, we will observe that some frames of reference are more useful than others. This chapter emphasizes criterion-referenced and norm-referenced interpretations of performance, which are typically the two most useful references in the classroom. However, we will also review the characteristics of two other widely used frames of reference.

This chapter helps you achieve four skills:

■ Identify frames of reference that help interpret student performance

■ Recognize the meaning of criterion-referenced and norm-referenced interpretations

■ Recognize when criterion-referenced and norm-referenced interpretations are preferable

■ Identify qualities desired in criterion-referenced and norm-referenced tests

FRAMES OF REFERENCE FOR INTERPRETING PERFORMANCE

We will consider four approaches to interpreting student performance:

Ability-referenced, in which a student's performance is interpreted in light of that student's maximum possible performance

Growth-referenced, in which performance is compared with the student's prior performance

Norm-referenced, in which interpretation is provided by comparing the student's performance with the performance of others or with the typical performance for that student

Criterion-referenced, in which meaning is provided by describing what the student can and cannot do

Table 2.1 summarizes characteristics of these four frames of reference.

Ability-Referenced Interpretations

Ability-referenced interpretations are a comparison of a student's performance to that student's potential performance. Statements such as, "That's about all this student can do" or, "This student can do better if given more time" are examples of ability-referenced interpretations.

The key to using ability as the frame of reference is having a good estimate of the student's maximum possible performance. Therein lies the problem. Teachers usually have only tentative, broad ideas of what each student can do. Although previous work and information from other teachers provide ideas about a student's ability, these estimates actually reflect what the student was observed doing rather than the upper limit of what the student is capable of.

Standardized aptitude tests also provide teachers with estimates of students' ability, but these estimates are general and of limited use in interpreting a student's performance. Furthermore, standardized tests typically indicate which students will achieve the most rather than how much a particular student can achieve. As with any estimate of ability, scores on aptitude tests are usually confounded by other variables, such as student background, prior achievement, and motivation.

Perhaps the greatest limitation of ability estimates is that we usually do not know precisely which abilities are prerequisite to the particular skills we are trying to teach. Because it is so difficult to obtain a good estimate of students' maximum possible performance, ability usually provides a weak frame of reference for interpreting student performance.

Table 2.1
Four references commonly used for interpreting classroom assessments

	Interpretation Provided by This Reference	Condition That Must Be Present for This Reference To Be Useful
Ability-referenced	How are students performing relative to what they are capable of doing?	Requires good measures of what students are capable of doing; their maximum possible performance
Growth-referenced	How much have students changed or improved relative to what they were doing earlier?	Requires pre- and post-measures of performance that are highly reliable
Norm-referenced	How well are students doing with respect to what is typical or reasonable?	To whom students are being compared must be clearly understood
Criterion-referenced	What can students do and not do?	Content domain that was assessed must be well defined

Growth-Referenced Interpretations

Growth-referenced interpretations compare a student's present skills to prior performances. This is a natural frame of reference in the classroom, since improvement in skills is highly relevant.

Growth of course implies change over time, that is, a change in performance between earlier and later measures of student performance. For the measure of growth to be reliable, both the earlier and present measures must individually be reliable. If the earlier measure is simply a teacher's present recollection of each student's earlier performance, this "measure" of earlier achievement will likely have very low reliability, and so will the growth-referenced interpretations.

Portfolio systems used by many teachers help get around this problem. They typically provide actual samples of earlier work to which present performance can be compared. As long as measures of the same skills can be obtained from the earlier and present work, and both work samples are reliably scored, then growth-reference interpretations can be meaningful. In fact, the reliable measure of growth is one of the potential strengths of portfolio systems.

Growth-referenced interpretations are often combined with what we later identify as norm-referenced interpretations. Norm-referenced interpretations involve the comparison of a student's performance to that of others. Statements such as, "This student has improved more than others" or, "This is one of the best classes I have had in terms of how much students have learned" combine growth- and norm-referenced interpretations. Interestingly, the reliability of interpretations that combine growth and norm references becomes very low as the correlation between how students perform on the earlier and present measure becomes high. This is because reliable differences observed on the present measure are subtracted out if the same relative differences are observed on the earlier measure.[1]

Both growth-referenced and ability-referenced interpretations of student performance tend to have significant problems, and when used should be supplemented by norm-referenced and criterion-referenced interpretations. For higher-impact settings such as in summative evaluations, only norm-referenced and criterion-referenced interpretations generally should be used.

Norm-Referenced and Criterion-Referenced Interpretations

Norm-referenced interpretations involve comparing the student's present performance to a range of previously observed performances, usually the performances of other students. We often make comparisons with other individuals or events to help interpret what we see. How well a student did on a test is often described in terms of how others in the class did. Similarly, measures such as how much it rained, how fast you were driving, and how you feel today are often interpreted through comparison with other similar events. It rained less than it usually does, I have never driven this fast, and so on. These are all norm-referenced interpretations.

For describing student performance, norm-referenced interpretations are limited in that they do not define what a student can and cannot do. However, they do help answer such questions as what is typical and what is reasonable.

Criterion-referenced interpretations, in contrast, involve comparing a student's performance to a well-defined content domain. Examples of content domains include the ability to locate a word in a dictionary; to associate famous composers of music with historical periods, such as baroque, classical, and romantic; or to solve an algebraic equation involving whole numbers and one unknown.

The key to making a criterion-referenced interpretation is having a well-defined domain. A criterion-referenced interpretation describes student performance within that domain. That is, a criterion-referenced interpretation indicates what a student can and cannot do with respect to the content domain. However, unlike norm-referenced interpretations, criterion-referenced interpretations do not answer questions of what is typical and what is reasonable.

Criterion-referenced and norm-referenced interpretations are generally the most useful frames of reference for describing student performance; hence our focus on these two references.

---

[1]Expressed as a formula, the reliability of growth-referenced scores becomes

$$r_{\text{growth}} = \frac{\dfrac{r_A + r_B}{2} - r_{AB}}{1 - r_{AB}}$$

where r_A and r_B are the reliability of scores on the earlier and present measures of students' achievement and r_{AB} is the correlation between scores on the earlier and present measures.

MEANING OF CRITERION-AND NORM-REFERENCED INTERPRETATIONS

Criterion-referenced means that a score is being interpreted in terms of the skills the test measures. To permit a criterion-referenced interpretation, the description of what is being measured does not necessarily have to be elaborate, but it must be concise. Indicating that a student can type 37 words per minute allows a criterion-referenced interpretation of an individual's performance. So does stating that a student can perform 12 chin-ups, list the 50 states, spell 2-digit numbers, or convert temperatures from the Fahrenheit to the Celsius scale. Each of these examples establishes a specific skill that a student can perform and, therefore, represents a criterion-referenced interpretation. Note that each of these illustrations of student performance can meaningfully be interpreted with no reference to how other students performed.

In contrast, a test is said to be norm-referenced if it compares a student's performance with the typical range of performances. Indicating that a student can type faster than 60% of the students completing a typing class represents a norm-referenced interpretation of performance, as does indicating that a student can do more chin-ups than 30% of other students the same age, can spell better than half the other students in the class, or is the best violinist in the orchestra. The group of people to whom the student is being compared is the norm group.

Note that in these illustrations of norm-referenced interpretations, the student's skill is described in general terms. Saying that a student is "the best violinist in the orchestra" indicates that the individual performs better than other violinists in the orchestra but does not describe the violinist's specific skills—what this violinist can and cannot do. Norm-referenced interpretations can be made using more general descriptions of the content domain than can criterion-referenced interpretations. Stated differently, content domains that cannot be well defined favor, or even require, norm-referenced as opposed to criterion-referenced interpretations.

Although norm-referenced interpretations can be made with more general descriptions of the content domain, they do require a well-defined norm group. A description of the violinist as the best in the orchestra provides meaningful information only if we have a clear understanding of which orchestra is being referenced.

Box 2.1   *Apply What You Are Learning*

Do each of the following allow a criterion-referenced or norm-referenced interpretation of performance?

1. Katherine won the 100-meter race.
2. Arnold ran one mile in 5 minutes, 12 seconds.
3. Walter scored near average on the final chemistry exam.
4. Carmen can separate alcohol from water through distillation.
5. In geometry, David cannot bisect an angle.
6. Heidi obtained the best score on the geometry test.

Answers can be found at the end of the chapter.

Both criterion-referenced and norm-referenced interpretations can be and usually are applied to a performance. For instance, we might observe that the student who types 37 words per minute is faster than 60% of the other students in the class. Both perspectives provide useful information.

It is possible for a test to be neither criterion-referenced nor norm-referenced. This condition is undesirable because without a good reference, a score lacks meaning. This point was illustrated at the opening of the chapter, when we observed that a score of 37 had no meaning when given without reference, such as what the test measured or how others did on the test. This fact is so obvious that few teachers would report a score in this manner without elaboration.

For less obvious reasons, however, many classroom tests lack both criterion-referenced and norm-referenced interpretations. This situation typically occurs when a teacher wants to use a criterion-referenced test but does not understand that a criterion-referenced interpretation requires a well-defined content domain. The following examples illustrate this point.

> Ellen scored 92% on an algebra exam. This performance cannot be given a criterion-referenced interpretation because the specific skills measured by the exam are not detailed. We do not know what Ellen can or cannot do. Nor is it possible to specify what instruction she should now receive. Scoring 92% may represent a high degree of competence if the exam measures difficult skills, but it probably represents low competence if the exam measures exceptionally easy skills. Converting scores to percentages does not in itself allow a criterion-referenced interpretation of a test. Ellen's performance cannot be norm-referenced either, unless comparison scores are also given.

> Natalie surpassed the criterion score of 80% and, therefore, passed the spelling test. Again, this performance cannot be given a criterion-referenced interpretation because the specific skills measured by the test are not described. Unless the types of words sampled by this test are known, we cannot tell whether scoring above 80% (or any other passing score) indicates a high or low proficiency in spelling. Establishing a passing score, sometimes called a criterion score, does not by itself allow for a criterion-referenced interpretation. We will see later that passing scores are applicable to both norm-referenced and criterion-referenced tests. Also, both norm-referenced and criterion-referenced interpretations can be given to test scores with or without specifying a passing score.

Criterion-referencing of tests began to gain popularity in the 1970s. This trend has been healthy because knowing what students can and cannot do is an important part of instruction. With the increased popularity of criterion-referencing, however, numerous, varying definitions have emerged, not all of which are appropriate. Nitko (1984) emphasized the importance of a well-defined domain of skills to making criterion-referenced interpretations. According to Nitko, the nature of a well-defined domain may be ordered or unordered. When a domain is ordered, indicating a student's position within the domain also indicates what that individual can and cannot do. Here are examples of well-defined, ordered domains:

■ A list of words ordered according to their spelling difficulty
■ A series of pictures depicting finger positions on piano keys ranging from an untrained position through progressively more appropriate finger positions
■ A series of math items ordered such that correctly answering each item (or a group of items) requires mastery of a skill more complex than the skill needed to master the preceding item in the series

In the first example, noting the most difficult word a student can spell identifies specific words the student can and cannot spell. Similarly, identifying the picture that most closely resembles a student's finger positions on piano keys indicates what the student must still learn. A similar interpretation can be given to a student's score on an ordered series of math items. In practice, domains tend not to represent perfect orders. For instance, a student may be able to spell some more difficult words and not some easier ones.

Nitko (1984) pointed out that a large number of important skills taught in schools represent unordered behavioral domains. The skills and, consequently, the test items that are included in a domain are clearly established (well defined), even though the skills cannot be ordered. Here are examples of well-defined, unordered domains:

- The addition of pairs of three-digit numbers that require regrouping
- Correctly lighting a Bunsen burner
- Locating words in a dictionary

These examples may require a student to perform a particular sequence of behaviors; however, measuring the student's proficiency with these skills would probably not pinpoint that individual's performance on a continuum within the domain. In contrast, if a student's mastery of the lighting of Bunsen burners required knowledge of gas burners whose complexity in lighting ranged from simple to complex, this would represent an ordered domain.

Nitko proposed various approaches to defining unordered domains. Two of them are to specify the stimulus and response attributes or to specify only the stimulus attributes of test items that belong in a domain. Another approach is to define a domain in terms of a common error made by students, for example, erroneously inverting the letters *ie* when spelling words.

Note that a passing score is not essential to a criterion-referenced interpretation of test performance. For either criterion-referenced or norm-referenced tests, however, a passing score may be administratively convenient and useful. For instance, tests used by colleges and employers to help select the best applicants are norm-referenced. Cutoff scores are commonly used with these tests. A teacher who uses a mastery learning strategy establishes a cutoff score to determine which students will be provided further instruction. Unless the test measures a well-defined domain, however, the presence of a cutoff score does not facilitate a criterion-referenced interpretation. Educators often mistakenly believe that a cutoff score, rather than the well-defined domain, allows for criterion-referenced interpretations.

Box 2.2   *Apply What You Are Learning*

Indicate whether each of the following allows a criterion-referenced interpretation, a norm-referenced interpretation, or neither.

1. Leroy obtained a score of 100.
2. Using a periodic table, Donna can name each of the elements.

3. Using graph paper, a ruler, and a protractor, Kristin can determine the sine, cosine, and tangent of angles.

4. Ray scored 90 on a history exam.

5. Using a map of the United States, Richard can show the location of the ten largest Civil War battles.

6. Suzanne passed the geography test.

7. David can select the specified number of objects when verbally given the numbers 1 through 12.

8. In terms of grade-point average, Lawrence graduated 194th among 210 students in his high school class.

9. Donna passed the oral portion of her Spanish final exam.

10. Henry knows more vocabulary words than 80% of his second-year German class.

Answers can be found at the end of the chapter.

We must emphasize that the usefulness of a test depends largely on how well the domain being measured is defined or how adequately the norm group to whom students are being compared is described. Not all classroom or standardized tests are equal regarding these important qualities. The best criterion-referenced tests determine within a specific domain exactly what each student can and cannot do. The best norm-referenced tests give a statement of a student's ability through comparison with a clearly defined and relevant group of other individuals. Many tests deviate from these ideal standards. Unfortunately, some classroom and standardized tests provide no reference at all from which to interpret their scores.

CHOOSING THE APPROPRIATE INTERPRETATION

The type of interpretation to use depends on the parameters available and the information needed from the results. Criterion-referenced interpretations are appropriate when content domains can be well defined and it is important to determine what students can and cannot do. Norm-referenced interpretations are appropriate when a relevant and well-defined norm group can be established and it is important to describe student performance in terms of what is typical or reasonable. As noted earlier, it is common to use both references, with one emphasized over the other based on the situation.

The type of evaluation often influences the reference used for the interpretation. For instance, assessments used for preliminary evaluations may occur in the absence of norms. In such a case, assessments should be criterion-referenced. On the other hand, measures used for summative evaluations may involve content domains too broad to be well defined. These measures then have to be norm-referenced. Let us examine the influence of type of evaluation on the selection of a frame of reference.

Interpretations for Preliminary Evaluations

Preliminary evaluations occur when you first meet students, usually within the first two weeks. Either norm- or criterion-referenced interpretations are emphasized, depending on circumstances.

When preliminary evaluations involve general or overall assessments of students' knowledge and attitudes, norm-referenced interpretations are required. These assessments of what students know or what their attitudes are involve domains too broad for criterion-referenced interpretations. As always when norm-referenced interpretations are used, it is important to identify your norm group. Are you comparing the new students with each other, with previous students when they were new, with previous students at the end of last year, or possibly with what you consider to be ideal students? Each reference may be appropriate, but it is important to recognize what the comparison group is.

Although norm-referenced interpretations are often thought to involve comparisons to others, a student may be her or his own norm group. Instead of establishing what is typical for a group of students, one is asking what is typical for one particular student. During preliminary evaluations, you often establish what is reasonable or typical for individual students. This norm becomes useful for interpreting later performance.[2]

Assessments leading to preliminary evaluations may be criterion-referenced instead of or as well as norm-referenced. Is a student a loner? Does he volunteer ideas or ask questions? Does she know the names for numbers? Does he know what is meant by electrolysis? Each of these can be a well-defined domain. Each is a domain that can be used to describe what a student can and cannot do (or in the case of attitudes, does or does not do). Each can also be norm-referenced when used to describe what is reasonable or typical.

Interpretations for Diagnostic Evaluations

Diagnostic evaluations are used to judge students' level of performance prior to instruction or to establish the source of the problem when students seem unable to achieve during instruction. Diagnostic evaluations are concerned with prerequisite or enabling skills.

Diagnostic evaluations usually require criterion-referenced interpretations because they involve knowing what a student can and cannot do. Thus prerequisite or enabling skills must be expressed as well-defined domains. However, it is often difficult to understand fully what the prerequisite skills are or to have the time to measure each of them. For this reason, diagnostic evaluations tend to be sporadic or constrained.

---

[2]A student's performance can be referenced to what he or she has done in the past. Is this norm-referenced or growth-referenced? Well, it depends. It is norm-referenced when you compare a student's performance with her or his range of previous performances. You are answering the question, "How does the present performance compare to what is typical for this student?" In contrast, the interpretation is growth-referenced if you are asking, "How much has this student improved or otherwise changed compared to a previous observation?" Growth-referenced interpretations often are problematic because of low reliability. Using norm- and criterion-referenced interpretations is generally better.

Although diagnostic evaluations always should emphasize criterion-referenced interpretations, they also may involve a norm reference, for instance, if you want to know whether a student's problem is typical. You may respond differently if the problem is common to most students rather than unique to a few students.

Interpretations for Formative Evaluations

Formative evaluations occur during instruction. Their purpose is to monitor learning in order to determine whether instruction should continue, should be modified, or should cease. Determining what students can and cannot do is central to formative evaluations. Criterion-referenced interpretations are required.

Most classroom assessments lead to formative evaluations. The majority of these assessments involve the teacher's informal observations and questions. To be criterion-referenced, these frequent assessments must involve well-defined domains. This process becomes a significant challenge for teachers—in terms of both difficulty and importance. During instruction, the teacher must always perceive instructional goals in terms of well-defined domains. The domains must allow the teacher to describe what students can and cannot do.

As with diagnostic evaluations, formative evaluations may also involve norm referencing. Comparison of student performance to that observed in previous classes or even the present class helps establish what is typical and reasonable. The emphasis with formative evaluations, however, should always be on criterion-referenced interpretations.

Interpretations for Summative Evaluations

Summative evaluations follow instruction and typically involve unit tests, midterm and final exams, and projects or other end-of-unit assignments. Summative evaluations usually use general or global content domains. Often, only a sample of specific content domains is assessed. Summative evaluations typically require norm-referenced interpretations.

Portfolios are being used increasingly for some academic subjects to accumulate samples of students' work. If these samples represent well-defined domains, criterion-referenced interpretations of these summative evaluations are possible. This kind of information is particularly useful for parents and other teachers because it describes what the student can do rather than simply indicating how the student compares with others.

QUALITIES DESIRED IN CRITERION- AND NORM-REFERENCED TESTS

As we have noted, the terms *criterion-referenced* and *norm-referenced* pertain to the interpretation of performance. The interpretation of a particular test might be criterion-referenced, norm-referenced, or both, and, unfortunately, it might be neither. However, there are a number of qualities concerning the development or analysis of a test that facilitate a norm- or criterion-referenced interpretation. Several of these qualities must be addressed later. Those discussed here pertain to the difficulty of items, the sensitivity of items to instruction, and the number of items needed to measure student performance.

Item Difficulty

The difficulty of test items affects the variability of scores. If all students correctly answer every item, there will be no variability in test scores because each student obtains the same perfect test score. Likewise, there will be no variability in scores if all students incorrectly answer each item. A large difference among students' scores can occur only when each item is answered correctly by some but not all individuals taking the test.

As a result, the difficulty of items affects how adequately scores can be given a norm-referenced interpretation. If all individuals obtained the same score, it would not be sensible to make statements such as "This student scored higher than 60% of individuals taking the test." *Norm-referenced interpretations require variability in test scores.* Also, norm-referenced interpretations tend to be more accurate if students achieve a wide range of test scores. Therefore, when constructing norm-referenced tests, it is best to avoid items that will be answered correctly by all (or none) of the students.

A criterion-referenced interpretation does not depend on comparisons among students. In this sense, the difficulty of items and the resulting effect on score variability is irrelevant. Does this mean it is appropriate to use items on criterion-referenced tests that are correctly answered by all students? The answer is yes and no. A criterion-referenced interpretation is not diminished if all students obtain the same score because each student's score is interpreted independently of other students' scores. On the other hand, there is no reason to spend time assessing each student's proficiency with a domain if it is known in advance that every student will correctly answer each item. A wiser use of time would be to assess skills for which student proficiency is not yet known.

A common misconception is that items used in criterion-referenced tests should be easier than those of norm-referenced tests. This belief probably results from the need to use criterion-referenced tests in mastery learning and other strategies that integrate testing and instruction. With each of these strategies, students are retested until a certain proficiency is obtained. Conceivably, this level could be 100%, meaning that each student would ultimately be expected to achieve a perfect score. However, as students majoring in economics, meteorology, education, and many other disciplines know very well, many skills are not perfected even following the most comprehensive and effective instruction available. Criterion-referenced tests are applicable to each of these disciplines. However, even when testing is integrated with instruction, certain skills will always cause some or all students considerable difficulty.

Sensitivity to Instruction

Authors sometimes suggest that items used in criterion-referenced tests should be difficult to answer before instruction and easy to answer following instruction (see for example, Haladyna & Roid, 1983). This approach is appealing because it proposes that test items be sensitive to instruction, but caution is needed here. Items that are highly sensitive to instruction tend to measure knowledge of simple facts and other skills that are easy to learn. Such skills are important and often provide a foundation for subsequent learning. However, neither instruction nor testing should be restricted to easily learned skills.

Some criterion-referenced tests in fact are quite insensitive to instruction. Consider a test designed to measure word comprehension. The domain of words to be defined could range from those learned in early elementary grades through college. Knowing the level of words a student can define will help determine the individual's reading proficiency. Most of the words included in the list, however, would be insensitive to short-term instruction. A typical student would have already learned the meaning to many of the easier words, and many of the more difficult words might never be learned.

On the other hand, items on norm-referenced tests *are* often sensitive to instruction. For instance, a comprehensive final exam usually must be norm-referenced because the set of skills being measured is too broad for a meaningful criterion-referenced interpretation. Many items included on a final exam would be difficult for students before instruction but would be correctly answered by the majority of students following instruction. The issue of whether items should be sensitive to instruction depends on the nature of the skills being measured and not so much on whether a criterion-referenced or norm-referenced interpretation of scores is appropriate.

Number of Items

In general, more items are required in criterion-referenced than norm-referenced testing. This is because a norm-referenced test is often used to sample content from a broad content domain, whereas criterion-referenced tests tend to measure more focused domains. The following example illustrates this point.

A ten-item arithmetic test could be devised to measure how well students multiply pairs of two-digit numbers that require regrouping. This would qualify as a criterion-referenced test because it measures a well-defined domain. Such a test is able to provide a fairly accurate indication of whether a student has mastered this multiplication skill. An alternative ten-item test could be constructed that samples the arithmetic skills taught over the period of a year. This alternative test can measure how a student's mathematics achievement compares to that of other students. However, the broad sampling of content prohibits the criterion-referenced interpretation that is allowed with the first test. A number of criterion-referenced tests, however, would be required to cover the same content sampled by a single norm-referenced test. Criterion-referenced testing requires the use of more items to cover a given subject area. On the other hand, criterion-referenced testing is more able to determine what a student can and cannot do and allows for better integration of testing and instruction.

Because criterion-referenced tests usually require more items to assess a given content domain, it may be necessary to use criterion-referenced tests to measure a subset of critical skills and use norm-referenced tests to obtain comprehensive measures of student achievement. Broadening the domain measured by each test can reduce the total number of items required by criterion-referenced tests, although this reduces the ability to establish specifically what a student can and cannot do.

SUMMARY

To be interpretable, scores on a test or any measure must have a frame of reference. Four interpretations commonly used by teachers are ability-referenced, growth-referenced, norm-referenced, and criterion-referenced. Of these, the norm-referenced and criterion-referenced interpretations are the most useful. Norm-referenced interpretations require a clearly defined norm group. Criterion-referenced interpretations require a well-defined content domain.

Often, both norm and criterion references are used to interpret student performance, although specific settings tend to emphasize one interpretation more than the other. Diagnostic and formative evaluations emphasize criterion-referenced interpretations. Preliminary evaluations rely heavily on both. Summative evaluations emphasize norm-referenced interpretations.

ANSWERS: APPLY WHAT YOU ARE LEARNING

2.1 1. Norm-referenced; 2. Criterion-referenced; 3. Norm-referenced; 4. Criterion-referenced; 5. Criterion-referenced; 6. Norm-referenced.

2.2 Items 2, 3, 5, and 7 allow criterion-referenced interpretations because each refers to a well-defined domain. From each of these items, one can indicate what the student can and cannot do relative to the domain. Items 8 and 10 allow norm-referenced interpretations. Although the specific skills that are referenced by these two items are not well defined (e.g., all that is known for sure about the vocabulary words is they are German), both of these items relate student performance to the performance of others. Items 1, 4, 6, and 9 allow neither criterion-referenced nor norm-referenced interpretations. None of these latter items establishes a well-defined domain. For example, the skills that are included in the geography test or the oral portion of the Spanish exam are not specified. In addition, none of these latter items relates student performance to the performance of others.

SOMETHING TO TRY

■ Think of a paper-and-pencil test you recently administered as a teacher or a test you took as a student. Was an ability-, growth-, norm-, or criterion-referenced interpretation used with this test? Why did you come to this conclusion? (Very often, more than one reference is used to interpret a particular test.) If an ability-referenced interpretation was used, was the ability of each student well understood? If a norm-referenced interpretation was used, was the group with which students were being compared clearly understood? If a criterion-referenced interpretation was used, was the content domain well defined?

■ Think about a recent assessment that was not a paper-and-pencil assessment, such as a portfolio assessment or an informal observation or question. What were its references? Why did you come to that conclusion?

ADDITIONAL READING

Berk, R. A. (Ed.). (1984). *A guide to criterion-referenced test construction.* Baltimore, MD: Johns Hopkins University Press. Each chapter focuses on an issue important to criterion-referenced testing, such as describing alternative types of criterion-referenced tests, specifying what is to be measured by a test, determining test length, validating a test, and estimating the reliability of test scores.

Bloom, B. S., Madaus, G. F., & Hastings, J. T. (1981). *Evaluation to improve learning.* New York: McGraw-Hill. Chapters 4 through 6 provide a detailed discussion of formative, diagnostic, and summative evaluations.

Glaser, R. (1994). Criterion-Referenced Tests: Part I. Origins. *Educational measurement: issues and practice,* 13(4), 9–11. Glaser introduced criterion-referenced testing in a 1963 address to the American Educational Research Association. In this article, the author reflects on that speech with respect to what has changed over the 30 years, and identifies anticipated problems that still remain.

CHAPTER 3

Measurable Objectives

This chapter is concerned with making learning visible. Unless a teacher can see, hear, or use other senses to detect a student's learning, the teacher cannot know whether learning has taken place. A teacher cannot assess a student's learning unless there is observable evidence of that learning.

Making learning visible, however, is difficult. Most of a person's knowledge and mental actions are invisible to others. Because we cannot see a person's thoughts, we depend on indicators that suggest the nature of his or her knowledge. To illustrate, consider the following:

How could you indicate that you know the universe is very large and that it contains a very large number of objects?

How could you indicate that you know the concept of multiplication?

In both cases, you might provide evidence of your knowledge as follows:

Regarding the magnitude of the universe, you might say the universe is large because it contains Earth, other planets, and our Sun. The Sun is one of billions of stars in our galaxy, and individual stars are light-years away from each other. Our galaxy, although very large, is but one of millions of galaxies in the universe.

Regarding the concept of multiplication, you might use several illustrations to show that multiplication is repeated additions. For example,

$$4 \times 3 = 3 + 3 + 3 + 3$$

To provide evidence of your knowledge, you must do things that others can see. Likewise, to assess a student's knowledge, a teacher must ask students to do something visible that indicates presence of that knowledge. A description of what students will be asked to do is called a performance objective. (Alternative names for performance objectives are behavioral objectives or instructional objectives; these names are interchangeable.) A performance objective describes an observable event that will indicate that a student has learned the targeted knowledge.

Performance objectives can be categorized by underlying capabilities or learning outcomes. Associating each objective with one of these categories helps assure that the correct learning outcome is being measured. Otherwise, as performance objectives only describe a visible manifestation of a skill, the visible performance may be the result of a capability other than the one being assessed. For example, a teacher may ask a student to solve a multiplication problem, such as 4×3, intending to measure the student's comprehension of multiplication; in fact, however, the teacher is measuring knowledge of multiplication tables.

This chapter helps you achieve five skills:

- Recognize categories of learning outcomes
- Identify characteristics of performance objectives
- Select your own performance objectives
- Communicate performance objectives to students
- Distinguish between performance objectives and instructional goals

CATEGORIES OF LEARNING OUTCOMES

The following exercise will help demonstrate that different types of learning are involved. Two people or two groups of people are needed.

> Ask the first person to watch you, and tell the second person seated nearby to look away. Hold up three fingers, and ask the first person to state how many fingers are shown. The first person will say three. Ask the person who is looking away to state how many fingers are being shown. The second person will also say three. The demonstration can be continued using different numbers of fingers.

From outward appearances, the performance of both persons in this demonstration is the same. However, very different capabilities are involved. The first person is illustrating the capability of counting. The second person is illustrating the ability to recall information. Although the first and second person may each have both capabilities, this may not be the case for students in the process of learning the concept of counting. A teacher must carefully structure observations so that the student's performance is a true indicator of the capability being measured.

You can improve the chances of measuring the appropriate capability by knowing the types of capabilities involved. Research in cognitive psychology has identified two dominant categories, *declarative knowledge* and *procedural knowledge*. As shown in Table 3.1, Bloom (1956) and Gagné (1985) proposed the same basic categories. Bloom refers to declarative knowledge simply as knowledge, whereas Gagné calls it verbal information. Bloom refers to his remaining five categories as intellectual skills,

Table 3.1
Categories proposed by Bloom and Gagné

	Bloom's Taxonomy	**Gagné's Capabilities**
Declarative Knowledge	*Knowledge:* Information such as specific facts, principles, trends, criteria, and ways of organizing events	*Verbal Information:* Same as what Bloom calls knowledge
Procedural Knowledge	*Intellectual Skills*	*Intellectual Skills*
	Comprehension: Use of information without necessarily applying this information to new situations and without fully understanding the implications of this knowledge	*Discriminations:* Reacting to stimuli such as visual images and determining whether they are the same or different
	Application: Use of an abstract concept in a specific but previously unused situation	*Concrete Concepts:* Identifying physical objects or images that have a specified characteristic
	Analysis: Breaking a concept or communication into its component parts	*Defined Concepts:* Understanding of an abstract classification
	Synthesis: Putting elements together into a cohesive whole	*Rules:* Applying principles that regulate the relationship among classes of objects or events
	Evaluation: Making a judgment about the value of products or processes for a given purpose	*Higher Order Rules:* Combining a series of rules into a single more complex rule or into the solution of a problem

Note: In addition to the categories shown in the table, Gagné adds *cognitive strategies, motor skills,* and *attitudes.* Bloom lists motor skills and attitudes as separate domains that he refers to as the psychomotor and affective domains. Other individuals have proposed taxonomies for these two domains.

and Gagné also uses the term to identify other categories, although Bloom and Gagné divide intellectual skills into very different subcategories.

Because they are assessed differently, it is important to look at the difference between declarative and procedural knowledge. We will also briefly look at motor skills and attitudes, two other qualities that are assessed in the classroom, typically through informal assessments.

Declarative Knowledge

Declarative knowledge refers to information one can state verbally. Declarative knowledge includes the recall of specific facts, principles, trends, criteria, and ways of organizing events. An example is recalling that you saw three robins as opposed to looking at the robins and determining that you saw three birds. Other examples include recalling the definitions of words, recalling physical and chemical characteristics of elements and compounds, and recalling that the trend each year is for an increase in the number of cars on the highway. Recalling that books can be categorized as fiction and nonfiction is also an example of declarative knowledge, as is recalling that Ohm's law pertains to the relationship among electrical resistance, voltage, and amperage.

It is important to understand the difference between declarative and procedural knowledge. Asking students to state what they know measures only declarative knowledge, not procedural knowledge. A very broad range of questions can be used to ask students what they know. For example,

Tell me what is meant by relative humidity.

What is the difference between air and oxygen?

Why do interest rates affect the stock market?

Contrast the geography of northern and southern Africa.

Why do heavy objects like ships float in water?

Each of these examples measures declarative knowledge. None measures procedural knowledge, which we will learn requires the use of very different types of questions.

In discussing the theories of Bloom or Gagné, the importance of declarative knowledge is often downplayed, even to the extent of discouraging the teaching and assessment of this type of knowledge. This happens in part because declarative knowledge is wrongly thought of as being limited to memorization of facts. Although knowledge of facts is part of declarative knowledge, so is knowledge of trends, abstractions, criteria, and ways of organizing events. In their writings, Bloom and Gagné clearly establish the importance of knowledge that can be declared.

Procedural Knowledge

Procedural knowledge is knowledge of how to do things. Examples of procedural knowledge include demonstrating conversions between the Fahrenheit and Celsius scales; correctly classifying whales, sharks, porpoises, salmon, and other sea animals as fish or mammal; and identifying which object in a picture is a tree. Other examples include visually discriminating between a $1 and a $5 bill, and generating rules that predict whether an object will float or sink in water.

Although the same content is often involved in both declarative and procedural knowledge, these two capabilities are distinct. For example, being able to state that most assessments in a classroom are informal rather than formal (declarative knowledge) is different from being able to observe and correctly classify assessments as informal or formal (procedural knowledge). Unfortunately, it is common to assume that a student has achieved both types of knowledge after examining only one of these two capabilities.

Box 3.1   *Apply What You Are Learning*

One situation in each of the following pairs is an example of declarative knowledge, whereas the other is an example of procedural knowledge. Indicate which (A or B) is an example of procedural knowledge.

1.   A.   Knowing that a touchdown in football is worth 6 points
     B.   Distinguishing between a touchdown and a safety

2.   A.   Looking at the fish caught by each of several individuals and determining who caught the most fish
     B.   Recalling the next day who caught the most fish

3.   A.   Naming the capital cities of each state
     B.   Given descriptions of several cities, identifying which are capital cities

4.   A.   Describing the difference between declarative knowledge and procedural knowledge
     B.   Classifying descriptions as examples of declarative knowledge and procedural knowledge

Answers can be found at the end of the chapter.

Both Bloom (1956) and Gagné (1985) refer to procedural knowledge as intellectual skills. As already noted, Bloom and Gagné divide intellectual skills into different subcategories. Bloom devised his categories through a series of informal conferences that he led from 1949 to 1953, during which a large number of performance objectives, primarily from college-level courses, were reviewed. The development of his taxonomy was governed by educational, logical, and psychological considerations, in that order of importance, with emphasis placed on developing categories that matched "the distinctions teachers make in planning curricula or in choosing learning situations" (Bloom, 1956, p. 6). Bloom's taxonomy remains widely used, although his subcategories of intellectual skills depart substantially from what is now known about procedural knowledge.

Our discussion of procedural knowledge involves an adaptation of capabilities identified by Gagné. Table 3.2 lists the category names we will use, along with descriptions of how each type of capability can be assessed. Declarative knowledge is referred to as information. Procedural knowledge is divided into subcategories that we will call discriminations, concepts, rules, and complex skills.

Discriminations.   Discriminations are the most basic procedural skill. They involve reacting to stimuli, such as visual images, and determining whether they are the same or different. Examples are determining whether two pencils are the same or whether two sounds are the same. The student is not told what characteristic is being compared, nor asked to give a name to what is being observed or to describe in what ways (if any) the stimuli are different. Instead, discriminations are concerned with whether students are sensitive to relevant differences.

Table 3.2
Techniques for assessing various capabilities

Capability	Assessment Technique
Declarative Knowledge	
Information	Ask students to state what they know
Procedural Knowledge	
Discriminations	Ask students to identify the object that is different in some way
Concepts	Ask students to distinguish between examples and nonexamples of the concept
Rules	Give students a specific relevant situation and ask them to apply the rule
Complex skills	Give students a specific problem to solve that requires use of the complex skill
Attitudes	Observe students' typical behavior
Motor Skills	Ask students to demonstrate the physical skill

Students, particularly older students, learn most relevant discriminations on their own. However, when a student is having trouble learning a skill involving procedural knowledge, the problem may be that he or she is missing an important discrimination. For example, if a student is having problems using words that contain the letters *p* and *q*, it may be that the student does not see the critical difference between these two letters. A student who exclaims, "Now I see what you are talking about," may be conveying the importance of a missing discrimination.

Concepts.   Concepts involve a characteristic that can be used to classify physical objects or abstractions. To assess concrete concepts, have students point at or otherwise identify objects or images that have the specified characteristic. Examples include identifying which objects are balls or circling the letter *d* within words.

The examples to be classified should be provided by the teacher rather than the student. The examples should involve previously unused illustrations. For instance, one would assess students' knowledge of the concept *ball* by using objects not used previously while learning the concept of a ball. Some but not all of the objects would be balls. If students provide the examples, or if previous illustrations are reused, it is possible that knowledge of information is being assessed rather than knowledge of the concept.

Because a concept involves a class of things, it should be assessed under a variety of conditions. If, for example, the concept of rectangle is being taught, the student should be asked to identify rectangles that have light or heavy lines, those with lengths close to and much longer than the widths, and those displayed at different angles. To demonstrate mastery of a concept, a student must perceive all qualities relevant to the concept and disregard all qualities irrelevant to the concept. To learn a concrete concept, a student must have already learned discriminations that are inherent in the concept.

Abstract concepts involve understanding a classification of nontangible objects, events, or relations. Unlike concrete concepts, abstract concepts involve things that cannot be touched or directly sensed. Examples include the concepts of sailing, the game of basketball, or a mystery novel. Another example is the idea of a tax shelter. Abstract concepts typically incorporate concrete concepts. For instance, sailing involves boats, wind, water, sails, and many other concrete items that can be touched or otherwise sensed. However, the concept of sailing also involves abstractions such as right-of-way rules and the boat's center of gravity. Because abstractions cannot be touched or pointed at, students are asked to distinguish between examples and nonexamples of the concept. Here again, students should be assessed under a variety of conditions.

The distinction between concrete and abstract concepts is not always clear, and often concrete and abstract concepts share the same name. For example, the basic shape of a rectangle is learned as a concrete concept. However, conceptualizing a rectangle as "a closed plane figure formed by four line segments that intersect at right angles" is an abstract concept.

Rules.   Rules involve the application of principles that regulate the relationship among classes of objects or events. For example, a rule pertains to using the indefinite article *a* or *an* in sentences. Another example is applying Boyle's law (the product of the volume of a confined gas and its pressure is a constant) by calculating what the pressure of air in a pump would become if its volume were decreased by 90%.

To assess a rule, students should be asked to apply the rule. Rules regarding the use of the indefinite article *a* or *an* in sentences can be assessed by asking students to supply the indefinite article within sample sentences. Boyle's law can be assessed by having students solve problems in which air pressure and volume must be computed for varying conditions.

As with concepts, the teacher and not the student should provide the situations to which the rule is to be applied. Directions to the student might even suggest which rule is to be applied, as in the problem "Convert 75° Fahrenheit to Celsius." The examples should involve previously unused applications of the rule. Creating unused applications often is very simple, such as using a different Fahrenheit temperature for calculating the Celsius equivalent, or using unknown words when measuring students' knowledge of spelling rules that involve *ie*.

Being able to state a rule (information) is different from using the rule. Stating, "The product of the volume of a confined gas and its pressure is a constant," is not equivalent to applying Boyle's law, nor is stating Boyle's law a prerequisite to understanding this rule. Information often facilitates learning concepts and rules but is not a prerequisite to and certainly is not equivalent to a working knowledge of concepts and rules.

Complex Skills.   Complex skills combine a series of rules into a single, more complex rule or into the solution of a problem. An example of a complex skill is demonstrating that if a is a nonzero real number and n is a positive integer, then a^{-n} equals $1/a^n$. Another example is determining where to position one larger and one smaller float under an object so that the object floats level in the water.

Complex skills are assessed in a manner somewhat similar to that used for assessing rules. Both involve presenting a specific situation in which students can apply their skill. However, in assessing complex skills, students are not told which relationships are involved; instead, they are asked to generate a new rule from the rules they know or, more simply, to solve a problem. Often, any of several responses represents a legitimate solution to the problem. Thus written tests involving multiple-choice or even essay items do not provide effective measures of complex skills. Performance assessments, in which students are observed often individually and under controlled conditions, are a better alternative.

It is important to see the distinction between rules and complex skills. Many rules can be complicated, but being complicated, in itself, does not make the skill a complex skill. For instance, if the rules are known, it is fairly complicated determining where in the local night sky the International Space Station will disappear as a result of entering Earth's shadow. Because established rules are being applied, they can be used over and over again in varying circumstances to determine when the space station will disappear. Because the same procedure can be reapplied each time, solving this complicated problem involves a rule (or rules), not a complex skill. On the other hand, a complex skill would be involved if, in the absence of these rules, students were asked to establish variables that are relevant to determine when the space station will and will not be visible to a person on Earth. The kinds of variables students would have to address include locating the space station within its orbit, establishing whether or not it was daytime or nighttime at a particular point on Earth, and establishing where the space station's orbit intercepted Earth's shadow. This is a complex skill because, as the problem is presented, there is no set of rules that, if applied, would solve the problem. The students have to use previously learned information, concepts, and rules in various ways to solve the problem. Different students likely will solve the problem using different sets of information, concepts, and rules. They in fact may create rules and possibly concepts that are new, at least to them.

Box 3.2 *Apply What You Are Learning*

Listed here are some educational goals or general objectives. Which learning outcome (information, discrimination, concept, rule, or complex skill) does each reference?

1. Recalling information published in the newspaper
2. Correctly spelling words involving *ie*, such as *receive* and *piece*
3. Going to a farm and identifying animals by name
4. Stating names of animals that were seen at a farm
5. In football, determining which play to use next

6. Classifying an example as a preliminary, diagnostic, formative, or summative evaluation
7. Stating the difference between a rule and complex skill
8. Seeing a difference in marks made by a pencil and pen, although not being able to describe the difference in words

Answers can be found at the end of the chapter.

Motor Skills

Motor skills are skills the student uses to execute movements, such as climbing a rope, writing with a pencil, sanding a piece of wood, tuning a violin, lighting a Bunsen burner, or standing appropriately when delivering a speech. Motor skills often are linked to declarative or procedural knowledge. For instance, tuning a violin requires knowing which strings produce the higher pitch and that tensioning the peg raises the pitch.

Performance assessments are required to assess motor skills. A written test can measure related declarative and procedural knowledge, such as when to use different types of sandpaper for sanding wood and steps to follow when lighting a burner, but no written test can measure the actual performance of the motor skill.

Attitudes

Attitudes are the learned mental states that influence a student's typical behavior. Choosing to go to a movie rather than a play illustrates the existence of an attitude. So are many other choices a person makes such as looking for alternative points of view rather than accepting a single point of view, or rereading a sentence that is unclear rather than accepting what is understood on first reading. Cultures tend to reinforce selected attitudes, although often inconsistently.

Assessment of attitudes involves measuring typical rather than maximum performance. Teachers, however, measure maximum performance more often than they measure typical performance. In part, this is because it is difficult to structure an assessment that accurately elicits typical performance. Also, it is often unclear when an attitude should be measured with the intent of modifying behavior perceived as undesirable.

Box 3.3   *Apply What You Are Learning*

Listed here are descriptions of behaviors. Use the following options to identify the category each behavior represents:

A. Declarative knowledge   C. Motor skill
B. Procedural knowledge   D. Attitude

1. Listing the letters of the alphabet

2. Naming the letter of the alphabet being shown
3. Placing a coat on a hanger
4. Reading a science fiction book rather than a mystery
5. Classifying paintings by historical period
6. Naming the oceans of the world
7. Determining whether an individual is speaking French or Spanish
8. Identifying the category each of the foregoing behaviors represents (that is, what capability have you just been demonstrating?)

Answers can be found at the end of the chapter.

COMPONENTS OF PERFORMANCE OBJECTIVES

We can think of performance objectives as being divided into four components: capability, behavior, situation, and special conditions. As we discuss these components, it is useful to keep in mind the purpose of performance objectives. Performance objectives describe an observable event that indicates that a student has learned the targeted knowledge. The performance is an indication of knowledge; the performance itself typically is not the knowledge. The performance objective prescribes the observable events that provide a reasonable basis for concluding that knowledge has been achieved.

Capability[1]

For each objective, it is useful to indicate the type of capability being assessed. Again, as performance objectives only describe a visible manifestation of knowledge, it may be that the visible manifestation is the result of a capability other than the one being assessed. Stating the capability involved alerts us to the type of behavior we should use to assess that capability. To specify a capability, we simply identify it by name: information, discrimination, concept, rule, or complex skill.

Behavior

A learning outcome can be measured only if it can be observed. To create an observable event, a student must exhibit a behavior. The central role of a performance objective is to identify a behavior that indicates that the targeted learning has occurred.

[1]Different authors divide performance objectives into somewhat different components. Virtually all authors agree that the purpose of an objective is to specify an observable performance that will be used to indicate the targeted learning has been achieved. Consequently, most measurement books agree that a statement of that performance or behavior is a basic component of any objective. However, the type of capability involved strongly influences the type of behavior that should be used to indicate achievement of the targeted learning. Therefore, this book proposes that a performance objective should begin with a statement of the type of capability involved. With the type of capability in mind, focus is then placed on selecting a behavior that is appropriate for measuring that capability.

To be most useful, the behavior should be specified in a manner that can be observed directly; that is, no inferences should be required to indicate whether the behavior has occurred. The performance objective must specify exactly what you will see.

Box 3.4   *Apply What You Are Learning*

Listed here are pairs of events. Within each pair, one event can be observed directly, the other cannot. The event that can be observed directly is the better candidate for a performance objective. For each pair, select the event that can be directly observed.

1. A.   Knows letters of the alphabet
    B.   Orally names all letters of the alphabet
2. A.   Points to a specified letter in a word
    B   Describes the letter in the word to which you are pointing
3. A.   States the name of the historical period during which a painting was created
    B.   Is able to associate paintings correctly with historical periods
4. A.   Likes science fiction books
    B.   Chooses a science fiction book

Answers can be found at the end of the chapter.

Notice that in the first pair, one cannot directly observe "knows letters of the alphabet." Within the second pair, "describes the letter" requires an inference to determine whether a description has occurred; the event "described" is not directly observable.

By attaching the name of the capability to the statement of behavior, we create performance objectives. Here is what they would look like:

Information: Orally names all letters of the alphabet

Concept: Points to a specified letter in a word

Concept: States the name of the historical period during which the painting was created

Attitude: Chooses a science fiction book

Situation

Often the context in which the student exhibits the behavior is relevant. May a dictionary be used when translating sentences from another language? May a calculator be used when solving math problems? Will the student be allowed to select the topic when asked to give an extemporaneous speech? Most characteristics of a situation are not specified either because they are obvious (such as the language in which the speech is to be given) or because they are judged not to be critical to defining the skill (such as the topic of the material being translated to another language).

Judgments have to be made about which if any situations will be specified as part of the performance objective. Including the following situations might help clarify the preceding objectives:

Concept: Points to specified letter in a word *when the teacher points to a word in a book and names a letter.*

Concept: *When shown an unknown painting that is clearly characteristic of the period,* states the name of the historical period during which the painting was created.

Special Conditions

Sometimes it is appropriate to place conditions on the action, for example, indicating how quickly the student must point to the appropriate letter within a word, or to establish a standard, such as the need to make a correct identification 80%, or possibly 100%, of the time.

Special conditions are sometimes confused with situations. A situation specifies the context in which the behavior will occur. Special conditions, in contrast, specify conditions that must be present in the student's behavior in order to conclude that the targeted knowledge has been learned. As with situations, judgment must be used about which, if any, special conditions are to be specified. Here is an example of a special condition in a performance objective

Information: Orally names all letters of the alphabet *in ABC order.*

Special conditions are not always specified in a performance objective. Thus a performance objective does not necessarily include a performance standard or passing score. Not all authors agree with this point of view. For example, Mager (1984) proposes that a performance standard should always be included within the objective to define a successful performance. Later in the book, we will show that establishing a passing score on a test is not always possible or necessary. Even when passing scores are used, it may be appropriate to establish the passing score after the test has been administered and the performance of students evaluated. In some situations, then, it would be inappropriate to specify a performance standard in the objective.

Box 3.5   *Apply What You Are Learning*

Each of the three performance objectives listed here has been partitioned with brackets, and the partitions are numbered. Within these objectives, indicate whether each partition is a capability, behavior, situation, or special condition.

[Concept][1]: [Within two seconds,][2] [point to the specified letter within a word].[3]

[Rule][4]: [Given sentences orally spoken in English,][5] [orally state equivalent sentences in German].[6]

[Concept][7]: [Given two sounds whose pitches are discrepant in frequency by 1%,][8] [orally state whether the first or second sound has the higher frequency].[9]

Answers can be found at the end of the chapter.

SELECTION OF PERFORMANCE OBJECTIVES

Ultimately, the teacher selects or creates performance objectives for her or his own class. However, the following four guidelines may facilitate selection of a useful set of objectives:

1. Describe the results of learning rather than strategies for facilitating learning.
2. Use behaviors that are relevant indicators for the capability that is to be learned.
3. Obtain indicators of all critical aspects of the knowledge being assessed.
4. Obtain indicators for an appropriate sample of all knowledge that is to be learned.

Describe the Results of Learning

Performance objectives specify what one will be able to see the student do if the student has learned the targeted knowledge. According to Linn and Gronlund (1995), to describe consequences of learning that are observable, performance objectives should not be specified in terms of the following characteristics:

- Teacher performance, such as saying, "Students will be taught to spell correctly."
- Learning process, such as stating, "The student will learn how to add numbers."
- Course content, such as indicating, "The student will know the difference between criterion- and norm-referenced tests."

To avoid these problems, always ask what you will be able to see the student do after the knowledge being taught has been learned.

Use Relevant Behavior as Indicators

Performance objectives do not describe knowledge. They describe indicators of knowledge. Considerable care must be taken to make sure the behavior specified in the objective is relevant to the knowledge that is being assessed.

Again, for this reason you are encouraged to include the name of the capability as part of the performance objective. Although it does not assure that relevant behaviors will be used to indicate learning, naming the capability can help make you aware of the types of behavior that are appropriate.

Assess All Critical Aspects of the Knowledge

Because only indicators of knowledge are being described, it is probable that one performance objective by itself does not address all critical aspects of a particular knowledge. Attending to all critical aspects of the knowledge, more than anything else discussed in this chapter, requires the abilities of a highly intelligent and perceptive teacher. The teacher must have mastery of what is being taught so that critical aspects of a concept or rule are evident. The teacher must be perceptive of how these critical aspects can be seen in the behavior of another person. Reading periodicals, such as *Reading Teacher* and *Arithmetic Teacher*, among others, and talking with other teachers are useful tools in developing this knowledge.

Assess an Appropriate Sample of All Knowledge

It is likely that the teacher will not be able to assess all knowledge that is to be learned within the course of a school year. When this is true, the teacher must select an appropriate sample of knowledge, a sample that is representative of overall content and does not exclude important skills.

To determine areas for which performance objectives are to be selected, the teacher should work from a general domain to a specific set of objectives. A way to accomplish this is to prepare a table such as Table 3.3. Column headings are types of capabilities, and row headings are content areas. For this illustration, the content areas are for an elementary school math class. The Totals column provides estimates of the percentage of time to be associated with each content area. These percentages are judgments of the teacher and are used to help match objectives to priorities of the class.

The numbers within each cell are estimates of the emphasis to be placed within a content area on each of the capabilities. For example, the first content area is physical measurements. The first cell within this role indicates that 5% of overall learning will involve information within the physical measurements area. The numbers in each row add up to the total percentage for that row. The percentages in the table appear to be highly precise statements concerning the amount of learning that should occur in each pairing of content and capability. Precise they are not. These numbers represent subjective estimates that help identify where emphases within the class occur. In using such a table, whether this number is 2 or 3 is irrelevant; what is important is whether the number in a particular cell is relatively large or small.

In this math class, information involves estimating the approximate length, capacity, or mass of familiar objects using various units of measure. By recognizing the ways of assessing information, concepts, and rules, the table provides a structure for selecting performance objectives.

Table 3.3
Framework for selecting objectives in an elementary math class

	Information	Concepts	Rules	Complex Skills	Attitudes	Totals
Physical measurements	5	5	5	—	—	15
Time	2	3	—	—	—	5
Money	2	2	4	—	2	10
Counting numbers	2	3	5	—	—	10
Addition and subtraction	3	5	8	4	—	20
Multiplication and division	3	5	8	4	—	20
Fractions	2	3	5	—	—	10
Geometric shapes	4	4	—	—	2	10

Selecting performance objectives is tedious and time-consuming. It is work to be shared with others who are or have been teaching the same material. Curriculum supplements typically provide teachers with lists of objectives or cite sources of objectives. Many educational organizations and state agencies also have and publish lists of objectives. These objectives always need to be reviewed critically and must be selected within the context of content and capabilities to be taught in the class.

CONVEYING PERFORMANCE OBJECTIVES TO STUDENTS

Performance objectives should be communicated to students. Knowing what is expected can help motivate them and also helps students determine when a skill has been achieved.

Communicating performance objectives does not necessarily imply that students are to be provided with a list of objectives; a student who lacks the skill about to be taught may be unable to comprehend the meaning of the stated objective. Also, research for some time has revealed no improvement in learning when students are provided objectives before instruction (see for example Duchastel & Merrill, 1973; Melton, 1978). Teachers can convey performance objectives to students simply by illustrating the behavior that is to be learned.

The method used to communicate objectives should take into account the category of performance that is to be taught. Table 3.4 lists the categories we discussed earlier and proposes a technique for conveying each type of capability to students. For example, a teacher who wants students to learn the multiplication table for all single-digit numbers (information) might tell students they will be expected to state the number resulting from multiplying any two single-digit numbers. A teacher who is about to teach students how to multiply numbers involving decimals (rule) might convey what is to be learned by giving an example of the type of multiplication problem that will be involved.

Table 3.4
Techniques for informing students of the objective

Type of Capability	Instructional Technique
Information	Describe what students will be expected to recall
Discrimination	(Learner is informed later)
Concept or rule	Demonstrate the activity to which the learner will be asked to apply the concept or rule
Complex skill	Demonstrate the situation in which the learner will be asked to solve the problem
Motor skill	Demonstrate the expected performance
Attitude	(Learner is informed later)

GOALS VERSUS PERFORMANCE OBJECTIVES

Goals are broader than performance objectives. As we have noted, a performance objective details the specific behavior that indicates that the student has obtained the capability being assessed. For instance,

> **Rule:** Given sentences orally spoken in English, orally state equivalent sentences in German.

The assessment of a well-written performance objective requires no inference. The behavior to be observed is orally stating sentences in German: one does not need to infer whether a student can orally state equivalent sentences in German. One can observe this behavior directly.

Goals are stated more generally than objectives. For example,

> Orally translates from English to German

A goal is often the equivalent of several objectives. With performance assessments, it is quite natural to use an instructional goal rather than performance objectives, since the skills being assessed are often highly complex in terms of the number of behaviors involved. Similarly, a group of several goals is used to provide the context for a portfolio. The use of goals rather than equivalent sets of objectives allows brevity. With complex skills, instructional goals may provide descriptions that are more practical than those provided by performance objectives.

Inferences are required to assess whether a student has achieved a goal. This allows flexibility in terms of the specific criteria that will be used to judge a student's performance. This flexibility can be damaging, though, because it increases measurement error resulting from subjectivity in scoring. For this reason, when we discuss performance assessments and portfolios in later chapters, which tend to be based on goals rather than objectives, we give careful attention to how to score student work.

SUMMARY

Student performance can be categorized into capabilities. Research in cognitive psychology indicates the existence of two dominant types of capability: declarative knowledge and procedural knowledge. In this book we refer to declarative knowledge as information and divide procedural knowledge into four subcategories: discriminations, concepts, rules, and complex skills. We also include two other capabilities often assessed in the classroom: motor skills and attitudes. Being aware of the type of capability involved is important, because different kinds of student performance are used to assess the different kinds of capabilities.

Performance objectives specify the behaviors that indicate that targeted knowledge has been learned. Performance objectives include up to four components: the name of the capability, the behavior, the situation, and special conditions. Naming the capability helps the teacher focus on appropriate indicators of knowledge. The behavior is central to the objective and specifies what will be seen when learning has occurred. The situation describes the context in which the student will be asked to indicate achievement. The special conditions, if necessary, specify conditions that must be met for the student's performance to be judged successful.

Performance objectives are best selected from a general domain, such as a table that lists the content and capabilities to be learned. Objectives can be conveyed to students without actually being stated.

Particularly with performance assessments and portfolios, goals are substituted for objectives. Goals are stated more generally, and assessing whether a student has achieved a goal requires inference. The flexibility inherent in goals increases subjectivity when scoring student work.

ANSWERS: APPLY WHAT YOU ARE LEARNING

3.1 1. B; 2. A; 3. B; 4. B.

3.2 1. Information; 2. Rule; 3. Concept; 4. Information; 5. Complex skill; 6. Concept; 7. Information; 8. Discrimination.

3.3 1. A; 2. B; 3. C; 4. D; 5. B; 6. A; 7. B; 8. B.

3.4 1. B; 2. A; 3. A; 4. B.

3.5 1. Capability; 2. Special condition; 3. Behavior; 4. Capability; 5. Situation; 6. Behavior; 7. Capability; 8. Situation; 9. Behavior.

SOMETHING TO TRY

■ A student's outward performance may provide an inaccurate or misleading indication of the student's learned capabilities. Can you recall personal experiences when a teacher or other person used an individual's outward behavior to make an incorrect conclusion about that individual's knowledge or attitude? What are strategies you might use to reduce the number of inaccurate conclusions drawn from outward behaviors?

■ This chapter (and most of the other chapters in this book) includes several Apply What You Are Learning exercises. Look at some of these exercises and try to identify which capability is being assessed.

■ Think of a capability you would try to teach your students. (Be sure not to confuse capability with performance. An example of a capability is knowing the concept of addition or knowing a rule such as that describing the relation between the density of an object and its ability to float on water.) Then list student performances that would be good indicators of whether this capability has been learned. Identify by name the type of capability you have described (e.g., concept).

ADDITIONAL READING

Bloom, B. S. (Ed.). (1956). *Taxonomy of educational objectives: handbook 1. cognitive domain.* New York: McKay. Discusses the technique used to classify objectives, describes categories of the cognitive domain, and presents example objectives and test items within each category.

Gagné, R. M. (1985). *The conditions of learning* (4th ed.). New York: Holt, Rinehart, and Winston. Discusses the nature of learned capabilities and conditions required for students to learn each capability.

Gronlund, N. E. (2000). *How to write and use instructional objectives.* Upper Saddle River, NJ: Merrill/Prentice Hall. This small book describes how to write objectives for attitudes as well as intellectual and performance outcomes. Suggestions are given for using objectives within instruction.

CHAPTER 4

Validity

Validity pertains to the degree to which a test measures what it is supposed to measure.[1] More than on any other factor, the quality of a test depends on its validity. If a test does not measure what it is supposed to measure, it is useless. Validity is the most central and essential quality in the development, interpretation, and use of educational measures.

Validity is an abstraction. We cannot directly see validity any more than we can see the capabilities we wish to assess. Instead of observing validity, we depend on various evidence that indicates the presence or absence of validity. Much like the strategy used by Agatha Christie's famous detective Hercule Poirot to solve a mystery, an educator uses evidence to determine whether a test is measuring what it is supposed to measure. Evidence is often grouped into three interrelated categories; *construct-related* evidence, *content-related* evidence, and *criterion-related* evidence. As we will observe, the distinctions among these categories are not clear, and one type of evidence does not negate the need for other types. Validity is a unified concept based on a series of evidence (American Psychological Association, American Educational Research Association, & National Council on Measurement in Education, 1999).

Construct-related evidence establishes whether the student performance to be observed represents a legitimate indicator of the capability or psychological construct the teacher hopes to assess. Content-related evidence establishes how well the actual content of questions, tasks, observations, or other elements of a test

---

[1]As noted in Chapter 1, *educational measurement* refers to the process of determining a quantitative or qualitative attribute of an individual or group of individuals that is of academic relevance. *Test* refers to the vehicle used to observe that attribute, such as a written test, a performance assessment, an informal observation, or an oral question.

corresponds to the student performance that is to be observed. Criterion-related evidence indicates how well a student's performance on a test correlates with her or his performance on relevant criterion measures external to the test.

You have probably observed evidence (or sometimes lack of evidence) of validity in tests you have taken. For instance, you may have observed that some written tests developed by some teachers more adequately sample the content covered in the course than do others. You may have noticed that the wording or structure of questions on some tests more accurately measures what you learned and did not learn. Perhaps you have noticed how effective teachers are careful to substantiate conclusions they draw from informal observations. Each of these situations involves collecting evidence of validity. In this chapter, we will look at specific ways to develop and apply these types of evidence of validity.

Validity is relevant to both frequent informal classroom assessments and the more formal written tests, performance assessments, and other systematic observations. Furthermore, validity is relevant to the interpretation as well as the use of formal and informal measures.

This chapter helps you achieve three skills:

- Recognize types of evidence used to establish validity
- Apply these types of evidence to formal and informal classroom assessments and to published tests that are used in schools
- Recognize the role of validity in the interpretation and use of tests

CONSTRUCT-RELATED EVIDENCE OF VALIDITY

Construct-related evidence establishes a link between the underlying psychological construct we wish to measure and the visible performance we choose to observe. There are many psychological constructs, such as learned knowledge, intelligence, interest, motivation, anxiety, and self-efficacy, among others. In each case, the construct is invisible. Measurement of the construct requires use of some visible performance that provides an appropriate indication as to the status of the construct we wish to measure.

The constructs generally of greatest relevance to teachers are those of learned knowledge. As with any psychological construct, learned knowledge cannot be directly seen. We cannot see what a student knows or is thinking. Therefore, we need to establish whether the visible student behaviors we choose to observe are legitimate indications of the student knowledge we wish to evaluate.

It is important to recognize that different types of capabilities must be assessed using different types of performance. As mentioned earlier, research in cognitive psychology has identified two dominant types of knowledge, declarative knowledge and procedural knowledge. We are using *information* to refer to declarative knowledge; we have divided procedural knowledge into four subcategories: *discriminations, concepts, rules,* and *complex skills.* In Chapter 3, we identified, for each capability, the type of student behavior that indicates whether knowledge has been learned. Table

3.2 summarizes that discussion. Let us look in further detail at the types of perform-ance that can be used to assess the types of knowledge we have discussed.

Information pertains to knowledge that can be recalled including facts, such as historical dates or multiplication tables, as well as other knowledge, such as princi-ples, trends, and ways of organizing events. An example of a principle is knowing that deciduous trees lose leaves in the winter; an example of a trend is recalling that the population of cities has generally increased over time. All such information can be measured by asking students to state what they know. A teacher can measure a student's knowledge of information through oral questions or any format of items used in written tests.

Assessing procedural knowledge requires observing different types of perform-ance, and different types of student performance are used to assess the subcategories of procedural knowledge. For example, if a student knows a concept, the student can identify examples of that concept in very different settings. Take our earlier example of the concept of rectangle. Simply asking a student to define or describe a rectangle does not measure the student's knowledge of the concept. Instead, it measures infor-mation—the student's ability to recall the definition or characteristics of a rectangle.

Knowledge of the concept of a rectangle would be measured by asking a student to point to examples of a rectangle. The student should be expected to identify those examples within the context of other objects that are not rectangles. The student also would have to identify diverse examples of rectangles, for instance, rectangles with very similar or very different lengths and widths.

Knowledge of concepts can be measured through oral questions and by most formats used in written tests. For instance, true–false items can ask a student to se-lect which of several illustrations are correct examples of the concept. Completion items, however, tend not to provide a good format for measuring a concept. Having a student write one or even several words in a blank usually does not help deter-mine whether that student can distinguish between correct and incorrect illustrations of a concept.

Assessing a student's knowledge of a rule requires observing a different kind of performance. Consider, for example, knowledge of Ohm's law, an equation that spec-ifies the relationship among electrical voltage, amperage, and resistance. Having a stu-dent state or describe Ohm's law would not measure the student's knowledge of the rule. It would measure information—the student's ability to recall the definition or description of Ohm's law. Similarly, asking a student to provide an example of Ohm's law would involve recall of information if the student used previously learned ex-amples. To measure a student's knowledge of a rule, the teacher must ask the stu-dent to apply the rule to concrete situations. For example, a student might be asked to determine electrical voltage when given amperage and resistance. As with con-cepts, knowledge of rules is assessed by asking a student to apply the knowledge in diverse settings. For instance, the student might also be asked to describe what hap-pens to electrical voltage if resistance is decreased while amperage remains constant.

The same test formats used to measure knowledge of concepts can be used with rules (although items used to assess concepts versus rules would ask students to do different tasks). For instance, oral questions are an effective technique for asking stu-dents to apply a rule. With the multiple-choice format, students might have to select the options that represent a correct application of a rule. The essay format can be used to describe what a particular rule indicates will happen under specified conditions. Again, the completion format generally is not able to measure students' ability to apply a rule. There are, however, notable exceptions. For instance, when application of a rule, such as Ohm's law, results in a single number, a completion item can be used to elicit a student's response. Similarly, when application of a rule, such as selecting the appropriate tense of a verb, results in a single word, a completion item can be used to obtain a student's response.

The assessment of complex skills involves presenting a student a relevant problem, the solution of which will generalize to other, similar problems. The solution should require use of previously learned concepts and rules. An example of such a problem is asking the student to locate two floats of different sizes under an object so that the object floats level in the water. Students who are able to solve this problem would likely use various strategies and utilize different subsets of concepts and rules. To assess complex skills, a teacher must be aware of the characteristics of different approaches, each of which represents a legitimate solution of the problem. Of equal importance, the teacher must use assessment procedures that provide students flexibility in selecting appropriate and inappropriate approaches. Written tests, including the essay format, generally do not provide this flexibility. Student proficiency with complex skills usually must be determined through performance assessments. Portfolios may provide a useful approach to managing the assessment of complex skills.

In establishing validity, there is no substitute for the person developing the test knowing intimately the construct being measured. When measuring learned knowledge, the person developing the test must meaningfully answer the question, "How would I indicate to others that I have this knowledge?" Establishing a legitimate link between the invisible capability and an observable performance is the essence of construct-related validity. Again, measuring the various types of capabilities requires observing different types of student performance, and it is important to establish the capability involved before determining how to assess what students have learned. When measuring student achievement, construct-related evidence of validity entails establishing the capability involved in the skills you wish to assess and then establishing that an appropriate performance was selected for indicating proficiency with that skill.

CONTENT-RELATED EVIDENCE OF VALIDITY

Content-related evidence of validity indicates how well the content of a test corresponds to the student performance to be observed. (Remember, *test* covers written tests, performance assessments, portfolios, informal observations, and oral questions.) You can think of content-related evidence as an extension of construct-related evidence. Through construct-related evidence, we determine what knowledge we need to assess and establish student behaviors that will provide good indicators of that knowledge. Through content-related evidence, we determine how well the content of our test incorporates those behaviors.

Poor planning or lack of planning by the teacher may result in a test that does not incorporate targeted behaviors. You probably have found evidence of this in some of the written tests you have taken or in the poor choice of behaviors upon which some teachers focus when observing their class. You probably have also noticed how some teachers carefully plan what they are going to observe when they informally assess students during instruction.

Another reason that a test may not incorporate targeted behaviors is that a test always involves sampling, that is, it includes only a sample of the behaviors that could be assessed, mainly because of lack of time and other resources. With informal observations, there is only enough time to observe a small fraction of what goes on in the classroom. Some samples, however, are better than others. Including a representative sample of content within a written test or informally observing a representative sample of students is obviously better than using unrepresentative samples.

Content-related evidence of validity is often established while an assessment is being planned. It involves a systematic analysis of what the test is intended to measure. Two techniques are commonly used for defining the intended content of a test: the first involves the establishment of a table of specifications; the second uses performance objectives.

Table of Specifications

A table of specifications consists of a two-dimensional chart. The vertical dimension of the chart lists the content areas to be addressed by the test. The horizontal dimension lists the categories of performance the test is to measure.

Table 4.1 is a table of specifications developed for an end-of-chapter written test on validity. In other words, it could be used for delineating the content of a test for the chapter you are now reading. The vertical dimension of this table lists the three topics being addressed in this chapter. The horizontal dimension lists the three capabilities being addressed in this chapter.

Table 4.1
Table of specifications for a test on validity

	Information	Concepts	Rules	Totals
Recognizing types of evidence used to establish validity	6	4		10
Applying types of evidence to classroom and published tests			5	5
Role of validity in the interpretation and use of assessment outcomes		5		5

In Chapter 3, Table 3.3 provided an example of a framework for selecting performance objectives. Both Table 3.3 and Table 4.1 use the same two dimensions: content and capabilities. However, the framework for selecting objectives includes content for the entire school year or term. A table of specifications lists only the content to be covered by a single written test or other assessment.

In Table 4.1, the three capabilities judged to be the most relevant for a written test on validity are included: information, concepts, and rules. On another assessment, other capabilities might be listed, such as discriminations, complex skills, motor skills, and attitudes.

The numbers within the table of specifications indicate the number of test questions to be associated with each content area and capability. A greater number of questions indicates that more emphasis or importance is given to that particular content area and capability. To establish these numbers, the teacher must determine the following:

First, the total number of questions to be included in the test

Then, the number of questions to be associated with each content area, entering these numbers in the Totals column

Finally, the number of questions within a content area to be associated with each capability

---

Box 4.1   *Apply What You Are Learning*

Based on the table of specifications illustrated in Table 4.1, answer the following questions.

1. What is the total number of questions in this test?
2. How many questions should be concerned with recognizing types of evidence used to establish validity?
3. Of the questions that are concerned with recognizing types of evidence, how many should measure concepts?
4. How many questions on the overall test should measure concepts?

Answers can be found at the end of the chapter.

Performance Objectives

Creating a table of specifications is one approach to planning a test and helping establish content-related evidence of validity. Another common approach is to work from performance objectives.

Recall that a table of specifications has two dimensions. One dimension lists content areas, and the other lists categories of performance. A performance objective can be thought of as the intersection of a row and column within a table of specifications, because a performance objective identifies both the content and the performance category of a skill. Chapter 3 suggests that each objective begin by stating the performance category or capability that is involved. The content is then specified

Table 4.2
List of performance objectives for a test on validity

	Number of Questions
Information: Describe characteristics of each of the methods used to establish evidence of validity.	6
Concept: When provided an example of evidence used to establish validity, classify by type the evidence being illustrated.	4
Rule: When provided an example of a classroom or standardized test, identify relevant evidence of validity.	5
Concept: Given the interpretation or use of a classroom test, explain why construct-related evidence of validity is relevant to the interpretation or use of the test.	5

through the behavior, situation, and special conditions components of the objective. In essence, a list of performance objectives can substitute for a table of specifications.

Table 4.2 lists performance objectives that are equivalent to the table of specifications presented in Table 4.1. The number of questions that will be used to measure each objective is specified, indicating the emphasis each skill is to receive in the test.

Applications to Formal Classroom Assessments

A table of specifications or the list of objectives is developed before the written test or other formal assessment is constructed. This then becomes a blueprint or plan for determining test content. As the test is completed, the table or list of objectives is used to help assure the content of the test is appropriate. This provides content-related evidence of validity.

When developing a test, a teacher uses judgment to determine how specific the test plan should be. As with blueprints that guide constructing buildings, the amount of detail required in a test plan depends on the significance of the test. A birdhouse probably can be built without a blueprint; remodeling a porch might require establishing some specifications; building a three-bedroom house calls for a fairly detailed blueprint; and constructing a large commercial building requires highly detailed plans specifying how parts of the framework will be joined and where ventilation ducts will be routed.

Similarly, a short quiz often can be developed without a formal table of specifications or list of objectives, and content-related validity probably can be established by using the teacher's mental idea of what is to be measured. Even if a major error in judgment results and the quiz has low validity, the implications of constructing one invalid quiz are minor.

On the other hand, any assessment that covers several weeks of instruction should be based on formal specifications. Such assessments include written exams, such as essay or objectively scored tests, performance assessments, such as of a student's speech, and take-home projects used for summative evaluations.

As occasionally happens when carpenters build houses, teachers constructing important assessments may overestimate how well they can develop the assessment without a formal plan. For example, without a written plan, a teacher might develop a test by selecting the more innovative test questions from among those included with curricular materials. Likewise, a teacher might focus on questions that will challenge students, instead of first establishing the content that is to be assessed. The carpenter who misjudges the need for specifications must adjust for or sometimes accept the errors that result. The teacher who misjudges the need for specifications often uses an assessment whose content is inconsistent with the focus of the class. The resulting low validity of such an assessment is a significant concern because the quality of each classroom assessment depends on its validity more than on any other factor.

Box 4.2   *Apply What You Are Learning*

Indicate (yes or no) whether each of the following statements describes a correct procedure for establishing content-related evidence that a written exam is valid.

1. Look through all existing questions, remove questions that do not match one of the objectives, and use the remaining questions on the test.

2. First determine how many questions should be used to measure each objective. Then construct a test so that the number of questions measuring each objective matches this specification.

3. Use a set of test questions whose difficulties correspond to the range of students' abilities.

4. First develop a table of specifications. Then construct a test so that the content of questions included in the test corresponds to this specification.

5. Use questions that have been proven to distinguish between students who have acquired specific knowledge and those who have not.

Answers can be found at the end of the chapter.

Applications to Informal Assessments

Informal assessments are by nature spontaneous. Also, they typically are directed toward one student at a time, with wide variation across students. It is unlikely that a formal plan, such as a table of specifications or list of objectives, will be used, at least outwardly, with informal assessments.

Nevertheless, all assessments, including those that are informal, must be valid. Otherwise they are useless. Thus content-related evidence of validity is relevant to informal assessments.

With informal assessments, content-related evidence is addressed before and after the assessments. Before instruction, while instructional activities are being planned, establish what will be observed and the type of informal questions that will be asked to determine whether students are learning important skills. After instruction, or when planning the next day's activities, look back at what has been observed and ask what evidence, if any, confirms whether or not students have mastered critical skills. Frequently ask (1) what you *should* know about students, (2) what you *actually* know now about students, and (3) how you know what you know. Because informal assessments are spontaneous, it is easy to base evaluations on what was seen rather than on a representative sampling of content. By frequently looking back at what has been assessed, the representativeness of informal assessments can become quite good.

The content of what is observed varies widely from student to student. Knowledge about individual students gained through informal assessments, therefore, is much less complete than is knowledge learned about the class as a whole.

Applications to Published Tests

The nature of published tests varies more than that of classroom assessments. In schools, the most widely used published tests are achievement measures; however, measures of aptitude, interest, and other constructs are also used.

Because the nature of published tests varies considerably, so do the procedures for collecting evidence of validity. These differences in validation procedures are occasionally overstated. For instance, some would argue that content-related evidence is relevant to achievement measures but not measures of aptitude. Similarly, some argue that construct-related evidence is more critical to constructs like aptitude than achievement. This simply is not true. All educational and psychological tests attempt to measure invisible constructs. With all tests, it is important to establish evidence that the performance observed through the test is relevant to the construct being measured. It is not useful to establish specifications for an achievement test without establishing a meaningful link between behaviors to be observed on the test and the invisible capabilities the test is intended to measure. Likewise it is not appropriate to describe behaviors associated with the construct an aptitude test is intended to measure but fail to establish that the content of the test includes these behaviors. Construct-, content-, and also criterion-related evidence of validity are each relevant to all tests.

Content-related evidence for any test is established through specifications. For instance, a test designed to measure intelligence must specify the observable behaviors that are indicators of intelligence and demonstrate that the content of the test involves these behaviors. For published achievement tests, this specification is usually accomplished with a table of specifications or list of performance objectives; the same procedure is used with classroom tests.

In selecting standardized achievement tests, school districts should work from local specifications, such as a list of objectives, and select published tests that correspond closely to these specifications. If a school district selects a published test without closely evaluating the match between the content of a test and content of the local curriculum, critical evidence of validity is not obtained. Because published achievement tests are often used to help evaluate students and their teachers, a significant mismatch between local objectives and test content is an important concern. We address this issue later in the book.

Other Procedures Used to Judge the Relevance of Test Content

Content-related evidence of validity usually involves establishing the desired content of the test, such as through a table of specifications, and then using this specification to control the selection of items included in the test. Other procedures sometimes are used to judge the relevance of test content. One of these procedures, *face validity,* actually has nothing to do with what the test measures and probably should not be referred to as *validity.* Two other procedures, *curriculum validity* and *instructional validity,* pertain more to the interpretation and use than the development of a test.

Face Validity. Test questions are said to have face validity when they *appear* to be relevant to the group being examined. To illustrate the concept of face validity, let us assume that the skill being tested is the calculation of the area of a rectangle when given its dimensions of length and width. This skill could be measured with the following question:

How many square feet are contained in a 4-foot by 6-foot rectangle?

This test question could be edited so that it appears particularly relevant to various groups of individuals. The following examples illustrate how this question might be revised for tests given to carpenters, glass cutters, painters, and landscapers.

Group Tested	*Question*
Carpenters	How many square feet are contained in a 4-foot by 6-foot piece of plywood?
Glass cutters	How many square feet of glass are contained in a 4-foot by 6-foot window?
Painters	How many square feet of painted surface are contained in a 4-foot by 6-foot area?
Landscapers	How many square feet of sod are required to cover a 4-foot by 6-foot section of ground?

These examples illustrate that editing a test question to improve its face validity does not alter the skill it is measuring. Such changes generally would not be expected to affect how examinees respond to the question. The term *face validity* is a misnomer because it addresses appearances in contrast to determining if the test measures what it is supposed to measure. Most measurement specialists consider face validity to be a desirable quality within a test, but do not consider this quality basic to the validity of the test.

Curricular and Instructional Validities. Another term that has become associated with validity is *curricular validity.* Hills (1981) defined curricular validity to be "an evaluation of the extent to which the content of a test agrees with the content of instruction" (p. 161). Curricular validity concerns the agreement of test content with instructional content. If the content of a test is consistent with the set of skills it was designed to measure but lacks consistency with the instruction that actually has been provided students, then the test is said to lack curricular validity.

Notice that curricular validity pertains to how the test is used and not how the test was designed. A test might be a valid measure of skills it was designed to measure, but invalid if used in a school or classroom where these skills are not taught.

The issue of curricular validity originated within the context of minimum competency testing. If passing a test is a prerequisite to receiving a high school diploma, then knowing that the test measures the intended content *and* that the curriculum provides students instruction in this content becomes an important issue. A widely cited Florida court ruling (*Debra P. v. Turlington,* 1981) concluded that although a minimum competency test used in Florida had been shown to measure the content it was designed to assess, the test could not be used as a graduation requirement until Florida could show that students had been given an opportunity to learn this content. The test was later accepted as a graduation requirement when an audit demonstrated that skills measured on the test were being taught (Fisher, 1983).

Sometimes, curricular validity is subdivided into issues of curricular and instructional validity. Often the terms *curricular* and *instructional validity* are used interchangeably. When used as distinct concepts, curricular validity pertains to the content covered in curricular materials, whereas instructional validity refers to the degree that this content is actually taught students. In this book, curricular and instructional valdity are assumed to represent equivalent concepts.

As with face validity, one can question whether curricular and instructional validity actually represent forms of test validity. Yalow and Popham (1983) reason that curricular and instructional validity concern how adequately instruction prepares students for a test in contrast to how adequately the test measures what it should measure. In contrast, Messick (1989b) reasons that test interpretation and use are inseparable from validity. Definitions aside, it is obviously important for tests to be relevant to the instruction students receive.

CRITERION-RELATED EVIDENCE OF VALIDITY

Criterion-related evidence indicates how well performance on a test correlates with performance on relevant criterion measures external to the test. Conceptually, criterion-related evidence of validity is quite simple. It asks, basically, "If a test is valid, with what other things should performance on the test correlate?" If, for example, a teacher's informal assessment of a student is valid, observations made through the informal assessment should be expected to correlate reasonably well with other knowledge the teacher has about the student. If they do not, one is inclined to question the validity of the informal assessment.

(The terms *criterion-related evidence of validity* and *criterion-referenced interpretations of performance* are sometimes confused. The meaning of these terms is distinct. Criterion-referenced refers to the frame of reference used to interpret performance on a test. It indicates that performance is given meaning by describing concisely the domain being measured by the test. In contrast, criterion-related validity is concerned with whether performance on a test correlates with other measures that should provide similar results. In fact, criterion-related evidence of validity is appropriate for criterion-referenced and norm-referenced tests.)

With criterion-related validity, the adequacy of the criterion is an important concern. As an example, a teacher's present knowledge of a student is used as the criterion for informal assessments. Therefore, it is important to ask how adequate the teacher's prior perceptions are.

Applications to Formal Classroom Assessments

With formal classroom assessments, criterion-related evidence of validity is obtained casually, although most teachers appropriately believe that this evidence is important. If a student's performance on a test is atypical, particularly if it is lower than expected, the teacher might question whether the test is valid. If a student has difficulties with a particular test format, such as essay or multiple-choice, the teacher might become suspicious about the validity of that format for the student.

It is always appropriate to look at performance on other measures as an indication of the validity of a formal assessment. Although not an infallible indication of validity, performance on other measures does provide some evidence of what the assessment measures.

Applications to Informal Assessments

As with formal assessments, a teacher should use other indicators to help judge the validity of informal assessments. This is difficult, however, because of the spontaneous nature of informal assessments. By looking back intermittently at what else is known about individual students and the class in general, informal assessments can benefit from criterion-related evidence of validity.

Applications to Published Tests

Criterion-related evidence, as with all approaches discussed in this chapter, is also appropriate for establishing the validity of published tests. Statistical correlations are often used to provide that evidence. For example, correlations are calculated between scores on the standardized test and scores on another relevant test, or even with scores on some later measure of academic performance, such as course grades. With classroom tests, however, statistical correlations usually are less useful than is the teacher's determination of whether students' scores make sense in light of what else is known about their performance.

Particularly with published tests, criterion-related evidence is often subdivided into *concurrent validity* and *predictive validity*, referring to whether the external criterion is obtained concurrent to the administration of the test, or at some point in the future. For instance, scores on a standardized achievement test are often correlated with scores on other achievement tests administered at about the same time. This would refer to concurrent validity. Scores on college admissions tests, in contrast, are often correlated with later grades in college, which refers to predictive validity.

Appendix A shows a commonly used procedure for computing statistical correlation. The resulting correlation coefficient is a number between zero and one, with zero indicating no relationship between two variables (such as scores on a test and an external criterion), and a correlation coefficient of one representing the highest possible or a perfect relationship between the two variables. This correlation coefficient is a positive number when the relationship is direct (increasing scores on one variable are associated with increasing variables on the other), or a negative number when the relationship is inverse (increasing scores on one variable are associated with decreasing variables on the other). When statistical correlations are used to establish criterion-related evidence, the correlation coefficients are usually positive.

VALID INTERPRETATION AND USE OF TESTS

Discussions of validity have traditionally focused only on evidence of what a test measures. Messick (1989a, 1989b) has described how this perspective is limited. He reasons that test validation is inseparable from the interpretation and intended use of tests.

Table 4.3 summarizes Messick's ideas. As illustrated in the table, Messick views validity in two dimensions, or facets. One dimension pertains to outcomes of a test, specifically, test interpretation (What do scores on the test mean?) and test use (What

Table 4.3
An expanded view of validity

	Test Interpretation	**Test Use**
Evidence	Evidence of what the test measures	Evidence that the test is relevant and useful for its intended application *(requires evidence of what the test measures)*
Consequences	Knowledge of appropriateness of what the test measures in light of society's values *(requires evidence of what the test measures)*	Consequences to society of using the test *(requires (a) evidence that the test is relevant and useful for its intended application, and (b) knowledge of appropriateness of what the test measures in light of society's values)*

Source: Adapted from "Meaning and Values in Test Validation" by S. Messick, 1989, *Educational Researcher, 18*(2), pp. 5–11.

actions should result from having these scores?). The other dimension concerns justifications for the testing. It involves evidence that justifies interpretations and uses of the test as well as consequences of these interpretations and uses of the test.

This two-by-two matrix results in four cells. The upper-left cell concerns evidence supporting interpretations of the test, that is, evidence of what the test measures. Included here are the types of evidence discussed earlier in this chapter: how well the test measures relevant constructs, descriptions of test content, and awareness of how performance on the test correlates with other measures. All this evidence allows interpretation of test performance.

The remaining three cells within the matrix address issues traditionally not included in discussions of test validity. The upper-right cell concerns evidence supporting proposed uses of a test, in other words, evidence that the test is relevant and useful for its intended application. This aspect of validity is especially relevant to classroom tests. For instance, many classroom tests are formative in nature in that they are meant to help the students or the teacher determine what to do next. An important question, then, is whether such a test is relevant and useful for this formative role. For example, in language arts, does a writing assignment that the teacher intends to use in a formative role provide relevant and useful information for helping the student improve writing performance? In math homework or in a written test that requires solving binomial equations, does student performance provide the teacher relevant and useful information concerning how to help students solve binomial equations?

Published tests also play significant roles within the classroom. Among other applications, they are used to group students and to evaluate the effectiveness of teaching and of teachers. As with classroom tests, the validity of published tests depends on evidence that they are relevant and useful for their typical applications. Research shows, with some significant exceptions, that students do not benefit from being grouped. Evidence also shows that published tests often are not useful for evaluating teachers, in part because the content of a given test does not correspond fully with what teachers are expected to teach.

Evidence supporting the interpretation and use of classroom and published tests is also relevant to students with special needs. The following are some additional questions that must be addressed when special needs are involved:

■ What is the relevance or usefulness of a test administered in English to a student whose best language is Spanish or another language?

■ How can scores on an intelligence test be interpreted when the test depends on cultural experiences and language previously irrelevant or unknown to some of the students?

■ How useful are tests that require written and oral responses for students whose physical impairment affects how they write or speak?

These issues are relevant to valid interpretations and uses of tests. However, these issues also show that virtually any test is invalid for some and possibly many situations. A relevant question is, For which interpretations and uses is a particular test valid? It is inappropriate to conclude that a test is invalid for every application when evidence indicates that it is valid for some, but not all, applications.

The lower two cells of Table 4.3 pertain to consequences of test interpretation and use. The lower-left cell concerns consequences of test interpretation, specifically, knowledge of the appropriateness of what a test measures in light of society's values. It is unlikely that consequences are examined for each classroom test, but they have a very real role when a teacher formulates the overall assessment strategy. Furthermore, issues of societal values are relevant to issues that affect classroom tests, such as school policies, goals and content of instruction, establishment of expectations, and grade assignment.

The lower-right cell of Table 4.3 concerns consequences of test use, that is, the consequences to society of using the test. An example is using tests (including teacher observations) to place students in special education programs. One consequence is the labeling of students. Another is providing additional resources for the students. These consequences, in turn, result in other consequences.

As noted in the table, the consequences to society (including students) of using a test depend on (a) evidence that the test is relevant and useful for its intended application and (b) knowledge of the appropriateness of what the test measures in light of society's values. These prerequisites both require evidence of what the test measures. This dependence, Messick argues, shows how an examination of the evidence and consequences of the interpretation and use of a test is consolidated into an expanded, yet unified, view of validity.

SUMMARY

Validity pertains to how well a test measures what it is supposed to measure. It is the single most important quality in the development, interpretation, and use of any educational measure.

Validity is an abstraction. Instead of observing validity, we evaluate various evidence pertaining to the interpretation and use of the test. Evidence associated with interpretation is conventionally grouped into construct-, content-, and criterion-related categories.

Construct-related evidence establishes whether a test matches the capabilities or psychological construct that is to be measured. With classroom tests, learned knowledge is usually the construct of greatest relevance. Declarative and procedural knowledge are the two dominant types of learned knowledge.

Content-related evidence concerns how well elements of a test relate to the content domain being assessed. A table of specifications and list of performance objectives are two common techniques used to guide the establishment of content-related validity. Content-related evidence is gathered when the test is being developed.

Criterion-related evidence of validity indicates how well performance on a test correlates with performance on relevant-criterion measures external to the test. With informal and formal classroom assessments, the teacher gathers criterion-related evidence by observing whether performance on an assessment agrees with other relevant indications of student performance.

Test validity applies not only to evidence of what the test measures, but also to evidence supporting applications for which the test is to be used. Validity also pertains to the appropriateness of what a test measures and to the consequences that result from use of the test. These dimensions of validity are interrelated. An evaluation of validity often indicates that a test is valid for some, but not all, applications for which it might be used.

ANSWERS: APPLY WHAT YOU ARE LEARNING

4.1 1. 20 questions; 2. 10 questions; 3. 4 questions; 4. 9 questions.

4.2 1. No; 2. Yes; 3. No; 4. Yes; 5. No. Although the strategies suggested in questions 1, 3, and 5 may identify good items, collectively these items may not measure the skills the test should be measuring. Content-related evidence of validity will be established only if the skills to be measured and the emphasis to be given to each skill are specified first. Only then should the required test items be assembled. Experience (including yours) has shown that tests often are not content-valid unless such a plan is used when constructing the test.

SOMETHING TO TRY

■ For a subject area you would likely teach, think of specific examples of knowledge you would try to help your students learn. Try to think of separate examples for each of the following types of capability: information, discrimination, concept, rule, and complex rule. For each example, describe what you might ask your students to do to indicate what they have learned. Make sure each description takes into account the nature of the capability being assessed (see Table 3.2).

■ Prepare a lesson plan for a one-hour class you would likely teach. (An existing lesson plan would be fine.) Describe how you would informally assess students during this lesson. State types of construct-, content-, and criterion-related evidence that could be used to establish the validity of these informal assessments.

ADDITIONAL READING

Messick, S. (1989). Validity. In R. L. Linn (Ed.), *Educational measurement* (3rd ed., pp. 13–103). New York: American Council on Education. This chapter provides an extended discussion of test validation, beginning with a description of the historical development of concepts of validity.

CHAPTER 5

Reliability

The focus of the previous chapter was validity. Validity was characterized as the single most important factor in determining the quality of an assessment. This chapter is concerned with reliability. Second only to validity, reliability is a critical quality of any test, whether that test is a written test, a performance assessment, or an informal observation or question.

By definition, *reliability is the degree to which a test measures something consistently.* This definition includes an important subtlety. As long as *something* is being measured consistently, the observation is reliable. In other words, a test that consistently measures any entity is reliable, even though this entity is not what the test is supposed to be measuring. A test can be reliable (measuring something consistently) without being valid (measuring what it is supposed to measure).

The inverse, however, is not true. Test reliability is a prerequisite to test validity. The validity of many educational measures is limited by their less than optimal reliability.

The fact that reliability is a prerequisite to validity is one reason it is important for you to understand both reliability and validity. Another reason is that educators often confuse reliability with validity when they interpret student performance. Sometimes, one determines that a test is reliable, but then mistakenly assumes that the test measures what it is intended to measure.

Like validity, a test might provide quite reliable measures in one context or situation, but not in another. Also like validity, reliability is an abstraction. One cannot "see" reliability. Instead, we depend on various indicators of reliability.

This chapter helps you achieve five skills:

- Realize why reliability is a prerequisite to validity
- Identify typical threats to reliability

- Recognize commonly used indicators of reliability
- Identify techniques that improve reliability
- Clarify the difference between reliability and validity

WHY RELIABILITY IS A PREREQUISITE TO VALIDITY

Whenever one measures anything, the measurement must have reliability as a prerequisite to having validity. This relationship between validity and reliability holds true whether we are referring to educational, psychological, or even physical measurements.

Assume, for example, that we are measuring the height of pieces of furniture in a room, but the tape measure we use is made of elastic. Because the tape is elastic, when we repeat our measurements of a piece of furniture, we get different values. We do *not* have consistency in our measurement; therefore, the measurement lacks reliability. But our measurement problem is more significant than simply lacking consistency. We are also measuring something other than what we are supposed to be measuring. The measurements we get may be more of an indication of the amount of tension being placed on the elastic tape than a measure of the height of furniture. That is, our measurement lacks validity in addition to lacking reliability.

To generalize from our elastic measuring tape, whenever the quality being measured *does not change* but the scores obtained from the measurement *are changing*, the only explanation is that something is being measured that is not supposed to be measured. If the skill being measured by a test is not changing for a given student but this student's test scores are changing, then the test must be measuring something other than or in addition to what it is supposed to be measuring. *A test that lacks reliability must also lack validity.*

This relationship between reliability and validity is very important. If any assessment lacks reliability, it lacks validity. If scores assigned to students' papers or other homework lack reliability, they lack validity. If an innovative technique is used to assess student performance but the technique lacks reliability, then it lacks validity. If observations made by informally asking students questions lack reliability, they lack validity. It is *never* appropriate to conclude that a measure of student performance is valid when one has reason to believe that the measure lacks reliability.

When assessing students, it is very important to have reliable measures. For this reason, discussion throughout this book includes strategies that minimize threats to reliability. These strategies do not guarantee but do increase our chances of obtaining valid assessments of student performance. On the other hand, ignoring the need for reliable measures virtually assures our measures of student performance will be invalid.

COMMON THREATS TO RELIABILITY

A measure of student performance is reliable if it measures something consistently. Anything that causes inconsistency within the measure is a potential threat to its reliability. This section describes the more common sources of inconsistency that occur in educational measures.

Not all types of inconsistency are threats to reliability. An inconsistency in student performance is a threat only if the inconsistency is due to something other than differences in students. For instance, if students differ from each other with respect to how proficient they are with a particular skill, the inconsistency or difference in their performance on a test that measures the skill is desirable. This inconsistency is not a threat to reliability. If a student over time becomes more proficient with a skill, change in that student's performance over time is desirable. Again, this inconsistency is not a threat to reliability. On the other hand, if a test that measures students' vocational interests is supposed to provide stable results over time so that the test can help students select and prepare for future careers, then inconsistency over time is undesirable. Here, inconsistency over time would be considered a threat to reliability. The circumstances within which abilities or attitudes are measured determine whether a particular inconsistency is a threat to reliability.

Inconsistencies Between Earlier and Later Measures

Many things change over time. Therefore, it is common to see inconsistencies between student performance on earlier and later measures. As noted earlier, an important question is whether or not the inconsistency is undesirable.

There are many examples of inconsistencies over time. If students are administered tests before and after instruction, their performance normally changes. This inconsistency is desirable. If students are administered an aptitude test in third grade and again in sixth grade, there are likely to be inconsistencies from one administration to the other. This inability of the aptitude test to provide results that are stable over time is often considered undesirable, such as when the test is used to identity which students should be provided special education over the next several years. If high school students complete a vocational interest inventory in the eighth grade, their performance on the inventory will probably have changed by the time this inventory is readministered in the eleventh grade. Again, this lack of stability is considered undesirable because it reduces the usefulness of long-range vocational planning.

A source of inconsistency between earlier and later measures must be evaluated to determine whether it is undesirable. If it is undesirable, it is a threat to reliability. Otherwise, it is not relevant to the reliability of the measure.

Inconsistencies Between Test Items That Supposedly Measure the Same Skill

Typically, more than one test item is used to measure each skill being assessed on a written test. Similarly, a teacher will orally ask more than just one question to determine if students understand a particular concept. The use of multiple test items, oral questions, or other observations represents a good technique. Multiple measures increase our confidence in what we observe.

Inconsistencies in student performance between test items that supposedly measure the same skill is a concern. In fact, it is this anticipated lack of consistency between items that causes us to use multiple items to measure each skill. If we expected each student to perform the same regardless of which multiplication problem were used, then we would use a one-item test to measure students' multiplication skills. Were student performance consistent from item to item, more than one test item would be redundant. Instead, however, we use several items to average out the inconsistency and increase our confidence in the measure. We will later observe that the use of several test items, oral questions, or observations is one of the most effective techniques for offsetting low reliability in our measures.

Students perform inconsistently among items that supposedly measure the same skill for a number of reasons. One reason is that students often guess at the correct answer and their guesses are inconsistently lucky. This is a problem not only with multiple-choice and true–false items, but also to a lesser degree with other formats such as essays, performance assessments, and oral questions.

Another reason for inconsistent performance across items is that many test items pose vague questions. When this happens, students differ with respect to what they perceive is being asked and accordingly give inconsistent answers. To reduce this source of inconsistency, considerable emphasis in subsequent chapters is placed on techniques for asking concise questions.

Another reason students perform inconsistently across items is that a group of items designed to measure the same skill often ends up measuring different skills. As you know, the skills students are expected to learn are extremely complex. Even a skill as focused as knowing the multiplication tables involves different skills. This is why, for example, it is easier to multiply numbers by zero or by five than by, say, six or seven. Also, each student's prior experience influences what a test item measures. For instance, asking a student to use aerodynamics to explain why a kite flies would require recall of verbal information if the relevance of aerodynamics to kites had previously been explained to the student. On the other hand, the student would have to generalize aerodynamic principles from other applications it the student had not been taught or did not recall the application of these principles to kites.

Sometimes, two *groups* of items such as two versions or forms of a test that supposedly measure the same skill are involved. For example, if a teacher is using a mastery learning strategy, one form of a test might be used to evaluate student achievement after initial instruction, and an alternative and, we hope, equivalent version of the test would later be used with students who needed further instruction. Or two equivalent versions of a standardized test might be administered in order to help maintain test security. Although the intention is to include equivalent items in both versions of the test, there usually is some inconsistency with respect to how students perform on the alternate forms of the test. This inconsistency is undesirable and threatens the reliability of scores on these tests.

Inconsistencies Between Alternate Skills in the Same Content Domain

The complexities of skills that are taught in the classroom create another source of inconsistency within student assessments. Because of the complexity of skills, in order to make instruction and assessment manageable, we often combine distinct skills into a single performance objective or into a single content domain. Sometimes we simply are unable to subdivide a complex skill into fully meaningful subparts. A student who is proficient with one component of a skill may be less proficient with another component included in the same content domain. The particular set of skills the teacher happens to incorporate into the test then affects the judgment the teacher makes of the student's performance.

For instance, when assessing student ability to deliver a persuasive speech, it is impractical and inappropriate to divide the delivery of a speech into each of its hundreds of component skills. In fact, one is able to measure only a sampling of these skills when one assesses a student's speech. The particular skills that will be measured during a student's speech are largely determined by multiple factors that are not easily controlled. Factors might include the topic and illustrations a student selects for the speech, the student's and teacher's prior experience with the topic and illustrations, the instructional goals on which the teacher is concentrating, and even the confidence and attitude the student has going into the speech. The assessment the teacher makes of the speech does not fully generalize, such as to a persuasive speech the student would make on a different topic. The teacher's intention of measuring the student's ability to deliver a persuasive speech becomes a more limited measure of that student's ability to deliver a speech within particular circumstances.

Complex assessment techniques such as portfolios and performance assessments are particularly vulnerable to inconsistencies between alternative skills. The sample of work included in a portfolio and even the students' and teacher's understanding of how to appropriately select samples of work to include in a portfolio largely determine the assessment that will be made of each student's performance. Likewise, the attributes of student performance a teacher chooses to rate within a performance assessment significantly affect the score each student will receive as a result of her or his performance. It is common to accept inconsistencies obtained from portfolios and performance assessments as an inevitable characteristic of these techniques, or even as an attribute one would hope to obtain with these flexible procedures. However, inconsistencies that are caused by the assessment procedure and not from differences in student performance reduce the reliability of the assessments. The inability of these assessments to generalize beyond the specific sample of student actions that are included in the particular portfolio or performance assessment is a significant limitation and not an asset of these assessments. As we discuss portfolio and performance assessments in later chapters, particular attention is given to techniques that help improve their generalizability or reliability.

Other techniques used to assess students are also vulnerable to inconsistencies in performance among skills in a domain. The informal observation that a teacher does naturally during instruction is highly susceptible to the specific skills the teacher happens to observe. For instance in a chemistry lab, a student needs to use equipment correctly, make accurate measurements, follow a reasonable sequence of actions, and work safely. For a given student, the teacher will probably observe a subset of these actions. Had the teacher observed a different subset of actions, a different assessment of the student's performance may have been obtained. Observations are even affected by what students allow or encourage the teacher to see. Had the teacher been able to observe other actions, different judgments of performance may have occurred.

Scores on written tests are likewise affected by the sample of skills measured by the test. You know from the tests you have taken that, even when the test is well constructed, you would have obtained a somewhat different score on the test had different questions about the same concept been asked or had the same questions been asked differently.

Because skills taught in school are complex, virtually every performance objective or content domain includes diverse and distinct skills. Inclusion of a particular subset of skills in an assessment provides a different judgment of student performance than would have been obtained from an alternative subset of skills. Perfect reliability is unobtainable in educational measurement, to a large part, because of the complexities of skills being assessed. Our goal is to take deliberate steps in the development and administration of student assessments so as to maximize the reliability we do obtain.

Inconsistencies from Measuring Unrelated Qualities Within One Test

The potential exists to build into a test inconsistencies internal to that test. One cause of this internal inconsistency is the use of a single score to report student performance on multiple unrelated qualities. An example is using one score on an essay test to indicate both the correctness of answers to questions *and* the correctness of spelling. Scores on this essay test would not be internally consistent. For some students, a low score would indicate problems with answering the questions. For other students, a low score would indicate problems with spelling. Using one score to report performance on unrelated qualities lowers the reliability of test scores.

An analogy helps illustrate the problem. Automobiles have a sensor that measures the amount of fuel remaining in the tank and another sensor to measure the temperature of the engine. Information from these sensors is displayed on gauges inside the car and is of considerable use. However, readings of the fuel and temperature sensors have little or no relation to each other. If information from the fuel *and* temperature sensors were combined into a single gauge, then the gauge would not be useful.

For the same reason, one test score should not be used to report unrelated qualities. As with the combined fuel and temperature gauge, combining unrelated factors into a single test score reduces the internal consistency and the usefulness of the score.

A test has internal consistency if everything that contributes to the score is related. Table 5.1 lists some situations that will cause higher versus lower internal consistencies. Situations in the upper half of the table tend to have higher internal consistency because the students who do best in one quality that is being scored tend to be the students who do best on the other quality. For instance, the same students tend to do best on addition and subtraction problems or on listing historical dates and names of significant people. In contrast, students who are most knowledgeable in social studies often are not the best spellers. Higher internal consistency would result if separate scores were used to report knowledge in social studies and ability to spell. Similarly, technical quality and artistic interpretation in figure skating are not

Table 5.1
Some situations that tend to affect internal consistency

Situations That Tend to Cause Higher Internal Consistency

On a math test, the use of one score for addition and subtraction problems

On a history test, the use of one score for questions concerning significant dates and the names of significant people

On a French test, the use of one score for vocabulary and translation

Situation That Tend to Cause Lower Internal Consistency

Within a social studies essay exam, the use of one score for accuracy in contrasting democracy versus totalitarianism and accuracy in spelling

Withing a science homework assignment, the use of one score for quality of work and timeliness (i.e., turning in a late paper)

Within Olympic competition figure skating, the use of one score to indiate technical quality and artistic interpretation

highly related. For higher internal consistency, Olympic judges should and do use separate scores to report performance in these two areas.

Problems with internal consistency show up within every assessment technique. For example, a portfolio in writing might include assessments of student ability to communicate ideas in writing, to use appropriate grammar, to use good penmanship, and to assemble samples of work into a portfolio properly. If one overall score (such as an overall qualitative description) is given for each portfolio, this score will lack internal consistency. On the other hand, if separate scores or descriptions are provided for each of these attributes, each score will have higher internal consistency.

Informal observations such as ongoing observations and oral questions can lack internal consistency. The reliability of observations is improved if unrelated attributes such as a student's attitude, facial expressions, and performance with the skill are kept as separate assessments rather than combined into an overall judgment of the student. Unrelated attributes can help qualify or explain student performance, but they should be retained as distinct assessments.

Random attributes also threaten internal consistency. In fact, random attributes are typically a significant problem within student assessments. Students' guessing of the correct answer is an example of this type of threat. Other examples of random attributes include student attempts to guess at what is being asked by an ambiguous question and a teacher using inconsistent standards from paper to paper when grading student work. These random attributes are particularly problematic because it is not possible to separate out their effects. With attributes such as grammar and spelling, it is possible to establish separate scores. It is not possible, however, to determine separate scores for students' ability to identify correct examples of a concept versus students' good fortune to guess correctly at examples of the concept. Similarly, it is not possible to separate differences in students' scores caused by true differences in their proficiency from the differences in scores caused by ambiguities in the test items.

Problems with internal consistency caused by these random attributes are serious problems within educational measurement. We therefore will give considerable attention to techniques that reduce the effects of guessing, as well as those that improve the clarity of informal and formally presented questions.

Inconsistencies Between Different Raters in the Scoring of Student Responses

A useful practice when students' responses must be subjectively scored is to involve more than one rater. Although often not practical, it is beneficial to have more than one rater read students' papers, review portfolios, observe students during performance assessments, and even informally observe students in class.

When multiple raters are used, inconsistencies between raters become apparent. This inconsistency is an extension of the problem with internal consistency that occurs when just one rater scores each student's performance. When more than one rater is involved, however, this inconsistency becomes visible.

Since the use of multiple raters is usually impractical, we will emphasize techniques that reduce inconsistencies in one teacher's ratings. Reducing these inconsistencies would have the indirect benefit of improving consistencies among different raters were different raters used.

Inconsistencies in Decisions Based on Student Performance

Sometimes a passing score is established for a test. With standardized tests, passing scores are sometimes established to make decisions such as whether a student is eligible to receive a high school diploma or to be admitted to a particular college. With classroom tests, passing scores are used to determine whether further instruction should be provided or whether a student should be placed with a particular group of students. When test scores are numerical, the passing score is also expressed as a number, possibly a percentage. When test scores are qualitative descriptions, a passing score might be an explicit or implicit description of a minimally acceptable performance.

Particularly with standardized tests, a student's performance relative to the passing score is highly significant. Likewise, misclassifications relative to this passing score, such as failing to grant a high school diploma to a student whose true achievement is actually superior to the minimally acceptable performance, is obviously a reason for concern.

Misclassifications of students relative to a passing score are the results of inconsistencies in test scores. Because of less than perfect reliability, some students whose true performance is higher than the passing score will, on the test, score below the passing score and be misclassified. The reverse will happen among students whose true performance is lower than the passing score. Misclassifications will more commonly occur among students whose true performance is close to the passing score.

Misclassifications will also occur among many more of the students if the test contains substantial inconsistencies, such as from sources discussed previously.

Classroom measures, particularly those that involve informal assessments such as casual observation, include substantial inconsistencies. For the most part this is unavoidable, although steps discussed later can help minimize this problem. With classroom measures, it is important to be alert to the fact that many decisions based on observations of student performance are in error, that another, comparable observation might have resulted in a different decision.

CONVENTIONAL METHODS FOR DETECTING INCONSISTENCIES

Like validity, reliability is an abstraction. One cannot "see" reliability. Instead, one must become aware of sources of inconsistency that reduce the reliability of measurements, and then take actions to improve reliability.

Several *indicators* of reliability are commonly used. Most indicators are statistical. They also tend to be more useful with educational measures that result in a numerical rather than qualitative description of student performance. These indicators of reliability, although generally not complicated, tend to be too time-consuming to be computed by hand. With the increase in computerized scoring of tests, however, some of these techniques are quite practical for use in classroom settings. Also, the techniques described here are widely used with the standardized tests that are administered in schools. For these reasons, being familiar with some of the conventional methods for estimating the reliability of test scores is useful.

Most methods described here express reliability as a number that ranges from .00 to 1.00. A value of .00 indicates total lack of reliability, or total inconsistency. A value of 1.00 indicates perfect reliability, or total consistency. This number is called the reliability coefficient.

Test–Retest Method

Possibly the most obvious method for judging whether a test measures something consistently is to readminister the test to the same students. If, on the readministration, the students who originally obtained the highest scores continue to achieve high scores, the middle-scoring students continue to achieve the middle scores, and so on, then one would anticipate the test is reliable. The test is measuring something consistently.

With the test–retest method, a correlation coefficient[1] is computed between students' scores on the test and the retest. If there is high agreement between the test

---

[1]Most of the techniques described here for estimating reliability are based on correlation coefficients. The computation of a reliability coefficient is illustrated in Appendix A. Another group of techniques, involving generalizability theory, divides variability among test scores into component parts, referred to as *sources of variability*. This is accomplished through a statistical technique called *analysis of variance*. For a particular interpretation of test scores, desirable sources of variability are then distinguished from undesirable sources. Although more complex, the technique estimates how well one's performance on a test will generalize to other relevant administrations of a comparable test.

and retest scores, the correlation coefficient will approach a value of 1.00. If there is little agreement between these scores, the coefficient will approach zero.

The test–retest method is not appropriate for classroom tests. One reason is that teachers generally are not willing to readminister a test just to see if the test gives consistent results. Nor are students interested in retaking a test for that purpose.

Of greater importance, the test–retest method does not detect inconsistencies that are of greatest concern with classroom tests. By readministering the same test at a later time, the test–retest method *does* detect inconsistencies between earlier and later performance, but this type of inconsistency does not and should not bother teachers; inconsistency between earlier and later performance is often the result of learning. However, the test–retest method is not sensitive to most sources of inconsistency that are relevant to classroom assessments. Readministering the same test questions, for example, will probably not detect inconsistent interpretations of vague questions unless each student forgets the original interpretation of the questions when taking the retest.

On the other hand, the test–retest method is appropriate for tests expected to give consistent results over time. For example, if an intelligence test proposes to measure a general academic ability that is stable over time, then the test–retest reliability of the test is relevant. Similarly, if a vocational interest inventory is designed to help students select and prepare for future occupations, consistency in performance over time is important for this inventory.

Box 5.1   *Apply What You Are Learning*

For each of the following instances, indicate (yes or no) whether the test–retest method is appropriate for estimating reliability.

1. A teacher assesses a student's portfolio by comparing the student's present work with similar work completed earlier in the year.

2. A judgment of each student's ability to learn is made during the first week of school. This judgment is the basis for grouping students throughout the year.

3. A teacher informally observes the work of five students in class. The teacher wonders if these five students' work is a good indication of what the rest of the class is doing.

Answers can be found at the end of the chapter.

Alternate-Form Method

Another strategy for estimating reliability involves administering two forms or versions of a test to the same students. This results in each student obtaining two scores, one on each test form. The correlation coefficient between the students' two scores is then calculated.

It is appropriate to use the alternate-form method whenever two or more forms of a test are developed and used interchangeably. This verifies that the alternate test forms are measuring the same thing. When both forms of a test are administered at the same time to a group of students, the correlation between scores on the two forms indicates the degree to which the alternate forms give consistent results.

Although the alternate-form method is appropriate when more than one form of a test is used, a teacher seldom has the opportunity to administer the multiple forms simultaneously to students. Therefore, different procedures are needed. If the purpose of using the multiple forms is simply to control copying, a preferred solution is to generate two forms by using the same items but in different orders on the two forms. Research has shown that the order in which items are presented on a test has minimal or no effect on the scores of examinees (Marso, 1970). Consequently, there is little reason to use the alternate-form method when the only difference between alternate forms is the order in which the test items are presented.

When alternate forms are developed so that students can, at a later time, be administered a retest, then distinct (although similar) items should be used on the different forms of the test. In this situation, the optimal procedure is to compute the correlation between scores on the two forms. As noted earlier, however, this is usually an impractical option for teachers.

A reasonable alternative is to take steps to ensure the equivalence of the forms. This might include writing items from carefully developed specifications and then randomly assigning items that measure each skill to the respective forms of the test.

Developers of commercially prepared tests sometimes prepare alternate forms of each test. As part of their test development process, the developers will estimate the equivalence of alternate forms by simultaneously administering both forms to a group of students. The correlation coefficient between these examinees' scores is then computed. If the alternate forms are measuring the same skills, this reliability coefficient approaches 1.00.

Split-Half Method

The split-half method is similar to the alternate-form method in that the correlation between scores on two forms is computed. Unlike the alternate-form method, the split-half method involves the administration of only one form of a test. Splitting test questions from a single test into two groups artificially creates two forms. Often, the odd-numbered questions versus the even-numbered questions make up the two groups. The correlation coefficient is then calculated between students' scores on the respective halves of the test.

Because the split-half method involves the administration of only one form of a test, this method may be practical for use in the classroom. However, the computations are tedious. Some computer programs are available for scoring tests by means of the split-half method, and fairly inexpensive calculators have built-in correlation programs.

A disadvantage of the split-half method is that it underestimates reliability. This is because there are fewer test questions in each half of the split than there are in the test as a whole. The use of fewer questions lowers reliability. Later in the chapter we see how this low estimate of reliability can be readjusted with the easy-to-use Spearman–Brown formula.

Kuder–Richardson Method

Kuder and Richardson (1937) devised several methods for estimating the reliability of scores from a single administration of a test. Their 1937 publication included numerous derivations. The 20th and 21st formulas within these derivations have become the most widely used of their methods for estimating reliability, and have become known as the KR-20 and KR-21 formulas. These formulas, particularly the KR-21, are fairly easy to use. The KR-21 formula estimates reliability using only the arithmetic mean and standard deviation of scores on a test, and it can be computed quickly with a calculator that has built-in mean and standard deviation functions. Although easier to compute, the KR-21 formula somewhat underestimates the reliabilities of scores when some items within the test are considerably more difficult than others. The use of the KR-21 formula is illustrated in Appendix A.

When only one form of a test is involved, the Kuder–Richardson formulas, particularly KR-20,[2] are generally preferred over the split-half method. The Kuder–Richardson methods are more sensitive to sources of internal consistency. A Kuder–Richardson reliability coefficient is often provided when objectively scored tests are scored by computer.

Box 5.2   *Apply What You Are Learning*

Which method of estimating reliability (test–retest, alternate-form, or Kuder–Richardson) best answers each of the following concerns?

1. Do vocational interests, as measured by a vocational preference inventory, remain stable over time?

2. Is a subtest within an arithmetic diagnostic test measuring a single ability?

3. Is a teacher-prepared test fairly free of random error that would be caused by ambiguous items?

4. Can two forms of a standardized achievement test be used interchangeably?

Answers can be found at the end of the chapter.

Inter-Rater Method

With subjectively scored assessments such as essay tests and judgments of products produced by students, considerable inconsistency may arise in the scoring of the assessments. That is, two raters, if they separately review the students' work, may come up with very different judgments of each student's performance. The inter-rater method can be used to detect this inconsistency. Basically, two or more teachers

---

[2]The Kuder–Richardson technique has one particular disadvantage: It can only be used with tests whose questions are scored right or wrong. Questions, such as the essay format, that allow partial credit for answers will not work with the Kuder–Richardson formulas. A generalized form of the KR-20 formula, referred to as the Cronbach (1951) coefficient alpha, can be used in those situations.

independently score each student's performance and obtain two scores for each student. The correlation coefficient is then computed between the teachers' scores.

Methods for Estimating Consistency of Decisions

Estimates of reliability should consider not only sources of error, but also types of decisions that will be based on the test scores (American Psychological Association, 1985). In mastery learning, criterion-referenced tests are used to decide whether further instruction will be provided to each student. It is appropriate to determine whether the same mastery decisions would have been made had a comparable but different form of the test been administered.[3]

Various methods have been proposed to estimate the consistency with which a test assigns students to mastery versus nonmastery categories. Swaminathan, Hambleton, and Algina (1974) described two methods. The first is the *agreement coefficient* and is easy to compute, although not likely used in classroom situations because they require the simultaneous administration of two forms of a test to the same students. The agreement coefficient is simply the proportion of students who are classified consistently on both forms (that is, consistently pass or consistently do not pass on both forms). However, the agreement coefficient is not expected to obtain a value lower than .50 even if there is no consistency in the way the two test administrations classify students, much as two flips of a coin will be in agreement 50% of the time.

The second method proposed is called the *kappa coefficient.* The kappa coefficient is conceptually the same as the agreement coefficient, but has the more conventional range of .00 to 1.00.

These coefficients are appealing when a mastery learning strategy is being used, although limited by the need for two administrations of a test. Procedures that estimate consistency of classification from a single test administration have been developed (Huynh, 1976; Subkoviak, 1976); however, their computations are more complex.

The agreement and kappa coefficients approach their minimal values as the KR-20 estimate of reliability approaches .00; the agreement and kappa coefficients approach their maximum values when the KR-20 estimate approaches 1.00 and students' scores are distributed away from the passing score (Subkoviak, 1988).

How Reliable Should One Expect Measurements to Be?

Several methods of estimating reliability have been discussed. Most of these methods produce a reliability coefficient that ranges from .00 to 1.00. In each case, the ideal value for a reliability coefficient is 1.00. Because the reliability of scores on tests seldom achieves this ideal value, a reliability coefficient should be interpreted in terms of what is realistic for a particular type of test.

---

[3]Classification of students in a consistent manner is important when a passing score is established. Remember, though, that establishing a passing score does not automatically allow a criterion-referenced interpretation of student performance. A test must measure a well-defined content domain to be criterion-referenced. In fact, a criterion-referenced interoperation can be accomplished without establishing a passing score. Nevertheless, when testing and instruction are integrated, a passing score is useful for determining for each student whether further instruction should be provided.

In general, alternate-form, split-half, and Kuder–Richardson reliabilities of commercially prepared standardized tests should be near or above .90 to be considered acceptably high. If a test measures a quality for which students' performance is expected to remain consistent over time, then the test–retest method should be used to estimate reliability. A test–retest reliability greater than .80 is realistic when the retest is administered within a few months of the initial test administration. As the amount of time between administrations increases, lower consistency between scores on the test and retest should be expected, with a corresponding decrease in the test–retest reliability coefficient.

The reliability of teacher-made tests is typically lower than that of commercially prepared tests. Diederich (1973) proposed that if a teacher's test requires a full class period to complete (approximately 50 minutes), its Kuder–Richardson reliability should be between .60 and .80. Shorter tests would be expected to have lower reliabilities.

Kane (1986) has pointed out that if the Kuder–Richardson reliability for a test is less than .50, the stability of scores is too low for the test to provide information useful for individualized instruction. If the KR-20 reliability of test scores is under .50, one cannot differentiate the performance of a student from the average performance of the class as a whole. Under such a condition, providing different instruction to students in a class based on their test scores is unwarranted.

Although the KR-20 and KR-21 reliability estimates are more applicable to norm-referenced interpretations, they can provide useful and, with computer programs, fairly easy to obtain indications about the stability of criterion-referenced measures. If the KR-20 or KR-21 reliability of a criterion-referenced test is found to be less than .50, the reliability usually can be improved by increasing the number of questions in the test. If reliability greater than .50 cannot be obtained, scores on a criterion-referenced test should be used to guide instruction given to the class as a whole rather than instruction given to individual students.

TECHNIQUES FOR IMPROVING RELIABILITY

To improve reliability of classroom assessments, one must anticipate the conditions that cause inconsistency within educational measures and then take actions that will control those conditions. For example, the complexity of the content domains being taught in the classroom is a major cause of inconsistency in measurement. A student's score on a given test is a function of the sample of specific skills from the domain that are measured by the test. One can generalize from the student's performance on this test only to the extent that the test adequately samples all relevant skills within the content domain being measured. To improve the reliability of this test, one must improve the sample of skills measured by the test by increasing the number of items or student observations in the test and/or improving the representativeness of skills measured by the test.

Four general techniques for improving the reliability of test scores are described here. The first includes a series of actions that can be used to improve the quality of observations of student performance. The second technique involves improvements in how the student performances observed are scored or judged. The third technique involves increasing the number of observations included in a test. The fourth technique is concerned with including a sufficient sample of diverse tasks within the assessment.

Improving the Quality of Observations

The next several chapters describe in detail a variety of techniques that are used to improve the quality of observations. Chapters 6 through 9 describe techniques that apply to written tests, such as those using essay and multiple-choice questions. Chapters 11 through 14 describe how to improve observations of student performance obtained from informal assessments, performance assessments, and student portfolios.

Ambiguities in a test are a major threat to reliability. When a test presents a vague task, students' reactions and responses are inconsistent. Ambiguities can be reduced by a variety of means, depending on the test format. For example, with multiple-choice items, using a stem that presents a concise problem to be addressed by the student reduces ambiguity. Problematic words and sentence structures in the stem and options can be avoided. With completion items, the item needs to be constructed so that only a homogeneous set of words will represent a correct answer when written in the blank. For portfolios, the categories of work samples to be included are identified, and within each category, the concise conditions or characteristics that a work sample should have are specified. Conciseness can work against the flexibility that is an asset of some formats, such as essays and portfolios. The trick is to determine the conditions that must be specified or controlled while providing students flexibility in how to meet those conditions.

Observations can also be improved by controlling students' ability to guess the correct answer for reasons unrelated to the skill being tested. Guessing presents a significant problem, particularly with the true–false and multiple-choice formats. We will look at ways to make the wrong answer plausible to students who lack the knowledge being tested without decreasing the likelihood that knowledgeable students will select the correct response. Guessing is also a serious problem with casual oral questions. Leading questions may tell students the correct answer, even if they do not have the knowledge being assessed. Although leading questions motivate students and help them reason through a problem, ultimately a student's proficiency should be assessed without the prompts.

The quality of test items—and ultimately reliability—can also be improved *after* the test items are used. A procedure called *item analysis* uses student responses to help detect ambiguities and other problems within items. This information is then used to improve items before they are reused within later tests. Item analysis is a technique most commonly used with multiple-choice items, although the general principles being used apply to other formats, including performance assessments and portfolios. Item analysis is addressed in Chapter 10.

Improving the Scoring of Performances

The scoring process can pose a serious threat to reliability, particularly for some formats, such as the essay items. Two raters may assign quite different scores to the same paper. Because the student's written answers obviously do not change, the difference between raters is caused by something other than the proficiency being assessed. Any inconsistency between raters is undesirable.

A teacher would not score a multiple-choice test without first developing a scoring key, yet even though essays are much more difficult to score, many teachers do read answers to essay tests without first creating a scoring plan. An effective way to increase the reliability of essay tests is to improve the scoring procedures.

Development of a scoring plan is also an integral part of constructing performance assessments and portfolios. A scoring plan can be used with either quantitative or qualitative scoring of performance. Procedures for developing scoring plans are discussed in chapters concerned with the use of these formats.

Observations and oral questions are also subjectively scored. Observations and oral questions are usually informal and spontaneous. Thus, their scoring plans have to be spontaneous. Having clear goals for these assessments is central to the ability to determine spontaneously how to score and interpret what is observed.

Previously, we addressed the potential for inconsistencies internal to a test caused by the use of a single score to report student performance on multiple, unrelated qualities. In formal assessments, such as essays, performance assessments, and portfolios, unrelated aspects of students' performance need to be divided into separate scores. For instance, with essays the completeness of a student's answer to the question, grammar, and spelling should be scored separately. Similarly, with portfolios the adequacy of students' work and the degree to which they follow directions in preparing their portfolio should be scored separately.

Increasing the Number of Observations

Increasing the number of observations is an effective way to improve reliability for educational measures just as it is for physical measures. When you use a micrometer to measure the thickness of an object, you obtain multiple observations by repeatedly loosening and retightening the instrument's screw. These observations are then averaged to obtain one best measurement. Similarly, the pH of soil is established from several samples. With physical measurements, the degree of consistency among the repeated measurements is often evaluated as evidence of the reliability of those measurements.

In educational measurement, various ways exist to increase the number of observations, any one of which increases reliability. One method is to include more items in a test. Another is to have more than one person score each assessment. Still another is to combine the observations of individual students to obtain a measure of performance of a *group* of students.

Increasing the number of observations improves reliability because it tends to average out the randomness that is inherent in scores that are less than perfectly reliable. For instance, including several multiple-choice items in a test averages out the gains made from a student's guessing. Including more than one sample of each type of work in a portfolio increases the reliability with which assessments will be made from that work. Using multiple readers to score an essay test averages out the inconsistency among persons scoring the test. Likewise, estimates of how the class as

Table 5.2
Reliability expected from increasing the number of items in a test

If present reliability is this value	Then the new reliability is expected to become this value when the number of test items is increased this many times				
	× 1.25	× 1.50	× 2	× 5	× 10
.20	.24	.27	.33	.56	.71
.33	.38	.43	.50	.71	.84
.50	.56	.60	.67	.84	.91
.67	.72	.75	.80	.91	.95
.80	.83	.86	.89	.95	.98

a whole is performing are more reliable than are estimates of how individual students in the class are performing. In each instance, consistency of the measure is improved by increasing the number of observations.

The amount that increasing the number of observations will improve reliability is predictable. If the overall characteristics of items remain the same, the Spearman–Brown formula shown in Appendix A predicts what the reliability will be as the number of observations is increased or decreased. Table 5.2 applies the Spearman–Brown formula to different reliabilities and different changes in the length of a test. For example, increasing the number of items by 1.5 times, such as from 12 to 18 questions, is expected to increase the reliability from .67 to .75.

Reading across each row in Table 5.2 illustrates how reliability continues to increase as the number of test items increases. In fact, if the length of any test were increased ten times, the reliabilities would be high, almost regardless of how low the reliability was initially. Although a tenfold increase in test length is usually impractical, the table does illustrate the major impact the number of test items has on reliability.

Box 5.3   *Apply What You Are Learning*

Use Table 5.2 to answer the following questions:

1. The reliability of scores on a teacher's 20-minute test was found to be .50. If doubling the available time allowed for administration of twice the number of similar items, what reliability would be expected on a 40-minute test?

2. With similar items, what reliability would be expected on a 10-minute test?

Answers can be found at the end of the chapter.

Recall that Diederich (1973) proposed that a test lasting a full class period should be expected to have a Kuder–Richardson reliability between .60 and .80. Because of the effect of the number of test items on the reliability of scores, one should expect lower reliabilities from a shorter test. Applying the Spearman–Brown formula to the standards proposed by Diederich, a test requiring half the class period (assuming only half as many items could be administered) should be expected to have reliabilities near .40 to .70. This reduction in reliability can be estimated by working backward in Table 5.2.

Recall also that Kane (1986) indicated that a test with a KR-20 reliability of less than .50 has insufficient stability to differentiate the performance of an individual student from the class as a whole. This means that if one uses Diederich standards (which practically speaking are fairly high standards), tests that require half a conventional class period to administer (approximately 25 minutes) would often have reliabilities too low to provide a basis for individualizing instruction.

On the other hand, because of the greater number of observations, a half-period test would likely provide a highly reliable measure of performance for the class as a whole. This is because the collective number of observation across all students in the class is much higher than the number of observations of individual students. Abbreviated observations can provide precise estimates of how the class as a whole is performing, while estimates of how individual students are performing, based on the same observations, will be quite unreliable.

Expanding the Breadth of Observations

Only a sample of tasks can be included in any formal or informal assessment. An important question to address is whether the sample of tasks we observed will generalize. Would student performance on the test be the same had a different sample of task from the same content domain been used? An assessment is of limited value if what we observed does not generalize to the portion of the content domain we did not observe.

The need for observations to generalize to related performances that were not observed is relevant to each of the basic types of capabilities. We have learned, for example, that many capabilities involve information, knowledge that can be recalled, such as naming the letters of the alphabet, stating the names of countries, or listing physical and chemical characteristics of elements. If a student can name one letter of the alphabet, can the student name the other 25 letters? Will a student who is able to name one country in the world, or even in North or South America, also be able to name the remaining countries? Will a student who is able to list the physical and chemical characteristics of one element, for instance, oxygen, also be able to list the characteristics of the other elements? Similar questions concerning generalizability apply to the other types of capabilities as well, such as concepts, rules, and complex skills involving problem solving.

Research by Shavelson, Baxter, and Pine (1992) suggests that performance does not generalize very well across tasks. Their study included a performance assessment of fifth- and sixth-grade students conducting science experiments. The performance assessment incorporated three experiments: determining which paper towels absorbed the most water; identifying the electric-circuit components hidden in different "mystery boxes"; and determining which physical environments were preferred by bugs. Although the three science experiments were quite diverse, the tasks with which students were assessed within each experiment were quite similar. In each case, students were asked to describe the steps they followed in conducting the experiment and to explain the basis for arriving at their conclusion. The study found that on each of the three experiments, different students performed best, that is, performance of the task in one context did not generalize well to performance of the task in a different context.

As important as this finding is, it is not new. When assessing knowledge that can be recalled, such as naming the letters of the alphabet, we know that some students can name one letter but cannot recall another letter. With concepts, such as recognizing a rectangle, we know that students often cannot consistently identify the shape that is a rectangle if geometric objects are presented in diverse shapes, orientations, and contexts.

A particularly effective way to increase generalizability is to observe a student during performance of a task across multiple, diverse instances of the task. Thus, a teacher should ask a student to name several letters from the alphabet rather than just one, or to identify rectangles presented in diverse situations and orientations.

The Shavelson, Baxter, and Pine study points to the need to incorporate multiple instances within performance assessments and other assessments of complex skills. Because of the high costs of performance assessments, there is a natural tendency to avoid reassessing a student's performance of a particular skill in more than a single setting. However, the student performance observed within a single setting will probably not generalize to other settings. For complex skills, then, as for information and concepts, increasing the breadth of observations used in the assessment increases the generalizability of those assessments.

In terms of breadth of observations, standardized tests are at a substantial disadvantage, particularly when the test includes only a few exercises because of the amount of time required to complete each task. When the breadth of observations is limited, the performance of each student usually will not generalize as it would if different samples of work were used. For instance, with writing skills, the performance of most students would be different if they were required to use a different style of writing or to write about a different topic. With classroom assessments, the teacher can usually base evaluations on a greater breadth and number of observations than can be included in a standardized test.

Increasing the breadth of observations is a particularly effective technique for increasing the generalizability and thus the reliability of assessments. Each of the three previous techniques, however, is prerequisite to this concern. Recall that the first technique involves improving the quality of observations, such as by reducing ambiguities in questions or tasks presented to the student. The second technique involves improving the scoring of observations. Unless observations are of high quality and performances are carefully scored, the individual components of an assessment will contain considerable error, and students' performance will not generalize, even if the breadth of observations is increased. All assessments contain random error, and a particularly effective way to reduce this error is to implement the third technique: increasing the number of observations. The fourth technique, expanding the breadth of observations, is actually a form of increasing the number of observations. To help assure that what we do observe regarding students will generalize to what we did not observe, each of these four techniques for improving generalizability must be implemented.

Box 5.4   *Apply What You Are Learning*

For each pair, indicate which strategy (A or B) improves reliability.

1. A. Asking students to perform a large number of tasks
   B. Asking students to perform a small number of tasks
2. A. Based on an assessment, inferring what individual students can do
   B. Based on an assessment, inferring what the class as a whole can do
3. A. Being flexible about which qualities will be scored in each student's answer
   B. Being structured about which qualities will be scored in each student's answer
4. A. Within the content domain being assessed, asking a student to perform several very similar tasks
   B. Within the content domain being assessed, asking a student to perform several diverse tasks

Answers can be found at the end of the chapter.

DIFFERENCE BETWEEN RELIABILITY AND VALIDITY

The reliability of an assessment has an important relationship to its validity. Basically, an assessment cannot have a high degree of validity unless its reliability is also high. Recall that validity is concerned with whether a test measures what it is supposed to measure. Validity is critical because a test is of no use unless the capability being evaluated is in fact being measured. Reliability therefore represents a very important attribute, because it is a prerequisite to validity.

The following example illustrates why reliability is a prerequisite to validity. Two teachers have agreed on the criteria to be used for scoring an essay test that students have completed. However, as is often the case, the teachers assign inconsistent scores to many of the students' tests. The students have completed the essay test, so the inconsistency in students' scores has nothing to do with changes in students' performance. Therefore, the scores assigned by the teachers are being influenced by something other than the students' performance on the test. When there is inconsistency in scores, something is being measured instead of, or at least in addition to, what the test was designed to measure. Inconsistency in the scores indicates that the validity of the test is threatened.

Reliability, therefore, is a prerequisite to validity. The need for test scores to be reliable as a prerequisite to validity applies to all sources of inconsistency, including inconsistencies among test items that supposedly measure the same skill, inconsistencies among alternative skills in the same content domain, and inconsistencies among different teachers who might potentially score the test. For this reason, subsequent chapters place considerable emphasis on techniques that are known to improve the reliability of our measures.

Although reliability is critical to validity, consistency is not by itself a sufficient condition for validity. Unfortunately, we can measure the wrong capability with consistency. Reliability in what we observe is a necessary but not a sufficient condition for validity. This book emphasizes techniques that reduce inconsistency in students' scores on written tests, performance assessments, and portfolios. At the same time, we must be very careful to ensure that in addition to being reliable, our assessments are also valid measures of the abilities we are trying to evaluate.

Box 5.5 *Apply What You Are Learning*

Indicate (true or false) whether each of the following statements accurately describes a relationship between reliability and validity:

1. If the procedures used for scoring an essay test have low reliability, the resulting test scores must have low validity.

2. If two forms of one test are found to correlate highly with each other, the validity of this test is probably high.

3. If a teacher's test is found to have high Kuder–Richardson reliability, it probably has high validity.

Answers can be found at the end of the chapter.

SUMMARY

Reliability is the degree to which a test or other observation measures something consistently. Reliability is prerequisite to having validity, although reliable measures are not necessarily valid.

A number of conditions diminish the reliability of educational measures. These include inconsistencies between earlier and later measures, between test items, between alternative skills in the same content domain, and between raters, as well as lack of internal consistency within one test. A variety of conditions, such as ambiguous test items and guessing, can be the source of any of these inconsistencies. Not all inconsistencies are bad. For instance, inconsistency over time in student achievement may be the result of learning and therefore would be desirable. Inconsistency over time in measures of students' vocational interest, however, may be undesirable if it seriously inhibits vocational planning

Several methods are used to estimate reliability. Common methods include test–retest, alternate-form, split-half, the Kuder–Richardson formulas, and the use of multiple raters. These methods are sensitive to inconsistency from different subsets of sources, some of which are more relevant to classroom assessments than others. Some methods are also easier than others to use in classroom settings.

Methods for estimating the consistency of decisions or the stability of a score within a content domain were developed specifically for criterion-referenced measures. Estimates of internal consistency, such as the Kuder–Richardson formulas, can help determine the reliability of criterion-referenced measures, even though these methods are designed primarily for norm-referenced tests.

Most methods for estimating reliability produce a reliability coefficient that ranges from near 0 to 1.00. Published achievement and aptitude tests should be expected to have reliabilities near .90 or higher. Longer classroom tests (those requiring a full class period to complete) should be expected to have reliabilities between .60 and .80. Reliabilities will be lower on shorter classroom tests.

ANSWERS: APPLY WHAT YOU ARE LEARNING

5.1 1. No. The test–retest method is not necessary because the teacher is not trying to generalize from earlier achievement to later achievement. 2. Yes. The teacher is assuming that the earlier groupings of students would still be obtained had students' ability to learn been reassessed. Reusing the assessment that was originally used to group students would help determine whether the earlier assessment generalizes to the present, even if readministered to only a sample of students. 3. No. In a way this is a trick question. Notice that different students would be involved in the subsequent assessment. The test–retest method involves reassessing the same students, because the test–retest method is used to see whether student performance is consistent over time.

5.2 1. Test–retest; 2. Kuder–Richardson; 3. Kuder–Richardson; 4. alternate-form

5.3 1. .67; 2. .33 (*Hint:* The second question involves a decrease in test questions and requires you to use the table backward.)

5.4 1. A; 2. B; 3. B; 4. B. Increasing the number of tasks improves reliability. This can be accomplished simply by using a large number of questions or by making inferences about the class as a whole rather than to individual students. Using a carefully structured scoring plan when scoring students' answers considerably reduces error. With essays, performance assessments, and portfolios, a structured scoring plan specifies what qualities will be scored, but provides students flexibility in how they will demonstrate the qualities. Selecting diverse rather than highly similar tasks from a domain to include in a test improves generalizability, that is, consistency between what was and was not sampled by the test.

5.5 1. True; 2. False; 3. False. The test described in the first statement has low reliability; therefore it must have low or no validity. The high reliability described in the second and third statements is a prerequisite but not sufficient condition for high reliability.

SOMETHING TO TRY

■   At the beginning of this chapter, in the section entitled Common Threats to Reliability, six sources of inconsistencies are described. Try to list at least one example for each of the six. If possible, use examples from recent assessments that were administered to you or recent assessments that you administered to students. Examples involving either formal or informal assessments can be used.

ADDITIONAL READING

Ebel, R. L. (1979). *Essentials of educational measurement* (3rd ed.). Englewood Cliffs, NJ. Prentice-Hall. Pages 282–284 illustrate the use of the Cronbach alpha coefficient to compute the reliability of an essay test.

Mehrens, W. A., & Lehmann, I. J. (1987). *Using standardized tests in education* (4th ed.). New York: Longman. Pages 67–69 discuss the reliability of "difference scores" such as scores that indicate how much achievement students gained over a specified period of time. As noted in an earlier chapter of the present book, the reliability of such scores is generally very low.

PART TWO

Written Tests

CHAPTER 6

Completion and Short-Answer Items

For all practical purposes, the completion and short-answer formats are equivalent. Their most significant distinction is appearance. A completion item consists of a sentence containing one or more blanks; the student is expected to identify the word or short phrase represented by each blank.

The Italian artist who painted the ceiling of the Sistine Chapel is Michaelangelo).

A short-answer item rewords this incomplete sentence as a question.

Which Italian artist painted the ceiling of the Sistine Chapel?

Virtually any completion item can be rewritten as an equivalent short-answer item and vice versa. For expediency, the term *short-answer item* will be used when discussing attributes common to both completion and short-answer formats.

Short-answer items are widely used in classroom quizzes and exams, and even in academic contests in which small teams of students from different schools compete against each other. Short-answer items are used more often than written items in all other formats.

Because short-answer items are used frequently, you should be familiar with their characteristics, including their advantages, limitations, and desired attributes. Evaluation of short-answer items used in the classroom reveals some major flaws. For example, many items present ambiguous questions for which diverse responses would qualify as appropriate answers. This chapter describes and illustrates the characteristics preferred in short-answer items. After discussing these characteristics, you will be asked to apply your understanding of these characteristics to evaluate a series of short-answer items.

This chapter helps you achieve three skills:

■ Identify the advantages and limitations of short-answer items
■ Identify qualities desired in short-answer items
■ Evaluate short-answer items for these qualities

ADVANTAGES AND LIMITATIONS OF SHORT-ANSWER ITEMS

Advantages of Short-Answer Items

Short-answer items have three advantages over written items in other formats. First, short-answer items are easy to construct. Second, as with the essay format, short-answer items require students to produce an answer rather than to select an answer from alternatives. Third, unlike the essay format, many short-answer questions can be included in a single exam.

1. *Short-answer items are easy to construct.* The ease of constructing short-answer items is a function of two characteristics. First, short-answer items generally can measure recall of information, but not procedural knowledge, such as concepts and rules: items that measure recall of information are easier to construct. Second, creating short-answer items does not require the detailed scoring plans needed to create essay items or to construct the options associated with multiple-choice items. For settings in which the short-answer format is appropriate, this efficiency in item construction is a major asset.

2. *Short-answer items require the student to supply the answer.* The multiple-choice and, even more so, the alternate-choice formats are negatively affected by guessing. Students often give the correct answer to items without solving the problem presented. Because guessing lowers test-score reliability, short-answer tests tend to be more reliable than multiple-choice or alternate-choice tests that contain the same number of items.

3. *Many short-answer items can be included in a test.* The inclusion of many items allows one test to provide a more adequate sampling of content, particularly compared with the essay format. This ability increases the reliability of test scores and potentially also their validity. The short-answer format, however, often has difficulty measuring procedural knowledge that can be assessed using other formats.

Limitations of Short-Answer Items

Short-answer items have two limitations. First, as already noted, short-answer items are generally restricted to measuring recall of information. Second, they are more likely to be scored erroneously than are objectively scored formats, such as multiple-choice and alternate-choice tests.

1. *Short-answer items are generally limited to measuring recall of information.* You may have noticed that most short-answer or completion-item tests you have

taken or given examined knowledge of facts, such as names of people, places, and procedures. Because the student must answer this format of items with a short sentence or often a single word, the skills that short-answer items measure are limited.

Many short-answer items are exceedingly difficult, such as those used in local and regional competitions staged for teams of high school students, in spelling bees, in game shows such as "Jeopardy," and even in popular board games that test players' knowledge of trivial facts. These questions test declarative knowledge rather than procedural knowledge such as concepts and rules.

The importance of declarative knowledge must not be understated. Declarative knowledge represents the foundation on which many cognitive actions must be based. However, virtually every ability that can be tested by short-answer items, including math completion items, represents the category of skills that in this book we refer to as information. Knowledge of concepts and rules generally must be assessed using other item formats.

2. Short-answer items are more likely to be scored erroneously than are the objectively scored formats. Short-answer questions often can be answered with a variety of responses, any one of which might be the desired response. The question "Who discovered America?" could be referring to the name of a person, a nation, or a culture from any of a variety of historical periods. Errors are likely to be involved in scoring potentially correct but divergent responses to short-answer items. To reduce this problem, each short-answer item should be constructed so that knowledgeable students respond with homogeneous answers.

Box 6.1   *Apply What You Are Learning*

In this part of the book, four different formats of written tests are discussed: short-answer, essay, multiple-choice, and alternate-choice (such as true–false items). Try to anticipate the item formats described by each of the following statements.

1.   These two formats require the student to produce rather than to select an answer.

2.   These two formats are the fastest to score.

3.   These two formats are least likely to involve errors in scoring.

Answers can be found at the end of the chapter.

IDENTIFYING QUALITIES DESIRED IN SHORT-ANSWER ITEMS

This section examines specific criteria for evaluating short-answer items. In the next section, you will be asked to use these criteria to evaluate some short-answer questions.

1. *Does this item measure the specified skill?* For a test to have content validity, its items must collectively measure the skills specified in the performance objectives or outlined in a table of specifications. An item should be selected or constructed only after the skill to be measured has been identified. Therefore, with every test

item, regardless of format, it is essential to ask whether the item is measuring the targeted skill. Short-answer items are generally limited to measuring recall of information. If the skill to be assessed is a concept or rule, an alternative format may have to be selected.

2. *Is the level of reading skill required by this item below the students' ability?* Chapter 5 described how internal consistency is decreased when a test measures more than one trait. If a test measures a student's proficiency in (1) a given content area and (2) reading ability, the internal consistency of the test decreases because more than one quality is being measured simultaneously. Students should learn to value good reading skills. However, unless the purpose of a test is to measure reading proficiency, the classroom test is not the place to measure reading ability. The level of reading skill required for understanding each item on a test should be *below* that of the students taking the test.

3. *Can this item be answered using one or two words or a short sentence?* Most short-answer items can be answered using one or two words. If more than a few words or a short sentence is required to answer the question, the item is probably a brief-response essay item and should be evaluated with the criteria discussed in Chapter 7.

4. *Will only a single or very homogeneous set of responses provide a correct response to the item?* The major cause of errors in scoring short-answer items is the use of questions for which several responses represent legitimate answers. Construction of items so that only a single or very homogeneous set of responses represents a correct answer reduces this kind of error. Also, if potentially correct answers are restricted, teaching aides and students can assist with scoring tests.

Box 6.2   *Apply What You Are Learning*

Correct answers to two of the five items are restricted. Which two items are they?

1. A high-quality classroom test must be _____.
2. The item format that allows assessment of how well a student expresses ideas in writing is _____.
3. The difference between Bloom's taxonomy and Gagné's capabilities is _____.
4. How long should a test be?
5. Which item format is generally limited to measuring a student's ability to recall information?

Answers can be found at the end of the chapter.

To develop items with restricted responses, Ebel and Frisbie (1986) proposed that teachers first determine the desired answer and then construct a question for which that answer is the only appropriate response. This is a very effective technique.

5. *Does the item use grammatical structure and vocabulary different from that contained in the source of instruction?* A common but unwise approach to constructing completion items is to select important sentences from a textbook or other source and replace a key word with a blank. Two problems are associated with this practice. First, it encourages students to memorize rather than comprehend what is read. Second, because most sentences derive some of their meaning from adjacent sentences, extracting sentences creates vague test items. Note the vagueness of the following items. Each is an important sentence appearing earlier in this book.

> **Although norm-referenced interpretations can be made with more general descriptions of the content domain, they do require a _____.**

> **The distinction between concrete and defined concepts is _____.**

The intended answers are "well-defined norm group" and "not always clear."

The suggestion made by Ebel and Frisbie (1986) is again relevant: First determine the word or phrase that represents the correct answer, and then construct the question for which that answer is the only appropriate response.

6. *Does the format of the item (and the test in general) allow for efficient scoring?* Short-answer items are more time-consuming to score than are questions written in the multiple-choice and alternate-choice formats. Except for the youngest students, the efficiency of scoring can be improved by having students write answers in a column to the side as illustrated here.

1. The artist who is responsible for the artistic style known as   1. Picasso
   Cubism is ____(1)____.

2. The French artist who did a series of paintings of water lilies   2. Monet
   is ____(2)____.

3. The artist who created the painting entitled *The Scream*   3. Munch
   is ____(3)____.

7. *If the item requires a numerical response, does the question state the unit of measurement to be used in the answer?* Consider the following question:

> What is the sum of 24 inches and 12 inches?   ____36____ inches

Had "inches" not been specified to the right of the blank, correct answers would have included 3 (feet) and 1 (yard). You can score answers more quickly and accurately if students use a common unit of measure.

The remaining criteria pertain only to completion items.

8. *Does the blank represent a key word?* If the blanks in completion items fail to represent key words, the test will measure reading comprehension more than knowledge of a particular content area. In fact, a technique for measuring reading comprehension is to have students fill in blanks representing every fifth word of a paragraph. Taylor (1953) named this procedure the "cloze" technique. Because every fifth word versus key words is substituted with blanks, the cloze technique does not (and is not intended to) provide an effective measure of the knowledge portrayed in the paragraph.

Box 6.3   *Apply What You Are Learning*

To make a completion item, which underlined word in each sentence is the key word and could be replaced with a blank?

1.   Validity is generally regarded as the most essential quality of an educational test.
2.   A test that measures something consistently would be considered reliable.
3.   More than any other format, it is difficult measuring a representative sample of content when using essay items.

Answers can be found at the end of the chapter.

---

9. *Are blanks placed at or near the end of the item?* The efficiency with which students answer completion items can be improved somewhat by placing blanks at or near the end of each item. This way, students can answer the items when they first come to a blank and avoid having to reread part of the item. Therefore, item 1 in the preceding examples should be rewritten as follows:

1. The quality generally regarded as most essential in an   1. validity
educational test is _____(1)_____ .

10. *Is the number of blanks sufficiently limited?* An excessive number of blanks within a completion item can cause problems. Having too many blanks increases the amount of time required for students to determine what is being asked. If fewer blanks are used, more items can be included in a test, improving coverage of content and hence potential validity.

Another problem caused by the use of too many blanks is that the resulting test item often has a variety of unintended but legitimate answers. How many answers can you generate for this item?

A _____ is _____ of _____.

Some possibilities include the following:

A gulf is south of Pensacola.

A midget is kind of small.

A branch is part of a tree.

A great aunt is the sister of your grandparent.

Although this example is rather extreme, completion items tend to have multiple solutions as the number of blanks increases. Remember, multiple correct answers are the major source of errors when scoring short-answer items.

11. *Is the physical length of each blank the same?* The tendency to provide a longer blank when the correct response is a longer word gives a clue to the answer.

1. Does this item measure the specified skill?

2. Is the level of reading skill required by this item below the students' ability?

3. Can this item be answered using one or two words or a short sentence?

4. Will only a single or very homogeneous set of responses provide a correct response to the item?

5. Does the item use grammatical structure and vocabulary different from that contained in the source of instruction?

6. Does the format of the item (and the test in general) allow for efficient scoring?

7. If the item requires a numerical response, does the question state the unit of measure to be used in the answer?

Additional criteria for completion items

8. Does the blank represent a key word?

9. Are blanks placed at or near the end of the item?

10. Is the number of blanks sufficiently limited?

11. Is the physical length of each blank the same?

Figure 6.1
Criteria for evaluating short-answer items

PRACTICE WITH APPLYING THESE DESIRED QUALITIES TO SHORT-ANSWER ITEMS

The previous section examined 11 criteria for evaluating short-answer items. Figure 6.1 lists these criteria. This section will help you apply these criteria by examining some example items.

The objective being assessed by the following items and the proposed correct responses are provided to help you evaluate each item. Each example fails to meet at least one of the criteria listed in Figure 6.1. A critique follows each item. Numbers in parentheses preceding each critique indicate which of the criteria the example item has failed to achieve. Try to identify these problems before reading the critique.

The following example items are intended to measure this objective:

Information: When given its definition, name the literary figure of speech being defined.

Example 6.1

1. A ____(1)____ compares two different things by using the word   1. simile
like or *as.*

Critique for Example 6.1

(9) This completion item should be worded so that the blank appears near the end of the sentence. This improves the item's efficiency by allowing students to respond immediately. Here is an improved version of this item:

1. A comparison of two different things made by using the word   1. simile
   like or *as* is called a(n) ___(1)___.

Example 6.2

2. The statement "He eats like a bird" illustrates what figure of   1. simile
   speech?

Critique for Example 6.2

(1) This is a good short-answer item but it does not measure the objective. Also note that this item is doing something relatively few short-answer items are able to do: It measures a *concept*. An effective way to measure concepts is to provide students illustrations not previously used, and ask the students to classify the example.

Example 6.3

3. ___(3)___ imply resemblances such as from human   1. Metaphors
   physiology to other objects, for instance, "the mouth of
   a river" or "the eye of a needle."

Critique for Example 6.3

(9) Again, this completion item should be worded so that the blank appears near the end of the sentence. Here is an improved version of this item:

3. Implied resemblances such as from human physiology   1. metaphors
   to other objects, for instance, "the mouth of a river" or
   "the eye of a needle" are called ___(3)___.

Example 6.4

4. In what way are similes and metaphors similar and different?

Intended answer: Both similes and metaphors use vocabulary that is already familiar to describe what is less well known. Similes accomplish this through comparisons, typically using *as* or *like,* for instance, "He eats like a bird." In contrast, metaphors attribute a resemblance to a familiar object, for example, "the mouth of the river."

Critique for Example 6.4

(1, 3) This item does not measure the objective. Also, students should be able to answer short-answer items with one or two words or a short sentence. This is an example of a brief-response essay item. (The essay format is discussed in the next chapter.)

SUMMARY

Despite differences in appearance, the completion and short-answer formats are equivalent and can be used interchangeably. Completion and short-answer items are the most widely used item format in written tests. There are three basic advantages to the short-answer format: ease of construction, student-generated answers, and the option of including many items within one test. Short-answer items have two basic limitations: They are generally limited to measuring recall of information, and they are more likely to be scored erroneously than are objectively scored items. Several desirable qualities of short-answer items were discussed and are listed in Figure 6.1.

ANSWERS: APPLY WHAT YOU ARE LEARNING

6.1   1. essay and short answer; 2. multiple-choice and alternate choice; 3. multiple-choice and alternate choice.

6.2   Correct answers to items 2 and 5 are restricted. Possible answers to item 1 include "valid," "reliable," "constructed from a list of objectives," and "a priority of all teachers." Possible answers for item 3 are "how they subdivide intellectual skills" and "Gagné's inclusion of cognitive strategies, attitudes, and motor skills." Assuming that item 4 is referring to administration time, the answer depends on a variety of factors, such as the age of the students, the content area, and the purpose of the test.

6.3   1. validity; 2. reliable; 3. essay.

SOMETHING TO TRY

- If you have access to some previously written short-answer items, use the qualities listed in Figure 6.1 to evaluate these items.

- Prepare some short-answer items that measure this objective:

  Information: Given a geological feature, name the region of the country in which this feature exists.

  Use Figure 6.1 to evaluate these items.

- Similarly write and then evaluate several items for an objective within your academic specialization.

ADDITIONAL READING

Wesman, A. G. (1971). Writing the test item. In R. L. Thorndike (Ed.), *Educational measurement* (2nd ed.). Washington, DC: American Council on Education. This chapter reviews the item-writing literature and discusses ideas for producing various formats of objectively scored test items.

CHAPTER 7

Essay Items

The essay question represents a very flexible test format. It can potentially measure any skill that can be assessed with other formats of written tests. An essay item is also uniquely able to assess a student's ability to communicate ideas in writing. On the other hand, the essay format has a number of weaknesses, which, if uncontrolled, can substantially reduce the usefulness of a test. For example, answers to essay questions are often scored differently depending on which teacher does the grading. Also, a variety of student characteristics other than the adequacy of the student's response often affect essay scores.

Some essay items more effectively exploit the advantages of the format and avoid the limitations. This chapter describes characteristics typically associated with the better-quality essay items. You will be asked to apply these characteristics by evaluating a series of essay questions. Many of the limitations of the essay format pertain to the scoring of students' responses. A variety of techniques that can improve scoring accuracy are described in this chapter. These include using a model answer, concealing the identity of students, and grading all responses to one question at a time.

This chapter helps you achieve four skills:

- Identify advantages and limitations of essay items
- Identify qualities desired in an essay item
- Evaluate essay items for these qualities
- Score students' responses to essay items

ADVANTAGES AND LIMITATIONS OF ESSAY ITEMS

Advantages of Essay Items

Essay items have three advantages over test questions written in other formats. First, essay items tend to measure more directly the behaviors specified by performance objectives. Second, essay items examine the student's ability to communicate ideas in writing. Third, as with short-answer items, essay items require the student to supply the response instead of selecting from among responses provided by the test.

1. *Essay items tend to measure more directly behaviors specified by performance objectives.* All the popular item formats can measure students' knowledge of information. In later chapters, we discuss how objectively scored formats, such as multiple-choice, can also measure knowledge of concepts and rules or relationships. Unlike other formats, however, the essay item often can directly measure the performance specified by the performance objectives. For instance, if the objective is that students will be able to state the relative advantages of criterion-referenced and norm-referenced interpretations, the corresponding essay item might simply be

State the relative advantages of criterion- and norm-referenced interpretations.

Other test formats, as illustrated by the following true–false items, often must infer student performance through a series of indirect measures:

Compared with criterion-referenced tests, norm-referenced tests can be used with more broadly defined content domains. (true)

The final exam in a high school class is more likely to be criterion-referenced than norm-referenced. (false)

As we will see later, the tendency for essay items to measure more directly the performance specified by an objective may be a result of how the objectives are stated rather than a characteristic of the essay format. Research has not been conclusive on whether the essay format provides a more valid measure of learning than do other types of written tests.

2. *Essay items can examine students' ability to communicate ideas in writing.* Given the importance of writing skills, this quality of essay items is significant. However, when essay items are used to assess a student's ability to communicate ideas, writing proficiency and comprehension of content should be reported in separate scores. Recall that the usefulness of test scores is reduced when a single score is used to describe simultaneously more than one outcome of instruction.

Caution must be used not to overgeneralize the advantage of essay items in assessing writing skills. For example, the essay test does not represent an appropriate environment for training students to write. Students are more inclined to learn appropriate grammar and to develop their writing skills when their abilities are shaped through frequent writing experiences outside examination settings. The use of essay items as a means of improving writing skills is likely to fail because of examination pressure, such as the need to write answers quickly.

3. *Essay items require the student to supply the response.* The multiple-choice and alternate-choice formats both allow the student to select an answer from among

options provided on the test. In working from a list of alternative answers, students may actually generate correct responses that they would have been unable to generate had no answers been suggested.

The essay format prevents students who have not acquired the knowledge from giving a correct answer through a blind guess. Guessing reduces the precision of test scores. If a guess is truly blind (i.e., based on no information), the student's response represents a random action that tends to lower the reliability of the scores. However, because test reliability can be improved by increasing the number of items on the test, ability to include a greater number of items in a multiple-choice or alternate-choice test more than offsets this particular advantage of the essay format.

Box 7.1   *Apply What You Are Learning*

Can you remember the three advantages of the essay format? List these advantages on a separate piece of paper and then check your answers.

Answers can be found at the end of the chapter.

Limitations of Essay Items

Essay items have three limitations relative to test items written in other formats. First, exams that use the essay format tend to provide a less adequate sampling of the content being tested. Second, the scoring of essay items is less reliable. Third, essay items take longer to score.

1. *Essay items usually provide a less adequate sampling of the content.* Time constraints usually allow inclusion of only a few essay items on one exam. As a result, one essay test will measure a relatively small portion of skills that students are expected to learn. Some time ago, Posey (1932) demonstrated that when as few as ten items are included in a test, a student's score is largely determined by whether these items happen by chance to sample content with which the student is knowledgeable. One conceivably might use broad essay questions to cover a greater percentage of skills with each item. This strategy, however, reinforces the weaknesses of the essay format. For instance, broad questions are very difficult to score accurately.

It is interesting to note that most of a student's time during an essay test is not spent solving the problem posed by the question. Most of the time is spent writing out the answer. If a student is fairly knowledgeable about the concept being questioned, relatively little time is needed to read the essay item and formulate a response. If some way other than writing could be established for recording the students' answers to essay questions, substantially more skills could be assessed by one test. If students did not write out their answers, however, the essay's distinctive advantage of being able to assess the ability to communicate ideas in writing would be eliminated.

Because so few items can be included in an essay test, instructors often conclude that an advantage of the format is that less time is required to develop a test. The time required to develop each high-quality essay item, however, is generally greater than that required to develop a good item written in any alternative format. The inclusion of fewer items in an essay test results from a limitation of the essay format; time constraints allow for the measurement of only a few skills.

Furthermore, teachers often think that essay tests are easier to develop because they construct essay items without creating a plan for scoring these items. This important issue is discussed later in the chapter.

2. *The scoring of essay items is less reliable.* Because of the subjective aspect of scoring essay items, scores assigned to a set of student responses are often inconsistent. Different readers will assign scores ranging from very low to very high to a given essay response. This discrepancy results largely because the qualities being assessed by an essay question vary as a function of who reads the responses. Factors such as penmanship, expected achievement, difficulty in reading the responses, and sex and race of the student have been found to affect significantly scores assigned to essays. Chase (1986) and Rafoth and Rubin (1984) found that the content of responses had only a moderate effect on the scores assigned. The subjective scoring of essay tests, combined with the relatively small number of items that can be included, usually reduces the reliability of these tests. Techniques described later in this chapter can help reduce this significant limitation of the essay format.

3. *Essay tests are more time-consuming to score.* Scoring essay exams is obviously time-consuming. No other written test format takes as long to score. If fairly detailed scoring procedures are followed and student responses are graded by more than one reader (both techniques are desired), the amount of time required to score essay items can be substantial.

Box 7.2   *Apply What You Are Learning*

Can you remember the three limitations of the essay format? List these limitations on a separate piece of paper and then check your answers.

Answers can be found at the end of the chapter.

IDENTIFYING QUALITIES DESIRED IN ESSAY ITEMS

Before considering specific qualities, a distinction should be made between brief-response and extended-response questions. Although extended-response essay items have unique assets, these same qualities limit the usefulness of the essay format in classroom tests.

Desirability of Using Brief-Response versus Extended-Response Questions

An essay question qualifies as a brief-response item if students can read and fully answer the item within ten minutes. A question requiring a longer response is considered an extended-response item. The required length of the answer is generally established by the nature of the task presented to the students. An extended-response item presents a broader task. The task may be broader simply because it asks students to do quantitatively more rather than to do a qualitatively different kind of task. Alternatively, an extended-response item may allow students to demonstrate such skills as creativity, selecting and organizing a number of ideas relevant to a given issue, and communicating ideas in writing. Either way, the appropriateness of using an extended-response essay question to achieve these characteristics should be evaluated.

If the purpose of using an extended-response question is to have students demonstrate a greater number of skills, the extended-response question can generally be broken into shorter questions that, individually, can be answered within ten minutes. This tactic will significantly improve the consistency with which answers are scored and will generally allow assessment of a better cross section of skills.

Not all extended-response essay questions can be subdivided. To determine whether subdivision is possible, look at the types of capabilities that are being assessed. If the capabilities involve recalling information or demonstrating knowledge of concepts or rules, the extended-response question generally can be rewritten as a series of brief-response questions, and doing so will be advantageous.

On the other hand, if the extended-response question requires complex skills, such as problem solving where students can use diverse strategies to solve the problem, then brief-response questions may not suffice. Be careful here. A task should not be classified as a complex skill simply because it is difficult, is academically important, or requires students to do a lot. A complex skill involves but does not require students to demonstrate their knowledge of information, concepts, or rules. If the extended-response question does require students to do these things, it likely is not measuring a complex skill. A complex skill requires students to draw on and synthesize information, concepts, and rules in order to solve a problem, and in solving the problem, the students' recall of information and knowledge of concepts and rules generally is not documented in their written responses. Again, if the essay question is asking for a statement of knowledge of information, concepts, and rules, the essay question generally is not assessing a complex skill and can be rewritten as a series of brief-response questions.

If a proposed essay question will require an extended response because it truly is measuring a complex task, such as problem solving, alternative formats other than a written test should be considered. Usually, complex skills are more adequately assessed through the use of portfolios and performance assessments. Asking a student to demonstrate a complex skill within the context of a written exam tends to be contrived, and more often than not distorts and invalidates an important assessment.

Criteria for Evaluating Essay Items

This section examines criteria that characterize high-quality essay items. In the next section, you will be asked to use these criteria to evaluate a series of essay questions. The last section of this chapter describes techniques that can be used to facilitate accurate scoring of essay tests.

1. *Does the item measure the specified skill?* As noted earlier, for a test to have content validity its items must collectively measure the skills specified in the performance

objectives or outlined in a table of specifications. An item should be selected or constructed only after the skill to be measured has been identified. Therefore, with every test item, regardless of format, it is essential to ask whether the item is measuring the targeted skill.

Box 7.3   *Apply What You Are Learning*

Here is an objective, and two essay items intended to measure that objective. Which item (A or B) provides the best measure of this objective?

Concept: Given descriptions of space vehicles, state with explanation whether or not they are satellites of Earth.

A. The mission of the Hubble Space Telescope is to photograph faraway objects from its orbit above Earth. Is the Hubble Space Telescope a satellite of Earth? Explain your reasoning.

B. What determines whether a space vehicle is an Earth satellite? Explain your reasoning.

Answers can be found at the end of the chapter.

Sometimes instructors allow students to choose the subset of essay items they will answer. This practice lowers the content-related validity of the test, because the set of questions included is determined by student preference rather than by a systematic plan. Allowing students to select questions creates two additional problems as well. First, to the degree that students avoid difficult questions, the test is less likely to detect areas with which they need help. Second, test scores based on subsets of items that measure different skills are difficult to interpret.

On the other hand, it often is appropriate to provide students options in how they respond to a question. For instance, students might be allowed to write about the scientist of their choice in order to illustrate the scientific method of inquiry. The essay question might even list the names of scientists from which the students may choose. Allowing students a choice in how they respond to a question is appropriate as long as the same capability is being assessed regardless of a student's choice and the same scoring plan can be applied to all students' responses.

2. *Is the level of reading skill required by this item below the students' ability?* As with other formats, measures of reading ability and achievement will be confounded unless the level of reading skill required to understand the test item is below that of the students taking the test. Each sentence should use simple construction and words with which all students are proficient.

3. *Will all or almost all students answer this item in less than ten minutes?* An essay question that requires students to take more than ten minutes to formulate and write a response is not a brief-response essay item. As discussed earlier, extended-response items should be avoided within the context of a classroom test.

4. *Will the scoring plan result in different readers' assigning similar scores to a given student's response?* Consistency in scoring is essential with all item formats. The need for consistency is more obvious for objectively scored items, such as multiple-

1. Total number of points assigned to the item based on its importance relative to other items
2. Specific attributes to be evaluated in students' responses
3. For each attribute, criteria for awarding points, including partial credit

Figure 7.1
Three characteristics to be included in the scoring plan of each essay item

choice items. For instance, if two people grade the same answers to a multiple-choice exam but derive quite different scores, the scoring process is likely to be judged inadequate. Consistency in scoring is equally important for essay items. Scoring inconsistency is as damaging to the reliability of an essay test (and therefore to its validity) as it is to any objectively scored tests. The scoring plan for each essay item must be designed so that different readers will assign similar scores to a given student's response.

To facilitate reliable scoring, the scoring plan should incorporate the three characteristics listed in Figure 7.1. First, the total number of points the item is worth must be specified. *The points associated with each essay item should be proportional to the relative importance of the skill being tested.* The importance of a test item should not be equated with the amount of time students need to answer the item. The increased time required to write a response to an essay item is not an appropriate reason for assigning more points to essay questions than to items in other formats.

Second, the attributes to be evaluated must be specified. Figure 7.2 provides an example of how attributes should be specified. First, let us state the objective being assessed:

Concept: Given a description of a storm involving strong winds, state with explanation whether or not it is a hurricane.

Test Item

A strong cold front approached Florida and a severe storm resulted. As the front approached, sustained winds from the southwest increased to 50 miles an hour with some gusts higher than 80. As the front passed, the wind switched to the northwest and then slowly diminished. Was this storm a hurricane? Explain your conclusion, briefly describing how <u>each</u> piece of information presented above was used in drawing your conclusion.

Attributes To Be Scored

1. Classifies the storm as not a hurricane
2. Identifies absence of a closed circulation around a calm center
3. Identifies absence of sustained winds above 75 miles per hour
4. Identifies three characteristics of this weather system that are not defining characteristics of a hurricane

---

Figure 7.2
Illustration of attributes with a scoring plan

Figure 7.2 shows an essay item that measures this objective and specifies the four attributes in students' responses that are to be scored. The essay question involves a concept, specifically that of hurricanes.

If these four attributes are judged to be appropriate for scoring this essay item, misspellings or errors in grammar will not count. Information that students provide that is superfluous to the criteria specified in the scoring plan will not count, regardless of the accuracy of this information. (Such qualities would be scored only if included in the scoring plan.) Therefore, answers to essay items often will include errors that are not scored. This does not mean that such errors are to be ignored; these errors can be marked (but not scored), and students can be required to correct important errors after test papers have been returned.

The third criterion to be included in a scoring plan pertains to how points will be awarded. The four criteria of a scoring plan are illustrated in Figure 7.3: The total number of points the essay item is worth has been set at 6, the attributes to be evaluated are specified, and the points associated with each attribute (or combination of attributes) are also specified.

A scoring plan must be precise enough for the reader to know when to and when not to award a point. If more than one point is associated with a given quality, the guidelines should indicate if and how partial credit is to be awarded. A scoring plan can be written using abbreviated or telegraphic statements.

There is an erroneous tendency to equate points to number of attributes being scored. For instance, the four attributes within Figure 7.3 might be thought to require a total of 4 points. Total points associated with an essay item should be influenced only by the relative importance of the skill being measured.

The scoring plan should be established for each essay item when the item is written. Creating an essay question without simultaneously establishing how it is to be scored is analogous to creating a true–false item without establishing whether the item is true or false.

One might incorrectly conclude that the presence of a scoring plan prevents essay items from measuring more than factual knowledge. This conclusion would be justified were a scoring plan thought of as a specification of the correct answer; but this is not what a scoring plan is. Instead of specifying the correct answer, the scoring plan specifies attributes of the correct answer. For instance, an essay item might ask students to take a position on a controversial issue and defend that position. The scoring plan would not be concerned with the position the students chose. Instead,

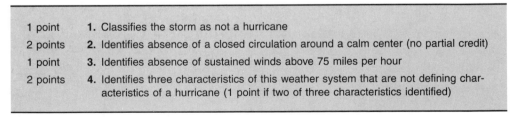

1 point	**1.** Classifies the storm as not a hurricane
2 points	**2.** Identifies absence of a closed circulation around a calm center (no partial credit)
1 point	**3.** Identifies absence of sustained winds above 75 miles per hour
2 points	**4.** Identifies three characteristics of this weather system that are not defining characteristics of a hurricane (1 point if two of three characteristics identified)

Figure 7.3
Illustration of a scoring plan

the scoring plan would be concerned with the conciseness with which students expressed their positions and the nature of the defense they gave in support of their respective positions. *The scoring plan delineates attributes that distinguish adequate from less adequate responses to the essay item.*

Box 7.4   *Apply What You Are Learning*

The preceding discussion identified three characteristics to use in developing a scoring plan. These characteristics are summarized in Figure 7.1. Which of these characteristics has not been addressed in the scoring plans to each of the following essay items?

Item 1. In an orchestra, what are the differences between wind and string instruments?

Scoring plan: 1 point for each correct answer

Item 2. Support or critique this statement: "The reading level of a test should be equivalent to that of the average student taking the test."

Scoring plan:

- Reference to need for reading level to be at or below that of all students taking the test
- Reference to idea that a difficult reading level confounds measurement of reading ability with the skill being tested

Answers can be found at the end of the chapter.

In this exercise, item 1 is vague. A variety of differences between wind and string instruments could be listed, probably some that the item writer did not anticipate. For instance, wind instruments are used in marching bands, they often are not made of wood, and they always are placed up to or partially into the player's mouth. Had the item writer thought through the scoring plan as the item was developed, the vagueness of this item would have been detected before the test was administered. Have you had to answer essay items where it was obvious a scoring plan had not been thought through?

5. *Does the scoring plan describe a correct and complete response?* The purpose of any test is to determine how proficient students are in a particular skill. This purpose can be realized only if test items are constructed so that students who have acquired that knowledge tend to give a correct answer and students who have not acquired that knowledge give an incorrect or incomplete response. This result can be accomplished, in turn, only if the person scoring the test can describe a correct and complete response. With an essay item, the correct response is described through the scoring plan.

It is difficult to construct a scoring plan that describes a correct and complete response if the essay item asks a broad question. This difficulty is a major reason for encouraging the use of essay questions that can be answered fully within ten minutes; items that require more than ten minutes tend to ask broad questions.

It is also difficult to develop a good scoring plan when the correct answer is a matter of opinion. Asking students to choose and defend a particular opinion or asking students to identify opinions is appropriate, as long as the scoring plan can specify characteristics of an appropriate response.

Box 7.5   *Apply What You Are Learning*

For which item (A or B) of the following pairs would it be more difficult to develop a scoring plan that content experts would agree describes a correct response?

1.   A.   What is a map?
     B.   Describe information that is included in a road map.
2.   A.   What are the major differences between a conservative and liberal economic policies?
     B.   Which is better, a conservative or liberal economic policy?

Answers can be found at the end of this chapter.

Colleagues who teach similar classes often can help each other develop or proof a scoring plan. One strategy is to ask a colleague to answer the essay question orally. If the colleague's response differs significantly from your own scoring plan, modify either the scoring plan or the item itself. An alternative strategy is to ask a colleague to score some of your students' answers using your scoring plan. Usually, a colleague will quickly detect significant problems that exist in your scoring plan.

6. *Is the item written in such a way that the scoring plan will be obvious to knowledgeable students?* If students proficient in the area being assessed are unable to describe how an item will be scored, the item cannot fulfill its role; that is, the item will be unable to determine the proficiency of students because it will not distinguish between students who have acquired the knowledge and those who have not. Proficient students will be able to give correct answers only if they can determine from the item the characteristics of a correct answer.

The same conditions that facilitate development of a scoring plan also help communicate to students the qualities desired in the answer. The essay item must pose a specific task for which the attributes of a correct response are not simply a matter of opinion. In addition to stating the essay question, it is sometimes helpful to state briefly the characteristics of a correct response. Also, to communicate how the item will be scored, state within the test how many points each essay item is worth.

PRACTICE WITH APPLYING THESE DESIRED QUALITIES TO ESSAY ITEMS

The previous section presented six criteria for evaluating essay items. Figure 7.4 lists these criteria. This section will help you apply these criteria by examining some example items.

1. Does this item measure the specified skill?
2. Is the level of reading skill required by this item below the students' ability?
3. Will all or almost all students answer this item in less than ten minutes?
4. Will the scoring plan result in different readers assigning similar scores to a given student's response?
5. Does the scoring plan describe a correct and complete response?
6. Is the item written in such a way that the scoring plan will be obvious to knowledgeable students?

Figure 7.4
Criteria for evaluating essay items

Each example states the performance objective that is to be measured, an essay item designed to measure that objective, and the scoring plan that was proposed for scoring responses to the item. When administered, only the essay item would be shown to students. Use Figure 7.4 to evaluate each example. Each essay item and/or its scoring plan fails to meet at least one of these six criteria. Compare your evaluation to the critique that follows each example.

Example 7.1

Objective: *Concept:* Given a description of heat being transferred, classifies the heat transfer as predominantly conduction, convection, or radiation (and provides logic behind this classification).

Essay item shown to students: A pan of water is being heated on the stove. Although the water is not being stirred, the water can be seen moving around within the pan as the temperature of the water increases. Is heat being transferred within this water mostly by conduction, convection, or radiation? What is happening in this water that causes this transfer of heat? (3 points)

Scoring plan: The student shows heat is being transferred by convection.

Critique for Example 7.1

The item, as written, is good. The scoring plan, however, does not provide criteria for awarding points. Without these criteria, different readers would likely assign dissimilar scores to each student's response. Here is a better scoring plan:

1 point   States heat transferred by convection

1 point   Indicates that convection transfers heat by movement and thus mixing of the heated fluid

1 point   Indicates that convection movement is caused by fluid expanding when heated, thus becoming more buoyant and rising

Example 7.2

Objective: *Concept:* When given an illustration of a change in a substance, classifies it as a physical change (i.e., altering the shape, form. volume, or density) or a chemical change (i.e., producing new substances with different characteristics).

Essay item shown to students: Explain the difference between a physical and chemical change in a substance. (3 points)

Scoring plan: Determine whether the student correctly explains the difference.

Critique for Example 7.2

Example 7.2 fails to meet almost all the criteria in Figure 7.4. Let us evaluate this item by examining each of the six criteria:

1. Asking the student to explain the difference between physical and chemical change does not measure the objective. Notice that this objective involves a concept. To measure a concept, students should be provided an illustration they have not previously used in this context, and then asked to classify the illustration. As worded, this essay item measures recall of information, specifically, the distinction between physical and chemical change. A better essay item for measuring this objective would be the following:

> **A piece of wood has burned. Is this an example of a physical or chemical change? Explain why.**

2. To this item's credit, the level of reading skill needed to understand this question is appropriately lower than the reading level of those taking the test, assuming the item is directed at typical readers of this book.

3. Again to this item's credit, most students can answer it within ten minutes.

4. The scoring plan is vague, and different readers will likely assign quite different scores to a given student's response. In essence, the scoring plan states students should give a correct answer, without specifying attributes to be evaluated or how points are to be awarded. Here is an improved plan for awarding the 3 points associated with this item (although improving the scoring plan does not negate this item's other problems):

2 points   Associates physical change with altering shape, form, volume, or density (or 1 point if 3 of 4 are listed); otherwise, 0 points

1 point   Associates physical chemical change with producing a different substance

5. The original scoring plan does not describe a complete response, to a large part because of the lack of conciseness in the scoring plan. As originally worded, content experts would differ with respect to what they believe constitutes a fully correct response.

6. The essay item does not communicate to the student how answers will be scored, mainly because the task presented to the student is vague. Often, vague essay items result from having only a vague scoring plan in mind when the item is

written. If the revised scoring presented in point 4 were used, here is how the essay item could be rewritten.

> What changes in a substance, if they occur, would be classified as a physical change? Likewise, what change in a substance would be classified as a chemical change?

Example 7.3

Objective: *Rule:* Given a constant force applied to an object moving through space, draw and explain the path this object will take through space as the force is continually applied to the object.

Essay item shown to students: An object is initially moving through space from left to right. A constant force from above, perpendicular to its initial movement, is applied to the object. Draw the path the object will take over an extended period of time as a result of the force being applied. Explain why the object will follow the path you have drawn. (4 points)

Scoring plan: An appropriate path is drawn and explanation given.

Critique for Example 7.3

The item is well written. It measures the objective and can be answered within ten minutes. This item is written so that the scoring plan probably would be obvious to knowledgeable students.

The scoring plan is carelessly written and as a result is vague. Assuming the person reading students' answers is knowledgeable, the scoring plan in this well-written item can be implied from the item; therefore, we may not have a serious problem here. Regardless, creating a vague scoring plan is a bad practice in part because it encourages writing vague essay items. The scoring plan should specify the attributes to be evaluated in students' responses, as well as criteria for awarding points for each attribute. Here is an improved scoring plan:

1 point   Drawing shows downward change in object's path

1 point   Change is smooth

1 point   From explanation, obvious that student recognizes rate of motion from left to right remains unchanged

1 point   From explanation, obvious that student recognizes downward motion increases at a constant rate

Example 7.4

Objective: *Rule:* Demonstrates that for a given perimeter, area of a rectangle increases as the length and width of the rectangle become closer to equal.

Essay item shown to students: An architect is drawing a classroom for a new school. The perimeter of the room is to be 160 feet. Determine whether the room will have more floor space if made in the shape of a rectangle or square. (3 points)

Scoring plan:

3 points   Uses square and sequence of at least three rectangles, all with perimeter of 160 feet, to demonstrate area increases as length and width become close to equal (2 points if proper sequence of at least four rectangles are given, but no square)

Critique for Example 7.4

The scoring plan matches the objective better than the essay item. Given the information provided in the scoring plan, the instructor who wrote this item probably had the objective clearly in mind when writing the item, but has not used the item to clearly communicate the intended task to students. Note that because students can fully answer the essay item by simply stating the square room has the larger area, a student would have a legitimate complaint if that answer received less than full credit.

In terms of criteria listed in Figure 7.4, the teacher failed to write the item in such a way that the scoring plan would be obvious to knowledgeable students. Here is an alternative essay item that more adequately conveys the scoring plan:

Drawing a sequence of four rectangular rooms and computing their areas, show that the maximum floor area is obtained when the length and width of the room are equal. Use a perimeter of 160 feet for all four rooms. (3 points)

This particular item might be considered a performance assessment rather than an essay item. (Chapters 12 and 13 discuss performance assessments.) In some cases, the distinction between essay items and performance assessments is unclear.

SCORING STUDENTS' RESPONSES TO ESSAY ITEMS

Analytical versus Holistic Scoring

Responses to essay items usually are scored analytically or holistically. Analytical scoring uses a detailed scoring plan to evaluate the answers to a given question. As described earlier in this chapter, the scoring plan identifies specific attributes to be judged in students' responses and indicates the number of points associated with each of these attributes. In a sense, the scoring plan can be thought of as a checklist, with the reader checking off the desired attributes contained in a given response.

As the complexity of an essay question increases or as students are given more flexibility in terms of how they may respond to a question, the quality of a student's overall response becomes less adequately represented by the sum of highly explicit parts. In such cases, holistic scoring is an alternative to analytical scoring. Holistic scoring involves reading the answer to each item in its entirety and then evaluating the overall quality of that answer.

One common approach to holistic scoring involves placing a student's paper into one of three groups, representing low, medium, and high categories of judged quality.

Often, the reader re-evaluates students' answers within each group to subdivide responses into additional categories. The final number of categories might correspond to the number of points associated with the essay item.

The advantages of holistic scoring are that it (1) is relatively fast and (2) can be used with items for which answers cannot be subdivided into components. Weaknesses of holistic scoring are that it (1) usually results in less reliable scores and (2) provides limited information to the student as to why an answer was judged appropriate or not so judged.

Because with holistic scoring less time is required to read students' responses, having a second reader independently score each response can offset the lower reliability. The two scores for each response are averaged. This approach is more practical in some situations, such as when teachers are working as a team or are using a common exam.

An alternative procedure for improving the quality of holistic scoring is to establish model answers for each question. Model answers help clarify the attributes sought in students' responses; in addition, distributing model answers to students can supplement the limited feedback associated with holistic scoring. When using a model answer, the teacher might read the responses of a few students before finalizing the model answer so that any unanticipated qualities may be included in the model.

A final procedure for improving holistic scoring involves what is called a scoring rubric. A scoring rubric consists of several different descriptions, each for a different level of quality, ranging from a poor response to an excellent response. Generally, descriptions at each level address the same elements within a response. Therefore, the scoring rubric defines the elements in students' responses that are to be scored. When scoring answers, a student's response is assigned to the one description within the scoring rubric that best matches the quality of that response. Typically, numbers are assigned to the descriptions within the rubric. For example, if the scoring rubric includes six descriptions, these descriptions are numbered 1 through 6, with 1 point assigned to the description of a poor response and 6 points assigned to the excellent response. In Chapter 12, we look more closely at scoring rubrics within the context of performance assessments.

Reading Responses to Multiple versus Single Items

With other formats, such as short-answer and multiple-choice, all of one student's answers are read before reading the responses of the next student. With essay items, all students' responses to a given item should be evaluated before reading responses to the next item. From a practical perspective, working with one item at a time focuses the reader's attention and speeds up the scoring process—significant advantages in grading essay exams. More important, reading all responses to a given item improves scoring accuracy. Focusing on a single item helps the reader maintain a clear perception of the standards being used to evaluate answers to that particular essay question. Also, reading the responses of all students to a single item reduces the tendency to bias the evaluation of one item in light of the quality of a student's response to previous items.

Reading Students' Papers in a Variable versus Consistent Order

A number of studies have shown that the quality of the previously scored essay affects the score assigned to a subsequently read response. Daly and Dickson-Markman (1982) and Hughes, Keeling, and Tuck (1980) demonstrated that a high-quality essay deflates the score assigned to a subsequent paper. Hughes and Keeling (1984) found this still to be true even when responses were being judged against model answers. To reduce the cumulative effect this biasing might have across items on each student's test score, the order of student papers should be rearranged after each question is read.

Concealing the Identity of Students

Previously referenced studies by Chase (1979, 1986) found that factors such as expected achievement, as well as the sex and race of the student, significantly affect scores assigned to essays. To prevent this biasing, student identity should be concealed to the extent possible when scoring essays. Such techniques as having students write their names on the back of a paper or using temporary identification numbers can facilitate this concealment. Unfortunately, a teacher is likely to learn to recognize the identity of students through writing style and penmanship. Full concealment of identity is generally not possible.

Using Multiple Readers

It is more practical to use multiple readers for holistic rather than analytic scoring because the former method takes less time. Averaging scores across multiple readers, however, will increase the reliability of tests, regardless of scoring technique. Coffman (1971) encourages having a different reader score each question when it is not possible for each reader to score the responses to all questions.

Using Diversity of Responses as an Indicator of Item Ambiguity

Often, students read questions other than those intended into an essay item. This problem can be minimized by carefully constructing the item and scoring plan, using the qualities listed in Figure 7.4 to evaluate the item, and having colleagues review questions before they are administered to students.

Diversity of students' responses, in which students appear to be interpreting the essay question differently, should be viewed as an indication of item ambiguity. If an essay question is ambiguous, the teacher, in essence, is giving students the option to interpret the question as they choose. This situation is similar to allowing each student to select questions to be answered and causes the same problems with content validity and with interpreting performance on the test. Essay questions that generate diverse responses should be revised before being reused.

SUMMARY

Essay items have some advantages over other written-test formats: They tend to measure targeted behaviors more directly, and they facilitate examination of students' ability to communicate ideas in writing. Relative to short-answer and completion items, essay questions much more readily assess intellectual skills. In contrast to objectively scored items, essay questions require students to supply the response. Essay items have basic limitations: They usually provide a less adequate sampling of content to be assessed; they are less reliably scored, and they are more time-consuming to score. Six qualities that should be incorporated into essay items were discussed and are listed in Figure 7.4.

When constructing essay items, it is also important to create a scoring plan. The scoring plan often specifies the characteristics as opposed to the content of a correct response. The plan may involve analytical or holistic scoring. The latter is appropriate when characteristics of a correct response cannot be subdivided into a series of separately scored characteristics. Other relevant scoring considerations include the desirability of scoring the responses of all students to one item before scoring the next item, rearranging the order of students' papers before reading the next item, concealing the identity of students when scoring responses, and using multiple readers whenever possible.

ANSWERS: APPLY WHAT YOU ARE LEARNING

7.1 The three advantages of essay items are that (1) they allow for direct measurement of behaviors specified in performance objectives, (2) they assess students' ability to communicate ideas in writing, and (3) they require students to provide an answer rather than to select one from alternatives provided.

7.2 The three limitations of essay items are (1) less adequate sampling of content resulting from the limited number of questions that can be included in one test, (2) errors in scoring answers resulting from inconsistency between readers and from evaluating irrelevant variables, and (3) greater time required to score students' responses.

7.3 Item A provides the better measure. Notice also that item B is asking students to recall information, whereas item A requires students to determine whether or not an illustration provided by the teacher is an example of a concept. Always be alert to the type of capability involved.

7.4 1. Neither the total number of points nor the attributes to be evaluated is specified. 2. Neither the total number of points nor guidelines for awarding points is specified.

7.5 1. A; 2. B. Within the first pair, item A is so general that a knowledgeable student could cite a variety of correct answers that were not included in the scoring plan. Within the second pair, the correct answer for item B is largely a matter of opinion or circumstance.

SOMETHING TO TRY

- If you have access to some previously written essay items, use the qualities listed in Figure 7.4 to evaluate these items, including the scoring plan.

- Prepare an essay item with a scoring plan that measures the following objective:

  Information: *Using an actual example, describe the procedure Congress is to follow for attempting to override a presidential veto.*

  Use Figure 7.4 to evaluate this item. An essay item written to measure this objective probably can be answered using two to four sentences. Although this represents a minimal essay question, it provides a useful context for writing a concise essay item and scoring plan.

- Prepare an essay item with a scoring plan that measures the following objective:

  Concept: *When given a specific and original example of a formal or informal assessment, provide examples of how construct-related, content-related, and criterion-related evidence of validity would be established for this assessment.*

  Use qualities listed in Figure 7.4 to evaluate this item.

- Similarly, write and evaluate several essay items for an objective within your academic specialization.

ADDITIONAL READING

Coffman, W. E. (1971). Essay examinations. In R. L. Thorndike (Ed.), *Educational measurement* (2nd ed.). Washington, DC: American Council on Education. This chapter provides a thorough discussion of advantages, limitations, and research issues related to essay questions as well as a description of procedures for improving the development and scoring of essay questions.

CHAPTER 8

Multiple-Choice Items

The multiple-choice format is one of the most popular item formats used in educational testing. Many group-administered standardized tests consist entirely of multiple-choice items. The multiple-choice format is also used extensively in classroom tests, particularly in the middle grades through college.

The multiple-choice item traditionally consists of a stem that describes a problem and a series of options, or alternatives, each representing possible answers to the stem. Normally, one option is correct, with the remaining alternatives referred to as distracters, or foils.

The suggestion is often made that the multiple-choice format is limited to testing recall of information. Because the correct response is always included among the item's alternatives, this type of item sometimes has been nicknamed multiple-guess and assumed to be unable to measure skills assessed by the essay and short-answer formats.

The multiple-choice format does have distinct limitations; however, effectively constructed multiple-choice items also have significant advantages. Many multiple-choice items used in classroom tests could achieve these advantages if they were constructed more effectively. Based on your own experience with multiple-choice tests, you probably will anticipate many of the qualities desired in multiple-choice items, such as a clearly expressed statement of the problem in the stem and judicious use of the "all of the above" option. This chapter will help you identify the qualities inherent in the better multiple-choice items. You will be asked to use these qualities to evaluate a series of multiple-choice items.

Considerable flexibility exists within the multiple-choice format. This flexibility will be easier to anticipate by broadening the traditional definition of multiple-choice options. Although the stem presents a problem to be addressed by students, the options should not be thought of as possible solutions to this problem. Instead, these options are the means through which students transform proposed solutions to a mark recorded in the test booklet or on an answer sheet. Look at the multiple-choice items illustrated in Figure 8.1. The directions serve as the stem in that they present the problem to be addressed. The multiple-choice options are the lines into which the individual sentences are formatted. These options do not represent alternative solutions to the problem presented by the stem. They do control how students mark their answer sheets. The options are designed so that students who are unable to solve the problem will typically mark a different answer than will those who understand the concept.

This chapter helps you achieve five skills:

- Identify the advantages and limitations of multiple-choice items
- Identify qualities desired in multiple-choice items
- Evaluate multiple-choice items for these qualities
- Identify variations of multiple-choice items
- Determine the optimal number of options to be included within a multiple-choice item.

ADVANTAGES AND LIMITATIONS OF MULTIPLE-CHOICE ITEMS

Advantages of Multiple-Choice Items

Multiple-choice items have four basic advantages over other test items. First, they provide a more adequate sampling of content. Second, these items tend to structure the problem to be addressed more effectively. Third, they can be quickly scored. Fourth, responses to multiple-choice items are objectively scored.

1. *Multiple-choice items allow a test to obtain a more adequate sampling of content.* Multiple-choice items can provide a more adequate sampling of content for two reasons. First, compared with essay items, multiple-choice tests can involve many more items, mainly because students need less time to record responses. Therefore, more content can be sampled by using the multiple-choice rather than the essay format.

Second, compared with the short-answer format, multiple-choice items (and essay items) can more readily measure procedural knowledge. Short-answer items require students to construct a response that consists of one or two words or, at most, a short sentence. Short-answer items, therefore, are usually limited to questions that involve the recall of information. In contrast, the stem to a multiple-choice item can ask students to identify an example of a particular concept. The options can include examples and nonexamples of this concept. The student can demonstrate knowledge of the concept by identifying the appropriate response. Multiple-choice items can similarly ask students to apply a particular rule. The options to such items can include correct and common incorrect solutions resulting from the application of the rule. The options might also contain descriptions of the characteristics of correct and

---

Directions: For each sentence, mark on your answer sheet the letter identifying the line that contains an adjective. Mark "E" if the sentence contains no adjective

1. A. Validity is
   B. the most
   C. fundamental issue
   D. in measurement.
   E. (no adjective)

2. A. Without validity
   B. a test
   C. is of
   D. no use.
   E. (no adjective)

Figure 8.1
Illustration of multiple-choice items using embedded options

common incorrect solutions instead of solutions. A short-answer item usually cannot do this.

   2. *Multiple-choice items tend to structure the problem to be addressed more effectively.* The responses to a multiple-choice item often help define the problem being addressed. Consider the following items:

Short answer: What should be the first step when constructing a classroom test?

Multiple-choice: Which of the following should be done first when constructing a classroom test?
   A. Determine the type of reliability to be computed.
   B. Establish the number of items to be used.
   C. Identify the skills to be tested.
   D. Review existing items.

A knowledgeable student answering the completion item might anticipate several actions, any of which could occur first when preparing a test. For example, determining the need to schedule a test must occur before a list of objectives to be tested is established. The options in the multiple-choice item more adequately define for the student the time frame being addressed. A test item written in any format should clearly specify a problem to the student. The multiple-choice item more easily achieves this goal than do the essay and short-answer formats.

   Because multiple-choice items structure the problem to be addressed, this item format usually cannot measure one of the important types of procedural knowledge, specifically complex skills. The assessment of complex skills requires students simultaneously to apply several concepts and rules. This assessment must allow students flexibility in deriving the solution to a problem. The difficulty in assessing complex skills is a restriction that applies not only to the multiple-choice item, but to all formats used with written tests.

3. *Multiple-choice items can be quickly scored.* Because students respond to each item with a single mark, multiple-choice items are scored very quickly. Scoring efficiency can be improved by having students mark responses in a blank to the left of each item, or on a separate answer sheet.

When responses are marked on a separate answer sheet, tests can be scored by machine. In the past, scoring machines were expensive and, if available at all, were located at a remote central site. Smaller, more economical scoring machines are now available and are accessible in many school buildings and in some individual classrooms. These machines score answer sheets for an entire class in a few minutes. Scoring machines often print each student's score on the answer sheet and mark incorrect answers. Many of these scoring machines will enter each student's responses into a computer for further analysis. (Analysis of items is discussed in Chapter 10.)

4. *Responses to multiple-choice items are objectively scored.* The reliability of essay tests usually suffers from inconsistencies in scoring students' responses. Inconsistency in scoring is negligible with multiple-choice items. When given the answer key, two individuals are likely to assign the same score to a given student's responses. Because multiple-choice items are objectively scored, they can be scored by students, teacher aides, or machine.

Although objectively scored, multiple-choice tests often contain measurement error. As with other formats, multiple-choice items are susceptible to error caused by asking ambiguous questions or measuring inappropriate skills. We will look carefully at this issue later in the chapter.

Box 8.1 *Apply What You Are Learning*

Which item format has each of the following qualities?

    A. Short-answer or completion

    B. Essay

    C. Multiple-choice

1. Students' answers can be quickly scored.
2. Test items can be quickly constructed.
3. Skills can be more adequately sampled within a single test.
4. Students' ability to express ideas in writing can be evaluated.
5. Students' responses can be scored with minimal error.

Answers can be found at the end of the chapter.

Limitations of Multiple-Choice Items

Multiple-choice items have three limitations. First, these items are somewhat susceptible to guessing. Second, multiple-choice items usually must indirectly measure targeted behaviors. Third, multiple-choice items are time-consuming to construct.

1. *Multiple-choice items are somewhat susceptible to guessing.* More so than with the essay and short-answer formats, multiple-choice items can be answered correctly by guessing. This would represent a significant problem were it not possible to include many multiple-choice items in a test. Relatively few items on multiple-choice tests are answered correctly by blind guessing.

The probability of successfully guessing improves if a student can eliminate some of the distracters to a number of items. The more distracters the student can eliminate in a test, the higher the test score. If the distracters represent common errors, this increase in score is desirable from a measurement perspective because a student who can avoid common errors should obtain a higher score.

Guessing does have a negative effect on test reliability. To the degree that guessing is involved, a student's performance will be inconsistent from item to item. Increasing the number of items on the test is an effective way to offset the results of guessing and to increase the reliability of test scores.

Because guessing is less of a problem for short-answer items, they tend to be more reliable than are multiple-choice items. Within the context of quantitative word problems, Oosterhof and Coats (1984) found that fewer than two-thirds the number of completion items would provide reliability comparable to that of multiple-choice items. Using the smaller number of short-answer items can reduce test preparation and administration times and potentially offset the greater scoring time required by the short-answer format.

2. *Multiple-choice items often must indirectly measure targeted behaviors.* Direct measures are always preferable to indirect measures. However, indirect measures are frequently used in many disciplines. An astronomer estimates the temperature of a star by measuring its color. Chemists measure the acidity of a liquid by judging the color of litmus paper. Similarly, an educator must frequently make judgments based on indirect observations. As long as the relationship is understood between a first quality that can be observed and the second quality that is of interest, measures of the second quality can be inferred from observations of the first.

In education, we are often unaware that indirect measures are involved. Let us assume that we want to determine whether a person can establish content-related evidence of validity for achievement tests. A direct way to assess this skill is to observe whether the person develops a test from specifications that define the test content, such as a list of performance objectives or a table of specifications. Better yet is to observe the person constructing several tests. However, asking someone to develop tests so that we can directly observe the person's ability to collect content-related evidence of validity is usually impractical. As an alternative, we could indirectly measure the person's skill using the following essay item:

> **Describe what a teacher must do to establish content-related evidence of validity for an achievement test.**

Often, we claim an essay item is a direct measure of our target skill by adjusting the wording of the performance objective. For instance, the previous essay item becomes a direct measure if our objective is written as follows:

> **Information:** Describe how to establish content-related evidence of validity for an achievement test.

Instead of the essay format, a series of multiple-choice items such as the one that follows might be used:

When establishing content-related evidence of validity for an achievement test, a teacher must be most concerned with the
- A. abilities of the students.
- B. adequacy of instruction.
- C. skills to be tested.
- D. total number of items to be included on the test.

As with all test formats, multiple-choice items do not allow teachers to observe directly what the student was thinking or why students selected particular wrong answers. Essay tests sometimes, but not always, provide an indication of the student's thought process. With multiple-choice math tests, worksheets often can be used to help diagnose problems. Similar documentation is usually not present in other content areas. On the other hand, the overall information that can be gained from using the multiple-choice format may be more useful than that obtained from an essay test. For example, more skills can be measured within a given amount of time by the multiple-choice test. Also, time saved by not scoring essay test items can be used to diagnose specific deficiencies through informal assessments and to prepare and deliver remedial instruction in areas found to be causing problems.

3. *Multiple-choice items are time-consuming to construct.* More time is required to build a test with multiple-choice items than is required with any other written format. Considerable time is needed to develop effective alternatives within each item. Essay tests, in particular, require less time to develop, primarily because fewer essay questions can be included in a test, although considerable time is needed to develop scoring plans for each item.

Usually, significantly more time is required to develop multiple-choice items that measure procedural knowledge than is required to develop items that measure recall of information. This is also true for other item formats. Because multiple-choice tests are time-consuming to construct, teachers often avoid this format unless they have access to previously developed items or unless the number of students makes scoring essay or short-answer items too formidable.

Box 8.2   *Apply What You Are Learning*

Identify the item format being described by items 1 through 5:

- A.   Short answer or completion
- B.   Essay
- C.   Multiple-choice

1.   Least likely to measure procedural knowledge such as concepts and rules
2.   Because of guessing, least likely for a student's performance on one item to generalize to performance on other items

3. Because of inconsistencies in scoring, least likely for a student's performance on one item to generalize to performance on other items

4. Because of the limited number of items used, least likely for a student's performance on the overall test to generalize to other skills in the same unit of instruction

Answers can be found at the end of the chapter.

IDENTIFYING QUALITIES DESIRED IN MULTIPLE-CHOICE ITEMS

This section examines criteria for evaluating multiple-choice items. In the next section, you will be asked to use these criteria to evaluate a series of multiple-choice questions.

1. *Does this item measure the specified skill?* As with any format, each multiple-choice item must be constructed or selected to measure a specific skill. Often, several multiple-choice items are needed to assess a particular skill, with each item within the set measuring a different aspect or perspective of that skill.

2. *Is the level of reading skill required by this item below the students' ability?* Again, this concern is relevant to test items written in all formats. Unless the level of vocabulary and sentence structure are sufficiently low, a test item will confound the measurement of reading ability with that of the skill being measured.

3. *Does the stem clearly present the problem to be addressed?* When the stem to a multiple-choice item is not self-sufficient, students end up reading the options without knowing what problem they are supposed to solve. The stem by itself should communicate what the student is expected to do.

Box 8.3   *Apply What You Are Learning*

Here are pairs of item stems. Within each pair, which stem more adequately presents the problem to be addressed?

1. A. Validity is
   B. A test is said to be valid if it

2. A. When riding a bicycle at night
   B. Which color of clothing is best to wear when riding a bicycle at night?

3. A. Which one of the following scales is used to measure the magnitude of an earthquake?
   B. Earthquakes are often very powerful and can be measured by seismographs over long distances. The Richter scale

Answers can be found at the end of the chapter.

A useful technique for improving the clarity of the stem is to present it as a question rather than as an incomplete sentence. Notice how this technique improved the clarity of the stems within items 2 and 3 in the previous exercise. Individuals who have had limited experience in constructing multiple-choice items find that writing the stem as a question helps formulate the problem being addressed and tends to improve the clarity of the entire item.

4. *Are all options parallel in type of content?* When options vary in type of content, the item is asking students to make a single judgment about two or more distinct qualities, like comparing apples to oranges. Note in the next example that because the options are not parallel in content, more than one alternative may represent the correct response.

Which of the following represents the warmest temperature?
  A. 100 degrees Celsius
  B. 200 degrees Fahrenheit
  C. 300 degrees Kelvin
  D. An oven set at medium

The first three options are all specific temperatures on well-defined scales. The fourth option represents a range of temperatures and uses an undefined scale (e.g., is this a drying oven used by a chemist or a food-baking oven?). The correct answer conceivably could be either A (the highest temperature among the first three options) or D.

Before constructing alternatives to a multiple-choice item, first think of the characteristics that all options will have in common. Then write options that match those characteristics. This approach helps maintain a focus for the item and reduces the chance of distracters' inadvertently becoming correct responses. Usually, options fail to be parallel in content because the stem does not present a concise problem. Unfortunately, two very common problems with multiple-choice items are failing to establish a concise problem in the stem and unintentionally creating multiple correct answers because the options are not parallel in content.

5. *Do the options avoid repetitive words?* The following item would be more efficient if the words repeated in each option were relocated to the stem:

Physics is
  <u>A.</u> the science that deals with the structure of matter.
  B. the science that deals with the composition, structure, and properties of substances.
  C. the science that is more concerned with solids than liquids.

Not only would this editing result in a more efficient use of words, but the modified stem would more clearly state the problem being addressed. Sometimes, a limited amount of repetition across options helps reinforce the idea presented in the stem or makes the options easier to read. However, excessive repetition should be avoided.

6. *Is extraneous content excluded from the stem?* The purpose of the stem is to present a specific problem to the student. The use of words or other content extraneous to this problem causes the item to measure how well students can determine what you are asking. The stem to each item should state the problem as simply as possible.

Box 8.4   *Apply What You Are Learning*

Listed here are stems to multiple-choice items. Within each pair, which stem is most free of extraneous words and content?

1. A. The percentage of homes that have at least one computer has increased each year, reaching what percentage at the end of last year?
    B. At the end of last year, what percentage of homes had at least one computer?
2. A. In miles per second, what is the speed of light?
    B. Although it is believed physical objects cannot go this fast, the speed of light is

Answers can be found at the end of the chapter.

---

7. *Are adjectives or adverbs emphasized when they reverse or significantly alter the meaning of a stem or option?* Whenever a single word significantly changes the meaning of a sentence or phrase within a test item, that word should be underlined or capitalized to draw attention to its presence. Otherwise, a student may read over the word and misinterpret the item. Here are some examples in which a word has been underlined because it alters the meaning of the phrase:

Which of the following conditions <u>least</u> affects the speed at which wind blows?

All of the following represent a field of science <u>except</u>

Which of the following is <u>not</u> a major cause of forest fires?

The word *not* is particularly troublesome within multiple-choice items because most phrases make grammatical sense if *not* is included or omitted, even though the meaning of the sentence changes dramatically. Potentially, then, the test item becomes a measure of how carefully students can read rather than a measure of the skill that the item was designed to target. The word *not* should be excluded from items whenever possible.

However, the negative is sometimes used within the stem to determine whether students can detect an exception (e.g., "Which of the following is <u>not</u> a major cause of forest fires?"). If it is important that students identify exceptions, replacing *not* with *except* and locating *except* at the end of the stem is more effective. This approach is illustrated in the second of the three previous examples.

The word *not* should always be excluded from the options of multiple-choice items. Its inclusion makes a normally correct response incorrect and, if it is a double negative, it makes a typically wrong response correct. The difficulties caused by using *not* are illustrated here:

Which of the following is not an item format?
    A. Not recall
    B. Not short-answer
    C. Not reverse video
    D. Not test–retest

Such a poorly constructed item would probably never be included in a test, but it demonstrates the confusion that can be generated by using *not* in the stem or in any of the options. (Note how clear the previous item becomes if all the *not*s are removed.)

8. *Is each distracter plausible?* Ideally, multiple-choice items should be constructed so that (1) students proficient with the skill select the correct option and (2) every student who has yet to achieve the skill selects a distracter. This ideal is unrealistic, however. Most academic skills are complex enough that students cannot simply be classified into two groups: those who have mastered and those who have not mastered the skill. The elusive perfect item is unable to divide students into such distinct groups because this grouping does not exist.

The perfect multiple-choice item is elusive for a second reason. Students who have not achieved the intended proficiency often select the correct answer by guessing, by detecting fallacies in the distracters, or by observing something in the correct response that is compatible with their misconception. Therefore, multiple-choice items can be substantially improved by making sure that each distracter is at least as attractive as the correct response for students who have not learned the skill being measured.

Techniques that make distracters more plausible are illustrated in Figure 8.2. First, distracters can represent common misconceptions as seen in items 1 and 2. In item 1,

---

1. When bicycling at night, which of the following colors of clothing is it best to wear?
   A. Blue
   B. Orange
   C. Red
   D. White

2. Although the duration of a lightning bolt is very short, the resulting sound of thunder usually lasts for several seconds. Why does the duration of thunder last so much longer than that of the lightning?
   A. Some parts of a lightning bolt are closer to the observer than other parts.
   B. The heat generated by lightning requires time to dissipate.
   C. Thunder echoes off nearby objects such as buildings and hills.

3. Which among the following represents the highest reliability coefficient?
   A. 0.00
   B. 0.80
   C. 100
   D. 1000

4. In educational testing, what term refers to how well a test measures the skills it is supposed to measure?
   A. Authenticity
   B. Conformity
   C. Objectivity
   D. Reliability
   E. Validity

Figure 8.2
Illustrations of plausible distracters

options B and C represent common misconceptions because orange and red, being bright colors, are thought to be highly visible at night. White clothing reflects more light and is the better choice when bicycling at night. (Clothing containing reflective tape is even better.) With respect to item 2, many people believe that echoing causes thunder to linger. In reality, because a lightning bolt is several miles in length, the sound from thunder caused by closer parts of the lightning bolt reach an observer several seconds before thunder caused by more distant parts.

Distracters also can be made more plausible by making them sound correct to the untrained reader, as illustrated by items 3 and 4. In item 3, uninformed students will likely find options D and E attractive, since 100 and 1000 sound like perfect or high scores (1.00 is the highest value of a reliability coefficient). In item 4, the words used for options A through C sound like labels one might associate with a test that measures what it was designed to measure. These distracters do not represent common misconceptions. Students would select "authenticity" because of ignorance rather than because of a misconception.

Distracters are often made plausible simply by being reasonably close to the correct answer. With items involving numerical answers, distracters will be more attractive if they represent common errors fairly close to the correct response. Students who can approximate but not correctly solve the problem presented by an item will consider such options. Although the use of distracters similar to the correct response improves their plausibility, care must be taken so that knowledgeable students continue to select the intended answer as the correct response.

Writing plausible distracters may seem devious. This perception is inaccurate when the purpose of the test item is kept in focus. To the degree possible, each item should distinguish between those students who have and those who have not gained a relevant skill. If knowledgeable students perceive distracters as the correct response, an item loses its usefulness. Similarly, if students who have not yet learned the relevant skill are more attracted to the correct response than to the distracters, the item again loses its usefulness.

9. *Is the grammar in each option consistent with the stem?* In the next illustration, can you identify the correct answer even though you may not know the concept being tested?

In item response theory, the one-parameter model assumes that each test item
    A. discriminates equally well.
    B. students perform equally well.
    C. students score the same across items.
    D. guessing affects all items the same.

In this item, the stem grammatically matches only option A, which happens to be the correct answer. The correct answer sounds correct.

All responses should be written so that they grammatically match the stem. When they do not, the item provides clues to the answer that are not relevant to student achievement. A grammatical mismatch usually occurs when the stem represents an incomplete sentence but one or more of the options do not adequately complete the sentence. This problem can be avoided by writing the stem as a question rather than as an incomplete statement. Whenever incomplete statements are used as a stem, each of the options should be checked for grammatical consistency with the stem.

10. *Does the item exclude options equivalent to "all of the above" and "none of the above"?* Phrases such as "all of the above" and "none of the above" are often included in multiple-choice items. Their typical role is to increase the number of options. "None of the above" is sometimes used to avoid giving clues to students when their incorrect solutions are inconsistent with each of the options included with the item. Although the rationale for using such options is good, their effect on test items is not beneficial.

When "all of the above" is used, a multiple-choice item actually behaves as if the number of options has been reduced. If any two of the options can be identified as correct, the student can be quite certain that "all of the above" is correct, in effect eliminating the role of the remaining responses. Similarly, if just one option can be identified as incorrect, the "all of the above" option can also be eliminated.

Sometimes, each of the distracters within a multiple-choice item contains a degree of truth, often unintentionally. When "all of the above" is used in this context, students are placed in an unfair dilemma by being expected to select between the superior option or "all of the above."

"None of the above" has similar problems. If a fallacy can be seen in each option, "none of the above" represents the logical response. Students, however, usually have difficulty determining whether the erroneous qualities were intentional and serious enough for the teacher to judge the option wrong. The only way to avoid this problem is to use options that are unequivocally correct or incorrect, and developing such options is difficult.

Spelling and computation skills do lend themselves to unequivocal statements. "None of the above" is often used in multiple-choice items testing these skills so that students will not assume that the correct solution is among the options. The effect of using "none of the above" with computational items was investigated by Oosterhof and Coats (1984). Replacing the last option with "none of the above" was actually found to lower reliability. "None of the above" served as an effective option only when it was the correct answer. As less knowledgeable students seldom selected "none of the above," it became an effective distracter only when it was the correct response. However, constantly using "none of the above" as the correct response is obviously not recommended.

11. *Unless another order is more logical, are options arranged alphabetically?* Correct answers should be distributed evenly among the alternative positions of multiple-choice items. Because items often are constructed before they are assembled into a test, this situation may be hard to achieve. Another approach is to alphabetize the options within each item. This strategy will counteract the tendency to place the correct option in the middle of the stack.

Sometimes, arranging options in an order other than alphabetical makes it easier for students to contrast the options. For example, options representing numerical values, dates, or points along a scale should be listed sequentially from low to high.

Box 8.5 *Apply What You Are Learning*

The options in each of the following items are alphabetized. With which items would an order other than alphabetical be appropriate?

1. What is the minimum number of alternatives that can be used in a multiple-choice item?
    A. five
    B. four
    C. one
    D. three
    E̲. two

2. Which best describes the relationship between reliability and validity? High validity is associated with
    A̲. high reliability.
    B. low reliability.
    C. moderate reliability.
    D. zero reliability.

3. Which item format will likely produce the highest reliability if used to construct a 30-minute test?
    A. Essay
    B. Multiple-choice
    C̲. Short-answer
    D. True–false

Answers can be found at the end of the chapter.

PRACTICE WITH APPLYING THESE DESIRED QUALITIES TO MULTIPLE-CHOICE ITEMS

Figure 8.3 lists the 11 criteria for judging multiple-choice items that we have just discussed. This section will help you apply these criteria by examining some example items. The objective being assessed and the proposed correct response are provided to help you evaluate each item. Each example fails to meet at least one of the criteria addressed in this checklist. A critique follows each item. Numbers in parentheses preceding each critique indicate the criteria within Figure 8.3 that the example item failed to achieve. Try to identify these problems before reading the critique.

The first examples pertain to a rule in astronomy; specifically, that objects in lower orbit travel faster than objects in higher orbit. Examples 8.1 through 8.3 are intended to measure knowledge of this rule, as expressed in the following objective:

Rule: Given smaller objects in orbit around a substantially larger object, the student uses the relative height of orbits to identify which object is traveling fastest in its orbit.

1. Does this item measure the specified skill?
2. Is the level of reading skill required by this item below the students' ability?
3. Does the stem clearly present the problem to be addressed?
4. Are all options parallel in type of content?
5. Do the options avoid repetitive words?
6. Is extraneous content excluded from the stem?
7. Are adjectives or adverbs emphasized when they reverse or significantly alter the meaning of a stem or option? Is the word *not* excluded?
8. Is each distracter plausible?
9. Is the grammar in each option consistent with the stem?
10. Does the item exclude options equivalent to "all of the above" and "none of the above"?
11. Unless another order is more logical, are options arranged alphabetically?

Figure 8.3
Criteria for evaluating multiple-choice items

Example 8.1

The artificial satellite with the highest orbital speed
    A. is the most recently launched satellite.
    B. is the satellite in the higher orbit.
    C. is the satellite in the lower orbit.
    D. is the satellite with an orbit closest to the equator.

Critique for Example 8.1

(3, 4, 5) The stem does not clearly describe the problem students are to solve. This is partly because each option repeats a significant amount of information that should be included in the stem. Because the stem fails to present a clear problem, the options are not parallel in content. Here is an improved version of the item:

Does the artificial satellite in higher or lower orbit have the higher orbital speed?
    A. The satellite in higher orbit
    B. The satellite in lower orbit
    C. The satellites have the same orbital speed.

Example 8.2

Ganymede and Callisto are moons of Jupiter with approximately equal mass. Ganymede orbits 1.1 million miles above Jupiter, whereas Callisto orbits 1.9 million miles above the planet. Ganymede has
    A. the faster orbital speed.
    B. more impact craters.
    C. will fall out of orbit sooner.

Critique for Example 8.2

(3, 4, 9, 11) Again, the stem does not clearly describe the problem students are to solve and the options are not parallel in content. Recall that the problem with using options not parallel in content is that more than one of the options often is unintentionally correct. That has happened here. For instance, more impact craters tend to exist on the moon closer to a planet because the planet's gravity attracts small objects in space, which tend to collide with the closer moon. If the item writer had first constructed a stem that clearly established the problem to be addressed, the options would likely have become parallel in content.

The present item has two other problems. Notice that option C is not grammatically consistent with the stem. When the grammar of an option does not match the stem, it provides clues to the answer that are not relevant to student achievement. The remaining problem with this item is that options are not ordered alphabetically. Unless another order is more logical, arranging options alphabetically helps randomize the location of the correct answer.

Here is an improved version of Example 8.2. The stem more clearly presents a problem, which in turn forces the options to be parallel in content. Although options are not listed alphabetically, they are in a logical order.

> Ganymede and Callisto are moons of Jupiter with approximately equal mass. Ganymede orbits 1.1 million miles above Jupiter, whereas Callisto orbits 1.9 million miles above the planet. Which moon has the faster orbital speed?
> **A.** Ganymede has the faster orbital speed.
> **B.** Both moons have the same orbital speed.
> **C.** Callisto has the faster orbital speed.

Example 8.3

> When a planet has more than one moon, which of the following best explains why the moon closest to a planet has the highest orbital speed?
> **A.** The closest moon has to travel faster to offset the greater gravitational pull of the planet.
> **B.** The closest moon tends to be the youngest moon and has maintained more of its original speed.
> **C.** The closest moon usually is smaller than the other moons and therefore travels faster.

Critique for Example 8.3

(1) The problem with this item might be harder to detect, but it is very basic. Mechanically, this item is well constructed, but it does not measure the specified objective. Because the objective pertains to a rule, the item should ask students to apply the rule to solve a previously unused problem. Instead, this item is measuring declarative knowledge, or knowledge of information. The item asks students to identify correct statements of factual information. Declarative knowledge is important and students must be able to state what they know; however, the present performance objective is concerned with knowledge of a rule, not declarative knowledge.

Items in Examples 8.4 through 8.6 are intended to measure the following objective:

Information: Identifies basic characteristics of instruments commonly used in a symphony orchestra.

Example 8.4

Which of the following characteristics is not a difference between a trumpet and a trombone?
    <u>A</u>. Both are made primarily of metal.
    B. Both can play notes an octave below middle C.
    C. Both change pitch primarily with valves.
    D. All of the above
    E. None of the above

Critique for Example 8.4

(7, 10) The word *not* should be underlined because it significantly alters the meaning of the stem. Better yet, *not* should be excluded from test items. In this case, the stem can be changed to a positive statement, as illustrated in the revision. The item includes "All of the above" and "None of the above" as options. Here is an improved version of this item:

Which of the following is true of <u>both</u> trumpets and trombones?
    <u>A</u>. They are made primarily of metal.
    B. They can play notes an octave below middle C.
    C. They change pitch primarily with valves.

Example 8.5

A symphony orchestra includes many instruments. They can be classified into strings, brass, woodwinds, and percussion sections. The percussion section
    A. includes the chimes.
    B. includes timpani, which can be tuned to different pitches.
    C. involves drums as well as other instruments
    D. is where you place the glockenspiel.
    <u>E</u>. All of the above

Critique for Example 8.5

(3, 6, 10) The stem contains extraneous content. Once again, the stem does not clearly establish the problem to be addressed. The intended answer, "All of the above," becomes the obvious answer to students who know any two of the preceding options are correct. ("All of the above" also causes problems if the options for the item vary from being fully correct to partially correct.) Here is an improved version of this item:

Within a symphony orchestra, the percussion section includes all of the following instruments <u>except</u>

   <u>A</u>. bassoon.
   B. chimes.
   C. drums.
   D. glockenspiel.
   E. timpani.

Example 8.6

Which one of the following instruments uses reeds to make sound?

   <u>A</u>. Oboe
   B. French horn
   C. Glockenspiel
   D. The conductor
   E. None of the above

Critique for Example 8.6

(8, 10, 11) Most students, even without knowing what a reed is, will recognize that the conductor is not an instrument; that option is not plausible and should be replaced. "None of the above" is more acceptable here than in many items because each of the options is unequivocally correct or incorrect. However, research cited earlier in this chapter indicates "none of the above" usually does not work as well as an option that directly answers the stem. Finally, unless there is another more logical order, the options should be alphabetized. This helps randomize the location of the correct response. Here is an improved version of the item:

Which one of the following instruments uses reeds to make sound?

   A. Flute
   B. French horn
   C. Glockenspiel
   <u>D</u>. Oboe
   E. Vibraphone

VARIATIONS OF MULTIPLE-CHOICE ITEMS

This section describes some of the variations possible within the multiple-choice format. In each variation, the stem presents a problem to be addressed by students. However, rather than presenting possible solutions, the options provide a means through which students transform proposed solutions to a mark in the test booklet or answer sheet.

Options Representing Ranges of Values

When computational skills are being tested, distracters to multiple-choice items usually represent solutions derived through common errors. These distracters do not usually represent all the errors that students are likely to make. Students who do not find their solution among the options are unintentionally told that an error has been made. Figure 8.4 illustrates how ranges of values can be used as options to computational items. Using ranges of values has two advantages: The solution to the problem presented in the stem is not included among the options, and it usually takes less time to construct options representing ranges of values than to construct distracters representing specific errors.

The following guidelines should be observed when constructing ranges of values for options:

■ Each range should have upper and lower limits that represent common numbers, such as multiples of 5, 10, and 25.

■ The width of intervals should be the same, except for the first and last options. Intervals should be selected that capture common student errors.

■ The interval containing the correct solution should not include common incorrect solutions.

Matching Items

Matching items are a special case of the multiple-choice format in which several items share a common set of options. All the qualities listed in Figure 8.3 apply to matching items.

Figure 8.5 illustrates two sets of matching items. For items 1 through 8, students must identify dates on which events related to the formulation of the United States Constitution occurred. To answer these items correctly, students are required to identify the sequence in which these events took place. For items 9 through 12, students must identify the role played by individuals in the development of the Constitution.

As with all multiple-choice items, options associated with a matching item should be parallel in content. This quality was established in Figure 8.5 by keeping the lists of options separate for the two groups of items. Unfortunately, teachers sometimes increase the list of answers, ostensibly to reduce guessing, by combining heterogeneous content into one set of matching items.

Figure 8.4

Illustration of multiple-choice items using options with ranges of values

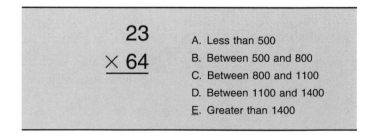

$$\begin{array}{r} 23 \\ \times\ 64 \\ \hline \end{array}$$

A. Less than 500
B. Between 500 and 800
C. Between 800 and 1100
D. Between 1100 and 1400
E. Greater than 1400

For items 1 through 8, use the options listed in the right column to identify the date on which each of the events listed in the left column occurred.

1. First Continental Congress is convened	A. 1770
2. Second Continental Congress is convened	B. 1771
3. Articles of Confederation are written	C. 1772
4. Articles of Confederation are revised in Philadelphia	D. 1773
5. Bill of Rights is written	E. 1774
6. Constitution of the United States is written	F. 1775
7. Articles of Confederation are ratified	G. 1776
8. Constitution of the United States is ratified	H. 1777
	I. 1778
Answers	J. 1779
1. E 5. T	K. 1780
2. F 6. R	L. 1781
3. H 7. L	M. 1782
4. R 8. S	N. 1783
	O. 1784
	P. 1785
	Q. 1786
	R. 1787
	S. 1788
	T. 1789
	U. 1790

For items 9 through 12, use the options listed in the right column to identify the person primarily responsible for each of the events listed in the left column.

9. Published proceedings of the Philadelphia convention in which the Articles of Confederation were revised	A. Franklin
10. Favored a government controlled by landowners	B. Hamilton
11. Authored the Bill of Rights	C. Madison
12. Refused to support ratification of the Constitution without inclusion of the Bill of Rights	D. Mason
	E. Washington

Answers
9. C   10. B   11. C   12. D

Figure 8.5
Illustration of matching items

Matching items represent a highly efficient means of testing students. A large number of matching items can be both developed and administered in a test within a short period of time. This efficiency also poses a danger to the matching format. Too much emphasis can be given to a single skill in a test by measuring that skill with a set of matching items. Planning in advance the number of test items to be used to assess each skill can prevent this problem.

Ranking of Options

Students can be asked to rank multiple-choice alternatives on a number of qualities. In essence, the first eight items in Figure 8.5 ask students to order historically a series of events. Other examples include asking students to identify the order in which steps should be completed in a laboratory experiment, to rank preferences for which of several medications should be given to patients, or to order alternative routes on a map according to distance.

As with all multiple-choice items, options must be parallel in content when students are asked to put them in some order. If a set of options represents more than a single dimension, knowledgeable students may use a defensible but unanticipated ordering.

Interpretive Test Exercises

Interpretive test exercises comprise a written presentation followed by a series of items examining students' ability to interpret the material. The written presentation might consist of a brief story, a newspaper article, a musical score, a patient's history, a chart, or a table, as illustrated in Figure 8.6. The questions can be concerned with facts contained in the presentation, interpretations and inferences, or issues requiring the student to draw on previously learned information. For example, within Figure 8.6, items 1 and 3 can be answered directly from information contained in the table. Item 2 requires a simple calculation. Items 4 and 5 require students to make an inference from the fact that Key West, being surrounded by water, has a smaller range in average temperatures than does Miami. Therefore, having freezing temperatures would be more abnormal for Key West, although Miami would be more likely to have a higher temperature on a given day in January. From a map of Florida, students could also answer questions about the effects of latitude and proximity to water on temperature.

Giving more than a brief introduction to interpretative exercises is beyond the objectives of this book. Wesman (1971) provides a good treatment of this assessment technique and is listed as additional reading at the end of this chapter. Interpretative exercises should be used prudently because they can require a substantial amount of time to develop and administer. Capabilities such as knowledge of concepts and rules often can be tested with less elaborate items. However, the interpretative exercise is a useful procedure for assessing students' ability to read and evaluate printed material. As with all multiple-choice items, it is very difficult for interpretive exercises to

January Weather Data for Selected Florida Cities

	Average Daily Low Temperature	**Average Daily High Temperature**	**Average Number of Days with Precipitation**
Jacksonville	45	65	8
Key West	66	76	7
Miami	59	76	7
Orlando	50	71	6
Tallahassee	41	64	10

Respond to the following questions using weather information obtained in the above table. The options for each these questions are

    A. Jacksonville
    B. Key West
    C. Miami
    D. Orlando
    E. Tallahassee

1. Which city tends to have the lowest temperature in January?
2. Which city tends to have the smallest range of temperatures in January?
3. Which city is <u>most</u> likely to experience precipitation on a typical January day?
4. Which city is <u>least</u> likely to experience precipitation on a typical January day?
5. Which city is likely to experience the <u>highest</u> temperature sometime during January?

Figure 8.6
Illustration of an interpretative test exercise

assess complex problem-solving tasks for which there are several possible successful strategies. Performance assessments, which are discussed in later chapters, provide a better approach.

OPTIMAL NUMBER OF CHOICES

For classroom tests, the most important factor in determining the number of options to include in multiple-choice items is the number of appropriate distracters that can be created. Incorporating distracters that are not plausible or are not parallel to the content of other options will contribute to the ambiguity of items.

The optimal number of choices to be included in an item might be less than expected. Lord (1977) compared four approaches for establishing this optimal number.

Results varied somewhat, depending on the theoretical assumptions being made. In general, however, three options per item were found to produce the most reliable test scores *as long as the total number of options across items in the test was constant.* For example, 20 items involving three options tend to provide more reliable scores than 12 items involving five options. Two options per item were found to be the next best. Four and then five options per item were found to be less effective.

This research into the optimal number of choices per item made one assumption that often is not true—that the total number of options a student can complete is the same regardless of how the options are grouped into items. It was expected that the same amount of time would be required to answer 60 alternatives divided into 30 two-option, 20 three-option, 15 four-option, and 12 five-option items. Budescu and Nevo (1985) investigated the appropriateness of that assumption with vocabulary, mathematical reasoning, and verbal comprehension tests. Each item in the vocabulary test could be read and answered quickly. The stems of the mathematical reasoning tests, however, required examinees to solve a computational problem before responding. The verbal reasoning items required examinees to read a paragraph before answering questions. Therefore, more time was required to administer 30 two-option mathematical reasoning items than 12 five-option mathematical reasoning items. The same was true with the verbal reasoning items. Adjusted for different amounts of testing time, five-option mathematical and verbal reasoning items were more reliable.

When a significant amount of time is required to solve the problem being addressed by the item, using fewer items, with more options per item, is the better strategy. If items can be answered quickly, it is preferable to use more items with fewer options per item. Thus, it seems that two-option items, such as alternate-choice items, have some potential! That is the topic of the next chapter.

SUMMARY

A multiple-choice item consists of a stem and a set of response options. The stem can be any stimulus or problem situation that might be presented to students. The response options may present correct and incorrect solutions to this problem. Alternatively, the response options can be very broadly defined; they simply represent any means through which students transform proposed solutions to a mark in the test booklet or on an answer sheet. This broader definition of response options provides considerable flexibility within the multiple-choice format.

The multiple-choice format has certain advantages. It can assess a relatively large number of skills within one test, it tends to structure a problem more effectively for students, and it can be quickly and objectively scored. Limitations of the multiple-choice format are its susceptibility to guessing, its more indirect assessment of procedural knowledge such as concepts and rules, and the amount of time required to construct each multiple-choice item. Eleven qualities that should be incorporated into multiple-choice items were discussed and are listed in Figure 8.3.

The best strategy for determining how many options to include in a multiple-choice item is to see how many plausible distracters can be created. It is counterproductive to include poorly constructed distracters just to obtain a certain number of multiple-choice options. For items that can be read and answered quickly, using more items, each with fewer options, is preferable. For items that require more time to answer, fewer items, each with more options, is best.

ANSWERS: APPLY WHAT YOU ARE LEARNING

8.1 1. C; 2. A; 3. C; 4. B; 5. C. *Item 1:* Short-answer items can be scored quickly, but multiple-choice items are more quickly scored, particularly when machines are used. *Item 2:* One short-answer item can be constructed more quickly than one essay item, largely because the essay format requires development of a detailed scoring plan. Considerable time is necessary to prepare options to multiple-choice items. *Item 3:* Multiple-choice allows better sampling than essay because more items can be included in a single test. Short-answer items often will provide less adequate sampling of content than will multiple-choice items when measurement of concepts and rules is involved. *Item 4:* With written tests, only the essay item format can assess students' ability to communicate ideas in writing. *Item 5:* Responses to multiple-choice items are more consistently graded than are responses to essay or short-answer items.

8.2 1. A; 2. C; 3. B; 4. B. *Item 1:* The short response required by short-answer items usually limits this format to measuring declarative knowledge, rather than procedural knowledge such as concepts and rules. Unlike with short-answer items, the student's response to multiple-choice items (usually an A, B, C, D, or E) is not the actual solution to the problem presented by the item. Instead, answers to multiple-choice items provide an indirect indicator of whether the student has solved the problem presented by the item. *Items 2–4:* Guessing significantly affects the reliability of multiple-choice items. However, inconsistency in scoring more significantly reduces the reliability of essay items. This is because, unlike the essay format, multiple-choice items can offset this threat to reliability by including a substantial number of items in a single test, but so can the short-answer format, whose reliability is not affected significantly by guessing. Therefore, the short-answer test is likely to have the highest reliability.

8.3 1. B; 2. B; 3. A

8.4 1. B; 2. A. Note that the stems with extraneous material are longer than necessary. This extraneous material may also unintentionally provide information that students can use to answer other questions within the test.

8.5 Options in item 1 should be ordered numerically, from one to five. Options in item 2 should be ordered from zero reliability to high reliability, or possibly the reverse. Within item 3, listing options alphabetically should be sufficient, although some writers may prefer a particular grouping of the item formats.

SOMETHING TO TRY

- If you have access to some previously written multiple-choice items, use the qualities listed in Figure 8.3 to evaluate these items.

- Prepare some multiple-choice items that measure this objective:

  Rule: *Distinguish between safe and unsafe bicycling practices.*

  With these items, be sure you are measuring a *rule*, not *information*. Use Figure 8.3 to evaluate these items.

- Similarly, write and then evaluate several items for an objective within your academic specialization.

ADDITIONAL READING

Carlson, S. B. (1985). *Creative classroom testing.* Princeton, NJ: Educational Testing Service. This book discusses types of objectively scored test items that teachers often overlook when constructing classroom tests. Several of the item types described are variations of the multiple-choice format. A number of examples and worksheets are provided in the discussion.

Haladyna, T. M. (1999). *Developing and validating multiple-choice test items* (2nd ed.). Mahwah, NJ: Lawrence Erlbaum. This book provides an extended discussion of developing multiple-choice items and validating item responses.

Osterlind, S. J. (1997). *Constucting test items: multiple-choice, constructed response, performance, and other formats* (2nd ed.). Boston: Kluwer Academic Publishers. This book provides an extensive treatment of constructing test items, particularly those using the multiple-choice format. Emphasis is on methods for identifying and minimizing measurement error during item construction and later review.

Wesman, A. G. (1971). Writing the test item. In R. L. Thorndike (Ed.), *Educational measurement* (2nd ed., pp. 113–128). Washington, DC: American Council on Education. This chapter reviews the item-writing literature and discusses ideas for producing various formats of objectively scored test items. See pages 113–120 for a discussion of the construction of multiple-choice and matching items; see pages 122–128 for the construction and characteristics of multiple-choice items within interpretive exercises.

CHAPTER 9

Alternate-Choice Items

Alternate-choice items present a proposition for which one of two opposing options represents the correct response. The most common example of the alternate-choice format is the true–false item. However, the alternate-choice format is quite general, and a number of its variations look nothing like the traditional true–false item. Because the true–false format is familiar, it does represent a useful starting point.

True–false items appear to have distinct limitations. Students with no knowledge of the content being tested can blindly guess the correct answer to half the items. Many true–false items measure trivia. True–false items are often stated ambiguously. On the other hand, because true–false items are quickly answered, they can sample a considerable amount of content within a single test. Also, true–false and other alternate-choice items when carefully constructed measure procedural knowledge such as concepts and rules.

This chapter describes qualities desired in alternate-choice items. You may anticipate many of these qualities, such as the need to use statements in true–false items that can be categorically classified as true or false. After we discuss qualities desired in alternate-choice items, you will be asked to use these qualities to evaluate a series of items.

The alternate-choice format can be used in a variety of creative ways. For example, Figure 9.1 illustrates a spelling test in which items are embedded in a paragraph. Students indicate whether each word is correctly spelled. Numbers given to the right of each word reference item numbers on the answer sheet. By listing words in the context of a paragraph, the test becomes a more authentic assessment of what students are expected to do, that is, check the spelling of words within a context rather than spelling words in isolation. As illustrated in items 2 and 4, this spelling check also requires students to verify that the appropriate word is being spelled.

Although response options are not limited to *true* and *false*, or even single words, options to an alternate-choice item always come in pairs. Each option represents an opposite of the other. As illustrated in Figure 9.1, an item does not need to be a sentence. Items can consist of a word within a sentence or, as will be demonstrated later, even an element within a checklist or matrix.

This chapter helps you achieve four skills:

- Identify variations of alternate-choice items
- Identify the advantages and limitations of alternate-choice items
- Identify qualities desired in alternate-choice items
- Review alternate-choice items for these desired qualities

VARIATIONS OF ALTERNATE-CHOICE ITEMS

The most familiar version of the alternate-choice format is a true–false item. Considerable variation from the true–false format is possible. At a superficial level, the options *true* and *false* can be replaced with words such as *yes* and *no*, or *correct* and *incorrect*. However, considerable flexibility also exists in the physical appearance of these items. This section describes some of these variations.

Traditional True–False Items

Most of us are very familiar with the true–false item. A single statement is made, usually consisting of one sentence. Students are asked to indicate whether the statement is true or false. When high school and college students are asked which item format they like the least, true–false items often come to the top of the list. This format suffers a terrible reputation. As noted earlier, true–false items are often thought to measure trivia and to be stated ambiguously. Some of this reputation is deserved. For example, true–false items are often ambiguous because subtleties make the item true or false. When writing the true–false item, it is difficult for the teacher to construct a statement that focuses students' attention on the element within the item that students are to judge as true or false without also giving away the answer to the item. We will look at a number of techniques for minimizing this problem.

True–False Items Requiring Corrections

A common variation of true–false items is asking students to rewrite false items as correct statements. Students' corrections can provide insights into how well they understand concepts. Giving students credit only when a false item is correctly rewritten

Indicate whether each underlined word is correctly spelled. For each word, mark your answer sheet as follows:

      A. Correctly spelled

      B. Incorrectly spelled

Construct validity is the most relavent[1] type of validity if their[2] is a need to determine whether a particuler[3] test, in affect[4], measures a psychological construct. Examples of psychological constructs include intelligense[5]; various[6] specific aptitudes, such as math aptitude, music aptitude, and creativity[7]; and personelity[8] traits, such as anxiety[9] and motivation[10].

Answers

1. B   6. A
2. B   7. A
3. B   8. B
4. B   9. A
5. B   10. A

Figure 9.1
Illustration of embedded alternate-choice items

may recover some of the test reliability lost when students give correct answers for the wrong reason.

Brown (1983) recommended that students identify the false element within each item instead of simply rewriting false statements as true sentences. This approach reduces trivial revisions. For example, most false true–false items can be made true by strategically inserting the word *not*.

Requiring students to correct false statements is equivalent to creating a series of short-answer or, possibly, brief-response essay items, and problems associated with this format would be expected to appear. For example, the number of items that can be included in the test will be reduced. Subjectivity in scoring answers will be increased. If students' responses are kept short, however, these limitations will be minimized.

Embedded Alternate-Choice Items

A series of alternate-choice items can be embedded in a paragraph. The spelling test illustrated in Figure 9.1 illustrates this approach. Each item consists of an underlined word or group of words. Students are asked to indicate whether each underlined element represents a particular quality such as a correctly spelled word or a factually correct statement.

Figure 9.2 illustrates embedded items used to determine if students can identify the verbs within a sentence. The items in Figure 9.3 test students' knowledge of historical facts. Figures 9.1 through 9.3 illustrate embedded alternate-choice items that can assess procedural knowledge such as rules and concepts, as well as recall of information.

Indicate whether each underlined word is used as a verb. For each item, mark your answer sheet as follows:

A. Used as a verb

B. Used other than as a verb

Sailing has[1] many advantages as[2] a recreational sport. You can[3] sail[4] by yourself or with[5] others. You can participate[6] in leisurely day sailing or competitive racing[7]. You need[8] not be physically strong to enjoy the sport. And while[9] important basic techniques[10] can be learned[11] quickly, you can spend[12] a lifetime developing your sailing[13] skills.

Answers

1. A	3. A	5. B	7. B	9. B	11. A	13. B
2. B	4. A	6. A	8. A	10. B	12. A	

Figure 9.2
Embedded alternate-choice items measuring knowledge of the concept of a verb

Indicate whether the underlined words make the sentence historically correct. For each item, mark your answer sheet as follows:

A. Correct

B. Incorrect

Christopher Columbus was a native of Italy[1]. His first voyage to the New World involved four[2] ships and over 100[3] men. This voyage began in Portugal[4] in 1491[5]. Approximately one year[6] was required to reach the Western Hemisphere. He first landed in what is now called Bahamas[7]. Columbus made a total of four[8] voyages to the New World. He was rich[9] and famous when he died in 1506. Before his death, he knew that he had yet to reach Asia[10].

Answers

1. A	3. A	5. B	7. A	9. B
2. B	4. B	6. B	8. A	10. B

Figure 9.3
Embedded alternate-choice items measuring historical knowledge

Multiple True–False Items

A conventional multiple-choice item consists of a stem and a list of options. Usually, one of the options is correct, and the others serve as distracters. An alternative would be to allow any number from none to all of the options to be correct. In essence, each of the options represents a true–false item. When a group of items shares a common stem in this manner, they are called "multiple true–false items."

Figure 9.4 illustrates multiple true–false items. Note that the options are numbered as separate items. This numbering procedure is important when scoring answers by machine. Many scoring machines compare the density of students' answers to each item and assume the darkest mark represents the student's intended response. Lighter

Read each option and indicate which are correct.

In comparison with multiple-choice items, advantages of the true–false format are

1. more items can be administered within a single test.
2. higher reliability is obtained from given number of test items.
3. each test item can be developed in less time.
4. students will select the correct answer only when they have achieved the skill being tested.

Correct options: 1, 3

Figure 9.4
Illustration of multiple true–false items

marks are presumed to be poor erasures. Treating each option as a separately numbered test item increases the accuracy of scoring.

Multiple true–false items are more similar to true–false than to multiple-choice items. Each of the series of items must present its own proposition, even though several items share a common stem. These propositions must be unequivocally true or false. In contrast, multiple-choice items allow students to select the best answer among a series of options, all of which may contain some truth and some falsity.

Sequential True–False Items

A series of true–false items can be presented in sequence, the correct response to each item being dependent on conditions specified in the previous item. For example, Figure 9.5 presents an incorrect solution of an algebraic problem. From the series of

Items 1 through 4 represent a student's attempt to solve for *x*. Evaluate this solution by determining whether each equation is equivalent to the *immediately preceding* equation.

In comparison with multiple-choice items, advantages of the true–false format are

A. This expression is *equivalent* to the preceding equation.
B. This expression is *not equivalent* to the preceding equation.

Solve for *x*:
$(4x - 3)(3x + 8) = (3x + 4)(3x + 6)$
1. $12x^2 - 24 = 9x^2 + 24$
2. $3x^2 = 48$
3. $x^2 = 16$
4. $x = 8$
Answers: 1. B   2. A   3. A   4. B

Figure 9.5
Illustration of sequential true–false items

four items following this incorrect solution, the student must determine where the solution is wrong. This item can measure the ability to locate inconsistencies in mathematical logic.

Sequential true–false items can be used in a number of settings where solution of a problem requires a series of steps, each providing information to the next stage. For example, many exercises in geometry and trigonometry can be divided into sequential items, as can problems in other subjects requiring students to apply logical reasoning.

Focused Alternate-Choice Items

A conventional true–false item requires students to classify a proposition as true or false. When constructing the item, it is often difficult to highlight the element within the proposition that is to be evaluated without also giving away the answer to the item.

The items shown in Figure 9.6 illustrate how the alternate-choice format can explicitly state the focus within each item. The student is asked to identify which of two key words or phrases accurately completes the statement. Notice that this is not simply a two-option multiple-choice item. Within any alternate-choice item, the two responses must have opposite or reciprocal meanings.

Ebel (1982) compared the reliability of scores from conventional true–false and the focused alternate-choice items. Students enrolled in a college course were administered eight unit tests. Each test included two forms consisting of true–false and focused alternate-choice items, respectively. For six of the eight tests, scores on forms using the alternate-choice items were more reliable. This increase in reliability probably results from helping students focus on the element within the item that is to be evaluated.

Checklists

A checklist consists of a series of statements. The student must read each statement and then indicate whether the quality described in the statement is present or absent. Checklists can be used to facilitate instruction or assess students in a variety of content areas. For example, the lists of characteristics that have been used within the last

---

1. The probability of precipitation increases as barometric pressure (A. increases; B. decreases).
2. The atmosphere near the equator flows to the (A. east; B. west).
3. Wind direction between centers of high low pressure is (A. parallel; B. perpendicular) to a line connecting the two centers.

Answers: 1. B   2. B   3. B

Figure 9.6
Illustration of focused alternate-choice items

several chapters to evaluate test items can be used as a checklist. You have been asked to use these lists to determine the status of various qualities within test items. These lists could also be incorporated into an exam to assess your ability to evaluate test items.

Language students can be given checklists to evaluate the grammatical structure of sentences. Student pilots can use checklists to facilitate instruction and examination in preflight procedures. Sometimes, students are expected to continue the use of a checklist after instruction has been completed. This is the case with the checklists used by airplane pilots. Teachers can also use checklists to structure observations of students, such as within performance assessments. This procedure is discussed in later chapters.

A checklist can be thought of as a series of alternate-choice items. Each element of the checklist represents an item. The two possible responses to each item have opposite meanings, although a variety of pairings can be used as responses such as yes/no or acceptance/nonacceptance.

ADVANTAGES AND LIMITATIONS OF ALTERNATE-CHOICE ITEMS

Advantages of Alternate-Choice Items

Alternate-choice items have four advantages. First, they allow a test to obtain a more adequate sampling of content. Second, they are relatively easy to construct. Third, alternate-choice items can be efficiently scored. Fourth, responses to alternate-choice items are objectively scored.

1. *Alternate-choice items allow a more adequate sampling of content.* As with the short-answer and multiple-choice formats, a substantial number of alternate-choice items can be included in a single test. This permits a more adequate sampling of content than can be achieved by particularly the essay format. In fact, students may be able to answer twice the number of alternate-choice versus multiple-choice or short-answer items within a given period of time. Unlike short-answer items, students need not write out a response. Unlike multiple-choice questions, students answering alternate-choice items need not read through a list of options. This makes the alternate-choice format particularly strong in its ability to sample content. As with the multiple-choice and essay formats, alternate-choice items can measure procedural knowledge such as concepts and rules, as well as recall of information.

2. *Alternate-choice items are relatively easy to construct.* Alternate-choice items do not require the construction of scoring plans associated with essay items or the list of options required by the multiple-choice format. As a result, more alternate-choice than essay or multiple-choice items can usually be produced within a given period of time.

The similarity of the structure of alternate-choice items to the way that we structure learning also may facilitate their construction. Ebel (1982) proposed that learning consists of formulating relationships among concepts. Assuming each relationship can be expressed as a proposition, achievement can be assessed by asking students to identify whether each in a series of propositions is correct or incorrect. The true–false format, in particular, parallels this pattern. If the teacher has identified the relevant propositions that express these relationships, the development of true–false items simply consists of writing a series of accurate and erroneous versions of these propositions.

3. *Alternate-choice items can be efficiently scored.* As with the multiple-choice format, alternate-choice items can be quickly scored by hand or machine.

4. *Responses to alternate-choice items are objectively scored.* Essay and, to a lesser degree, short-answer items are subjectively scored. As a result, two readers often assign different scores to a given student's answers. Essay tests in particular lose reliability because of scoring inconsistencies. Because multiple-choice and alternate-choice tests are objectively scored, their reliabilities are not threatened by inconsistencies in scoring. (However, students guessing at answers reduce the reliability of multiple-choice and particularly alternate-choice tests.)

Limitations of Alternate-Choice Items

Alternate-choice items have three limitations. First, these items are susceptible to guessing. Second, alternate-choice items can be used only when dichotomous answers represent sufficient response options. Third, alternate-choice items typically must indirectly measure performance objectives related procedural knowledge.

1. *Alternate-choice items are susceptible to guessing.* Because one of two responses to an alternate-choice item must be correct, the probability that a student will give the correct response from a blind guess is 50%. With no understanding of the skills being tested, a student is expected to correctly answer 5 items on a 10-item test or 50 items on a 100-item test.

This threat of guessing is more perceived than real. Student knowledge hopefully is never tested with just one item, regardless of item format. In addition, 5 of 10 items or 50 of 100 items generally would not be considered passing scores on a test. If students did answer alternate-choice items with blind guesses, fewer than 10% of the students would correctly answer *more* than 7 of 10, 13 of 20, or 56 of 100 items on the test. The chances of a student blindly achieving a score greater than 70% on a 100-item alternate-choice test is less than four in a million. Increasing the number of items included in a test will control the threat of guessing answers to alternate-choice items. Students typically can answer two alternate-choice items per minute. Therefore, including sufficient items within a test is feasible.

Nevertheless, guessing does reduce the reliability of alternate-choice items. Increasing the number of items included in a test reduces but does not negate this problem. In general, when comparing tests that require equal amounts of time to administer, short-answer tests provide the highest reliability, followed by multiple-choice, alternate-choice, and essay tests, in that order (Frisbie, 1973; Oosterhof & Coats, 1984; Oosterhof & Glasnapp, 1974). Even with the problems caused by guessing, tests that use the alternate-choice format can obtain acceptably high reliabilities (Ebel, 1982).

2. *Alternate-choice items can be used only when dichotomous answers represent sufficient response options.* Many statements cannot be answered with simply a "yes" or "no," or a "true" or "false." To function properly, an alternate-choice item must be

answered without qualification, using these or similar dichotomous answers. Later in this chapter we look at some techniques that help alternate-choice items address this constraint.

   3. *Alternate-choice items usually must indirectly measure performance related to procedural knowledge.* As noted in the chapter opening, educational measurement is not alone in its dependency on indirect measures. Most measures in the physical sciences, for instance, rely on well-understood indirect measures of phenomena and properties. Similarly, all measures of knowledge use student behaviors as an indirect measure of knowledge because teachers cannot directly see what a student knows or is thinking. Chapter 7 points out that essay tests in particular appear more able to directly measure skills one is trying to teach, but this often is simply the result of wording performance objectives in a manner more similar to the wording of essay questions. It is critical to recognize that student performance is always an *indirect* measure of a student's knowledge. More fundamental than choosing a particular item format is selecting the type of student behavior that provides a well-understood indirect measure of the knowledge being assessed. This is why, beginning in Chapter 3, emphasis has been placed on identifying the type of behaviors that provide good measures of different types of knowledge, such as information, concepts, rules, and complex skills. We must recognize that alternate-choice questions usually have to indirectly measure performance related to procedural knowledge. Our way of addressing this limitation will be to construct items that involve student behaviors known to be good indicators of procedural knowledge.

Box 9.1 *Apply What You Are Learning*

Indicate whether each of the following statements is true or false:

1. The reliability of a 20-item alternate-choice test is generally higher than that of a 20-item short-answer test.

2. Students tend to get higher scores on multiple-choice tests than on alternate-choice tests.

3. Scoring errors diminish the reliability of an alternate-choice test more than that of a short-answer test.

4. More time is usually required for students to complete a 30-item multiple-choice test than a 30-item alternate-choice test.

5. Students spend a greater portion of time solving problems on an alternate-choice test than an essay test.

6. The essay format more adequately measures knowledge of *concepts* than the alternate-choice format.

7. More time is required to construct an alternate-choice test than an essay test.

8. A multiple-choice item usually requires more time to construct than an alternate-choice item.

Answers can be found at the end of the chapter.

IDENTIFYING QUALITIES DESIRED IN ALTERNATE-CHOICE ITEMS

This section examines specific criteria for evaluating alternate-choice items. In the next section, you will use these criteria to evaluate a series of alternate-choice questions.

1. *Does the item measure the specified skill?* As with any format, each alternate-choice item must be constructed or selected to measure a specific skill. Often, several items are used to assess a particular skill, with each item within the set measuring a different aspect or perspective of that skill.

2. *Is the level of reading skills required by the item below that of the students' abilities?* Again, this concern is relevant to test items written in all formats. If reading skills are above or even at the limit of a student's capability, the test confounds the measurement of reading ability with that of the skill being measured.

3. *Is one of the two response options unequivocally correct?* This quality is relevant to all variations of alternate-choice items. It is particularly difficult to achieve with true–false items. The problem results from having to create a single statement that is, in isolation, unequivocally true or false. A technique that often eliminates the problem is to contrast two ideas. To illustrate, the following true–false item has been improved through such a contrast:

Without contrast: The reliability of short-answer tests is unaffected by guessing.

With contrast: The reliability of short-answer tests is less affected by guessing than are multiple-choice tests.

Because the short-answer format is generally not affected by guessing, the first item is basically true. Sometimes, however, students do get correct answers on short-answer items by guessing. An example would be correctly guessing the spelling of a word on a spelling test.

Alternate-choice items must function as unequivocally correct or incorrect propositions *from the perspective of students with whom the items will be used.* It may be unrealistic to write items that content experts, for instance, would judge to be unequivocal. If your knowledgeable students consistently answer an item correctly, this is evidence that the item is constructed appropriately. If, however, some students present defensible explanations for selecting the wrong response, you have reason to believe the item is deficient.

4. *Does the item present a single proposition?* An alternate-choice item becomes ambiguous when it contains two propositions, one that may be true and the other false. To avoid this source of ambiguity, alternate-choice items should always state a single proposition.

Box 9.2   *Apply What You Are Learning*

Indicate "yes" when the alternate-choice item contains *more than one* proposition; otherwise indicate "no":

1. Essay tests require less time to construct than multiple-choice tests; however, essay tests require more time to score.

2. The reliability of short-answer tests is less affected by guessing than multiple-choice tests.

3. Classroom tests should be reliable and should give consistent scores across time.

Answers can be found at the end of the chapter.

5. *Is the item stated as simply as possible?* This point parallels the need to exclude extraneous material from the stem of a multiple-choice item. In either format, the use of words or other content extraneous to the problems being presented may cause the item to measure how well students can determine what the question is asking. Identifying what is being asked represents an important skill. However, if that is not the skill being tested, including extraneous material in an item confounds the measurement of the intended skill. You will not know if students missed the item because they did not comprehend the question or because they have yet to master the skill being tested. Each alternate-choice item should state its proposition as simply as possible.

Box 9.3   *Apply What You Are Learning*

Listed below are pairs of true–false items. Within each pair, which item (A or B) is most free of extraneous words and content?

1. A. In the United States, high-definition television uses (A. analog; B. digital) signals.
    B. High definition television, more so in the United States than some countries, uses (A. analog; B. digital) signals.

2. A. One of the rules in volleyball is that a team scores points only when it serves the ball. (true)
    B. In volleyball, only the team that served the ball can score a point. (true)

Answers can be found at the end of the chapter.

Stating an alternate-choice item as simply as possible helps restrict the item to a single proposition. In these examples, when an item was not stated simply, multiple propositions were created. To state items simply, clearly establish in your mind the proposition to be addressed, and then include in the item only words that are critical to communicating that proposition.

6. *Are adjectives or adverbs emphasized when they reverse or significantly alter the meaning of an item?* Individual words that by themselves significantly change or reverse the meaning of the item should be underlined or capitalized to give emphasis. Failing to do so often results in students reading around these critical words. In effect, the item becomes a measure of reading ability that confounds the measurement of the skill being tested.

The word *not* is a particularly troublesome adverb in alternate-choice items. Demonstrate this to yourself. Which of the following statements are true?

Decreasing the number of items does *not* increase test reliability.

A test is *not* necessarily reliable if it is valid.

More alternate-choice than essay items *cannot* be included in a given test.

Only the first statement is true. Note how much easier these alternate-choice items become when the word *not* is deleted:

Decreasing the number of items increases test reliability. (false)

A test is reliable if it is valid. (true)

More alternate-choice than essay items can be included in a given test. (true)

Most adjectives and adverbs that significantly alter the meaning of a sentence can be used in alternate-choice items if they are emphasized. The adverb *not* is an exception and should be excluded from alternate-choice items.

7. *Are adjectives and adverbs that imply an indefinite degree excluded?* Words such as *frequent, often,* and *sometimes* specify indeterminate quantities. These and similar words have a broad range of meanings. The sentence, "Students *often* spelled the words correctly," could mean they correctly spelled several out of 100 or almost all of 100 words. Words with indefinite meanings should be excluded from alternate-choice items. They prevent items from being classified as unequivocally correct or incorrect. Which of the following alternate-choice items can be answered unequivocally?

Alternate-choice tests *usually* include *many* items.

Multiple-choice items *frequently* have three options.

Teachers *typically* use short-answer items.

None of these items can be answered unequivocally. The italicized words within each item have indefinite meanings. Here is how each of these items could be made unequivocally true or false:

A 20-minute test can include more questions if short-answer items are rewritten as alternate-choice items. (true)

A multiple-choice item can contain three options. (true)

Teachers use more short-answer items in classroom tests than any other format. (true)

8. *Are adjectives and adverbs with absolute meanings avoided?* Statements containing words such as *all, always, every, never,* and *no* are usually found to be false. Students who have not learned the concept being tested answer such items as incorrect because an exception to the *always* or *never* probably exists. Therefore, these words increase the effectiveness of *true* alternate-choice items because students unfamiliar with the concept anticipate the presence of exceptions. Conversely, these words lower the effectiveness of false statements and should not be used when the statement poses a false proposition. However, if absolute words are used too frequently in true statements, students will soon learn to reverse common logic. For this

1. True–false items more easily measure knowledge of concepts than do completion items. (true)

2. Multiple-choice items should contain at least four options. (false)

3. A test has content-related evidence of validity if its scores correlate highly with course grades. (false)

4. A test will be reliable if scored objectively. (false)

Figure 9.7
Examples of plausible true–false items

reason, you might occasionally use words with absolute meanings but, in general, should avoid their use in alternate-choice items.

9. *Is the incorrect response plausible?* Test items should be designed so that students who have achieved the relevant skill can easily give the correct answer whereas those who have yet to achieve this skill provide a wrong response. This represents a formidable task for alternate-choice items because students have a reasonable chance of giving the correct answer using only a blind guess. However, because students usually do not guess blindly at test items, the ability of an item to perform properly will be enhanced if the wrong response is plausible. The incorrect response should be at least as believable as the correct response for students who have yet to master the pertinent skill.

As with distracters to multiple-choice items, several techniques can be used to make the incorrect answer more plausible. First, the wrong response can represent a common misconception, as illustrated by the first two items in Figure 9.7. The first item is plausible because people often believe true–false items are limited to measuring recall of information. The incorrect response to the second item is also a common misconception. Because multiple-choice items commonly use four or five options, deviating from this norm seems inappropriate.

Again, as with multiple-choice distracters, the incorrect responses to alternate-choice items are more plausible if they sound believable. The third and fourth items in Figure 9.7 illustrate this approach. With item 3, it seems reasonable that tests should correlate with course grades, although it does not represent the procedure for establishing content-related evidence of validity. With item 4, superficial reasoning would also suggest an objectively scored test is reliable. Neither item represents common misconceptions. However, a student with limited comprehension of relevant concepts would find these incorrect responses to be attractive.

APPLYING THESE DESIRED QUALITIES TO ALTERNATE-CHOICE ITEMS

Figure 9.8 lists the nine criteria for judging alternate-response items that we have discussed. This section will help you apply these criteria by examining a series of example items. The objective being assessed and the answer proposed by the item

1. Does this item measure the specified skill?
2. Is the level of reading skill required by this item below the students' ability?
3. Is one of the two response options unequivocally correct?
4. Does the item present a single proposition?
5. Is the item stated as simply as possible?
6. Are adjectives or adverbs emphasized when they reverse or significantly alter the meaning of an item; is the word *not* excluded?
7. Are adjectives and adverbs that imply an indefinite degree excluded?
8. Are adjectives and adverbs with absolute meanings avoided?
9. Is the incorrect response plausible?

Figure 9.8
List of criteria for evaluating alternate-choice items

writer are provided to help you evaluate each item. Each example item fails to meet at least one of the criteria. A critique follows each item. Numbers in parentheses preceding each critique indicate the criteria within Figure 9.8 that the example item has failed to achieve. Try to identify these problems before reading the critique.

Examples 9.1 through 9.4 pertain to timing the delay between a lightning strike and the following thunder to determine the distance of the lightning from the observer. Because sound travels a little more than 1000 feet per second, the distance of a lightning strike can be determined by dividing by five the number of seconds it takes for the sound of thunder to arrive. The performance objective could be stated as follows:

Rule: Given the time delay between a lightning strike and the following thunder, calculates the distance between the lightning strike and the observer.

Example 9.1

If the time between lightning and thunder is 3 seconds, the lighting strike was not as far away as one mile. (true)

Critique of Example 9.1

(5, 6) This item does require the student to apply the rule specified by the performance objective. However, this item should be stated more simply. Also, words that by themselves significantly change the meaning of a statement usually can be used in alternate-choice items if they are underlined or otherwise emphasized. The word *not* is an exception. Because it potentially sets up a confusing double-negative, *not* should always be excluded. This item can be stated more simply and *not* can be removed by rewriting the item as a positive statement:

If the time between lightning and thunder is 3 seconds, the lightning strike was <u>less</u> than one mile away. (true)

Example 9.2

The time delay between a lightning strike and the sound of the thunder equals the distance of the lightning strike in miles. (false)

Critique for Example 9.2

(1) This is a well-constructed item, but it does not measure the objective. The item asks whether students can state the relationship between the distance of lightning and time delay of thunder (information), rather than the ability to apply the rule. When measuring student achievement, this distinction between declarative and procedural knowledge is important.

Example 9.3

If there is little time delay between lightning and the thunder, the distance of the lightning strike is (A. more; B. less) than one mile.

Critique for Example 9.3

(7, 9) The adjective *little* implies an indefinite degree. Such words prevent alternate-choice items from being classified as unequivocally correct or incorrect. Also, the incorrect answer to this item is not plausible. Students who do not know the rule concerning the time relationship between lightning and thunder will probably answer this item correctly. Here is a better alternative to this item:

If the time delay between lightning and thunder is 4 seconds, the distance of the lightning strike is (A. more; B. less) than one mile.

Example 9.4

Thunder is louder and follows the lightning more quickly when the lighting strike is closer. (true)

Critique for Example 9.4

(1, 4) This item does not measure the objective. As with Example 9.2, the item measures declarative knowledge (information), not procedural knowledge (rule) as specified in the objective. Also, this objective involves more than one proposition: thunder associated with closer lighting is louder, and thunder associated with closer lightning occurs more quickly. Here is an alternative item that involves a single proposition, although it still does not measure the targeted objective:

The more distant a lightning strike, the (A. sooner; B. later) the thunder is heard.

Examples 9.5 through 9.7 pertain to knowledge of when an emergency number is to be used to summon assistance. In many communities within North America, the 9-1-1 phone number is used for emergencies. The performance objective could be stated as follows:

Information: State whether 9-1-1 is used to summon various examples of needed assistance.

Example 9.5

You should always use 9-1-1 to call the police. (false)

Critique for Example 9.5

(8) Words with absolute meanings, such as *always* and *never*, should be avoided in alternate-choice items, particularly when the proposition posed by the item is false. Because there usually are exceptions, students usually guess the proposition to be false when they do not know the answer. In this case, police usually discourage the use of 9-1-1 for nonemergencies such as requests for information and traffic accidents not involving injuries. Here is how this item could be improved:

One should use 9-1-1 to ask the police about a parking ticket. (false)

Example 9.6

If there is smoke in your house and you do not know what is causing it, you should call 9-1-1. (true)

Critique for Example 9.6

(4) This item involves two propositions: There is smoke in the house, and the cause of the smoke is unknown. More than one proposition should not be included in an alternate-choice item because multiple propositions tend to make the item ambiguous; one proposition may be correct and the other incorrect. Here is a way to improve this item:

9-1-1 should be used if you believe your house is on fire. (true)

Example 9.7

Usually, you should not use 9-1-1 to make an emergency call to a plumber. (true)

Critique for Example 9.7

(6, 7) The word *not* should be excluded, as should words with indefinite meanings such as *usually*. Here is a better wording for this item:

9-1-1 should be used to make an emergency call to a plumber. (false)

Alternate-choice items are useful for measuring declarative knowledge (*information*), and most types of procedural knowledge, including *concepts* and *rules*. For instance, alternate-choice is a good format for determining whether students know the concept of a noun. As we learned, concepts are measured by having students classify previously unused illustrations as examples versus nonexamples of the concept. This is what each of the remaining items to be critiqued try to do. The objective they are supposed to measure is as follows:

Concept: Identify whether or not a word is a noun.

Example 9.8

The word *fire* is a noun. (true)

Critique for Example 9.8

(3) This item is not unequivocally correct. Although *fire* is often used as a noun, a sentence such as "He will fire the rocket engine" uses the word as a verb. Providing context can make a proposition indisputably true or false, as is the case with the following item:

In this sentence, is *fire* used as a noun? "Fire was used to cook the food." (true)

Alternately, embedded alternate-choice items such as illustrated in Example 9.2 can be used to provide context.

Example 9.9

Often the word *help* is used as a noun. (true)

Critique for Example 9.9

(3, 7) Words such as *often* that imply an indefinite degree should be excluded. Here, *often* could mean "most of the time" or possibly "frequently but less than half of the time." With indefinite meaning, the item is not unequivocally true or false. The following item avoids this problem:

The word *help* can be used as a noun. (true)

Example 9.10

A noun can be used as the subject within a sentence. (true)

Critique for Example 9.10

(1) Other than not measuring the targeted objective, this item is well constructed. As written, the item measures declarative knowledge pertaining to what a noun is. According to the performance objective, the item should be concerned with the *concept* of a noun. Knowledge of a concept is measured by having students classify unused illustrations as examples versus nonexamples of the concept.

SUMMARY

The true–false item is the best-known version of the alternate-choice item. Other variations include true–false items where students rewrite false statements to make them true and multiple true–false items that list several true or false statements following a common stem. Embedded items are another variation and involve a series of underlined words or phrases whose accuracy students are asked to judge. Embedded items have the potential advantage of requiring students to make judgments when the stimulus is presented in authentic context. Focused alternate-choice items are similar to the familiar true–false format, except that the specific contrast students are to evaluate is identified.

The alternate-choice format has several advantages. It allows more extensive sampling of content within one test, items using this format are relatively easy to construct, and these items are efficiently and objectively scored. Limitations of alternate-choice items are their susceptibility to guessing, their need for using dichotomous response options, and their use of more indirect measures when assessing intellectual skills. The negative effects of guessing, for the most part, can be offset by the greater number of alternate-choice items that can be included in a test. Problems brought on by use of dichotomous response options can be addressed by using statements that involve a contrast. Nine qualities that should be incorporated into alternate-choice items were discussed and are listed in Figure 9.8.

ANSWERS: APPLY WHAT YOU ARE LEARNING

9.1 1. false; 2. false; 3. false; 4. true; 5. true; 6. false; 7. true; 8. true. *Items 1 and 2:* For a given number of items, alternate-choice tests have lower reliability than multiple-choice tests, which in turn have lower reliability than short-answer tests. Reliability is diminished because students often select the correct answer by chance. For this same reason, students tend to get higher scores on alternate-choice than on multiple-choice tests. Increasing the number of items in a test increases reliability. Therefore, one can partially offset the lower reliability of multiple-choice and particularly alternate-choice tests by using more items. *Item 3:* Inconsistency in scoring is usually a minor problem for short-answer items but is almost nonexistent for alternate-choice items. This inconsistency does lower the reliability of short-answer tests somewhat. (The overall reliability of multiple-choice and alternate-choice tests is lower than that of short-answer tests because of the impact of selecting correct answers by chance.) Inconsistency in scoring has a major effect on the reliability of essay tests. *Item 4:* Thirty seconds is usually sufficient for completing an alternate-choice item, and 60 seconds for a multiple-choice item. A 30-item multiple-choice test could be completed in 30 minutes, and a 30-item alternate-choice test in 15 minutes. *Item 5:* Almost all the exam time on multiple-choice and alternate-choice tests is spent reading items and solving their problems. A considerable amount of time in an essay test is consumed by writing out the response, as opposed to resolving the mental problem posed by each item. *Item 6:* Alternate-choice and multiple-choice items can indirectly, although accurately, measure procedural knowledge. What is unique to essay items is their ability to determine whether students can express their ideas in writing. *Items 7 and 8:* More time is required to write one essay item than one alternate-choice item, particularly when the time for constructing the essay scoring plan is considered. A test, however, can include many more alternate-choice than essay items, resulting in more time being required to construct an alternate-choice exam. This shorter time for constructing an essay test is *not* an asset, since it results from the essay's weakness with respect to the number of skills that can be measured within one test. With respect to multiple-choice items, alternate-choice items require less time to develop, primarily because of the time required to devise multiple-choice options.

9.2 1. yes; 2. no; 3. yes. *Item 1:* The two propositions are "essay tests require less time to construct" and "essay tests require more time to score." This is a poor alternate-choice item because conceivably one statement could be true and the other false. *Item 2:* Although this item involves a contrast (short-answer versus multiple-choice formats), only one proposition is stated: Guessing affects the reliability of short-answer items less than multiple-choice items. *Item 3:* Two propositions are presented in this item. The first proposition is true: Classroom tests should be reliable. The second proposition is false: Scores on a given classroom test should not be expected to remain constant across time. (If student achievement changes, scores on achievement tests should reflect that change.)

9.3 1. A; 2. B. Within B of the first pair, the phrase "more so in the United States than some countries" is extraneous to the knowledge being measured. It actually formulates a second proposition in the item. Within item A of the second pair, referring to "one of the rules" does not clarify the proposition and should be eliminated.

SOMETHING TO TRY

■ If you have access to some previously written true–false or other alternate-choice items, use the qualities listed in Figure 9.8 to evaluate these items.

■ Prepare some alternate choice items that measure this objective:

Rule: *Identify the effect that Earth latitude has on the relative length of a winter day and a summer day, for different locales.*

(In the northern and southern hemispheres, locales closer to the poles have longer days in their summer and shorter days in their winter than locales closer to the equator. For example, the North Pole has continuous daylight at the beginning of its summer.)

Focused alternate-choice items work particularly well with this objective. Use Figure 9.8 to evaluate your items.

■ Similarly, write and then evaluate several items for an objective within your academic specialization.

ADDITIONAL MATERIAL

Carlson, S. B. (1985). *Creative classroom testing*. Princeton, NJ: Educational Testing Service. This book discusses types of objectively scored test items that teachers often overlook when constructing classroom tests. Several of the item types described are variations of the alternate-choice format. A number of examples and worksheets are provided.

Ebel, R. L., & Frisbie, D. A. (1986). *Essentials of educational measurement* (4th ed.). Englewood Cliffs, NJ: Prentice-Hall. Pages 155–157 describe procedures for helping true–false items discriminate between more and less knowledgeable students.

Wesman, A. G. (1971). Writing the test item. In R. L. Thorndike (Ed.), *Educational measurement* (2nd ed.). Washington, DC: American Council on Education. This chapter reviews the item-writing literature and discusses ideas for producing various formats of objectively scored test items. Pages 91–94 discuss construction of true–false items.

CHAPTER 10

Producing, Administering, and Analyzing Written Tests

Much like planning a lesson, producing a test is often time-consuming. Following particular steps can improve test preparation efficiency and the test instrument quality. Also, some test administration procedures are more effective than others. For instance, anticipating how to respond to students' questions and avoiding common distractions improve the efficiency with which students will complete the test. This chapter focuses on specific techniques to improve production and administration of written tests. It also describes how to improve items by analyzing patterns in students' responses.

One of the major considerations when constructing a test is determining how many items to use. This issue is tied to the development of a content-valid test because a teacher should establish the skills to be assessed and only then determine how many items will be used to measure each skill. The number of items included in a test also affects the reliability of test scores because, as we've learned, increasing the number of items is one of the most effective procedures for increasing reliability. The number of items also depends on practical issues such as how quickly students can answer items written in a particular format.

A second major consideration when developing a test is the use of items of appropriate difficulty. You have probably experienced tests that seemed too difficult or possibly too easy. Depending on the test's purpose, items that deviate considerably from optimal difficulties reduce the test's usefulness.

A third consideration pertains to the physical arrangement of items in a test. Should a test begin with easier items, or should items be organized by content? How should items be formatted on the page? What instructions should be included within the test?

In addition to addressing these issues, this chapter outlines steps to follow when constructing a test and factors to consider regarding the testing environment. You will also be shown how to analyze students' responses to improve the quality of your test items. The chapter helps you achieve six skills:

- Determine the number of items to include on a test
- Determine the appropriate difficulty of test items
- Determine the arrangement of items within the test
- Identify steps to follow when developing a test
- Establish an appropriate environment for administering a test
- Use item analysis to detect ambiguities in test items

NUMBER OF ITEMS TO INCLUDE IN A TEST

Ultimately, the number of items included in a test must be determined within the context of validity. How results of the test will be used and the nature of the skills to be assessed heavily influence the nature as well as the number of items that should be used. The total number of items that are included in a test, however, must also be based on how quickly students can answer test items and how reliable the resulting test scores must be.

Speed versus Power Tests

One factor influencing the number of items included in a test is the issue of speed versus power. A test is considered a speed test if the score each examinee receives is simply a function of how quickly the examinee can answer items. Easy items are used on speed tests. In fact, if time limits were not used, all examinees would achieve near-perfect scores. However, enough items are included in a speed test so that, given the time allowed, few if any of the examinees will complete the entire test. Such tests are used to measure certain clerical abilities and repetitive physical tasks such as assembling small objects.

A test is considered a power test if the score each examinee receives depends on how difficult an item the individual can answer correctly, regardless of time. Conceivably, the difficulty of items could be such that few if any examinees correctly answer all items. Time limits are often not used in the administration of power tests. When time limits are applied, they provide sufficient time for virtually all examinees to complete the test.

Pure speed and power tests represent extremes of a continuum. Most classroom tests are much closer to the power end of this continuum. The teacher is more interested in whether the student can accomplish a task as opposed to how quickly the student can complete that task. Practical constraints require that some type of time limit be imposed. The number of items and the time limit, however, should be such that almost all if not all students can complete the test.

Time limits *should* typically be used with classroom tests for three reasons. First, students tend to complete tests more rapidly when limits are imposed, which in turn allows for the administration of more items or additional time for instruction. Second, time limits generally encourage students to complete tasks efficiently. Third, students should learn to pace themselves when taking a test so as not to be at a disadvantage when completing tests within more constrained time limits.

The use of time limits must be an evolving process. Time limits should be shortened as students become able to work more efficiently with tests or as they become more competent with the tasks being examined. Time limits that prevent more than a few students from completing the test are to be avoided in classroom settings. Such limits weaken a test's most important attribute, specifically its ability to measure student competence with a specified set of skills. Skills tested by items that time limits prevent students from answering obviously remain unmeasured.

Time Required to Answer Items Written in Various Formats

The amount of time required to answer test items depends in part on the nature of the task being examined. For example, items concerned with mathematical problems often consume more time than those requiring the reading of a short verbal passage. Items assessing procedural knowledge tend to require more time than those measuring recall of information.

Some general benchmarks, however, can be identified. For instance, students can answer up to three to four simple alternate-choice items per minute. When alternate-choice items present more complex or difficult propositions, students can usually complete two items per minute as long as each item represents a fairly concise statement. Students can answer two multiple-choice items per minute if the stem and each of the options are brief and the items are testing recall of information. One multiple-choice item per minute is often a reasonable time when measuring procedural knowledge, particularly the application of rules. Additional time may be necessary if items require students to work through a computational problem or read a paragraph. Two short-answer items can normally be completed per minute when the answer requires only a single word. Items that must be answered with a phrase or sentence require a minute or more.

The amount of time required to answer an essay item depends on the task presented by the item. Chapter 7 discussed the importance of limiting the in-class essay to items that students will answer within ten minutes.

Each of these time estimates obviously depends on the skills being measured and the characteristics of the students being tested. These times assume students are experienced with the particular format. Therefore, these values sometimes represent underestimates for elementary students. All written items depend heavily on reading skills; these estimates therefore are inappropriate for students with limited skills in the language used with the test.

Retaining Intended Emphasis When Mixing Item Formats

Essay items clearly require more response time than objectively scored items. This fact is usually reflected in the greater number of points associated with each essay question. This higher weighting of essay items, however, should be based on the test plan and not simply on the proportional amount of time required to respond to each essay item. For example, if the table of specifications or objectives calls for 20% of the weight to be associated with skills measured by the essay items, then one fifth of the points on the test should be divided among the essay questions. Should answering these essay items consume half the test period, it would be wrong to give 50% of the total points to the essay items.

Sometimes, skills that can be tested quickly are unintentionally given excessive weight. For example, one matching item really represents a series of multiple-choice items that share common options. A series of ten matching items can be developed and answered more quickly than ten independent multiple-choice items. It is uncommon to use ten separate multiple-choice items to measure one objective, but the use of ten matching items would be quite practical. The speed at which matching items can be created and answered can result in skills measured by the matching items receiving an excessive amount of weight. When a relatively large number of matching items are used, you can reduce their weight by assigning them fewer points.

For an achievement test to be valid, the skills being measured must correspond to those the test is intended to measure. When item formats are mixed, it is easy to forget the emphasis planned for each skill. There is nothing wrong with mixing formats. However, the points associated with the skills that each format measures should be consistent with the weights planned for these skills before the construction of the test.

Obtaining Sufficient Accuracy

For a test to be valid, it must measure something consistently. Chapter 5 describes the reliability coefficient as an index of this consistency and identifies alternative methods of estimating the value of that coefficient. Table 5.2 within that chapter illustrates the relationship between the reliability coefficient and the number of items on a test. The reliability of scores improves as the number of items in a test increases.

In addition to consistent scores, teachers often are concerned with how accurately a test classifies students. If a test is used to determine whether a student receives further instruction, it is important to know how accurately the test determines each student's mastery. The reliability coefficient does not provide this information. Nevertheless, as with the reliability coefficient, accuracy of classification improves as the number of test items increases. A variety of techniques have been proposed for determining the number of items required for a given accuracy in classification (Hambleton, Mills, & Simon, 1983; Millman, 1973; Wilcox, 1976). The method discussed by Millman is used here to describe problems associated with accurately classifying students. (Each model is based on a series of assumptions and pragmatic considerations that are discussed in the literature. This chapter focuses on the implications of using small numbers of items in a test.)

You probably anticipate that errors associated with measuring achievement will often result in students being misclassified. You may not, however, anticipate the degree to which this misclassification error is a problem. The extensiveness of this misclassification problem is hidden by the fact that one never knows a student's true proficiency. Instead, one only has *estimates* of proficiency provided by the test. If only we could find out students' true proficiency, we could then compare that proficiency to the estimates provided by tests.

Actually, we can do something similar to this. Assume a teacher has determined that any students achieving less than 75% proficiency with a particular domain of skills should be given further instruction. This can be interpreted to mean that if all possible test items measuring these skills could be established, students who correctly answered less than 75% of the items would be given further instruction. But even if all items in the domain could be established, it would be practical to include only a sample of these items in a test. An important question is how many items would have to be sampled to be reasonably confident students are correctly classified.

Teachers usually include a number of items in a test, but let us consider what would happen if student proficiency were to be measured with only one item. Students *correctly* answering the one item would be judged proficient and therefore not given further instruction, whereas students *incorrectly* answering the one item would be given further instruction. The bad news is that many, maybe even a majority of students whose true proficiency is less than 75%, will *correctly* answer the one item and be misclassified. These examples illustrate why:

> Students with 60% true proficiency can answer 60% of all possible items measuring the skill in question. With less than 75% proficiency we should provide these students further instruction. However, if only one item drawn at random is used, a student with this proficiency has a 0.60 chance of correctly answering that one item and therefore being *misclassified*. That is, these students have only a 0.40 chance of being correctly classified.
>
> Similarly, students with 70% true proficiency can answer 70% of all possible items that measure the skill. With less than 75% proficiency, we should provide these students further instruction. However a student with this proficiency has a 0.70 chance of correctly answering the one item and therefore being *misclassified*. That is, these students have only a 0.30 chance of being correctly classified.

The news is better for students whose true proficiency is higher than the required 75%.

> For instance, students with 80% proficiency can answer 80% of all possible items that measure the skill. With *greater* than 75% proficiency, we need not provide these students further instruction. A student with this level of true proficiency has a 0.80 chance of correctly answering the one item and therefore being *correctly* classified.

Table 10.1 provides the probabilities of students being correctly classified at these and other levels of true proficiency, if a one-item test is used to classify the students. As the table indicates, students whose true performance is closer to the required performance will have the greatest chance of being classified. *The closer a student's true performance is to the passing score, the more likely it is that the student will be misclassified.* Particularly troublesome, *students whose true proficiency is below the required proficiency of 75% are likely to be misclassified.*

Fortunately, teachers typically do not use one-item tests. As the number of items in a test increases, the chance that a given student will be correctly classified also increases. Table 10.2 illustrates this increased accuracy. If a 40-item test is administered, a 30 of 40 passing score will result in a very high to moderately high chance that a student will be correctly classified if the required true proficiency is 75%.

Table 10.1
Probability of correctly classifying students, using one test item, if required performance in domain is 75%

Passing Score	True Performance in Domain					
	50%	60%	70%	80%	90%	100%
1 of 1	0.50	0.40	0.30	0.80	0.90	1.00

Table 10.2
Probability of correctly classifying students, using various numbers of test items, if required performance in domain is 75%

Passing Score	True Performance in Domain					
	50%	60%	70%	80%	90%	100%
1 of 1	0.50	0.40	0.30	0.80	0.90	1.00
3 of 4	0.69	0.52	0.35	0.82	0.95	1.00
6 of 8	0.86	0.68	0.45	0.80	0.96	1.00
9 of 12	0.93	0.77	0.51	0.79	0.97	1.00
12 of 15	0.96	0.83	0.55	0.80	0.98	1.00
15 of 20	0.98	0.87	0.58	0.80	0.99	1.00
18 of 24	0.99	0.90	0.61	0.81	0.99	1.00
21 of 28	0.99	0.93	0.64	0.82	1.00	1.00
24 of 32	1.00	0.94	0.66	0.83	1.00	1.00
27 of 36	1.00	0.96	0.67	0.83	1.00	1.00
30 of 40	1.00	0.96	0.69	0.84	1.00	1.00

Box 10.1 *Apply What You Are Learning*

Table 10.2 may be difficult to understand. Can you use the information in the table to answer the following questions?

1. Assuming the required performance is 75%, should students be provided further instruction if their true proficiency is 50%, 60%, or 70%?

2. If a student has a true performance of 70%, what is the probability that this student will be correctly classified if required to answer three items correctly on a four-item test?

3. If this same student were required to answer six items on an eight-item test, would the probability of correctly classifying the student get better or worse?

4. Do the probabilities of a test correctly classifying a student become better or worse as the student's true proficiency gets closer to the required performance?

Answers can be found at the end of the chapter.

Many teachers include sufficient items in tests to classify correctly a high percentage of students. But this is often not true when test results are used to identify specific content areas each student should review. For example, if a 40-item test uses 4 items to measure achievement on each of 10 objectives, then decisions about student mastery with each objective are based on 4-item tests, not the total of 40 items. If additional instruction is to be given to students with less than 75% proficiency, Table 10.2 indicates that the probability is only 0.52 that a student with a true proficiency of 60% will be correctly classified. Also, there is only a 0.35 probability that a student whose true proficiency is 70% will be correctly classified. Remember that each student's performance on a test is only a sample of a student's true performance that would have been observed had all possible test items relevant to the skill been administered. *Large percentages of mastery classification errors occur when decisions about individual skills are based on small samples of test items.*

Oosterhof and Salisbury (1985) identified several options for responding to the problems of small numbers of items. One option is to combine related objectives into broader domains of skills. If a test is divided into fewer although broader domains, more items can be used to measure each domain. However, this becomes an unacceptable solution if objectives cannot be combined meaningfully. If students are provided feedback on broad skill areas, the students may lack sufficient information as to what specific skills need to be reviewed.

Another option is simply to recognize that students whose true proficiency is near the required performance level will often be misclassified. A test is more able to classify students correctly whose true proficiency is considerably above or below the required level. These, in fact, are the students for whom it is most important to correctly classify. Nevertheless, it is important to be aware that test scores misclassify many students, particularly those close to targeted levels of performance.

So far, the number of items required to obtain sufficient accuracy has been discussed from the perspective of the individual student. In this setting, each test item provides a single observation of that student's proficiency. From the perspective of a group of 20 students, however, the single item provides 20 observations. Therefore, observations about the group of students are much more accurate than observations concerning individual students. If the vast majority of students in a class correctly (or incorrectly) answer an item, the teacher can assume this to be an accurate indication of what the class can do.

Although individual test items are quite accurate measures of group proficiency, they are limited in the sense that an individual item measures a highly specific skill. Students' performance on one item may or may not generalize to other similar skills.

However, if the teacher develops a test carefully so that a variety of relevant skills are sampled, collectively the test items will provide the teacher a clear indication of class performance. This, in part, is why it is so important for teachers to follow pre-scribed procedures for selecting items to be included in their tests.

USE OF ITEMS OF APPROPRIATE DIFFICULTY

With classroom tests, *item difficulty* generally refers to the percentage of students cor-rectly answering a given item. An item difficulty of 60% indicates that three fifths of the students answered correctly. With experience, a teacher can anticipate the ap-proximate difficulty of an item before its use in a test. This section shows how to use this knowledge to improve the usefulness of a test.

Relation of Item Difficulty to Determination of Student Achievement

There are two instructional advantages to knowing how well students have achieved. First, instruction can become responsive to students' needs. Second, instruction of future students can be adjusted and made more effective. A test is useful only if it contributes new information about student achievement. Consider two extreme situ-ations. If a teacher administers a test item that all students are known to be able to answer, this item does not provide new information about student achievement. It simply confirms what the teacher already knows. The same situation would occur if an item were used when it is known that none of the students will correctly answer the item. A test item is of greater use if some but not all students are expected to provide a correct answer. The purpose of the item is to determine *which* students can provide an appropriate answer.

Likewise, an item that just one student answers incorrectly (or correctly) provides less information than one for which substantial numbers of students give right and wrong answers. One might anticipate maximum information being provided by items that half the students correctly answer. Lord (1952) demonstrated that the potential reliability of tests is higher when item difficulty considers the effect of guessing. True–false items should be easier than completion items. Similarly, multiple-choice items with three options should be easier than those with five options. Table 10.3 lists these optimal difficulties.

Box 10.2 *Apply What You Are Learning*

Given the information discussed in Table 10.3, is the following statement true?

To obtain maximum reliability, items on a true–false test should range from fairly diffi-cult to fairly easy.

Answer can be found at the end of the chapter.

Table 10.3
Optimal difficulties to maximize information obtained from items written in various formats

Alternate-choice and two-response multiple-choice	85%
Three-options multiple-choice	77%
Three-options multiple-choice	74%
Three-options multiple-choice	69%
Short-answer and completion	50%

A teacher should use the values in Table 10.3 only as a guideline. It is often not possible and sometimes not desirable to use only items that obtain these optimal difficulties. As the importance of a skill increases, the selection of the item should be based less on its expected difficulty. For instance, if it is critical that every student achieve a particular skill before further instruction, then it is quite appropriate to measure that skill even if almost all students are expected to provide the correct answer. Also, if an item is used that all students *unexpectedly* answer correctly, that item was appropriately used in the test because it provided the teacher new information.

The use of only items that some students are expected to miss may appear to limit content validity and may appear to be somewhat sadistic. When planning a test, a teacher should focus on the most important skills, particularly those for which there is the most uncertainty regarding student mastery. It is not possible to take meaningful measures of everything that is taught. A classroom test should be designed to measure the most useful sample of student behaviors.

The use of test items that a number of students will likely miss is consistent with good teaching. An effective teacher focuses attention on important skills that have yet to be learned. A test is most useful when it identifies which students need further instruction. A test is less useful if it reconfirms what is already known about students. This does not suggest, however, that teachers should select test items simply because they will challenge students. Only items that measure important course objectives should be included in tests. Items of moderate difficulty may discourage some students. To encourage students, teachers should emphasize the diagnostic role of tests and should frequently point out during informal assessments skills that have been achieved. This helps students (and teachers) to maintain a useful perspective of written tests.

Relation of Item Difficulty to End-of-Term Grades

Some schools use checklists to report student progress. Limiting tests to those skills for which each student's status is unknown will not change a teacher's ratings on a checklist. If the teacher knew without a formal test that all students had achieved a particular skill, including that skill on a test would not change the rating. Of course, when the teacher does not know whether a skill has been achieved, this information must be obtained through examination. Again, tests should focus on gathering un-known information concerning students' achievements.

Most schools use letter grades to report student achievement. One might con-clude that grades would be lowered if items that all students answer correctly are ex-cluded from the tests. Excluding these items changes the scores on tests but does not alter what students have learned. Assuming that end-of-term grades are used to com-municate how much a student has achieved, grades should not be lowered simply because tests focus on the subset of skills for which student mastery is unknown. Chapter 18 describes how to set grading standards that take into account the diffi-culty of written tests and other measures.

ARRANGING ITEMS WITHIN A TEST

When arranging items within a test, the teacher should consider (1) the order in which items are presented, (2) the physical layout of items, and (3) the directions that accompany the items.

Ordering of Items

Leary and Dorans (1985) reviewed a number of previous studies concerned with how location of an item within the test impacts student performance on that item. Little evidence was found that suggests that item context affects examinee performance. For instance, student performance on each item did not change if items were ordered from easiest to most difficult, or the reverse, or in some random order. Placing an item in the context of other items that measure similar versus different content did not alter performance. Also, changing the order of items was not found to have dif-ferent effects on high- versus low-anxiety or high- versus low-achieving examinees.

The review by Leary and Dorans (1985) did find effects with speeded tests. Ex-aminees scored higher on speeded tests when easier items were placed toward the beginning. Often this was because placement of easier items at the end prevented examinees from reaching items that would have improved their overall scores. This finding ought not to have a bearing on classroom tests, where emphasis should be on power rather than speed.

Basically, the research indicates that as long as tests are not speed tests, item order matters little. The common practice of placing easier items near the beginning to "transition" students into an exam will probably not affect students' scores. Other factors such as ease in scoring, reviewing results, and possible retesting represent more significant considerations.

Ease of Scoring.   If tests are to be scored by hand, scoring efficiency is an important consideration. Items are easier to hand score when those of the same format are grouped together. When the short-answer format is being used, tests can be scored faster if items are grouped by the type of answer being sought. Items requiring numerical answers, definitions, and single-word answers might each be arranged together as groups to facilitate scoring.

Ease of Reviewing Results.   If you are going to discuss test items with students after they are scored, you should anticipate the order in which you will review items. This usually involves placing together items that measure similar content.

Ease of Retesting.   When testing is fully integrated into instruction, students are retested after reviewing problem areas diagnosed on the initial test. If retests measure only skills that each student did not previously master, the teacher may have to prepare different test forms for each student. An efficient alternative is to prepare a common retest form, but to group test items according to the objectives they measure. Each student then completes only the items associated with relevant objectives.

Physical Layout of Test Items

Test items should be formatted so that students can access all relevant information without turning pages. This means items should not be split between two pages. Directions pertaining to a specific item should appear on the same page as the item. Charts, tables, and other information used in answering an item ideally should also be on the same page. When space does not permit, this information can be placed on the back of the preceding page or in a separate handout.

Items should be formatted so that they are easy to read, answer, and score. Figure 10.1 illustrates that multiple-choice options are easier to read when listed vertically. Sufficient space should be provided for responding to short-answer items. If a test is to be hand scored, space should be provided in the margin for answers. In this way, students' responses can be scored by placing an answer key along the margin.

Sometimes test format is improved by printing items two columns per page. Multiple columns are used in newspapers and magazines to make sentences easier to

To obtain maximum reliability, which of the following formats should the greatest percentage of students answer correctly?

    A. Alternate-choice   B. Multiple-choice   C. Short-answer

To obtain maximum reliability, which of the following formats should the greatest percentage of students answer correctly?

    A. Alternate-choice
    B. Multiple-choice
    C. Short-answer

Figure 10.1
Comparison of multiple-choice options listed horizontally versus vertically

read. Using a narrower column also reduces the amount of space consumed by multiple-choice items when the width of their options is short. Word processing programs easily format text into multiple columns. Care should be taken not to split items between columns. Generally, printing more than two columns per page is not practical.

A test should always be proofed after it is produced. The best procedure is for the teacher to self-administer the completed test before distributing it to students. Answers should be written out in the same manner expected of students. All of the distracters to multiple-choice items should be read to verify they have not been erroneously changed.

Test Instructions

Except for the youngest students, printed test directions should be used. Directions should be complete but as brief and to the point as possible. The directions should indicate how students are to record their answers, how much time is available to complete the test, what to do when the test is completed, and how answers are to be scored. The directions should explain any special requirements of the test such as the use of scratch paper, where to show computations, and what materials students may use during the test. Even when a separate answer sheet is being used, having students print their name in the test booklet helps locate work that students completed in the booklet and helps assure all booklets are returned.

Directions to standardized tests are often read aloud by a proctor while students read a printed copy. With classroom tests, this technique might be used with slow readers and younger students. Younger students also benefit from working together through example problems. This is particularly true when a separate answer sheet is used. Written directions should be restricted or not used at all with early elementary students.

STEPS TO DEVELOPING A CLASSROOM TEST

The previous sections have discussed issues to be considered when developing a classroom test. These have included the number of items to include in the test, the appropriate difficulty of items, and the use of directions at the beginning of a test. This section outlines the steps to follow in conceptualizing and producing a classroom test. Most of our attention is placed on unit tests designed to measure student achievement after one to four weeks of instruction. Teachers also develop other types of written tests such as quizzes and final exams. Issues involved in the development of these types of tests are addressed later in this section.

Step 1: Determine How Results of This Test Will Be Used

In the classroom, written tests are most commonly used for formative or summative evaluations. Formative evaluations occur during a unit of instruction and are used to determine how instruction should proceed. Summative evaluations occur at the end of a unit of instruction. The focus of quizzes often is on formative evaluations; however, unit tests and term exams emphasize summative evaluations.

With formative evaluations, multiple items are required to measure each skill confidently, particularly when evaluations are used to plan instruction for individual students versus instruction for the class as a whole. With summative evaluations, significantly more objectives are covered by the test but fewer items are used to measure each objective.

Step 2: Determine the Type and Number of Items to Be Used

The *type* of skills limits which item formats may be used. Any of the formats can easily measure declarative knowledge. Being able to recall information represents an important set of skills and deserves considerable emphasis. At the same time, classroom tests are often justifiably criticized for measuring only this type of skill.

The essay, multiple-choice, and alternate-choice formats can more easily measure procedural knowledge than can the short-answer format. The essay format can also directly measure students' ability to organize and express ideas in writing. Complex skills are more easily assessed using performance assessments and other techniques described in Part 3 of this book.

The *number* of skills also influences the item format to be used. Essay items should be used only if the number of skills to be measured is quite limited. With all item formats, the amount of time available to administer the test ultimately limits the number of items that can be used.

Step 3: Determine the Number of Items Required to Measure Each Skill

Chapter 4 describes how a table of specifications or list of performance objectives is used to specify the number of items used to measure each skill. If a test is used for formative evaluation, one is trying to estimate students' proficiency with each skill. Table 10.2 illustrates the large amount of error that occurs with these estimates when a small number of items are used to measure a skill. With unit tests, the focus is usually on summative evaluations. Students' status on individual objectives is not the primary concern. Then the number of items should correspond to the relative importance of individual skills.

Step 4: Prepare the Required Test Items

After determining the number of items needed to measure each skill, these test items must be prepared. Developing items is usually very time-consuming. Often, textbook publishers help with this task by providing items in instructor's manuals. These items may be well constructed but should be used cautiously. The individuals writing these items often do not take into account the important distinctions between declarative and procedural knowledge. For example, we have learned that students should be asked to perform different kinds of tasks to measure information, concepts, and rules. Sometimes items provided with curriculum materials are simply not well written. The criteria summarized in Chapters 6 through 9 can be used to evaluate these items.

If a sufficient number of adequate items cannot be found from other sources, the teacher must produce the items. One way to reduce the time required to produce tests is to accumulate a pool of test items. This is done by retaining and reusing test items. Reusing items not only saves time, it also can improve the quality of items. Later in this chapter, we discuss a technique called *item analysis*, which uses patterns of students' responses to identify problems within items. Once found, these problems often can be fixed before the item is reused. Chapter 17 describes how a computer can help perform the item analysis and also maintain an item pool.

Step 5: Assemble the Items into a Test

The last step is to assemble items into a test booklet. This includes ordering the items, determining the layout of items within the booklet, and establishing instructions to be placed at the beginning of the test. Each of these points was discussed in some detail earlier in this chapter.

Developing Other Types of Written Classroom Tests

Similar steps are followed to produce other types of classroom tests. Comprehensive midterm and final exams, when used, are usually longer and cover more content than unit tests. Due to their comprehensive nature, it is common for a given objective to be measured by one item or not measured at all. This is appropriate given the summative role of these exams. Because of the limited sampling of objectives, a table of specifications is generally preferred over a list of objectives to plan which skills are to be measured.

Quizzes usually play a formative role. Their content is typically very focused, and quizzes can be developed rather quickly. Because a limited number of skills are tested, it is easy to determine how much emphasis to give each skill. Again, more items must be included if the purpose of the quiz is to establish the proficiency of each student as opposed to determining what the class overall has learned.

Some teachers give a pretest at the beginning of the course. Such tests play a diagnostic role and are particularly useful when the status of students with prerequisite skills is unknown, as is often the case in math and foreign language courses. If the pretest will be used to diagnose skills that individual students (as opposed to the class as a whole) have yet to learn, sufficient items must be used to classify accurately students' mastery on each skill. Because more items can be used to measure each skill if the number of skills tested is minimized, a pretest should be limited to those skills that are most critical to subsequent instruction or for which it is likely a number of students lack the required proficiency.

ESTABLISHING AN APPROPRIATE TESTING ENVIRONMENT

This textbook gives considerable attention to developing valid classroom tests, and with good reason: A test is of no use unless it measures the skills it is intended to measure. Likewise, a test loses its usefulness if it measures qualities in addition to those it is intended to measure. This is why it is important to administer tests in an appropriate environment. If students are seriously distracted while completing a test, the validity and therefore the usefulness of the test is reduced.

A number of important environmental considerations are obvious. A test should be administered in a quiet, physically comfortable environment with sufficient light for reading. Some less obvious yet significant factors are discussed in the following paragraphs.

Interruptions

Once test materials are distributed, any activity that distracts students from the test is an interruption. This includes directions concerning the test, verbal corrections of errors found in the test, students asking questions, visitors entering the classroom, and announcements over the school public address systems. Some interruptions are likely to occur during a test, but one should work hard to minimize them.

Except for younger students, written directions at the beginning of the test will eliminate or reduce the amount of required oral directions. When oral directions must be given, keep them brief! If necessary, give directions from written notes to avoid interrupting students later to address something that was neglected. Some students out of nervousness will ask questions concerning the directions. Minimize this behavior by referring the student to the written directions, if in fact the directions are clear and sufficient.

Interruptions to correct errors in the test will of course not occur if the test is free of errors. Proofing the test before it is reproduced will minimize these errors. If corrections must be made either before or during the test, first write the correction on the board and then announce the error. This minimizes further interruptions from students' questions. If an error detected during the test is unlikely to affect students' answers, do not announce it.

Students sometimes need to ask questions about individual items. Judgment must be used in responding to these questions. If the question results from a faulty copy or serious error in the item, then help should be provided. If the question results from the student's lack of comprehension of the skill being tested, helping the student reduces the validity of the test; encourage the student to work with the information in the test. If the question results from a student's legitimate but unanticipated interpretation of the item, clarification should be given.

Student Frustration

Classroom tests are often frustrating experiences for students. This is particularly true when tests play a summative role. Some actions unnecessarily raise the frustration associated with tests. A particularly inappropriate action is the use of tests as punishment or threat of punishment. Another is scheduling the test just before a holiday vacation or a particularly significant social event. Misplaced good intentions such as motivating students to do well on the test to avoid negative consequences are also a source of frustration. Tests are likely to measure factors in addition to achievement when students' frustrations are raised to a high level.

CORRECTION FOR GUESSING

Some teachers (and some standardized tests) use a correction formula to prevent guessing on multiple-choice and alternate-choice items. From an ethical point of view, guessing is sometimes frowned on because it implies a student is trying to get credit without mastering the skill being assessed. Guessing on a test is quite similar to guessing what to do in other decisions in life. Working from less than full information often is not the wisest course of action, but many decisions must be made within that context.

From a measurement perspective, guessing is undesirable because the examinee's random response confounds measurement of a skill. This reduces the reliability and validity of the test. However, evidence is inconsistent regarding whether a correction for guessing improves the situation (Diamond & Evans, 1973).

The most common correction uses the following formula:

$$Score = Right - \frac{Wrong}{Options - 1}$$

Where   *Score* is a student's corrected score

Right is the number of items the student answered correctly

Wrong is the number of items the student answered incorrectly

Options is the number of alternatives associated with the items.

On a test consisting of 20 five-option multiple-choice items in which a student correctly answered 14 items, incorrectly answered 4 items, and omitted 2 items, the corrected score would be as follows:

$$Score = 14 - \frac{4}{5 - 1} = 13$$

Notice that the formula subtracts a proportion of the *wrong* responses. It *assumes* that the more incorrect answers a student gives, the more the student has guessed. One cannot determine exactly how many items each student answered correctly by guessing. For example, with the 20-item test just referred to, all students who correctly answered 14 items and incorrectly answered 4 items would receive a corrected score of 13. Among these students, however, some probably answered 14 items correctly by successfully guessing 2 items, while others were unlucky and failed to get any points from guessing. Nevertheless, the formula gives each of these students a "corrected" score of 13. The formula *cannot* correct for guessing because it does not know with how many items each student guessed. The use of this correction formula, therefore, is commonly called formula scoring rather than a correction for guessing.

Although formula scoring cannot correct precisely for guessing, its presence can discourage examinees from guessing for fear of scores being corrected. Formula scoring is most commonly used with speeded tests to discourage examinees from guessing blindly.

Teachers generally are discouraged from using formula scoring with classroom tests for several reasons. First, as stated previously, its benefits to validity and reliability are unclear. Second, classroom tests should not be speeded, but should be designed so that most or all students complete the test. There should be little need for students to guess blindly because they are running out of time. Third, formula scoring often assumes that all items on a test have the same number of options. This is generally not true for classroom tests. Finally, students tend to underestimate their ability to answer items correctly. Students score better than chance even when they believe they are guessing blindly (Bliss, 1980; Cross & Frary, 1977; Frary, 1989). When formula scoring is applied, students who ignore directions about not guessing score higher than those who follow the directions.

Students are often unsure about what they should do regarding guessing on multiple-choice and alternate-choice tests. Therefore, this issue should specifically be addressed in the test directions. A statement such as "answer all questions, even if you must guess" is usually sufficient.

USING ITEM ANALYSIS TO IMPROVE TEST ITEMS

Item analysis is a name given to a variety of statistical techniques designed to analyze individual items on a test after the test has been given to a group of examinees. Some item analysis techniques are highly sophisticated and are useful only to individuals with specialized training. Other techniques are simple to interpret and can be useful to the classroom teacher in terms of both improving the quality of test items and identifying instructional problems.

The ability of item analysis techniques to improve the quality of existing test items is important to the teacher for two reasons. First, revising existing test items is more efficient than creating new test items. Second, a test that includes a number of previously developed and revised items typically provides a better measure of student achievement than a test consisting entirely of untried or unrevised test items.

Item analysis techniques can also help a teacher determine quickly which skills are causing students difficulty. Assistance of this type is invaluable to a teacher when assessment is used for formative evaluations.

Although the principles can be applied to a variety of formats, item analysis procedures are most commonly used with objectively scored formats, particularly multiple-choice items. The computations described here can be completed by hand, but usually are provided by a computer. In the past, classroom teachers often found obtaining item analyses of tests to be inconvenient because a remotely located computing center was used to obtain the item analysis report. The availability of small computers, however, has made it practical for the teacher to obtain an item analysis report immediately on completion of a classroom exam. The specific components of analysis discussed in this chapter are what Hills (1981) referred to as three levels, or degrees, of analysis of items, these being *item difficulty, item discrimination,* and *distracter analysis.*

Item Difficulty

The first level of an item analysis is *item difficulty*. The difficulty of an item refers to the proportion of students who answered the item correctly. For example, if 15 of 25 students correctly answered a particular test item, the item difficulty is $15/25 = 60\%$, or .60. The range of item difficulty is from .00, indicating no student taking the exam answered the item correctly, to 1.00, indicating all students answered the item correctly.

Box 10.3 *Apply What You Are Learning*

The following table presents several sets of values from which item difficulties can be calculated. For example the first row illustrates that if 12 of 50 students correctly answered an item, the item difficulty would be .24. Can you compute the item difficulties for items 2 through 7?

Item	Number of Students Answering Item Correctly	Number of Students Administered the Test	Item Difficulty
1	12	50	.24
2	12	20	?
3	20	20	?
4	1	10	?
5	0	37	?
6	7	20	?
7	14	40	?

Answers can be found at the end of the chapter.

Because item difficulty obtains higher numerical values for easier items, hindsight suggests that *item difficulty* may not have been the best term to apply to this concept. Be sure to avoid confusion by remembering that item difficulty refers to the proportion *correctly* answering the item.

Item Discrimination

The second level of an item analysis is *item discrimination*. The discrimination of an item refers to its ability to distinguish between more and less knowledgeable students.

A common method used to determine a numerical value for item discrimination involves the identification of two subgroups from the students who were administered the exam. The 25% of the students who obtained the highest scores on the test are defined as the *upper 1/4*. The similar number of students who obtained the lowest scores on the test are identified as the *lower 1/4*. For purposes of the analysis, it is assumed that students in the upper group are, in general, more proficient in the skills being measured by the exam than students in the lower group.[1]

A test item is said to "discriminate" if a larger proportion of students from the upper group correctly answered the item than in the lower group. Item discrimination is defined as the difference in proportion of students in the upper and lower groups who answered an item correctly. For example, if 90% of the students in the upper group and 50% in the lower group correctly answered an item, the discrimination of that item is as follows:

$$Discrimination = 90\% - 50\% = 40\% = .40$$

Box 10.4 *Apply What You Are Learning*

This next table presents several sets of values from which item discrimination can be calculated. For example, the first row illustrates that if 70% of the students in the upper group and 60% of the students in the lower group correctly answer an item, then the discrimination is .10. Can you compute the item discriminations for items 2 through 7?

Percentage of Students Answering Item Correctly

Item	Upper 1/4	Lower 1/4	Item Discrimination
1	70%	60%	.10
2	80%	10%	?
3	100%	0%	?
4	100%	100%	?
5	50%	50%	?
6	0%	50%	?
7	0%	100%	?

Answers can be found at the end of the chapter.

The numerical value of item discrimination ranges from 1.00 to −1.00. The highest possible value, 1.00, is obtained if every student in the upper group *correctly* answered the test item and every student in the lower group *incorrectly* answered the item. Obtaining such a high discrimination for an item would be unusual because it is not likely that every student in the lower group would incorrectly answer the

---

[1]When using the method described here, item discrimination is usually computed using only the highest and lowest scoring students. Students who scored in the middle are excluded from the computation. The reason for this is that item discrimination is trying to determine whether an item can distinguish between students whose achievement level is truly different. If students scoring in the middle are included in the computation, as would be the case if those scoring in the upper 1/2 were compared to those in the lower 1/2, the achievement of the two groups of students would be much more similar. It would be unrealistic to expect an item to be able to discriminate between two groups of students with such similar levels of achievement.

item. Even if the students in the lower group were totally unknowledgeable about the concept being tested and simply guessed blindly, 20% of these students would be expected to answer correctly a five-option multiple-choice item, and 50% would be expected to answer correctly an alternate-choice item.

Conversely, the lowest possible discrimination value, -1.00, would be obtained if no student in the upper group correctly answered the item and if every student in the lower group correctly answered the item. This also would be a very unlikely situation. Unless the teacher has miskeyed an item (i.e., indicated an incorrect option to be the correct answer), the discrimination is usually higher than zero.

It is important to recall that a primary role of tests is to help the teacher distinguish between students who need further instruction and students who have become proficient with a particular set of skills. For this reason, test items that have high item discrimination are desired. These are the items with which less knowledgeable students have difficulty but that more knowledgeable students tend to answer correctly.

An individual test item, by itself, is usually not a very reliable measure of a student's achievement. This is one reason a test must consist of numerous items. This is also the reason one should not expect the item discrimination of an individual test item to be particularly high. On teacher-constructed tests, item discrimination above .20 is generally considered sufficient. Item discrimination above .40 is quite high and is equivalent to the level of discrimination found on many commercially developed tests. Test questions with item discrimination near zero do not help (or harm) the ability of an exam to distinguish between more knowledgeable and less knowledgeable students. Questions with a negative discrimination do harm the quality of a test to the extent that they partially offset positive contributions made by other test items. Later discussion will indicate that test questions found to have near zero or negative item discrimination should be evaluated and possibly revised before being reused.

Item difficulty has an important effect on item discrimination. The data for item 4 illustrates that if 100% of the students in both the upper and lower groups answered an item correctly, the discrimination of that item is zero. This particular item is very easy in that virtually every student (at least 100% of the students included in the upper and lower groups) answered the item correctly. Similarly, in the unlikely event that every student answered an item incorrectly, the discrimination of that item would also be zero. The closer the difficulty level of an item is to 0% or 100%, the less likely an item is to obtain a favorable level of discrimination. Items that are of moderate difficulty (that is, neither extremely easy nor extremely difficult) are more likely to obtain a high level of discrimination.

Distracter Analysis

The third level of an item analysis is distracter analysis. Figure 10.2 illustrates what a distracter analysis might look like for a given multiple-choice item. The column headings A through E refer to the typical options of a multiple-choice item. "Upper 1/4"

	A	(B)	C	D	E
Upper 1/4	7	86	0	7	0
Lower 1/4	13	60	7	13	7
All students	12	70	5	10	3

(Correct response identified with parentheses)

Figure 10.2
Illustration of a distracter analysis

and "Lower 1/4" represent the highest and lowest scoring 25% of the students, the same groups used to calculate item discrimination. The percentage of students from the upper and lower groups who selected each of the multiple-choice options is also given. For example, 7% of the students scoring in the upper 1/4 answered the test item by selecting the A option, 86% selected B, and so on. Percentages listed for the upper and lower groups each total 100%, assuming all students answered the item. The numbers listed within the "All students" category indicate the percentage of all students (including the middle 50%) who selected each of the options. Parentheses are used to identify Option B is as the correct answer to this particular test item.

If a test item is performing satisfactorily, you should expect a greater percentage of students in the upper 1/4 to answer the item correctly than in the lower 1/4. This is the case for the item illustrated in Figure 10.2 because 86% of the upper group and 60% of the lower group selected the correct answer (option B).

Conversely, you should expect a smaller percentage of students in the upper 1/4 than the lower 1/4 to select each of the wrong answers or *distracters* to the item. The desired pattern of percentages has occurred for each of the distracters associated with the item illustrated in Figure 10.2. If this condition does not occur for a given distracter, you should review the item to determine why a greater percentage of the more capable versus less capable students are selecting that particular incorrect option.

Figure 10.3 presents the distracter analysis for five different test items. Within item 1, option A is identified to be the correct response to this test item. As the correct answer, option A performed appropriately because more students in the upper group selected this option than students in the lower group.

Among the four distracters to item 1, however, only option D performed appropriately. For some reason, a greater percentage of the more knowledgeable versus less knowledgeable students are selecting option C, which is a wrong answer. Furthermore, options B and E appear not to be distinguishing between the more and less knowledgeable students because the same percentage of students in the upper and lower groups selected these options. In fact, no students from either group selected option B. Before reusing this test item, the teacher should determine why most of the distracters performed inappropriately.

Figure 10.3

Exercise in interpreting a distracter analysis

Item 1	(A)	B	C	D	E
Upper 1/4	20	0	55	10	15
Lower 1/4	12	0	28	45	15
All students	15	0	47	20	18
Item 2	A	B	C	(D)	E
Upper 1/4	5	46	12	34	3
Lower 1/4	14	20	19	39	8
All students	11	33	14	36	6
Item 3	A	B	C	(D)	E
Upper 1/4	13	27	0	47	13
Lower 1/4	8	68	8	8	8
All students	11	44	4	30	11
Item 4	A	B	C	D	(E)
Upper 1/4	7	0	7	7	79
Lower 1/4	25	8	32	18	17
All students	15	4	22	7	52
Item 5	(A)	B	C	D	E
Upper 1/4	73	13	7	0	7
Lower 1/4	67	17	16	0	0
All students	70	15	11	0	4

(Correct response identified with parentheses)

Box 10.5 *Apply What You Are Learning*

Use the percentages within items 2 through 5 in Figure 10.3 to determine which options within each item are performing appropriately.

Answers can be found at the end of the chapter.

Note that although 15% from both upper and lower groups selected option E of item 1 in Figure 10.3, 18% of all students selected this option. This apparent inconsistency results from not knowing the responses of the 50% of students excluded from the upper and lower groups.

The numerical values associated with an item analysis can be unstable, particularly when based on less than 50 students. As a result, these values can change for a given test item if the item is reused, even when the item is unaltered. Ideally, an item analysis is based on 200 or more examinees. Sometimes college instructors can obtain analyses based on this number of students, as can the occasional teacher in secondary school who administers a common test across multiple sections of a course. These examples are exceptions. Typically, the teacher must interpret the results of an item analysis, recognizing that the indices may be unstable.

A distracter analysis may use percentages, as illustrated in this chapter, or it may list the actual number of students selecting each option. Both approaches have advantages. When a distracter analysis uses percentages, the totals for both the upper and lower groups always equal 100%. With percentages, one more quickly learns to anticipate the optimal numerical values associated with each option within a distracter analysis. Also, the calculation of difficulty and discrimination indices is more obvious when percentages are used in the distracter analysis. On the other hand, frequencies are somewhat easier to compute than percentages, although this is of limited significance, given that a computer usually produces item analysis reports. The use of frequencies rather than percentages has a significant advantage because this reduces the tendency to overinterpret item analyses based on a few students. Therefore, if percentages are used in the distracter analysis, the total number of students involved should be stated somewhere in the item analysis report.

Interpreting an Item Analysis

Let us now look at how to integrate information from item difficulty, item discrimination, and the distracter analysis to analyze an item. The strategy we will use is to evaluate item difficulty, item discrimination, and the distracter analysis in that order. Next a hypothesis regarding the quality of the item is established, including a statement of specific problems that the item being analyzed may contain. Finally, the hypothesis about the test item is evaluated by actually reviewing the test item being analyzed.

Applying this approach to the information in Figure 10.4, one first notes that 70% of the students taking the test correctly answered this item. Given that the item caused some students difficulty, the next concern is whether or not this difficulty is due to the item's ability to discriminate between more knowledgeable and less knowledgeable students. The item discrimination is .26; that is, 26 percentage points separate the upper and lower groups on the correct answer (option B). Because the discrimination is higher than .20, a probable reason this item is causing some students difficulty is that the test item appropriately discriminates between more and less knowledgeable students relative to the skill being measured. In other words, the difficulty students had with this item does not appear to be due to ambiguity inherent in the item.

The third step is to interpret the distracter analysis. When an item is found to discriminate appropriately, there typically is little reason to look at the distracter analysis in any great detail. A cursory look at the distracter analysis indicates that each of the options performed appropriately. A larger percentage of the upper group selected the correct option than the lower group. (This is the information provided us by the item discrimination.) A smaller percentage of the upper group selected each of the

Figure 10.4

An item analysis that incorporates item difficulty, item discrimination, and the distracter analysis

Item 6	A	(B)	C	D	E
Upper 1/4	7	86	0	7	0
Lower 1/4	13	60	7	13	7
All students	12	70	5	10	3

Difficulty = .70
Discrimination = .26

Figure 10.5

An item analysis for a test item that all students answered correctly

Item 7	A	B	C	(D)	E
Upper 1/4	0	0	0	100	0
Lower 1/4	0	0	0	100	0
All students	0	0	0	100	0

Difficulty = 1.00
Discrimination = .00

distracters than the lower group. Therefore, none of the distracters is working against the ability of the correct answer to discriminate between more and less knowledgeable students. Our hypothesis about this item should be that it causes some students difficulty because it appropriately discriminates between students who are more versus less knowledgeable in the skill area being measured.

Figure 10.5 presents item analysis data from another test item. Again, the first step is to look at item difficulty. Note that 100% of the students taking the exam answered this item correctly. This is a very easy item. Because everyone answered the item correctly, we can conclude without looking further that this item does not discriminate between the more and less knowledgeable students. Similarly, given that all students selected the correct response, we can anticipate that none of the distracters is perceived as plausible, even by the less knowledgeable students.

Measurement specialists commonly discourage the inclusion of very easy or very difficult items, partly because such items do not help identify which students are having difficulty with a particular set of skills. If a teacher knew in advance that all students would correctly answer the item, the teacher should have considered excluding this item; including it uses test time to confirm what the teacher already knows. As the proportion of test items answered correctly by all students increases, the amount of time available for determining which students are having difficulty with the remaining skills decreases. On the other hand, if an easy item is measuring a highly important skill, the inclusion of the easy item is very appropriate.

Figure 10.6 presents data for an item that has some problems. Again, the first step is to look at the item difficulty. Of the 60 students taking this exam, 55% answered the item correctly. The second step is to determine whether or not this difficulty is the result of the item discriminating between more and less knowledgeable students. The item discrimination indicates that only 3 percentage points separate the upper and lower groups of students. Therefore, it appears that something that is wrong with

Figure 10.6

An item analysis for a test item with moderate difficulty and low discrimination

Item 8	(A)	B	C	(D)	E
Upper 1/4	56	0	38	6	0
Lower 1/4	53	0	15	19	13
All students	55	0	23	13	9

Difficulty = .55
Discrimination = .03

the item appears to be causing student difficulty with this item. The third step is to use the distracter analysis to determine why this item did not discriminate. Based on the distracter analysis, option C is found to be inappropriately attracting a greater percentage of the more, rather than the less, knowledgeable students. Also, option B does not represent a plausible distracter because no student selected this option. Options D and E appear to be effective distracters.

Based on these observations, an appropriate hypothesis is that this item is causing students difficulty because of problems internal to the item. The specific problems appear to be associated with options A, B, and/or C, or possibly with the way students perceive these options in the context of the item's stem. If inspection of the item confirms any of these problems, the teacher can revise the item before reusing it. On the other hand, if inspection of the item fails to confirm the hypothesized problem, an alternative hypothesis would be that the problem is external to the item. That is, the item is not discriminating between students because in fact students who tend to be more knowledgeable are having as much difficulty with this item as students who tend to be less knowledgeable. This suggests that the specific skill being measured by the item was not effectively taught. This latter hypothesis can be evaluated by talking to a few students; particularly those who tend to do well on test items.

Box 10.6 *Apply What You Are Learning*

Here is the item analysis for two additional test items. Propose hypotheses about each items based on their item analysis.

Item 9	A	B	(C)	D	E
Upper 1/4	56	0	38	6	0
Lower 1/4	53	0	15	19	13
All students	55	0	23	13	9

Difficulty = .55
Discrimination = .03

Item 10	A	(B)	C	D	E
Upper 1/4	56	0	38	6	0
Lower 1/4	53	0	15	19	13
All students	55	0	23	13	9

Difficulty = .55
Discrimination = .03

Answers can be found at the end of the chapter.

Although the use of item analysis is helpful for improving the quality of multiple-choice items in particular, the time required for calculating the difficulty, discrimination, and distracter analysis for each item makes it impractical to use item analysis techniques unless a computer is performing the computations. Computer programs that perform these calculations are widely available, particularly from the vendors that manufacture the small optical scanners available in many schools. Some of these computer programs are more useful than others. For instance, programs are less useful if they only provide the overall percentage of students selecting each multiple-choice option without comparing the response patterns of students in upper and lower groups. Likewise, programs are less useful when they compare response patterns for students performing in the upper and lower halves rather than the upper and lower fourths. The vendors typically offer more than one item analysis program. Therefore, if you do not first find what you are looking for, ask to see some other programs.

The item analysis techniques described here obviously are most appropriate for multiple-choice items. However, the same basic strategies work well with all item formats, even including performance assessments. The essence of an item analysis technique is to first look at an item's difficulty. If virtually all students correctly answer the item, then you can assume the item is not discriminating because all students find it easy. If in fact an easy item is measuring a critical skill, then knowing that students are doing well with that skill represents good news and important information. However, unless highly critical skills are involved, easy items should be avoided on a test. This frees up testing time to focus on skills with which some are having difficulty.

If an item is not easy and therefore is incorrectly answered by some students, an important question regardless of item format is whether or not the item is discriminating. If higher achieving students correctly answer the item more often than lower achieving students, this suggests the item is doing its job. On the other hand, if the item is not easy but it is also not discriminating between higher and lower achieving students, then you want to find the source of the problem. With any item format, reusing items that have been analyzed and revised improves the quality of your tests.

SUMMARY

The number of items included in a test depends partly on how reliable test scores must be and how quickly students can answer the items. Increasing the number of items on a test usually improves reliability. When scores are used to establish whether students have reached mastery, increasing the number of items improves the accuracy of the classification. When mastery decisions are made for each skill measured by the test, the items associated with a given skill become a self-contained subtest. Often, this results in each decision being based on a few test items with a correspondingly low probability of correctly classifying each student.

The time required to answer each test item depends on the format and complexity of the item as well as the students' age. The number of items included in a test should allow virtually all students to complete the test within specified time limits.

It is inappropriate to base the number of points assigned to test items on the amount of time required to answer the items. Instead, points should be proportional to the emphasis each skill should be given to make the test content valid.

A classroom test is useful only if it provides new information about students' achievement. Therefore, the usefulness of a test is decreased when it knowingly includes items that all students will answer correctly. A similar problem exists if extremely difficult items are used. In this chapter, optimal difficulties were identified that maximize a test's potential reliability. The order in which items appear in a test appears to have little effect on student performance. Consequently, other considerations such as ease of scoring, reviewing results with students, and administering a retest should govern the order of items. Test items should be arranged so that students can access relevant information without turning pages. Except with younger students, written rather than oral directions should be given at the beginning of a test.

Six steps to developing classroom tests have been identified. These include determining how test results will be used, the nature of the skills to be measured, the type and number of items to be used, and the number of items to be used to measure each skill. Following these steps, the required number of items are developed for each skill. Finally, items are assembled into a test.

Tests should be administered in a proper environment. The room should be quiet and should have appropriate light for reading. Once a test has begun, interruptions such as giving directions, making announcements, or having conversations with students should be minimized. Care should be taken not to increase the frustration of students taking a test. To reduce student frustration, explain and demonstrate the test's instructional role, frequently reward students for achievement outside the context of testing, and never use tests for punishment.

Sometimes, a formula is used to subtract a portion of incorrect responses from each student's score. This formula scoring is intended to encourage students to omit rather than guess at multiple-choice and true–false items when they don't know the answer. Formula scoring is used most often with speeded tests. Research, however, suggests that most of the benefits expected from formula scoring are not realized, and use of formula scoring with classroom tests is discouraged. Test directions should encourage students to attempt to answer all items.

Item analysis is a useful tool for improving the quality of test items. Item analysis procedures are most commonly applied to objectively scored test items, particularly those written in the multiple-choice format; however, the same principles can be used with items of any format.

ANSWERS: APPLY WHAT YOU ARE LEARNING

10.1 *Item 1:* Students whose true performances are 50%, 60%, and 70% should be provided further instruction, given that the required performance is 75%. *Item 2:* The numbers in Table 10.2 indicate the probability that a student will be correctly classified. There is a 35% chance this student will answer *less* than 3 of the 4 items, and therefore be correctly classified as needing further instruction. *Item 3:* Increasing the number of items to 6 of 8 increases the chance of a correct classification to 45%. *Item 4:* A test does a worse job of classifying students correctly as their true performance approaches the minimal required performance.

10.2 The statement is false. For maximum reliability, *every* item on a true–false test should be correctly answered by 85% of the students. Therefore, each item should be fairly easy. It is often assumed that a test more effectively identifies which students need further instruction if it includes items with a full range of difficulties. This assumption is incorrect. A test more accurately distinguishes between more and less knowledgeable students if the difficulty of every item matches the values given in Table 10.3.

10.3 For items 2 through 7, the item difficulties are .60, 1.00, .10, .00, .35, .35

10.4 For items 2 through 7, the item discriminations are .70, 1.00, .00, .00, −50, −1.00

10.5 *Item 2:* Option D is identified as the correct response. However, this option is performing poorly because a greater percentage of lower-scoring students are selecting this correct response. Option B is a poor distracter, because more high-scoring than low-scoring students are selecting this option. Options A, C, and E are performing appropriately in that more low-scoring than high-scoring students are selecting these distracters. *Item 3:* Option D is performing appropriately. Options A and E are poor distracters, because greater percentages of high-scoring than low-scoring students have selected these options. Options B and C are performing as good distracters. *Item 4:* All options are performing appropriately. *Item 5:* With the exception of options D and E, the correct option and each of the distracters are performing appropriately.

10.6 *Item 9:* This item is of moderate difficulty. With 34 percentage points separating the upper and lower groups of students, a good proportion of this item's difficulty is due to its ability to discriminate between students who are more versus less knowledgeable in the skill being measured by this item. With such a high discrimination, it is generally not necessary to review the distracter analysis. This item might be improved, however, by determining what makes distracter B relatively attractive to the higher scoring students. Further improvement might also be realized by making distracter D more plausible. *Item 10:* This item is also of moderate difficulty. The discrimination index suggests that the item is ambiguous: therefore, the distracter analysis should be reviewed. The distracter analysis suggests that the item would be improved by determining what makes distracter C more attractive to high versus low scoring students. This item might also be improved by making options A and E more plausible.

SOMETHING TO TRY

- Using a written test you or someone else developed, use criteria discussed in this chapter to evaluate the physical layout of the test.

- Obtain an item analysis for a previously administered multiple-choice test and evaluate the items using procedures discussed in this chapter. For each item, use the item analysis to first form a hypothesis about the quality and possible sources of problems within a test item before actually looking at the test to confirm or reject your hypothesis.

ADDITIONAL MATERIAL

Thorndike, R. L. (Ed.). (1971). *Educational measurement* (2nd ed.). Washington, DC: American Council on Education. Part One of this book (Chapters 2 through 8) is concerned with test design, construction, administration, and processing. Three chapters are particularly relevant to the topics discussed here. Chapter 3 (written by S. N. Tinkelman) provides an extended discussion of the steps to developing objective tests. Chapter 6 (written by R. L. Thorndike) elaborates on procedures for formatting items within tests and reproduction of test booklets. Chapter 7 (written by W. V. Clemans) addresses a variety of factors concerned with test administration. Each of these chapters includes elements particularly relevant to larger scale testing such as district-wide assessments. Discussion in each chapter is highly structured so that is quite easy to identify topics of personal interest.

Millman, J., & Greene, J. (1988). The specification and development of tests of achievement and ability. In R. L. Linn (Ed.), *Educational measurement* (3rd ed., pp. 335–366). New York: American Council on Education. This chapter discusses options for establishing test specifications and developing a test. Its focus is on professionally developed tests.

PART THREE

Alternative Assessment Techniques

CHAPTER 11

Informal Observations and Questions

Observation and oral questions are by far the most common forms of assessment in the classroom. Estimates of the percentage of assessments that are based on observation and questioning are hard to find. Probably more than 90% of all measures of student performance involve casual observation and questioning, as opposed to written tests, performance assessments, and the other more formal types of assessment.

Relative to many other assessments, observation and questioning are efficient and adaptable. For example, numerous observations can occur simultaneously or at least in rapid succession. Subsequent observations can take into account whatever was observed just moments earlier. Similarly, follow-up questions can reflect a student's response to a previous question.

In spite of their tremendous efficiency and adaptability, however, informal observations and questions have significant limitations. Observations tend to be limited to student performances that occur naturally. Failure to see a student demonstrate a particular skill may result because the student lacks the skill or because, although the student has achieved the skill, he or she is not demonstrating it for any number of reasons. Furthermore, the teacher observes only a small proportion of students' behaviors. Because informal observations and questions are spontaneous, these techniques tend to be technically inferior to written tests and performance assessments. Another limitation is that most assessments based on observations and oral questions are undocumented. Unless recorded, the results of these assessments are easily forgotten or distorted.

Despite their limitations, observations and oral questions are absolutely essential to an overall strategy for assessing students. Other techniques do not adequately help the teacher maintain the spontaneity that is crucial to effective instruction.

For this reason, it is important to understand the characteristics of informal observations and questions and to review techniques that can help maximize their usefulness within assessment. This chapter helps you achieve three skills:

- Recognize characteristics of informal observations and questions
- Identify techniques for improving the quality of these observations and questions
- Identify techniques for recording results from informal assessments

CHARACTERISTICS OF INFORMAL OBSERVATIONS AND QUESTIONS

An important characteristic of both observations and questions is their familiarity. We constantly use observation and questioning as part of virtually everything we do, whether it's spending an afternoon at the shopping mall, being with friends, arriving at an airport, attending a class as a student, or leading a class as a teacher.

Let us review the characteristics of observation and questioning as they naturally occur within two very familiar settings: driving a car and talking with friends. As we review these characteristics, ask yourself whether your personal experience confirms their existence. Try to anticipate how these characteristics of observation and questioning apply to informal assessments within the classroom. Later, we will relate these characteristics to the classroom.

First, here are some characteristics of observations that occur while driving a car within the busy downtown area of a city.

- *Many events are observed either simultaneously or in very quick succession.* Within seconds, you observe each of many cars. You observe traffic signals and road signs. You observe pedestrians, bicycles, parked cars, debris on the road, potholes, and markings on the pavement, such as the centerline. Your observations are not only visual. You listen to the sounds of the car and the wheels on the road. You may be listening to the radio and what passengers in the car are saying.

- *Events are observed at different levels of detail.* While driving, some observations are detailed, such as when you read street signs. Other observations are more general, such as when you spot a traffic light in the distance.

- *Current observations help select and structure subsequent observations.* Seeing the distant traffic light may cause you to look at how closely cars are following you, just in case you have to stop quickly at a red light. You might also start looking for familiar landmarks to determine whether the approaching intersection is where you plan to turn.

- *Often, observations become focused on one event.* One event may command your complete attention out of necessity, such as when a car suddenly turns in front of you, or out of choice, such as when you hear an interesting announcement on the radio. When attention is focused, fewer or possibly no other events are observed.

- *When observations become focused, observation of other critical events must be maintained.* Many accidents occur when a driver's attention is diverted.

For example, cars get rear-ended when the driver in the following car focuses on a single event, such as tuning the radio. You establish which critical events must always be observed, even as your observations become more focused.

- *Experience and confidence with a task substantially increase the effectiveness of observations.* When you first learned to drive, you focused on things that would affect you immediately, such as the car next to you and the position of your car relative to the edge of the road. When you were a new driver, you probably avoided driving downtown simply because it would require observing too many things in quick succession. With experience, critical observations became more automatic and complex situations more easily handled. This experience now allows you to go places that you avoided as a new driver. Confidence, however, must accompany experience. If you lack confidence in your ability to drive, the effectiveness of your observations will not be optimal. For example, after an accident, a driver's confidence is reduced, and for a period of time the person becomes a less proficient driver until confidence is regained. The effectiveness of observations is highly related to experience and confidence.

- *Familiarity with surroundings increases the effectiveness of observations.* Familiarity with surroundings is a special form of experience. Familiarity also influences confidence. An otherwise experienced driver is more proficient when driving in a familiar downtown area than when driving through a new city. When surroundings are familiar, your observations become more automatic and you can observe more events simultaneously.

- *One depends heavily on the observations of others.* To keep the number of observations manageable, you often depend on others observing you. You could not safely drive through heavy traffic unless the drivers of other cars were observing you. Other drivers may have to initiate actions to avoid problems you do not see or alert you to problems that are developing. You usually take actions to help others observe you, such as driving in a predictable manner or using the horn when necessary.

- *Most events go unobserved.* Although you observe a phenomenal number of events while driving, you never see most things that occur around you. For example, you probably do not read the license plates of most nearby cars. You do not observe the type of clothes worn by most people in other cars and on the sidewalk. You may not observe that the driver of a car up ahead is trying to get out of a parking space. You cannot possibly observe everything. Many, possibly all, of these events are not relevant to your act of driving the car. Some may be relevant. For instance, if the driver of the car leaving the parking space also has not observed you, your cars may collide.

- *Most observations are not remembered or are distorted when recalled.* Because of the huge number of observations that occur, most details are not remembered. Unlike a tape recorder or computer disk, the mind does not retain verbatim what is received. Instead, the mind organizes what is observed in ways that are expected to be useful later. Over time, the mind reorganizes these perceptions. After you arrive home from driving downtown, you retain very few observations. Many of them, such as how long you waited at a traffic light, can be reconstructed, although often inaccurately. Witnesses to an accident similarly construct contradictory descriptions of what recently occurred. Immediately writing down details of what was observed substantially improves the accuracy of recollection. Your idiosyncrasies, such as your values, interests, and habits, influence what you remember and how you remember it. Your idiosyncrasies also influence what you observe in the first place.

Although driving a car is obviously very different from teaching a class, the characteristics of observations that occur in both settings are similar. In both the car and the classroom, you observe many events simultaneously or in quick succession. Within a few seconds while walking around in the classroom, you may have looked to see if students are staying on task with seatwork, briefly read what a nearby student wrote on her or his paper, noticed the unusual way another student holds a pencil, heard conversation in the hallway, and heard a click over the school intercom suggesting that someone is about to make an announcement.

These events are observed at different levels of detail. Reading what the student wrote on her or his paper, for instance, would be a detailed observation, whereas the overall check of whether students are staying on task would be a general observation. Current observations help select and structure subsequent observations. Anticipating an announcement over the intercom may cause you to continue watching students in general rather than to focus attention on the student whose paper you briefly read. The conversation in the hall may cause you to walk closer to the door so that you can observe what is happening.

Classroom observations often become focused on one event. When this happens, the number of other events that can be observed is decreased. For example, if you find it necessary to watch what is happening in the hallway, even if you stay in the classroom you will be less able to monitor what students are doing in the classroom. Similarly, if you begin working closely with the student whose paper you had scanned, you will be less able to observe what other students are doing. As you focus your attention, you must maintain your observation of certain critical events. For instance, if you focus attention on one student's paper, you must continue to observe how much time is passing, what other students are doing, and overall trends in student behavior. When you focus your attention, the tendency will be to stop all other observations. Doing so must be avoided.

Experience and confidence significantly improve the effectiveness of observations in the classroom. Just as when you first learn to drive a car, when you first begin teaching, your observations are much less effective. New teachers tend to focus narrowly on what they will do next. With experience, many actions become automatic, and teachers become able to observe several events simultaneously and to handle highly complex situations.

It is ironic that teaching may be the only profession in which responsibilities are as or even more complex on the first year as they are on the last year of employment. During the first year, a new teacher typically prepares for and teaches multiple subjects. Often, these preparations are in content areas other than those with which the new teacher is most proficient. Experienced and higher paid teachers have earned the right to teach the less demanding students and classes.

In contrast, when learning to drive a car, a new driver progresses from simpler to more complex situations. After training, the new driver has the option and usually tries to avoid complicated situations until he or she gains more experience. Although in some ways an inexperienced driver may be more dangerous than an inexperienced teacher, the classroom environment is much more complex. A teacher who successfully employs informal observations in the classroom is performing an act more complicated than effectively using observations while driving through downtown traffic.

Confidence, in addition to experience, enhances observation abilities in the classroom. Being comfortable in the classroom setting, being in a school whose administration and other teachers encourage confidence, and being certain of your knowledge of the subject matter help you effectively observe students.

Teaching students with whom you are familiar helps automate classroom observations. Your observations are less effective if, as is common at the beginning of the year, you confuse students with one another or lack preliminary evaluations of each student's characteristics. Likewise, observations are less effective when new curriculum materials are introduced. After becoming familiar with new materials, your observations tend to be more automatic.

As with driving in traffic, the teacher depends heavily on the observations of others. A teacher has to depend on students' observations to keep events in the classroom manageable. Students must learn how to observe and be comfortable with initiating observations and taking corrective actions. The teacher can help structure students' observations by asking timely questions, being encouraging, and showing students how and when to get the teacher's attention.

Most events that occur in the classroom go unobserved. There are just too many events happening in the classroom for all of them to be observed. In addition, most of the events a teacher would like to observe are invisible. As we have noted before, one cannot directly observe what students know or are thinking.

Although most events in the classroom are never observed, what is observed is often quickly forgotten or distorted when recalled. Writing down what was observed helps retain accuracy, although it is practical to write down only a fraction of what is observed. Careful and continuous observation, as an assessment technique, is unbeatable when it comes to immediate, *formative evaluations* of student performance. Most classroom assessments are based on informal observations. No other assessment technique provides the information necessary to monitor student progress continually. However, because details are quickly forgotten or distorted, the role of informal observation must diminish when *summative evaluations* are involved.

Box 11.1 *Apply What You Are Learning*

In Chapter 5, several sources of inconsistency were identified that reduce the likelihood that what we observed will generalize to what we did not observe. Scan through the ten characteristics of informal observations we have just discussed, which are listed on the next page in Figure 11.1. Which one of these ten characteristics makes it so important to determine whether observations of student performance will generalize to other settings?

Answer can be found at the end of the chapter.

1. Many events are observed either simultaneously or in very quick succession.
2. Events are observed at different levels of detail.
3. Current observations help select and structure subsequent observations.
4. Often, observations become focused on one event.
5. When observations become focused, observation of other critical events must be maintained.
6. Experience and confidence with a task substantially increase the effectiveness of observations.
7. Familiarity with surroundings increases the effectiveness of observations.
8. One depends heavily on the observations of others.
9. Most events go unobserved.
10. Most observations are not remembered or are distorted when recalled.

Figure 11.1
Characteristics of informal classroom observations

So far, we have drawn analogies between observations that occur when driving a car and those that occur in the classroom. In the classroom, however, most observations are of an indirect nature. We generally cannot directly see what students have learned and must depend on outward indications that learning has indeed occurred. Furthermore, in the classroom we often augment these observations with oral questions. Questions can compel, or at least encourage, student actions. Oral questions put you in the driver's seat.

To facilitate our discussion, we are going to use as a reference several characteristics of informal observation and questioning that occur when friends interact with each other. We will then relate these characteristics to what goes on in the classroom. It is useful to note that the characteristics discussed previously also apply to our interactions with friends. For instance, when interacting with friends, we observe many events simultaneously or in quick succession. Previous observations affect subsequent observations. Observations often become focused with a corresponding reduction in other observations. Also, experience and confidence greatly facilitate observations among friends.

Here are some additional characteristics of observations and questioning that occur when interacting with a group of friends:

■ *Observations often require inference.* You cannot see what your friends are thinking or what they know. Instead, you have to make inferences from things you can observe, such as what they say, their tone of voice, and their facial expressions. If, for instance, conversation among friends is focusing on a recent video that some members of the group have seen, paying attention to their words and expressions provides only an indication of what they know or are thinking about the video. Inferences drawn from what you observe typically include some distortion of what your friends actually know or are thinking.

■ *Subsequent observations substantiate or modify earlier observations.* When interacting with friends, you have opportunities to use additional observations to confirm or modify your judgments. This situation differs from what typically happens with serial activities, such as driving a car. When driving, it is often not practical to go back and make additional observations. When interacting with friends or teaching in a classroom, however, there are many opportunities to follow up with more observations, and this is important because so many judgments in these cases are based on inference rather than on direct observation.

■ *Questioning can set up subsequent observations.* Not only can you make follow-up observations, but you can also ask questions that shape or encourage ensuing observations. For instance, you can ask friends for details about a movie to find out if it is scary or has graphic content.

■ *Questions are obtrusive.* Asking a question indicates that observations are occurring and identifies what is being observed. Setting up observations, in fact, is often the purpose of asking a question. However, questions undo a major asset of observations, being unobtrusive. When observations are unobtrusive, they provide an excellent technique for determining typical behaviors, such as attitudes. A question that implies that a movie was boring can cause others to camouflage their real attitudes. A friend might outwardly accept the view that the movie was boring if for no other reason than to try not to be offensive.

■ *Questions have to be interpreted by others, so clarity is important.* Since you cannot see another's thoughts, you have to infer what thoughts underlie the questions being asked. For instance, you might say, "My parents are visiting. Would renting this video be appropriate?" Possible inferences include "Would I be embarrassed to watch this movie with my parents?" "Would older people enjoy the plot?" or possibly, "Would my parents relate to the issues the movie is raising?" Asking a concise question helps communicate what you are thinking: "My parents enjoy only G-rated movies. What's the rating of this video?" Certainly an advantage of informal questions is the ease with which ambiguous questions can be clarified.

■ *Questions can be directed to individuals or to the group.* A question directed at the group encourages others to participate. For instance, you might ask, "Do you all think this video is worth renting?" Most individuals in the group who have seen the movie will at least answer the question to themselves if not verbally. Although questions directed at the group encourage greater participation, this approach reduces control over who will respond to the question. Also, if questions are directed at the group for an extended period, the number of individuals participating tends to decrease because of the lack of personal feedback.

■ *To remain involved, individuals to whom a question is addressed must perceive that their response was listened to and used appropriately.* Because oral questions affect subsequent observations, ignoring or misusing an individual's response is detrimental to later interactions. Friends realize that this is important. They are generally attentive to each other's responses and demonstrate they are empathetic to what is said.

■ *Individuals to whom a question is addressed will typically forget their answers, as will the person who asked the question.* As we noted earlier, the mind does not memorize knowledge; it organizes knowledge in ways that are expected to be useful later. Writing down what we learn facilitates later recall. Otherwise, the details of even significant events are usually distorted. In casual conversation with friends, forgetting details of what transpired is often of no significance. Questions and observations are used to formulate ideas and impressions rather than to generate a list of details. When details are to be recalled, such as a phone number, a future date, or a joke you wish to tell others, writing it down even in abbreviated form substantially improves the chances that we will recall it.

Each of these characteristics applies to the informal observations and questions that occur in a classroom. For instance, when observing students, you cannot directly observe what they know or what they are thinking. Instead, you make inferences from what you see—and that inference may be in error. If you watch a student writing an essay and see that student make a grammatical mistake with subject–verb agreement, you might conclude that the student does not understand how to match the plural form of a verb with a plural subject. It may be, however, that the student mentally switched from a singular to plural subject but forgot to compensate for this switch when writing out the sentence. Similarly, if you happen to see a student holding a pencil incorrectly, you may infer that the student does not know how to hold the pencil, but the student might have just grasped the pencil incorrectly.

Subsequent observations can be used to modify earlier observations. For example, continuing to watch the student write will help clarify whether the student understands rules concerning subject–verb agreement; continuing to watch the student hold the pencil will help determine whether he or she typically holds the pencil incorrectly or simply happens to be holding it that way at a particular moment.

Questions directed at students can set up subsequent observations. Asking the first student about subject–verb agreement or talking to the second student about how he or she is holding the pencil can quickly help clarify what these students know. However, questions are obtrusive. The student writing the paper will focus on subject–verb agreement, which in itself might be productive. However, knowing what is being observed, the student is likely to focus on subject–verb agreements and thus might begin to demonstrate maximum rather than typical performance in this area. Similarly, the second student might adjust the pencil grip and later, when you are not observing, revert to the incorrect grasp.

Questions require the students to make inferences from what they observe you saying, since they cannot see what you are thinking. The accuracy of their inferences is influenced by the clarity of your questions.

Questions within a classroom setting are often directed at the group rather than at an individual. For instance, if discussion in the class focuses on how drinking water becomes contaminated, you might ask, "Who can identify a source of water contamination?" Addressing questions to the group tends, at least momentarily, to encourage broader participation. Students who do not respond verbally usually answer the question to themselves. Individual students, however, must perceive that their response to the teacher was listened to and used appropriately. Otherwise, students tune out.

1. Observations often require inference.
2. Subsequent observations substantiate or modify earlier observations.
3. Questioning can set up subsequent observations.
4. Questions are obtrusive.
5. Questions have to be interpreted by others, so clarity is important.
6. Questions can be directed to individuals or to the group.
7. To remain involved, individuals to whom a question is addressed must perceive that their response was listened to and used appropriately.
8. Individuals to whom a question is addressed will typically forget their answers, as will the person who asked the question.

Figure 11.2
Characteristics of interactive observations and questions

With all informal assessments, the details of what was asked and observed are soon forgotten, whether they are observations that occur while driving a car, listening to what friends say, or observing students' responses to questions. Students forget the details of questions they were asked and the responses they gave. Questions are a useful assessment technique only when short-term recall of observations is required, for instance, in assessments used for preliminary, formative, and diagnostic evaluations. Unless students' responses are documented, they are not useful for later summative evaluations.

Box 11.2 *Apply What You Are Learning*

Chapter 4 discusses the need to establish evidence that an assessment is valid and describes common techniques for doing so. In that discussion, one type of validity evidence is called criterion-related evidence. It involves using observations outside the assessment to substantiate what was observed within the assessment. Figure 11.2 lists the eight characteristics of informal assessments we have just discussed. Which one of these characteristics is most closely related to using outside observations to substantiate informal assessments?

Answer can be found at the end of the chapter.

GUIDELINES FOR USING INFORMAL OBSERVATIONS

When driving a car, interacting with friends, or helping students learn, we depend heavily on experience to become proficient at observing. Reading a textbook cannot provide this experience. However, we can develop some basic principles of observation that guide what we learn through experience.

Know What to Observe

When we sit around a table with friends, our goal is often simply to enjoy being with each other. We typically are not trying to bring about deliberate changes in our friends. In this respect, a teacher's role is very different. The goals of a teacher are centered on intentionally generating significant improvements in students' capabilities. These goals are the basis of activities in which a teacher involves students and should also be the basis for determining what actions are observed.

We have noted the important distinction between students' capabilities and performance. We cannot see what students know and are thinking. Instead, we infer students' capabilities from their performance, which we can see. Our goals for students are typically stated in terms of capabilities. When establishing goals and determining what to observe, we must be careful to select student performances that are reasonable evidence of relevant capabilities. Doing so, in turn, requires knowledge of the characteristics of capabilities. Matching what we measure to the construct we wish to measure is central to obtaining valid assessments.

Although characteristics of capabilities are not fully understood, classifications such as those we are using in this book provide useful references. For instance, a distinction has been drawn between declarative and procedural knowledge, with procedural knowledge divided into subcategories that include concepts and rules. Most goals involve several capabilities. Knowledge of multiplication, for example, includes declarative knowledge ("Tell me what three times seven is."), concepts ("What is multiplication?"), and rules ("How do you multiply fifty-three times twenty-seven?"). To observe capabilities, we must first identify the characteristics of the capability and then identify which observable student performances will indicate whether a student has achieved that capability.

Declarative knowledge, for instance, is measured by asking students to recall specific facts, principles, trends, criteria, and ways of organizing events. Continuing the example with multiplication, we can measure declarative knowledge by observing whether a student can recall multiplication tables and by asking students to explain what is meant by multiplication. In contrast, knowledge of a concept is measured by asking a student to distinguish between illustrations and nonillustrations of the concept. For instance, a student should recognize that illustrations of multiplication include finding the area of a rectangle, the total cost of 12 objects costing $3 a piece, or the total number of blocks arranged in 3 rows of 7 blocks. The student should recognize that the concept of multiplication is *not* involved in measuring the length and width of a rectangle or totaling the cost of several items of unequal value. As you recall, knowledge of a rule is measured by observing a student apply that rule to solve new problems. For instance, a student who knows rules of simple multiplication should be able to solve problems where knowing multiplication tables is not sufficient, such as 53×27.

Box 11.3 *Apply What You Are Learning*

Here are some observations that might be used to assess a student's knowledge related to placing a fulcrum between two unequal weights so that a bar holding the weights balances. Indicate whether each of the following observations would indicate that the student has learned a skill involving

- declarative knowledge (information)
- procedural knowledge involving a concept
- procedural knowledge involving a rule

1. Observing whether the student uses the word *fulcrum* correctly in casual conversation.
2. Observing whether the student correctly states the definition of *fulcrum*.
3. Observing whether the student can place the fulcrum so that the bar with the weights is balanced.

Answers can be found at the end of the chapter.

Knowing what to observe involves first establishing the goals of instruction and then breaking these goals into meaningful capabilities that students are expected to achieve. For our observations and questions to be useful, these capabilities must be classified as representing declarative or procedural knowledge. As we have noted, different types of behavior must be observed to assess these two basic types of knowledge.

The best time for determining what to observe is when the lesson is being planned. At that point, we must establish where declarative and procedural knowledge are involved and accordingly select student performances to be observed.

Know When to Limit How Much Is to Be Observed

One of the characteristics of observation is the ability to observe several things simultaneously or in quick succession. Focusing the observations, however, allows you to observe a limited number of events in greater detail. Focus is often necessary when observing students, especially when the performance being observed is complex or when the observation is critical. A critical observation is one used to determine whether further instruction is necessary.

When planning instructional activities, it is useful to consider whether that day's activities involve complex or critical skills. If they do, you should plan to focus observations on a limited number of skills, possibly on only one. With experience, you learn to observe a number of events simultaneously. At the end of the day, however, if you cannot recall students' performance with a critical skill, the number of skills being observed probably needs to be reduced.

Be Familiar with What Is Being Observed

When you are driving a car, being experienced and familiar with your surroundings significantly improves the efficiency of your observations. An experienced driver is much more adept at observing what is going on than is a person who is just beginning to drive. Also, a person makes more efficient observations when driving through a familiar but busy area of town than when driving through an unfamiliar but equally busy area of town.

Likewise, familiarity substantially affects a teacher's ability to observe. A teacher who is knowledgeable about the content being taught is much more effective at observing students than a teacher who has superficial content knowledge. An example of superficial knowledge is knowing the content a little bit better than the best students. A teacher who is knowledgeable about content can differentiate between information that students can be asked to recall and concepts that they must demonstrate through other means, and can detect subtle characteristics in student performance that indicate that the student is learning a misconception. This level of knowledge is difficult to obtain. Experienced teachers tend to be more knowledgeable than new teachers. To a degree, the teacher's insights and ability to learn influence the level of knowledge. For the most part, level of knowledge is influenced by persistence, looking for limitations and misconceptions in your own knowledge, talking through ideas with colleagues, and reading ideas described in the several widely available professional magazines. Familiarity is also obtained by gaining experience with a particular set of instructional materials and strategies. However, thorough knowledge of the content being taught is the teacher's single most important means for being familiar with what is to be observed.

Avoid Extended Inferences

Because we cannot see what a student knows or is thinking, inferences are required to make judgments about the student's capabilities. Any inference is based on assumptions. For example, if a student correctly spells the words *achieve* and *receive*, we may infer the student knows how to use *ie* versus *ei* when spelling words. This inference assumes that the student did not simply guess at the order of these letters; it also assumes that the student is applying the rules pertaining to *ie* and *ei* rather than memorizing the spelling of selected words.

Inferences that involve fewer or less significant assumptions are called limited inferences. Those that involve many or highly significant assumptions are called extended inferences. Conclusions drawn from extended inferences are more likely to be in error simply because of the increased chance of one or more of the critical assumptions being untrue. Observations that require limited inferences should be favored over those requiring extended inferences. Inferences drawn from multiple observations tend to be more limited than inferences drawn from one observation, since more opportunities are provided for detecting false assumptions.

Box 11.4 *Apply What You Are Learning*

Listed here are several observations, each followed by two possible inferences. For each observation, identify which inference is the limited and therefore the preferred inference.

1. **Observation:** Gary volunteered to spell *hippopotamus*. He spelled it correctly.

   Inference A: Gary is good at spelling.

   Inference B: Gary knows how to spell *hippopotamus*.

2. **Observation:** When asked how to balance a checkbook, Jerome described specific (and correct) steps used by his mother.

   Inference A: Jerome knows the steps followed when balancing a checkbook.

   Inference B: Jerome knows the importance of balancing a checkbook.

3. **Observation:** Alice described how to focus the astronomical telescope she has at home.

   Inference A: Alice enjoys astronomy.

   Inference B: Alice knows how to focus an astronomical telescope.

4. **Observation:** Gretchen slept while the class was discussing historical events.

   Inference A: Gretchen did not participate in the discussion of historical events.

   Inference B: Gretchen is very tired.

5. **Observation:** After being asked to read a lesson on Japan, none of four students asked could identify Tokyo as the capital of Japan.

   Inference A: Students in the class do not know that Tokyo is the capital of Japan.

   Inference B: Students did not carefully read the lesson.

Answers can be found at the end of the chapter.

Form and Then Substantiate Hypotheses

When observing students, it is best to form hypotheses concerning what a student or group of students knows. *Hypotheses are tentative, reasonable explanations* of what we have observed. Hypotheses are not conclusions.

Because what a student knows cannot be seen, it is better to form hypotheses than to draw conclusions from what we observe. By forming hypotheses, we deliberately plan to use additional observations to confirm (or reject) our explanation of student performance. The additional observations may simply be replications of earlier observations. Often they involve different sources of information, such as other things we have seen the student do or possibly information provided by other students, teachers, counselors, and parents.

Forming and then substantiating hypotheses helps us avoid making extended inferences. The earlier illustrations of extended and limited inferences included the observation that Gretchen fell asleep while the class discussed historical events. The teacher might form several initial hypotheses at this point, such as, Gretchen finds the present discussion boring: Gretchen finds history in general boring; Gretchen is very tired; or Gretchen is protesting some earlier treatment. Each of these hypotheses would involve extended inferences. The number of assumptions required to make each inference can be reduced, however, by using additional observations to substantiate or refute each of these hypotheses. As a general rule, an initial hypothesis should be substantiated with at least one additional observation. Interpretations drawn from two or more observations tend to be much more accurate than those drawn from just one observation.

When forming a hypothesis to explain what was observed, the temptation will be to remember the explanation of what we saw and forget the event that helped create the hypothesis. This is an undesirable practice. The appropriateness of a hypothesis assumes a valid interpretation of what was observed. Keeping a clear distinction between what was observed and the interpretation of what was observed makes it much easier to use additional observations to substantiate the hypothesis.

Recognize That Observations Overestimate Achievement

Most observations occur while learning is taking place or shortly thereafter. If observations were made long after instruction, the effects of short-term memory would become apparent. Students soon forget or are unable to recall much of what they have learned. Part of this results from natural forgetfulness. However, retention also drops because many of the cues that supported a student's response are removed, modified, or forgotten within a short period of time. Because most observations occur near the time of instruction, they tend to overestimate student achievement.

Observations also overestimate achievement because knowledgeable students are more likely to be observed than are less knowledgeable students. When informally observing students, we usually look for evidence of learning rather than evidence of an absence of learning. Students who first learn the skill being taught are more likely to encourage the teacher's observation by answering questions, establishing eye contact, and taking other actions that invite observation.

Help Students Participate in Observations

As when driving a car or interacting with friends, we observe a small fraction of events that occur in the classroom. It is impossible to do otherwise. When driving or when interacting with friends, we depend on the observations of others. For instance, you could not possibly drive safely through a busy downtown district if other drivers were unable or unwilling to observe you. The same situation exists in the classroom.

Students will naturally participate in classroom observations, although a teacher can take steps to encourage and direct this involvement. Students become better observers if they know where the teacher is going, and students are more responsive if the teacher's intentions are concise and predictable. Teachers can provide this information to students in a variety of forms, including statements of goals, advanced organizers, and illustrations of what students will be able to do when skills are learned.

Students can participate in observations only if they have the opportunity to do so. Lecture provides fewer opportunities to participate than does discussion. Asking for recitation provides fewer opportunities than allowing students to originate questions and challenge ideas. Working with a large class as a whole provides fewer opportunities than dividing the class into smaller groups of students.

Students' participation in observation is influenced by their interest in what is going on and by the reinforcement they have received from earlier participation. Knowing the ultimate goal of instruction and its importance increases students' interest. Is not your own ability to learn more about classroom assessment heavily influenced by your having a clear idea of what you will be learning and the degree to which you believe this knowledge will improve your effectiveness in education?

Students maintain or increase their involvement if rewarded. A student tends to feel rewarded if the teacher values his or her thoughts and if the teacher helps the student determine parts of observations that are insightful and important. Students' active participation in informal observations and other assessments is critical because the teacher, without student help, is able to observe a small fraction of what occurs in the classroom.

Document Observations That Must Later Be Recalled

We recognize that unless documented, observations are forgotten shortly after they occur, or, at the very least, they become seriously distorted. Documentation usually involves a written or electronic record.

Most observations are not documented because of the amount of time needed to record any more than a small portion of what is observed. Fortunately, most observations in the classroom are for immediate use and need not be retained for extended periods. However, when information needs to be retained, it must be documented or it will be lost.

It is easy to assume that the details of an important event will not be forgotten. Such details are extremely clear at the time the event happens. But within the hour, many details of an important event are gone! Later in this chapter, we describe some techniques used to document the more significant observations.

GUIDELINES FOR USING INFORMAL QUESTIONS

By asking questions, a teacher can often quickly gather evidence concerning what students have learned. If only informal observations, but no questions, are used, the teacher might not be able to obtain useful evidence within a reasonable amount of time. Questions greatly expedite informal assessment. However, because questions are obtrusive and can affect what a teacher will be able to observe, they need to be presented carefully and prudently. In this section, we address several guidelines that should facilitate the use of informal questions.

Develop Questions from Instructional Goals

By basing questions on instructional goals, we can anticipate which capabilities need to be assessed. Different capabilities require different kinds of questions. Consider, for example, these two questions about the presidential primary elections in the United States:

> What is a primary election?
>
> Which state holds the first presidential primary election?

Now contrast those questions to the following:

> If all states decided to hold their presidential primaries on the same day, how would this influence which candidates are nominated?
>
> If separate primaries in each state were replaced with one national primary, how would this affect where political parties invested their funds?

These two groups of questions assess very different capabilities. The first two questions involve declarative knowledge or recall of information. The second two questions measure procedural knowledge. Both capabilities are important. Unfortunately, we often ask questions that measure one type of capability and then assume we are measuring both.

By determining what capabilities are implicit in an instructional goal, we can determine which observations need to be made and what questions will facilitate these observations.

As instructional goals often form the basis for planning activities for students, knowing the types of capabilities implicit in each goal can enhance the usefulness of these activities. Informal observations and questions should be established at the same time instructional activities are planned. To be effective, student activities, informal observations, and questions all must reflect the types of capabilities implicit in each instructional goal.

Establish a Clear Problem for Students to Address

Chapters 6 through 9 were concerned with the development of written test items. Considerable emphasis was placed on preparing items that establish a clear problem for the student to address. Doing so is important because one of the major threats to the reliability of students' responses is ambiguity within the items. The quality of informal questions is similarly threatened by this ambiguity.

Informal questions have a major advantage over items in a written test. With written tests, questions must be fully developed before the test is administered. With informal assessments, outlines and a teacher's telegraphic notes are often sufficient for preparing the questions. The specific wording of an informal question is established spontaneously as it is being asked. Questions can be clarified on the spot, and even body language can be used to help communicate the intention of a question.

The spontaneity of informal questions, however, can become a crutch that encourages lack of planning on the teacher's part. If students often ask for questions to be clarified or if the nature or content of students' responses departs significantly from the intent of the question, it is a warning sign that the questions are failing to present clear problems to be addressed.

As with written tests, questions that measure procedural knowledge, such as concepts and rules, are more difficult to create than those that measure recall of information. Therefore, even with informal assessments, it is useful to prepare the details of these more sophisticated questions prior to class. Think through the list of details the question must communicate to students, the reasoning students should go through in answering the question, and the characteristics of a full and correct answer to the question. A series of related questions must often be asked to assess a skill involving procedural knowledge.

Allow Sufficient Time for Responses

When questions are being asked informally in the classroom, it is common for a teacher to pose several questions within the period of one minute. Students also respond quickly to questions; two or three seconds of silence before a student responds is often considered lengthy. This rate of questions and responses may be appropriate for recalling information, but it is often inadequate for measuring procedural knowledge.

To draw an analogy with written tests, informal questions are most similar to the short-answer and essay formats. Declarative knowledge involving the recall of information might be tested using the short-answer format, but the assessment of procedural knowledge typically would require essays. Essay questions cannot be answered at the rate of several a minute, even if we subtract the large amount of time required to write out the answer to the essay question. Likewise, a student requires some time to think through possible strategies for conceptualizing an answer to an essay question even before the response is structured.

Informal questions are different from written test items, though, so the analogy to an essay question is somewhat flawed. For instance, a teacher and student can carry on a dialogue during the response to an informal question, which could not occur with essay questions. Several supplementary questions might be asked as part of that dialogue. Nevertheless, when using informal questions to measure procedural knowledge, questions should be asked at a slower rate. Also, periods of 5 to 10 seconds of silence prior to a response are reasonable when concepts, rules, and complex skills are involved.

Avoid Embarrassing or Intimidating Students

One disadvantage of informal questions is that they are public. When asked within a group, the student needs to respond in front of others. This raises the possibility of embarrassing or intimidating the student, often unintentionally. Even when the teacher is working one on one with a student, the student has to perform in front of the teacher. In contrast, with a written test, a student works in almost total privacy. Intimidation or embarrassment can motivate students when used in moderation. However, their effects vary widely across students and are often counterproductive. The teacher's reactions to students' answers tend to be the major source of embarrassment and intimidation.

Recognize the Importance of Reactions to Answers

A teacher's reactions to students' answers are an important part of informal assessments. Many of these reactions do not have counterparts in formal written tests. For example, a teacher can immediately summarize what a student said or ask the student to expand on a point. A teacher can use facial expressions to communicate satisfaction, ask for clarification, or discourage further response.

Kissock and Iyortsuun (1982) believe that listening is the principal tool that teachers have in reacting to students' responses. They propose two parts to effective listening. The first is understanding what a student has said. The second is knowing the feelings of the student who provided the response. Both understanding the content of the response and accepting the student's feelings are important to encouraging further participation by the student.

Kissock and Iyortsuun (1982) also list a number of ways in which a teacher can react to a student's response. Here is a sample from that list:

Acknowledge and reinforce a student's response by rephrasing the answer.

Clarify a student's answer by expanding it or comparing it to another student's answer.

Probe responses by asking for clarification, further evidence, or definitions.

Use nonverbal gestures instead of verbal reactions to encourage other students to respond to what has been said thus far.

Ask another student to evaluate a response.

Use a student's response as the basis for the next question.

Provide an overview of progress that was achieved through discussion.

RECORD KEEPING

The observations from most informal assessments are not documented. This statement is in part a simple recognition that far more observations occur than could ever be recorded. There also is no need to record most observations, since information gained from the typical observation is used immediately. Informal observations and questions are used mostly for preliminary, formative, and diagnostic evaluations.

When an observation has unusual significance or when a particular performance is part of a list of important skills the student is expected to demonstrate, however, the details of observations do need to be retained. Thus, they must be documented. Details of observations that are not documented are not usually remembered beyond one hour. The basic techniques used to document observations are anecdotal records, checklists, and rating scales.

Anecdotal Records

Anecdotal records are often used to document a student's behavior for later reference by the teacher or by parents, counselors, and other teachers. An anecdotal record consists of a short narrative describing both a behavior and the context in which the behavior occurred. The record may also include an interpretation of that behavior and possibly a recommendation. Figure 11.3 illustrates an anecdotal record. Anecdotal records are often used to describe social adjustments. Unlike checklists and rating scales, anecdotal records are unstructured; therefore, they are particularly useful for describing unanticipated or unusual behaviors. Anecdotal records provide a useful way to record significant observations that are not part of a formal assessment.

Because anecdotal records are unstructured, the following guidelines should be followed so that the record communicates information effectively:

1. The anecdotal record should objectively report specific and observed behaviors.

2. If interpretations of a behavior or recommendations are included in a record, they should be separated from the description of the student's performance.

3. Information contained in a record should be self-sufficient. Whoever reads it later will be unaware of circumstances surrounding the observation; therefore, pertinent

---

Student _Jimmy Watson_ ———————————— Date _2/9/01_

Observer _H. James_

This behavior is (TYPICAL)   ATYPICAL
(circle one)

Observation: The class was asked to orally list causes of the Civil War. Students were raising their hands to volunteer a possible cause. Jimmy raised his hand. When called on, he asked if a movie would be shown in class.

Interpretation (optional): Jimmy often becomes detached from class activities. This has increased in frequency since the beginning of the year and occurs about twice during a class period. He does not seem to be trying to disrupt the class or draw attention to himself. I presently have no explanation for this behavior.

Recommendation (optional):
    None

Figure 11.3
Example of an anecdotal record

information about what was happening just before and during the observation must be provided.

4. There should be a specific reason for writing an anecdotal record. The narrative should make that reason obvious to anyone reading it.

5. An anecdotal record may be read in isolation from other records. Therefore, the narrative should clearly indicate whether the observation represents a typical behavior and should state the nature of any trends relevant to the behavior.

6. Each anecdotal record should record one event pertinent to one student. Separate records should be prepared, if necessary, to describe the actions of more than one student.

Checklists and Rating Scales

A checklist is a list of actions or descriptions; a rater checks off items as the particular behavior or outcome is observed. In previous chapters checklists were used to list qualities sought in written test items. Checklists can be used in settings where the presence or absence of a series of conditions is to be established. They also help structure complex observations. For example, pilots use a preflight checklist to verify that an aircraft is ready for takeoff.

Separate copies of a checklist are usually prepared for each student. If the number of items included in the checklist is limited (usually five or fewer), observations of all students in the class can be recorded on a single checklist. For example, students' names might be listed vertically down the left side of the page and characteristics to be checked listed as column headings. This format is particularly useful when observing the class as a whole rather than individual students.

Cartwright and Cartwright (1984) describe a variation of the checklist in which the frequencies of each student's behaviors are tallied rather than checked as present or absent. They call this variation a "participation chart." All students in the class, or at least a group of students, are listed on one chart. Because several students are being observed simultaneously, the number of behaviors being observed must be limited.

A rating scale is another technique for recording the frequency or degree to which a student exhibits a characteristic. Instead of checking the presence or absence of a characteristic, the teacher uses a scale to describe the student. Such scales often use numbers, such as 1 to 5. Descriptions, for instance, ranging from "never" to "always," are associated with each number. Later chapters describe in some detail the construction and use of checklists and rating scales.

SUMMARY

The vast majority of classroom assessments involve informal observations and questions. These techniques are very efficient and adaptable. Meaningful preliminary, formative, and diagnostic evaluations cannot exist without this type of assessment.

On the other hand, the technical quality of spontaneous observations and questions tends to be inferior to techniques associated with formal assessments. Informal assessments also tend to overestimate student achievement.

Our experience in using observations and questions in other settings provides a good base for understanding their characteristics when used in the classroom. From this experience, we recognize that many events can be observed quickly. Focusing our observation reduces the number of events that can be observed but increases the amount of detail that is examined. Current observations structure subsequent observations. Experience and confidence are both prerequisites to making efficient observations.

Because of their immense number, most events go unobserved. Many events in the classroom cannot be observed because they are invisible; that is, we cannot directly observe what another person knows or is thinking. Inferences must be made from behaviors that can be observed. Limited inferences are preferred over extended inferences. The use of multiple observations as well as careful selection of what is observed helps limit inferences. A useful strategy for formulating inferences is to form and then substantiate hypotheses that explain what has been observed.

Questions can greatly facilitate observations. Clarity of questions is important, since students cannot observe what the teacher is thinking. Each student must perceive that his or her responses are being observed and used appropriately. Questions are obtrusive and tend to encourage maximum rather than typical performance.

Observations and questions should be devised at the time student activities are planned. Outlines and telegraphic notes are often sufficient. Instructional goals provide a useful base for this planning; however, capabilities implicit in each goal should be identified. The distinction between declarative and procedural knowledge is important, as it is within all classroom assessments.

Informal assessments are usually not documented, and details of student performance are soon forgotten or distorted. This limitation is often not a concern, since information gained through observation is typically used immediately. Information that is to be retained must be documented. Techniques used to record informal observations include anecdotal records, checklists, and rating scales.

ANSWERS: APPLY WHAT YOU ARE LEARNING

11.1 The ninth characteristic is most relevant to generalization: "Most events that occur in the classroom go unobserved."

11.2 The second of the eight characteristics is most closely related to gathering criterion-related evidence of validity: "Subsequent observations substantiate or modify earlier observations." In essence, performance observed within the informal assessment is being correlated with subsequent observations.

11.3 1. Probably both declarative knowledge (information) and procedural knowledge involving a concept; 2. declarative knowledge (information); 3. procedural knowledge involving a rule.

11.4 1. B;   2. A;   3. B;   4. A;   5. A.

SOMETHING TO TRY

■ Think of some techniques that you have used to avoid being called on when you did not know the answer. This kind of avoidance procedure is common. What negative consequences do such procedures have on the teacher's ability to assess informally what each student (and the class as a whole) knows and does not know? What techniques can a teacher use to prevent these problems?

■ The mind quickly forgets or more often distorts factual details that are not immediately documented. A good illustration of this is our recollection of a traumatic event, such as the explosion of the *Challenger* space shuttle. Try answering these questions:

In what month did the explosion happen?

How many women were aboard?

Who was the U.S. president at the time?

Compare your answers to those of a classmate. What implication does this have for a teacher's informal assessments in which what was observed is to be recalled later?

■ Informal observations often depend on interactions with those being observed. This is necessary to keep the number of observations manageable. List some techniques that a teacher can use to get students to participate actively in the process of informal observations.

ADDITIONAL READING

Cartwright, C. A., & Cartwright, G. P. (1984). *Developing observation skills*. New York: McGraw-Hill. This book discusses principles of observing and recording student behaviors. Many examples are included. Ideas will be most useful to individuals working in special education and with early elementary students.

Dillon, J. T. (1989). *The practice of questioning*. London: Routledge. This book provides a research-based discussion of questioning in a variety of settings, including the school classroom, clinical settings in medicine, and the courtroom.

Guerin, G. R., & Maier, A. S. (1983). *Informal assessment in education*. Palo Alto, CA: Mayfield Publishing. This book focuses on the use of day-to-day observations when evaluating students. Skill areas discussed include sensorimotor development, spelling, handwriting, reading, and arithmetic. Various rating forms are illustrated.

Kissock, C., & Iyortsuun, P. (1982). *A guide to questioning: Classroom procedures for teachers*. London: Macmillan Press. This book discusses and illustrates the use of informal questions within each of the six levels of Bloom's cognitive categories and the five levels of Krathwohl's affective categories.

CHAPTER 12

Considerations When Using Performance Assessments

Written tests cannot meaningfully measure a number of important skills. Often this is simply because the particular skill does not involve writing. Certainly written tests cannot measure how well a student can deliver a speech, focus a microscope, play a musical instrument, hold a pencil, or interact socially. Written tests also cannot measure students' ability to solve complex problems when highly diverse solutions to the problems are possible. A well-constructed written test presents students a problem and structures how students will resolve the problem. Skills that in this book we have been calling *complex skills* can be assessed only if the structure of the problem's solution is not fixed. For instance, to create a well-written, persuasive letter, two different individuals could and probably would combine different information, concepts, and rules to develop their arguments. The only effective way to measure a complex skill such as this is to give students a task that requires direct, yet flexible application of that skill. One might ask students to do the following:

> Write a letter that could be published in the newspaper about using tax money to support students attending private schools. Your letter should be written to persuade others to agree with your point of view.

This task provides direct observation of student performance and is called a performance assessment.

In recent years, considerable attention has been given to what is referred to as authentic assessment. All authentic assessments are performance assessments, but the inverse is not true. An authentic assessment involves a real application of a skill beyond its instructional context. In an interview Shepard (cited in Kirst, 1991) stated that the term *authentic assessment* is intended to convey that the "assessment tasks themselves are real instances of extended criterion performances, rather than proxies or estimators of actual learning goals" (p. 21). Linn, Baker, and Dunbar (1991) describe authentic assessments as involving a "performance of tasks that are valued in their own right. In contrast, paper-and-pencil, multiple-choice tests derive their value primarily as indicators or correlates of other valued performances" (p.15).

Writing a persuasive letter would be an authentic assessment in a language arts class. In a physics class, an authentic assessment might require students to create hypotheses from their existing knowledge that explain why binary stars orbit around each other at a particular rate. In a class concerned with educational measurement, an authentic assessment would involve the actual development of classroom tests.

Portfolios (discussed in Chapter 14) are sometimes described as authentic assessments. For our purposes, we recognize that portfolios typically include the products of authentic assessments but often include other material, such as annotations written by the student or teacher, paper-and-pencil tests, and other items that help document student progress. We will not equate portfolios with authentic assessments. We will, however, use *performance* and *authentic* assessment interchangeably, since our discussion of performance assessments will be limited to situations in which the content of the task that students are asked to perform is authentic.

Performance assessments are typically used in conjunction with written tests. Although performance assessments are needed to measure complex skills, written tests tend to be more efficient at assessing the information, concepts, and rules that provide the fundamental knowledge for complex skills. For example, before a performance assessment asks students to create hypotheses about the behavior of binary stars, written tests can be used to establish students' knowledge that is prerequisite to creating these hypotheses, such as concepts and rules related to gravitation, mass, and centrifugal force.

Performance assessments have a variety of unique characteristics. For example, they can measure a process as well as products resulting from a process. They can occur in natural or structured settings. Most important, performance assessments can measure skills that paper-and-pencil tests cannot. However, performance assessments have significant limitations. For instance, they are usually time-consuming to develop, administer, and score. Also, as with essay tests, subjectivity in scoring, unless controlled, results in substantial measurement error.

The next chapter describes how to create performance assessments. In this chapter, we will examine some important characteristics of performance assessments and discuss their implications. We will also describe three procedures for scoring performance assessments: checklists, rating scales, and scoring rubrics. We conclude by discussing some tasks that should precede creation of a performance assessment. This chapter helps you achieve three skills:

■ Identify characteristics of performance assessments

■ Recognize qualities desired in a performance assessment

■ Recognize characteristics that checklists, rating scales, and scoring rubrics should have when used to score performance assessments

CHARACTERISTICS OF PERFORMANCE ASSESSMENTS

Specifying the characteristics of performance assessments depends in part on deciding exactly what a performance assessment is. The qualities associated with written formats such as multiple-choice and essay are more established. The nature of performance assessments is highly diverse and may include observation and evaluation of lab experiments, artwork, speaking, work habits, social interactions, and feelings about issues. For our purposes, a performance assessment will be limited to those situations that meet the following criteria:

1. Specific behaviors or outcomes of behaviors are to be observed.
2. It is possible to judge the appropriateness of students' actions or at least to identify whether one possible response is more appropriate than some alternative response.
3. The process or outcome cannot be directly measured using a paper-and-pencil test, such as a test involving a multiple-choice, essay, or another written format.

Defining performance assessments in this manner narrows our focus. For example, determining whether an individual can swim is too global to be evaluated through a performance assessment; determining whether a person can use the breaststroke or can stay afloat without assistance for five minutes is specific and thus would represent a performance assessment. To take another example, determining whether a student is more likely to listen to jazz or rap would not be a performance assessment because one response is no more appropriate than another. Narrowing our focus in this way does not imply that observing general behaviors is inappropriate or that providing students with experiences for which there is no correct or preferred solution should be avoided. Our definition of performance assessments is restricted so as to focus on procedures other than written tests to which educational measurement principles can be readily applied.

Categories of Performance Assessments

Performance assessments can be categorized in several ways. This chapter contrasts performance assessments that measure a process versus a product, use simulated versus real settings, and depend on natural versus structured stimuli.

Process versus Product Measures.   A process is the procedure that a student uses to complete a task. A product is a tangible outcome that may be the result of completing a process. For example, the way in which an individual uses woodworking tools to build a piece of furniture would be a process; the piece of furniture resulting from working with the tools would be the product. Generally, a performance assessment is concerned with only the process or only the product, or at least emphasizes one over the other. For instance, the completed watercolor might be assessed, but not the student's technique in producing the painting.

Simulated versus Real Settings.   Many performance assessments represent simulations because the real situations are too expensive or dangerous to use, unavailable, or impractical for other reasons. Some simulations are so realistic that they unquestionably represent adequate substitutes for the real thing. Sophisticated flight simulators train and examine new pilots so thoroughly that the student pilots can safely pilot basic aircraft solo without prior in-flight experience.

Performance assessments in the classroom often depend on simulations. The realism of the simulation may represent an important quality of the performance assessment or nothing more significant than superficial appearance. The need for realism must be judged in light of the reason for giving the assessment. For instance, if the principles that affect stock prices are being taught, a performance assessment need not have any consequences associated with students' investing wisely or poorly. Although the assessment may seem more realistic and exciting if the exchange of money is simulated, doing so would have little benefit or might even hamper the teacher's ability to determine whether students know what factors influence stock prices. On the other hand, including information in the simulation about changes in interest rates and the price of bonds would represent important aspects of the assessment, because these significantly affect the price of stock.

Authentic assessments place considerable emphasis on realism, simulated or otherwise. As with any performance assessment, however, realism must go beyond appearances. Having an assessment look real is not sufficient to make an assessment authentic. The appearance of realism may not even be necessary. Instead, an authentic assessment must incorporate all conditions relevant to the realistic use of the assessed knowledge.

Natural versus Structured Stimuli. A stimulus is natural when it occurs without the intervention of the observer. For instance, a student's social skills are typically evaluated without prompts. In some situations, however, a stimulus may be structured to ensure that the behavior being evaluated occurs or occurs in a particular setting. Examples of structured stimuli include asking a student to prepare and deliver a speech, perform a lab experiment, or read aloud.

Natural stimuli facilitate observation of typical performance, whereas structured stimuli tend to elicit maximum performance. Therefore, natural stimuli are preferred for assessing personality traits, work habits, and willingness to follow prescribed procedures such as safety rules. Structured stimuli are needed to determine how well a student can explain a concept orally, write a paper, play a musical instrument, or perform other tasks.

Structuring the stimulus also ensures that the performance to be observed will occur. Observation time can be reduced by asking a student to do something rather than waiting for it to happen naturally. Structuring also helps determine whether the lack of a particular performance results because the student is avoiding a behavior in which he or she is not proficient or because the appropriate condition for eliciting that behavior has yet to occur.

Advantages of Performance Assessments

The most significant advantage of performance assessments is that they allow evaluation of skills that cannot be assessed by written tests. As we have noted, many skills fall into this category because they rely heavily on motor skills; such skills are involved in speech, writing, foreign language, science labs, music, art, and sports. Other skills can be measured only by performance assessments because of constraints posed by written tests; these skills, as mentioned earlier, are complex skills. A complex skill draws on previously learned information, concepts, and rules, and involves problems that can be solved in a variety of ways. A written test can measure students' understanding of grammar rules; however, a performance assessment must be used to determine whether students can apply these rules when writing. Parallel examples exist in every academic area. The learning of complex skills is often the ultimate justification of many subjects taught in school. Without performance assessments, proficiency with these skills generally cannot be evaluated.

A second basic advantage of performance assessments is their effect on instruction and learning. If, for example, you and I are learning grammar rules, the way in which we expect our grammar skills to be tested will probably influence what we learn. We will more likely be motivated to learn the difference between the active voice and passive voice if we anticipate being asked to make this distinction on a written test. We will learn to write in the active voice if our writing performance is also going to be assessed. Furthermore, our teacher is more likely to teach us how to write in the active voice if the performance assessment is part of the lesson plan. Our teacher may also be more likely to use performance assessments if the school district uses standardized tests that incorporate performance assessments to evaluate writing skills.

A third advantage is that performance assessments can be used to evaluate the process as well as the product. Whereas written tests (and portfolio assessments) focus on the product that results from performing the task, the focus of a performance assessment is often on the process a student uses to get to that product. Examples include observing how students formulate a hypothesis or techniques they use in a science lab. Observing the process is particularly important in diagnostic evaluations. If a student is having difficulty solving a math problem, an effective way to diagnosis the problem is for the teacher to watch the student work through the problem. This activity is a performance assessment.

Limitations of Performance Assessments

One major limitation of performance assessments is the considerable amount of time they require to administer. Although written tests are usually administered simultaneously to an entire class, performance assessments often must be administered to one student or to a small groups of students. This limitation makes it difficult to use performance assessments for measuring a substantial number of skills. Because administering performance assessments is time intensive, more efficient techniques, such as written tests, should be used when possible.

A second limitation of performance assessments is that the student responses often cannot be scored later. In particular, when a process rather than a product is being assessed, the observer has to score or record events as they happen. If a pertinent behavior goes unobserved, it goes unmeasured.

A third limitation pertains to scoring. Like that of essay tests, the scoring of performance assessments is susceptible to rater error. Bias, expectations, and inconsistent standards can easily cause teachers to interpret the same observation differently. As with essay tests, this problem can be controlled by developing a careful scoring plan.

A fourth limitation involves the inconsistencies in performance on alternative skills within the same domain. Will a student who can deliver a persuasive speech also be able to deliver an entertaining speech? Will a student who is able to create a demonstration of factors affecting electrical voltage also be able to demonstrate factors affecting amperage? Will an individual who can create a good short-answer test also be able to create a good essay test or a good performance assessment? Performance often does not generalize across alternative skills of a domain. The way to resolve this problem is to observe the student performing each task. However, doing so is often not possible because performance assessments are time-consuming to administer.

Performance Assessments in Standardized Tests

A standardized test is a test designed to be administered the same way even when administered by different individuals at different locations. Examples of standardized tests include many of the commercially developed aptitude and achievement tests as well as tests developed and mandated by states or school districts. Until quite recently, standardized achievement tests used multiple-choice items or other paper-and-pencil formats. Most standardized testing programs have now incorporated or sometimes converted entirely to performance assessments. As with many fundamental changes in education, using performance assessments with standardized tests brings significant good news and bad news. Let us look at some of the issues.

As with classroom assessments, standardized tests should include performance assessments because important skills in language, science, math and other basic content areas cannot be assessed using other formats. A traditional written test cannot determine whether students can write a letter to communicate a point of view, search the Internet for information, or use scientific procedures to compare physical properties of two compounds. Unless performance assessments are used, entire areas of the curriculum go unmeasured. Limiting standardized tests to traditional formats has important implications when these tests are used to certify student achievement or evaluate the effectiveness of instruction. As with classroom assessments, the content of standardized tests not only determines what we know about student achievement, but also influences the content of the curriculum itself.

The limitations of performance assessments also become particularly acute with standardized tests. Performance assessments are expensive to produce and to score. Unless the budget for standardized testing is increased, fewer skills can be assessed when performance assessments are used. In addition, the amount of time allocated to administering standardized tests is restricted. This time constraint, even more than the cost, limits the number of skills that can be assessed when performance assessments are used with standardized tests.

We have learned that limiting the amount of content sampled by a test raises an important question: Does that which we observed generalize to that which we were unable to observe? If the answer is no, then conclusions we make about each student's achievement would be different had a similar but different sample of content been included in the test. Because the number of observations is so limited when performance assessments are used with standardized tests, this issue of generalization is significant.

Research has shown that generalization is a serious problem. For example, Um (1995) investigated a statewide writing assessment being piloted in Florida. She found that the performance assessment would have to be increased to an impractical length to obtain an acceptable level of generalizability. When Um changed her analysis from individual students to the school as a whole, the results improved, because conclusions about all students in a particular school are based on more observations than are conclusions about each individual student. You may recall that one of the most effective ways to improve reliability or generalizability is to base assessments on more observations. The implication of Um's study is that a standardized test cannot, with confidence, use a performance assessment to certify the writing ability of an individual student, but a standardized test can use a performance assessment format to establish writing performance for the school as a whole.

Similarly, Yen (1997) examined a performance assessment administered annually in Maryland to help evaluate school effectiveness. Performance in this assessment is reported for each of five content areas (math, science, reading, writing, and language usage) along with overall performance. As is common practice, school performance is reported in terms of the percentage of students achieving above a cutoff previously established as an acceptable level. An important question is whether the performance observed on this assessment would generalize to a different sample of similar observations. Yen concluded that the enrollment in most elementary schools was too small to obtain the targeted precision for each of the five content areas. Sufficient precision was obtained when observations were combined across the five areas.

As with classroom tests, the performance assessment represents an important item format for standardized tests. Complex skills cannot be measured effectively with other formats. Evidence to date, however, suggests that performance assessments within standardized tests do not generalize adequately unless a large number of observations is involved. Ways to obtain a sufficiently large number of observations include using the performance assessment to evaluate all students in a large school as a group rather than to evaluate individual students. When performance assessments are used to evaluate multiple content areas, it may be necessary to evaluate school performance on the test as a whole rather than for individual content areas. The frequent assessment that occurs within the classroom makes it more likely that teachers can adequately use performance assessments to evaluate the achievement of individual students.

OPTIONS FOR SCORING PERFORMANCE ASSESSMENTS

As with essay tests, performance assessments can be scored analytically or holistically. With analytical scoring, the appropriateness of a student's response is judged on each of a series of attributes. Checklists and rating scales are used with analytical scoring. The scoring of many performance assessments, however, cannot be broken into distinct attributes. Instead, an overall or holistic judgment is made. Scoring rubrics are used to facilitate holistic scoring.

Scoring amounts to making a summary statement concerning a student's performance. This summary may, but does not need to, involve numbers. Although numbers are convenient, the actual descriptions provided by the checklist, rating scale, or scoring rubric are generally more useful than numbers generated through the scoring process. However, numbers are particularly helpful when summative evaluations are involved, such as when grades are to be assigned. With formative evaluations, the completed checklist, rating scale, or scoring rubric provides a framework for discussing results with students.

Anecdotal records, which are discussed in Chapter 11, can also be used to document a student's behavior and facilitate later feedback. Creating anecdotal records generally does not constitute scoring a performance assessment.

Checklists and Rating Scales

A checklist is a list of actions or descriptions; a participant or rater checks off items as the given behavior or outcome is observed. Checklists can be used in a variety of settings to establish the presence or absence of a series of conditions. They also help structure complex observations. We have noted that pilots use a preflight checklist to structure the complex observations that occur before takeoff. A checklist can similarly structure observations of a student within a performance assessment.

The checklist in Figure 12.1 is from part of an assessment of students learning to use a word processor. Students were provided both a disk and a printed copy of a short paper. Changes that the students were to make were handwritten on the paper copy. The checklist was used to observe each student's use of a word processor to make the

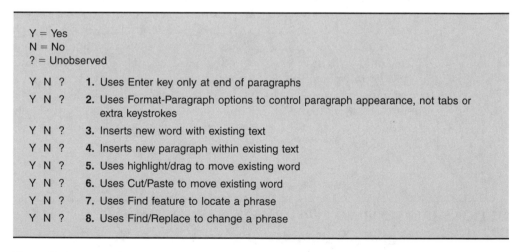

Figure 12.1
Partial checklist for scoring performance with a word-processing program

Figure 12.2
Illustration of a rating scale

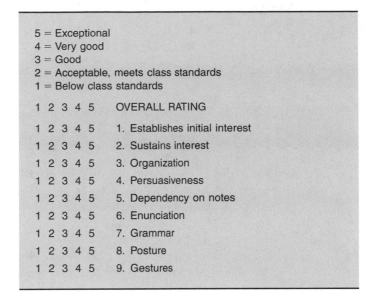

5 = Exceptional
4 = Very good
3 = Good
2 = Acceptable, meets class standards
1 = Below class standards

1 2 3 4 5   OVERALL RATING

1 2 3 4 5   1. Establishes initial interest

1 2 3 4 5   2. Sustains interest

1 2 3 4 5   3. Organization

1 2 3 4 5   4. Persuasiveness

1 2 3 4 5   5. Dependency on notes

1 2 3 4 5   6. Enunciation

1 2 3 4 5   7. Grammar

1 2 3 4 5   8. Posture

1 2 3 4 5   9. Gestures

required changes. Using a checklist is appropriate here because each attribute can be reported as satisfactory or unsatisfactory. Notice that an option is provided for recording a "did not observe."

Rating scales are similar to checklists, except they provide a scale or range of responses for each item. Figure 12.2 illustrates a series of rating scales. In this example, students are assigned a score between 1 and 5 on different qualities associated with delivering a speech.

Rating scales can assume a variety of forms. For instance, the scales in Figure 12.2 use words involving comparisons among students. Ratings such as "exceptional," "good," and "class standards" gain meaning through prior experience with other students. Instead of comparing students with each other, points on a rating scale can reference specific behaviors, as shown in Figure 12.3.

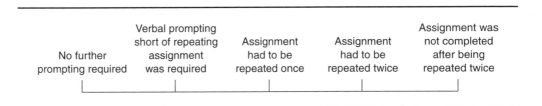

| No further prompting required | Verbal prompting short of repeating assignment was required | Assignment had to be repeated once | Assignment had to be repeated twice | Assignment was not completed after being repeated twice |

Figure 12.3
A scale for rating the amount of additional prompting required before the student completed an assigned task

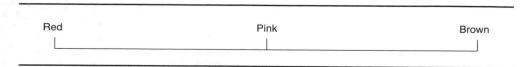

Figure 12.4
A scale for rating the color of meat at the center of the steak

Rating scales also can differ on how ratings are recorded. For example, the scales in Figure 12.2 are marked by circling the appropriate number. In contrast, a mark can be placed anywhere within the range of the scale in Figure 12.4.

With any rating scale, words used to describe the meaning of various points on the scale should be carefully chosen so that they have the same meaning to different raters. The words must also describe only one dimension or characteristic per scale. Note that in the scale shown in Figure 12.5, two dimensions are addressed. This scale should be divided into two separate scales, one concerned with the adequacy of the sanding and the other with how well the wood was cleaned.

Each rating scale should have four to seven divisions. Words should define the scale at least at its two extremes. Preferably, intermediate points within the scale, the midpoint in particular, should also be defined. If the same descriptions are used for a series of scales, numbers can be associated with descriptions and then used throughout the scales, as in Figure 12.2.

There is a tendency for raters to use only a portion of each scale, for example, to rate more individuals as above average than as below average. This practice negates the usefulness of part of the scale and reduces the reliability of scores. To minimize this problem, verbal descriptions used throughout the full range of a scale should depict plausible behaviors or levels of performance that actually do occur among the students being observed.

The efficiency of a checklist or rating scale has a major impact on how complex the performance assessment can be. The following characteristics improve efficiency:

■ The fewest words possible should be used within each item of the checklist or rating scale. Similarly, the fewest words possible should be used to define points on a rating scale. Minimizing the words increases the speed with which the items

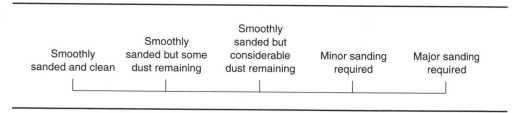

Figure 12.5
A scale that is incorrectly constructed because it rates two distinct qualities

can be read. Telegraphic phrases that represent incomplete sentences but clearly communicate ideas to the rater are appropriate. Using a redundant phrase in each item such as "the student will" is inappropriate.

■ Key nouns and verbs that indicate the essence of the quality being addressed should appear early within each item. This helps the practiced rater recognize each item within the checklist or rating scale simply by reading the first few words.

■ Items should be grouped in the order in which they are likely to be rated. When a process is evaluated, the order should correspond to the sequence in which behaviors are likely to be observed. When a product is evaluated, items of similar content or various stages of the evaluation should be grouped together.

■ All items should have the same polarity. For checklists, all items should describe either a desired quality or an undesired quality. For rating scales, the left end of scales should always describe either the most desired or the least desired performance.[1]

■ The checklist or rating scale should be easy to mark. For right-handed observers, a space for placing a check should be provided to the right of each item in the checklist. The rating scales, along with words used to define points on the scales, typically are listed vertically down the right side of the page. Any narrative used to describe what is being rated is located to the left of each scale. These relations are reversed for left-handed observers.

It is often necessary to write comments on the checklist or rating score to qualify ratings or to describe significant events. Writing comments on the back of the page slows down the rating process and may draw undesirable attention to the rating procedure. Designating a space for comments or simply using wide margins can solve this problem.

A numerical score for a student's performance can be obtained from a checklist by associating points with each item and then adding up the points associated with items for which the student received credit. With rating scales, a numerical score can be obtained by associating points with each scale, such as 1 through 5, and then summing these points across items. In many situations, such as discussing results with students, ratings on individual items are more informative than is a totaled score.

As illustrated in Figure 12.2, it is often useful to provide an overall or holistic rating in addition to ratings on more narrowly focused items. It is common to place the "overall" rating following the other items, although it is actually better to place such an item at the beginning. When placed at the end, overall ratings are heavily influenced by ratings on the preceding items. In essence they become averaged or totaled ratings, which if desired can be obtained by simply summing points across

---

[1]In contrast, when developing opinion questionnaires, one should reverse the polarities of some items so that respondents will carefully read each question before answering. Unlike questionnaires, a checklist or rating scale is used repeatedly by the same observer. Once experienced, the observer does not read through items sequentially or in great detail. Reversing the polarity of some items slows down the experienced observer and increases the risk of her or him marking the checklist incorrectly.

these items. If the overall rating is meant to be holistic, it is better to place it ahead of the other items.

Scoring Rubrics

Performance assessments sometimes must be scored holistically because it is not always possible to analyze performance into a series of separate attributes. Sometimes holistic scoring is used simply because it is faster than analytical scoring; it is quicker to obtain an overall impression than to make a series of judgments. Scoring rubrics are often used when performance is being holistically scored.

The term *scoring rubric* is sometimes used to reference any scoring plan associated with performance assessments, including checklists and rating scales. In this book, *scoring rubric* refers specifically to complex and holistic descriptions of performance.

In a way, a scoring rubric is like a rating scale. It consists of a scale with descriptions of performance that range from higher to lower. Unlike a rating scale, though, a scoring rubric addresses several qualities simultaneously within the same scale. Also, only one scoring rubric is used to score a student's performance, whereas a series of rating scales are used to collectively describe the student's performance.

A restaurant uses a scoring rubric, in essence, to describe how meat can be cooked. In the series of descriptions shown in Figure 12.6, notice how the same set of variables—in this case, color and temperature—is present at each level of the rating. Each variable changes from lower to higher as the overall rating changes from one end of the continuum to the other. This use of the same set of variables across the full range of the continuum is a common characteristic of scoring rubrics.

With performance assessments, a scoring rubric provides a series of holistic descriptions of performance. The rater observes the student's performance and then assigns the student to the category that best describes her or his performance.

Figure 12.7 illustrates a rubric for scoring writing samples. Notice, again, that the same set of variables is used across the range of the continuum. When developing a scoring rubric, it is important first to list the variables that are to be judged and then to establish specific descriptions of these characteristics for each point along the continuum.

These characteristics should fit together at each point. That is, it is not sufficient for each variable to change from lower to higher across the continuum. Instead, the

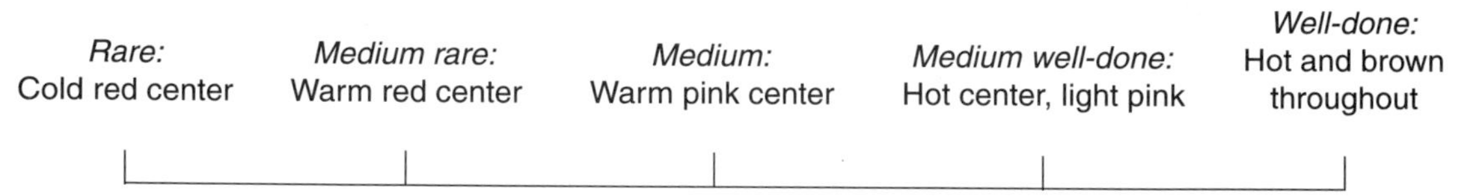

Figure 12.6
Descriptions of cooked meat

Writing is focused on the topic
Logical organization pattern
Ample supporting ideas or examples
Demonstrates sense of wholeness
Word choice is precise
Few errors in spelling
Various kinds of sentence structures used

Writing is focused on the topic
Organization pattern has some lapses
Supporting ideas or examples used
Demonstrates sense of wholeness
Word choice lacks some precision
Errors in spelling uncommon words
Various kinds of sentence structures used

Writing is generally focused on topic
Organizational pattern evident, with lapses
Occasional supporting idea or example
Demonstrates sense of wholeness
Word choice adequate
Errors in spelling mostly uncommon words
Different simple sentence structures used

Writing contains ideas extraneous to topic
Organization pattern attempted, with lapses
Supporting ideas not developed
May lack sense of wholeness
Word choice adequate but limited
Common words misspelled
Different simple sentence structures used

Writing slightly related to topic
Little evidence of organization pattern
Supporting ideas inadequate or illogical
Limited sense of wholeness
Word choice limited or immature
Common words frequently misspelled
Simple sentence structure used

Figure 12.7
Illustration of a rubric for scoring a writing sample

description of all variables should match what is typically seen in students perform-ing at a particular level. For instance, in the previous rubric describing how meat is cooked, meat that is light pink in the center will also be expected to have a hot tem-perature in the center. In Figure 12.7, a student who uses ample supporting ideas or examples (listed in the highest category of the rubric) will typically use words pre-cisely and exhibit few errors in spelling. A student who includes but does not de-velop supporting ideas (fourth category in the rubric) will also demonstrate an ade-quate but limited word choice and will misspell common words. If descriptions of variables at a particular point on the continuum represent a combination that is un-likely to be seen in students, the scoring rubric will be difficult to use and inconsis-tencies in scoring will increase.

Scoring rubrics make scoring of student performance more rapid than using a list of items within a checklist or a series of rating scales. Rubrics are also developed more quickly than comparable checklists and rating scales. A scoring rubric, however, tends to result in greater inconsistencies in scoring than occurs with a series of check-list items or rating scales. Lower consistency reduces the degree to which ratings of student performance will generalize. Therefore, scoring rubrics should be used for less critical ratings of student performance or in situations where performance must be scored holistically. When scoring rubrics are used in critical situations, consistency in scoring can be improved by averaging the scores assigned by two or more raters.

ACTIONS TO TAKE BEFORE CREATING A PERFORMANCE ASSESSMENT

The next chapter describes how to create performance assessments. Before beginning that discussion, it will be useful to identify other tasks that should be completed be-fore the performance assessment is produced. Performance assessments are a very valuable tool. They can assess skills that other techniques cannot assess, and these skills tend to represent the ultimate goals of instruction. At the same time, perform-ance assessments are our most expensive assessment tool. They should be imple-mented judiciously. Here are some strategies that can be useful in this regard.

Identify Authentic Tasks

Performance assessments should focus on authentic tasks. Here are qualities that make a task authentic:

- The task is an actual performance outcome that students are to achieve through your class. The task is not a convenient substitute of that performance or an in-direct indication that students have achieved that performance.
- The task requires students to draw on previously learned knowledge.
- The task clearly involves important themes and ideas associated with the content being taught.
- The task involves a real-world application of the content being taught.

This last point is often confusing. Involving real-world applications does not necessarily refer to activities in which students will directly participate later in life. Instead, real-world applications involve direct applications of knowledge that are highly relevant to situations outside the classroom. Authentic tasks in science, for instance, relate to real-world situations in which the science is applied or discussed. Likewise, authentic tasks in math relate to real-world situations in which mathematicians or other consumers of mathematics use math knowledge.

Identify Concise Goals That Will Be Assessed

Prior to creating a performance assessment, the goals to be assessed must be identified. Whereas a performance objective identifies the specific behavior, a goal is stated more broadly. Performance assessments normally are used to evaluate broader objectives or goals. An example of a performance objective is

Information: Identify qualities desired in short-answer items.

An example of a goal is

Produce a short-answer test.

A goal is often the equivalent of several objectives. Goals rather than performance objectives typically have to be used with performance assessments because the task cannot be meaningfully expressed as a series of specific behaviors. Alternatively, listing the full series of specific performances associated with the task may be impractical.

Nevertheless, to develop a performance assessment, a goal must be expressed in operational terms. The actual task to be performed may represent one of several options for operationally expressing the goal. The task that is selected must be a meaningful representation of the goal.

When constructing performance assessments, there is a temptation to increase realism by involving associated skills irrelevant to the goal being assessed. Including such skills, even when they increase realism, is equivalent to including irrelevant information in a written test item. This extraneous information tends to confuse students and, more important, confounds the assessment. When a student performs unsatisfactorily, the teacher cannot determine whether the student has yet to achieve the goal being assessed or simply is unable to work through the irrelevant material. When determining content to be included in a performance assessment, keep it free of irrelevant skills.

Determine Whether the Assessment Will Focus on Process or Product

As we have noted, a performance assessment is uniquely able to evaluate the process that a student uses as well as the product that results from completing the task. The process is particularly important for diagnostic evaluations when a teacher is trying to find out why a student is having difficulty. For some tasks, the way in which a student tackles the problem is more relevant to the instructional goal than is the specific solution the student derives.

Generally, the performance assessment focuses on either process or product, not both. The particular focus affects the directions given to students and the plan you must devise to score students' responses.

Tell Students What Will Be Expected of Them

One advantage of performance assessments is that you usually can tell students exactly what is on the test. This cannot be done with a written test. With performance assessments, telling students what they will be asked to do, right down to the actual scoring criteria, is a very effective way of communicating instructional goals. (This also is an effective way to help assure that your instruction is consistent with your goals!) Telling students what they are to do increases the likelihood that they will successfully perform the task. Given that performance assessments are time-consuming to administer, you can save yourself and your students considerable time by explaining what you expect them to accomplish. Performance assessments on which students have performed well are much more quickly scored than performance assessments with which students have had significant problems.

Determine That Students Have Mastered Prerequisite Skills

When used appropriately, performance assessments require students to integrate knowledge. Obviously, without knowledge of prerequisite information, concepts, and rules, students will not succeed with the performance assessment. Considerable time will be saved if prerequisite skills are identified and students' achievement of these skills is evaluated before the performance assessment is administered. Again, performance assessments on which students perform well are much more quickly scored.

SUMMARY

A performance assessment is the only way to measure many skills. A performance assessment is authentic when the performance to be observed consists of actual versus indirect indications that a student has achieved an instructional goal and involves a direct application of knowledge that is highly relevant to situations outside the classroom. Performance assessments can be used to evaluate a process or a product. They can assess behaviors resulting from natural or structured stimuli. Performance assessments are considerably more expensive than written tests to develop, administer, and score. They effectively communicate instructional goals to students, and can assess capabilities, including complex intellectual skills, that cannot be evaluated through written tests.

Performance assessments can be constructed with minimal planning if implications of the evaluation are limited. However, a performance assessment needs to be systematically developed when used to measure complex or critical outcomes of instruction or when used to assign grades. In such cases it is important to develop specifications for structuring a performance assessment and a list of qualities for evaluating the assessment.

Checklists, rating scales, and scoring rubrics facilitate judging and recording observations from performance assessments. Checklists are appropriate when the process or product can be broken into components that are judged to be present or absent, or adequate or inadequate. A scoring rubric is used when performance is to be scored holistically. Performance assessments usually are scored more quickly with scoring rubrics, although the resulting scores tend to have lower reliability than when checklists or rating scales are used. Scoring procedures should be constructed to facilitate the efficient use of these scoring instruments. Checklists, rating scales, and performance assessments should be formatted so that brief comments can be quickly inserted during observations. Usually, qualitative scoring of performance assessments is preferable, although numerical scores can be derived when needed, such as for assigning letter grades.

SOMETHING TO TRY

■ List three instructional goals for a class you might teach that would be assessed with a performance assessment. Do you believe the performance of students who achieved each of these goals would be considered authentic? Why or why not?

ADDITIONAL READING

Flexer, R. J., & Gerstner, E. A. (1993). *Dilemmas and issues for teachers developing performance assessments in mathematics.* (CSE Technical Report 364). Los Angeles: University of California, National Center for Research on Evaluation, Standards, and Student Testing. This case study examines issues related to implementing alternative assessments in the classroom, including logistics, changes in teachers' instructional and assessment practices, and effects on student learning. Articles such as this report are available from the CRESST web site.

Messick, S. (1994). The interplay of evidence and consequences in the validation of performance assessments. *Educational Researcher,* 23(2), 13–23. This article provides a detailed discussion of validity issues related to performance assessments. Topics addressed include the need for targeting the underlying capability when designing an assessment rather than focusing on students' outward performance. The article also discusses the role of structured assessments such as objectively scored tests.

Shavelson, R. J., Baxter, G. P., & Pine, J. (1992). Performance assessments: Political rhetoric and measurement reality. *Educational Researcher,* 21(4), 22–27. This article summarizes research studies by the authors related to performance assessments. Issues addressed include factors affecting student performance on the assessments, reliability of scores, and correlation of scores on performance assessments with traditional written tests. Their research involved fifth- and sixth-grade students participating in a special hands-on science curriculum.

Solano-Flores, G., Shavelson, R. J., Ruiz-Primo, M. A., Schultz, S. E., & Wiley, E. W. (1997). *On the development and scoring of classification and observation science performance assessments* (CSE Report 458). Los Angeles: University of California, National Center for Research on Evaluation, Standards, and Student Testing/Center for the Study of Evaluation (Available online at *http://www.cse.ucla.edu/CRESST/Reports/TECH458.pdf*). This report describes how to conceptualize hands-on performance assessments in science. The report also illustrates the problem performance assessments often have with generalizability across tasks; altering what students are asked to do changes which students perform well.

CHAPTER 13

Creating Performance Assessments

The previous chapter discussed considerations when using performance assessments, including options for scoring results. This chapter uses that information to describe how to create performance assessments. This creation involves three basic steps. First, the capability to be assessed is established. Then, the performance students will use to demonstrate proficiency with the capability is determined. Finally, a plan for scoring students' performance is created.

Performance assessments can be used to measure any type of capability, although their cost requires us to use them judiciously. When a performance assessment is used to measure information, a concept, or a rule, we will call it a single-task performance assessment. Single-task performance assessments are easy to set up, although they usually require more time to administer than do their written-test counterparts.

When a complex skill is involved, we will call the assessment a complex-task performance assessment because the student is being asked to apply a complex of information, concepts, and rules to solve a problem.

In this chapter, we will first talk through the three steps of developing a performance assessment. This discussion will be illustrated with the creation of a complex-task performance assessment. We then will use these three steps to create four additional performance assessments. Three of these are single-task performance assessments, and the final example is a complex-task assessment.

As we discuss the creation of performance assessments, it is useful to keep in mind considerations that should precede their development. As is true with instruction, our assessments of student performance must be goal driven. We also should limit performance assessments to tasks that are authentic; that is, these assessments should involve real-world applications of the content being taught. For each goal, we need to determine whether the focus of instruction and, likewise, the assessment is on the process or the resulting product. We need to establish for each goal what is expected of students, again both to guide instruction and to provide the basis for designing and scoring the assessment. Because of the relatively high cost of performance assessments, we should identify prerequisite skills that can be assessed through more efficient assessment techniques.

This chapter helps you achieve two skills:

- Recognize the three basic steps to producing a performance assessment
- Apply these steps to the creation of single-task and complex-task performance assessments

ESTABLISHING THE CAPABILITY TO BE ASSESSED

When creating a performance assessment, it is useful to structure the process using a *specification*, such as the one illustrated in Figure 13.1. The specification breaks the construction of a performance assessment into three major components, the first involving a specification of the capability to be assessed.

Specifying the capability to be assessed is the most fundamental step in creating a performance assessment. Throughout this book, a very deliberate distinction has been made between the student's capability and the student's performance. The capability is the student's knowledge, which we would like to assess but cannot assess directly, because we cannot see what another person knows or is thinking. Instead, we must identify a performance that provides an indication of the student's knowledge.

A performance assessment is used to observe this performance systematically. The selection of the performance to be observed must be based on a clear awareness of the capability being assessed. Identifying that capability helps us determine the type of behavior we should observe and how broadly our observation must generalize. For instance, if we are trying to learn whether a student can find the meaning of an unknown word without the help of others, we might ask the student to look up a few words in a dictionary. However, we may want our observations to generalize to both paper and electronic dictionaries and possibly to other resources. We must clearly establish the capabilities we are trying to assess and use this framework to control the content of our performance assessments.

With performance assessments, the capability is often expressed as a goal. Goals involve statements such as these:

Using commercial references, find the meaning of unknown words.

Produce a short-answer test.

Summarize the plot of a short story.

Calculate the volume of an irregularly shaped object.

Use ratios of area to solve common problems.

CAPABILITY TO BE ASSESSED

Goal to be assessed: Produce a short-answer test
    (Focus of goal is on formatting items within a test so as to facilitate easy reading and scoring. Attention also given to using appropriate header information, such as title, test directions, date, and student name.)

Type of capability involved: Complex skill

PERFORMANCE TO BE OBSERVED

Description of performance: Using previously developed short-answer items, the student will produce a copy-ready test.

Required materials: Previously developed short-answer items

Guidelines for administration: Other than making a brief reference to procedures discussed previously for producing a written test, provide no prompts beyond the instructions given below. Test can be hand-written as long as it is copy-ready.

Instructions to student:

- Use the previously developed items and produce a short-answer test.
- The test is to be ready for photocopying.
- Students will write answers directly on the test.

Which will be scored, process or product? Product

SCORING PLAN

Heading
___   Test title present (1 pt.)
___   Date of test provided (1 pt.)
___   Directions easy to understand (2 pts.)

Format of Items
___   Items numbered in left margin (1 pt.)
___   Items measuring similar content grouped together (2 pts.)
___   All material relevant to each item is accessible without turning page (2 pts.)

Space for Students' Answers
___   Blanks lined up vertically in wide margin to right of items (2 pts.)
___   Blanks numbered to match item number (1 pt.)
___   Blanks of equal length (2 pts.)
___   Blanks of sufficient size for answers (2 pts.)

Figure 13.1
Specification of a performance assessment related to producing a short-answer test

As noted in earlier chapters, goals may incorporate several performance objectives. Goals generally do not identify the specific behavior that will be observed but often represent a summary statement or a title for the capability we are trying to assess.

When creating a performance assessment, it may be necessary to elaborate on the goal in order to define the capability adequately. In Figure 13.1, for instance, simply stating that the student will "produce a short-answer test" does not adequately establish a target for creating our first performance assessment. Therefore additional detail is given parenthetically.

When establishing the capability to be assessed, we must also identify the type of knowledge involved. We know that the two basic types of knowledge are declarative and procedural. In this book, the term *information* is used to reference declarative knowledge and the terms *concept, rule,* and *complex skill* are used as the names for the subtypes of procedural knowledge. Identifying the type of knowledge involved is important, because different types of student performance are used to indicate whether a particular type of capability has been learned. Table 13.1 lists examples of each type of capability along with the type of performance that can be used to indicate achievement of these capabilities.

Only performance assessments are able to measure complex skills. To assess this type of capability, students must have the flexibility to use their choice of appropriate and previously learned information, concepts, and rules to solve the problem presented in the assessment. Written tests do not provide this flexibility and therefore are not useful for this purpose. Written tests can, however, measure information, concepts, and

Table 13.1
Types of performance used to assess the different categories of capabilities

Category	Examples of Goals	Performance Used to Assess Capability
Information	Name the vowels within the alphabet Recall the plot of important short stories	Ask students what they know
Concept	Identify triangles among previously unseen objects Identify the statement of the plot within descriptions of previously untold short stories	Ask students to classify diverse and previously unused illustrations as examples versus nonexamples of the concept
Rule	Using commercial references, find the meaning of unknown words Correctly use *ei* and *ie* when spelling unknown words	Provide students a relevant but previously unused example and ask them to apply the rule
Complex Skill	Read and then summarize the plot of a previously unseen short story Calculate the volume of a previously unseen irregularly shaped object	Ask students to generate solutions to a previously unused problem that requires use of the complex skill

rules, and should be used instead of performance assessments whenever possible because of their efficiency.

Performance assessments often have to be used regardless of a capability's category because of the characteristics of students or skills being evaluated. For example, written tests cannot be used to test young children or to test older students who have conditions that make written tests inappropriate. Many noncomplex skills require the use of performance assessments simply because they involve extensive motor skills. Examples include skills learned in music, art, sports, science labs, speech, and language acquisition.

Box 13.1 *Apply What You Are Learning*

Which of the following skills must be evaluated using a performance assessment?

1. Identifying characteristics of different elements within a periodic table
2. Running the 40-yard dash
3. Writing a play
4. Communicating orally in Spanish
5. Determining how individual words are used in a sentence (identifying a noun, verb, or adjective)
6. Knowing what is meant by the word *tardy*

Answers can be found at the end of the chapter.

ESTABLISHING THE PERFORMANCE TO BE OBSERVED

As illustrated in Figure 13.1, the second major component of a performance assessment specification establishes the performance to be observed. We divide this second component into five parts:

Description of performance is a brief narrative description of what we will see the student do. In some cases, particularly when the goal to be assessed is clearly stated, this description of performance is very similar or even identical to the goal. With many goals, however, any of a number of performances could be used in the performance assessment. For instance, either an electronic or book version of a dictionary might be used to see if students can find the meaning of unknown words. Or any of a number of tasks could be selected to see whether students can use ratios of area to solve common problems. This part of our specification establishes the specific behavior to be observed in the performance assessment.

Required materials identifies physical items that will be required in the performance assessment.

Guidelines for administration establish what the teacher must do in order to administer the performance assessment. This particular part of the specification also identifies prompts that can be provided students during the performance assessment.

Instructions to students state either verbatim or in outline form the directions that will be provided students at the beginning of the performance assessment.

Which will be scored, process or product? Here we simply establish whether the performance assessment will focus on a process or a product. This decision usually affects the performance to be observed, and certainly influences the scoring plan.

When establishing the performance to be observed, four issues should be considered.

1. *Does this performance assessment present a task relevant to the instructional goal?* As with all tests, to be valid, a performance assessment must involve an appropriate behavior. This means that the student performance to be observed must correspond to the goal being assessed, including the type of capability represented by the goal. Our illustration in Figure 13.1 involves producing a short-answer test, a capability that is a complex skill. Table 13.1 indicates that to assess complex skills, the student should be asked to generate a solution to a new problem that requires use of the targeted skill. In this case, the student should generate a short-answer test.

2. *Are the number and nature of qualities to be observed at one time sufficiently limited to allow accurate assessment?* It is possible to assess too many qualities. This is more of a concern when the focus of the performance assessment is on the student's process rather than on the product. If an assessment is too comprehensive and the behaviors being observed occur rapidly, it may not be possible to judge all behaviors simultaneously.

One technique for observing a complex process is to score it at its conclusion. This procedure is used in some competitive sports, such as gymnastics and diving. Other performances that can be rated at their conclusion include looking up a word in the dictionary, providing the correct change after a purchase, and parking a car. When ratings are assigned at the conclusion of the performance, the duration of the observation must be short so that the rater can remember exactly what occurred.

The number of qualities being observed is less critical when a product rather than a process is being scored. One way to reduce the number of qualities is to divide a task into a series of subtasks. In Figure 13.1, this was accomplished by having the items for the short-answer test developed at an earlier time. The present performance assessment is then limited to producing the short-answer test. By restricting the number of qualities being evaluated at one time, the evaluation becomes more focused. The assessment also becomes more efficient because time is not spent evaluating later tasks until prerequisite performances are achieved.

Often, the complexity of assessments can increase as you become more proficient with the rating procedures. You should initially use performance assessments that measure few qualities. If a complicated assessment must be used, you can improve your assessment skills by first rehearsing its administration.

3. *Are the conditions under which the performance assessment will occur clearly established?* Any measurement must occur under a controlled condition. Electrical measurements of an electronic component must occur in the presence of specified

voltages. The effects of a chemical on plants must be determined within controlled temperature and moisture conditions.

When preparing a performance assessment, particular care must be taken to ensure that the conditions under which the measurement is to occur have been clearly established. The specification illustrated in Figure 13.1 helps delineate conditions by indicating equipment and other items the student must use and by specifying instructions to the student.

With performance assessments, one can either wait for a student's behavior to occur naturally, without prompting, or one can structure the stimulus by telling the student what to do. When the stimulus is structured, the instructions to the student play the major role in specifying conditions. If a naturally occurring stimulus is to be used, the instructions to the observer must address the following issues:

- The conditions that must exist for the observation to begin or what conditions will cause the observation to begin

- How long the observation is to be or what condition will terminate the observation

- To complete the assessment, how many times a student must be observed

- During the observation, what actions by others and what circumstances nullify the assessment

4. *If the stimulus is structured, are instructions to the student concise and complete?* When the stimulus is structured, the instructions should cause proficient students to meet all the qualities listed in the scoring criteria. Professional judgment is used to determine the adequacy of instructions. In Figure 13.1, the instructions indicate that a short-answer test is to be produced using existing items, the test is to be ready for photocopying, and students will be writing their answers on the test. The directions do not specify how the test is to be formatted or that information is to be included with the test, such as a test title and date. The expectation is that an individual who is proficient at developing a test will do these things without being told. Experience with a performance assessment helps determine whether directions are adequate. If proficient students fail to meet some of the scoring criteria, the directions (or the scoring criteria) should be altered.

ESTABLISHING A PLAN FOR SCORING STUDENTS' PERFORMANCE

As illustrated in Figure 13.1, the third major component of a performance assessment specification establishes the scoring plan. The scoring plan may result in a numerical score, but often, particularly in classroom assessments, it produces a qualitative description of a student's performance. The scoring plan establishes what the teacher will observe within each student's performance.

The content of a scoring plan is heavily dependent of whether the process or product of a student's response is to be scored. Fitzpatrick and Morrison (1971) propose that the process should be scored if generally accepted procedures for completing the task have been taught and a student's departure from these procedures can be detected. On the other hand, the product should be scored if a variety of procedures are appropriate, particular procedures have not been explicitly taught, or the use of appropriate procedures cannot be ascertained by watching the student's performance. With respect to the illustration in Figure 13.1, the student's actual construction of the short-answer test will not be observed; however, characteristics that should be present in a copy-ready short-answer test have been established. The scoring of this performance assesment, therefore, focuses on the product rather than on the process.

Three issues should be considered when establishing a scoring plan.

1. *Is each quality to be measured directly observable?* A process or product can be measured only if it can be observed. When possible, qualities to be scored should be described so that no inference is required to determine that the quality being scored does in fact exist. Note that most of the descriptions given in the scoring criteria within Figure 13.1 are directly observable. One can determine, without inference, whether all blanks within the short-answer test are of equal size or whether the title of the test is present. Some inference is required, however, to determine whether the directions are easy to understand.

Box 13.2 *Apply What You Are Learning*

The following are descriptions used to judge the adequacy of student performance with various skills. The first five descriptions pertain to process assessments and the second five to product assessments. Within each group of five, three of the descriptions require inferences because the specified qualities are not directly observable. Therefore, those descriptions are less desirable as scoring criteria in a performance assessment. Which descriptions require an inference?

Process Assessments

1. The student demonstrates good sportsmanship.
2. The student uses fingertips to depress valves on the trumpet.
3. The student knows how to sand a piece of wood.
4. The student places a lighted match next to the burner before turning on the gas.
5. The student correctly views the needle on the voltage meter.

Product Assessments

1. The painted piece of wood is free of brush marks.
2. The chair is solidly constructed.
3. The steak is properly cooked.
4. The fingernails are free of dirt.
5. The student understands the directions.

Answers can be found at the end of the chapter.

2. *Does the scoring plan delineate essential qualities of a satisfactory perform-ance?* The importance of this characteristic to a scoring plan is obvious. Particularly with complex performance assessments, it is easy to accidentally exclude some essential qualities in the scoring plan. A way to reduce this problem is to ask a colleague to look at your performance assessment and independently list important qualities to be scored or at least provide feedback to your scoring criteria.

3. *Will the scoring plan result in different observers' assigning similar scores to a student's performance?* Once the desired characteristics of a performance are established, the scoring plan should result in independent observers' giving consistent ratings to a particular performance.

ADDITIONAL EXAMPLES OF CREATING PERFORMANCE ASSESSMENTS

The preceding sections divided the creating of a performance assessment specification into three basic steps:

1. Establishing the capability to be assessed
2. Establishing the performance to be observed
3. Establishing procedures for scoring the performance

These three steps were illustrated with a performance assessment that involved production of a short-answer test. In this section, these three steps are used to create three single-task and one complex-task performance assessment. Recall that a single-task assessment is used to measure knowledge of information, concepts, and rules. A complex-task performance assessment involves the measurement of complex skills.

Both single-task and complex-task performance assessments are formal assessments in that they are created before they are used. In contrast, the teacher's large number of informal assessments involve casual observations and oral questions. Although informal assessments are (or should be) systematically planned, they are improvised as instruction progresses.

When complex-task measures are involved, the teacher generally has no choice but to write out the full specification for the performance assessment. As illustrated in Figure 13.1, this specification includes listing a description of the performance, required materials, and guidelines for administration, along with the scoring plan. There is too much involved with the assessment of complex skills to develop the performance assessment without written specifications.

With single-task measures, these same specifications can often be devised mentally and not written out. Nonetheless, the teacher should probably formally state the goal to be assessed and prepare a formal, albeit brief, scoring plan. In the following examples of performance assessments, we will write out the entire specification to facilitate discussion. However, a teacher will typically need to develop full written specifications only when complex-task performance assessments are involved.

Example 1: Identifying Tense of a Verb within a Spoken Sentence

Capability to Be Measured.   As Figure 13.2 indicates, the goal to be measured by this performance assessment is identifying the tense of a verb within a spoken sentence. In this assessment, students listen to an orally stated sentence and then identify the tense of a verb in the sentence. The capability is a concept. According to

Figure 13.2

Specification of a performance assessment related to identifying verb tense

CAPABILITY TO BE ASSESSED

Goal to be assessed: Identifying tense of a verb within a spoken sentence

Type of capability involved: Concept

PERFORMANCE TO BE OBSERVED

Description of performance: Student indicates whether verb in sentence is past, present, or future tense. Sentence does not include an infinitive or gerund. Sentence can involve past or future perfect tense. Sentence presented orally without visual cues. Verb within sentence identified to student.

Required materials: Cue cards for teacher from which sentences are read.

Guidelines for administration: Administer 10 sentences in random order, two each representing past, past perfect, present, future, and future perfect tense. Name but do not provide the meaning of the five verb tenses. Sentences can be reread when necessary.

Instructions to student:

• At beginning of assessment, tell student that you will read some sentences and ask the student to name the tense of the verb.

• After reading each sentence, restate the verb and ask the student what tense it is.

Which will be scored, process or product? Product

SCORING PLAN

Student correctly identified the verb tense (Yes or No)

Table 13.1, this type of capability can be assessed by asking students to distinguish between examples versus nonexamples of a particular verb tense. Alternatively, as will be done here, students can be asked to classify examples according to verb tense. Either way, the examples should involve illustrations the student has not used previously. (Were students asked to recall their own illustrations of verb tense, the performance assessment would be testing information rather than a concept. The choice of task that the performance assessment asks students to perform is always a critical decision.)

Performance to Be Observed.   Because this is a single-task performance assessment, this part of the specification probably could be developed without writing it out. Figure 13.2, however, illustrates some of the qualities that need to be thought through. For instance, should verb forms such as infinitives and gerunds be included in a sentence? How many different sentences should be used with each student? May the student be told the names of the verb tenses? May the meaning of the various tenses be told?

Notice that the teacher will be reading the sentences from a set of cue cards. Given the number of factors to be considered, writing out sentences prior to the performance assessment will make its administration easier and more consistent with the specification.

In this performance assessment, the product rather than the process will be scored. The assessment is examining whether students recognize the appropriate tense, not the logic they apply to make their determination.

Scoring Plan.   The scoring plan is very simple, consisting of a one-item checklist. For each sentence, the teacher simply determines whether the student identified the appropriate verb tense. This scoring plan appropriately involves a directly observable event: The student states the tense of the verb. Also, different observers who are knowledgeable about verb tense will similarly score each student's performance.

This skill could also be assessed by a written test. After reading each sentence, the student would specify the verb tense. Short-answer, multiple-choice, or alternate-choice formats could be used. By orally stating the sentences, this performance assessment involves listening rather than reading skills. As with many single-task performance assessments, this one can be administered simultaneously to a number of students, with students writing their responses on paper rather than responding orally.

Example 2: Telling Time Using an Analog Clock

Capability to Be Assessed.   Figure 13.3 illustrates the specification for this performance assessment. The goal being assessed is telling time using an analog (versus digital) clock. The capability is a rule, because the student can apply the same procedural knowledge to tell the time in each situation. Hence, this capability can be assessed by providing students previously unused examples of a clock face and asking them to state the time.

Performance to Be Observed.   The student looks at the clock face and states the time. As with most single-task performance assessments, this assessment involves

Figure 13.3
Specification of a performance assessment related to telling time

CAPABILITY TO BE ASSESSED

Goal to be assessed: Tell time using an analog clock

Type of capability involved: Rule

PERFORMANCE TO BE OBSERVED

Description of performance: Student views the face of an analog clock and states the displayed time

Required materials: Clock face with movable hour and minute hands

Guidelines for administration: Use 8 different time settings, two times with the minute hand within each of the quarter hours. Vary the hour hand through its full range. The minute and hour hands should be distinctly visible in all settings.

Instructions to student:

• Say to the student, "What time does this clock show?"

Which will be scored, process or product? Product

SCORING PLAN

Time stated by student is correct within one minute.

some details that need to be addressed prior to its use with students. For instance, to help assure that observations will generalize, eight different time settings are used, with the minute hand presented within each of the quarter hours. Also, only times are used for which the minute and hour hands are visually separate.

The specification is for a physical clock with movable hands. Alternatively, clock faces drawn on cards should work. This particular performance assessment can be administered simultaneously to a group of students. It could be replaced with a written test in which students view the pictures of clock faces and indicate the displayed times.

In this performance assessment, the product rather than the process will be scored, as somewhat different but acceptable procedures might be used to derive time from the clock display. The correctness of each student's procedure is determined from the outcome or product of that procedure.

Scoring Plan.   Figure 13.3 indicates that a one-item checklist is used to score a student's response. The scoring plan specifies that an answer within one minute of the displayed time is scored as correct.

Example 3: Showing How to Phone the Police from Home in an Emergency

Capability to Be Assessed.   This example (Figure 13.4) involves demonstrating how to use the phone to call the police in an emergency. Unlike the other examples, this skill involves declarative knowledge, or what in this book we are calling information. This particular skill requires the student to restate what he or she can do. No application of a concept or rule to a new situation is involved. Instead, the student recalls what is to be done.

Performance to Be Observed.   With this skill, the important performance is the immediate dialing of the police emergency number. The specification in Figure 13.4 indicates that the phone used is to be similar to what the student would use at home. At the beginning of the assessment, the phone is some distance from the student but the student is aware of its presence. Once the emergency situation is conveyed to the student, no further prompts are provided.

With this performance assessment, the process rather than the product is scored. The police are not actually contacted; therefore, the teacher is not focusing on the product. Students are being tested to determine whether they follow a specifically taught procedure.

Scoring Plan.   Figure 13.4 shows the rating scales used to score students' performance. A checklist could have been used to indicate whether or not students adequately met the criteria. The rating scales allow the observer to specify the degree to which the criteria are met.

A scoring rubric is not appropriate here. In a scoring rubric, several levels of a holistic description are established. With this performance assessment, the criteria can be scored separately. For instance, a student might promptly go to the phone (a desirable behavior), but then dial the emergency number before removing the handset (an undesirable behavior).

The rating scales in Figure 13.4 include numbers. The use of numbers is not necessary, although numbers can expedite recording the observed performance. As is often the case with performance assessments, scores from this particular assessment provide a criterion-referenced interpretation. (Recall that criterion-referenced interpretations indicate what a student can or cannot do.) Using numbers to score this assessment does not facilitate or detract from its being criterion-referenced. On the other hand, were the numbers recorded and the descriptions associated with the numbers removed, the numbers by themselves would not be interpretable.

CAPABILITY TO BE ASSESSED

Goal to be assessed: Demonstrate how to use the phone to call the police in an emergency

Type of capability involved: Information

PERFORMANCE TO BE OBSERVED

Description of performance: Student shows how to dial the emergency number used for contacting the local police agency

Required materials: A disconnected phone, similar to what the student has access to at home, to use for prop

Guidelines for administration: The assessment begins with the telephone clearly visible but approximately 10 feet away from the student. Student is to be aware of the phone's presence. Instructions are to be clearly stated to the student but not repeated. No additional cues are to be provided.

Instructions to student:

• Using the phone in this room, show how you would call the police in an emergency.

• Do this right now.

Which will be scored, process or product? Process

SCORING PLAN

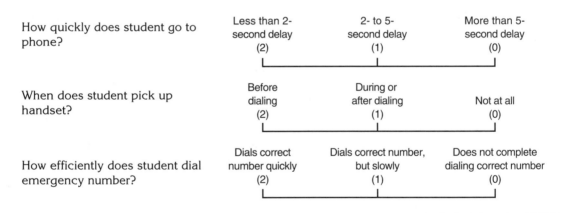

Figure 13.4
Specification of performance assessment related to using the phone to report a fire at home

Example 4: Using Ratios of Area to Solve Common Problems

Capability to Be Assessed.   The last example involves using ratios of area to solve common problems. To assess this skill, students might be asked to compute the area of a field to be planted with seed and, using directions provided with the seed, to determine how many packages of seed are needed to plant the entire field. Alternatively, students might be asked to use information provided on a paint can to determine how many cans are required to paint the interior walls of several rooms. In each case, students would not be told that they need to calculate areas or that a ratio of areas must be determined in order to solve the problem.

A third way to assess this skill, as illustrated in Figure 13.5, is to ask students to create a gauge for measuring rain to the nearest 0.1 inch. A problem with measuring rain is that high accuracy is usually required; in this case, within 0.1 inch. The solution to this problem is to collect rain using an object with a relatively large area—in this case a funnel—and to let the rain flow into an object with a relatively small area—a tall glass cylinder such as may be found in most chemistry labs. The ratio of the areas of the funnel and glass cylinder is used to calibrate the cylinder. For instance, if the top of the funnel has 10 times the area of a cross section of the cylinder, then 1 inch of water in the cylinder corresponds to 0.1 inch of rain falling into the funnel.

Performance to Be Observed.   The capability being measured here is a complex skill. This is the one type of skill that only performance assessments can adequately measure. To demonstrate proficiency with a complex skill, the student must have flexibility with respect to applying previously learned information, concepts, and rules to solve the problem. With this and any complex skill, two students relying on somewhat or possibly quite different knowledge may both derive perfect solutions to the problem.

In this book, considerable importance has been given to matching the test item to the category of capability being measured. Had we asked students, for instance, to explain how they would construct a rain gauge, we provide students the option to recall from memory and state what they know. Such a test item would be measuring information, not a complex skill. Similarly, had we asked students to contrast the advantages of alternative ways of constructing a rain gauge, we again would have been asking students to recall what they know. Knowledge of information as well as concepts and rules is always essential, and likewise the assessment of these categories of knowledge is very important. However, the assessment of these categories with the exclusion of complex skills is a mistake. The assessment of complex skills requires the use of performance assessments in which students use previous knowledge to solve authentic problems.

As with any assessment, an important question is whether the observed performance will generalize to relevant performances that were not observed. The present performance assessment is trying to determine whether students can use ratios of area to solve common problems. Will our observations generalize? If students can satisfactorily use ratios of areas to calibrate a rain gauge, will they also be able to determine how much seed they need to plant a given field or how much paint they

CAPABILITY TO BE ASSESSED

Goal to be assessed: Use ratios of area to solve common problems

Type of capability involved: Complex skill

PERFORMANCE TO BE OBSERVED

Description of performance: The student creates a rain gauge by placing a funnel into a tall glass cylinder. The student calibrates the rain gauge by measuring the cross-sectional area of both the cylinder and top of the funnel, determining the ratio of their areas, and placing calibration marks on the cylinder accordingly.

Required materials: 12-inch ruler, funnel, tall and narrow non-graduated glass cylinder, paper, pencil, and transparent tape

Guidelines for administration: The required materials are to be placed on a table in front of the student such that it is obvious all of the materials are part of the assessment. Other than the instructions to the student that follow, no additional information is provided the student by the teacher. In response to questions by the student, the teacher may provide the formula for area within a circle. The teacher may also answer other questions not relevant to the goal being assessed.

Instructions to student:

- Use the funnel and glass cylinder to create a rain gauge.
- The rain is to fall through the funnel and collect in the cylinder.
- Calibrate your gauge so that it measures rainfall to the nearest tenth of an inch.
- Mark your calibrations on the paper. Use the tape to secure the paper to the cylinder.

Which will be scored, process or product? Process

SCORING PLAN

Area of cross section of cylinder	Computed with major error (more than 50% or not computed)	Computed with moderate error (20% to 50%)	Computed with minor error (10% to 20%)	Computed with no significant error (less than 10%)
Area of cross section of top of funnel	Computed with major error (more than 50% or not computed)	Computed with moderate error (20% to 50%)	Computed with minor error (10% to 20%)	Computed with no significant error (less than 10%)
Ratio of areas of funnel to cylinder is established, using whatever areas were computed[1]	Ratio is not computed	Ratio is computed with error that affects results by more than 10%	Ratio is computed with error that affects results by less than 10%	Ratio is computed with no error
Cylinder calibrated throughout its length, using whatever ratio of areas was computed[2]	Cylinder not calibrated	Measures differences in rainfall with less than 0.1 inch precision	Measures differences in rainfall with 0.1 inch precision	Measures absolute rainfall with 0.1 inch precision

[1]When computing ratios, use student's erroneous areas if errors were made in their computation.

[2]When calibrating cylinder, use student's erroneous ratio if error was made in its computation.

Figure 13.5

Specification of performance assessment related to using ratios of area to solve common problems should purchase to paint the interior walls of a house? Likewise, if we find that a student is unable to use ratios to calibrate the rain gauge, will this student also be unable to determine the required amount of seed or paint? We conceivably might answer this important question of generalizability by administering multiple assessments to assess students' ability to solve problems involving ratios, but would this be practical? Would we have sufficient time, given that other skills must also be assessed? The issue of generalizability is important, but it is also especially problematic with the assessment of complex skills.

Scoring Plan.   Satisfactorily completing this particular performance assessment results in a product; specifically, a calibrated rain gauge. The focus of the scoring plan for this assessment, however, is on the process. Can the student use ratios of area to calibrate the rain gauge?

The scoring plan shown in Figure 13.5 indicates that four steps within the process are examined, beginning with computing the areas for the funnel and cylinder and concluding with the calibration of the glass cylinder. Arguably, the rating scales focus on the product at various points within a student's solution of the problem, as opposed to the process the student is using. The scoring plan does, however, attend to the process of using ratios of areas to create the rain gauge rather than focusing on characteristics of the completed rain gauge.

The scoring plan appropriately uses qualities that are directly observable. The plan also attempts to delineate qualities essential to a satisfactory performance. The rating does not dictate how areas of the funnel and glass cylinder will be computed, but does stipulate that the process of producing the rain gauge will involve a ratio of areas that is appropriately determined. Each rating scale addresses a single dimension. Each scale is constructed so that different observers would likely assign similar ratings to a student's performance.

SUMMARY

The creation and scoring of a performance assessment is divided into three basic steps. First, one establishes the capability to be assessed. Although the assessment requires observation of each student's performance, that performance is used only to indicate the degree to which a student has achieved the targeted capability. Our knowledge of the capability being assessed guides our selection of observable student behaviors to be used in the performance assessment.

The category of capability is also very important. We have illustrated four categories. If the capability is declarative knowledge, we call the capability information. Procedural knowledge has been divided into three subcategories: concepts, rules, and complex skills. Table 13.1 provides examples of instructional goals involving these categories, along with types of performance that can be used to assess knowledge within each category.

The second step in developing a performance assessment is establishing the performance to be observed. This performance must be relevant to the capability being evaluated and must be practical in terms of the number and nature of qualities that must be scored. Conditions under which the performance will occur must be clear, and instructions to the student need to be concise and complete. A performance assessment specification helps guide the establishment of a performance that achieves these qualities. Specifications are illustrated in Figures 13.1 through 13.5.

The third step in developing a performance assessment is the creation of a scoring plan. This plan should involve qualities that are directly observable and that collectively represent the essential qualities of a satisfactory performance. The scoring plan should result in different observers' assigning similar scores to a student's performance. A scoring plan typically involves a checklist, rating scales, or a scoring rubric.

ANSWERS: APPLY WHAT YOU ARE LEARNING

13.1 Skills 2, 3, and 4 must be evaluated using a performance assessment. These skills can be assessed with written tests. Skill 2 requires a performance assessment because it involves significant physical activity. Communicating orally in Spanish (skill 4) cannot be assessed through writing. Speaking in a nonnative language also is a complex cognitive skill because it requires application of numerous, previously learned concepts and rules, and because many different strategies or dialogues provide a correct response. Skill 3, writing a play, similarly represents a complex skill. Skills 1, 5, and 6 can be evaluated using a written test. Skill 1 involves recall of information, skill 5 requires application of rules, and skill 6 pertains to a concept. With these skills, a written test should be used unless inappropriate for the abilities of the student.

13.2 Among the process descriptions, items 1, 3, and 5 require an inference about what is being observed. In contrast, the following alternatives directly would describe what is to be observed: *Item 1:* The student helps teammates score points. *Item 3:* The student sands the wood parallel to the grain. *Item 5:* The student views the voltage meter in a way that will eliminate parallax error. Among the product descriptions, items 2, 3, and 5 require inferences. Alternatives to these items include the following: Item 2: The chair supports 500 pounds. *Item 3:* The steak is pink in the center. *Item 5:* The broom was placed (as directed) in the closet.

SOMETHING TO TRY

■ Devise a performance assessment for assessing this instructional goal: Be able to determine the density of a solid object. (*Density* is defined here as an object's mass relative to water. An object with twice the mass of water would have a density of 2.0. Similarly, an object with half the mass of water would have a density of 0.5.) Using criteria given in this chapter, select a task that is authentic through which one can assess a student's achievement of this instructional objective.

■ Prepare a performance assessment for a class you might teach. Use the specification format illustrated in Figures 13.1 through 13.5.

ADDITIONAL READING

Berk, R. A. (Ed.). (1986). *Performance assessment: Methods and applications.* Baltimore, MD: Johns Hopkins University Press. This book includes several chapters on the development and use of performance assessments. Specific chapters discuss listening, speaking, and writing assessments.

Cartwright, C. A., & Cartwright, G. P. (1984). *Developing observation skills* (2nd ed.). New York: McGraw-Hill. Chapters 2 through 4 include examples of checklists, rating scales, and other techniques for recording observations during performance assessments, particularly at elementary grade levels.

Fitzpatrick, R., & Morrison, E. J. (1971). Performance and product evaluation. In R. L. Thorndike (Ed.), *Educational measurement* (2nd ed., pp. 237–270). Washington, DC: American Council on Education. This chapter discusses the development and production of performance assessments. Examples are provided in a variety of content areas. Issues such as the reality of simulations, reliability, validity, and cost factors are addressed.

Zigmond, N., Vallecorsa, A., & Silverman, R. (1983). Assessment for instructional planning in special education. Upper Saddle River, NJ: Prentice Hall. This book presents a 12-step process for developing, administering, and interpreting an assessment of individual students. The process is then illustrated in the areas of reading skills, written expression, and mathematics.

CHAPTER 14

Portfolios

In recent years, portfolios have become widely used in many elementary and secondary schools. In some classrooms, they have become the only procedure for formally assessing students.

The practice of developing a portfolio comes from professions such as architecture, advertising, art, photography, and journalism. In these professions, a person assembles a portfolio containing examples of work to be shown to prospective clients and employers. The portfolio generally includes the person's best work. The content of the portfolio, however, must also be responsive to the interests and needs of the client or employer.

A student's portfolio also contains samples of work. Within guidelines established by the teacher, the student typically selects the material to be included. As with professional portfolios, this material tends to represent the student's best work. Usually, the material is placed in an expandable file folder that is maintained for each student. This portfolio becomes the basis on which the teacher and student collaboratively assess the student's achievement.

Many characteristics of portfolios match qualities often sought in education. For example, the preparation and evaluation of a portfolio emphasize the performance of the individual student. A portfolio also focuses on the accomplishments of the student, with particular emphasis on the student's best work. The evaluation of a student's work is collaborative in that it involves both the student and teacher.

Some characteristics of student portfolios are fundamentally different from those of portfolios prepared for prospective clients or employers. For instance, professional portfolios are ultimately evaluated by clients and employers, not by the person who developed the portfolio. In the classroom, the teacher and student develop and evaluate the portfolio. The teacher and student must assume a fuller responsibility for determining the appropriateness of the portfolio's content and also for scoring the content. Validity and generalizability are crucial issues within this responsibility.

Professional and student portfolios also differ with respect to their roles. Professional portfolios emphasize summative evaluations, whereas student portfolios often emphasize formative evaluations. That is, with student portfolios, emphasis is given to determining what instruction should occur next. To play this formative role, student portfolios must be evaluated frequently and they must contain more detailed examples of work than are required for summative evaluations.

This chapter helps you achieve two skills related to student portfolios:

- Recognize characteristics of portfolios when used for student assessment
- Become familiar with procedures for designing portfolios

CHARACTERISTICS OF PORTFOLIOS

As with any assessment technique, the characteristics of student portfolios include both advantages and limitations. Some of these advantages and limitations are unique to portfolios. Because portfolios represent a relatively new approach to assessing students and because their popularity has grown rapidly in recent years, their use in the classroom is sometimes accepted without critical evaluation. Ignoring significant limitations then causes critics to reject portfolios as a useful tool for assessing students. As we review some of the main characteristics of portfolios, it is important to keep a balanced perspective. We will observe that portfolios represent a useful assessment technique when their unique advantages are relevant to the teacher's instructional goals. However, their limitations must also be addressed. Because of these limitations, portfolios often must be supplemented with other formal, and certainly with many informal, assessments of student achievement. We will discuss the advantages and limitations of portfolios in the context of seven qualities.

Adaptable to Individualized Instructional Goals

Portfolios can be easily adapted to the instructional goals of individual students because each student prepares a separate portfolio and the teacher reviews the portfolio with the individual student. Written tests and performance assessments, in contrast, are more difficult to individualize.

Written tests often involve a common set of items administered simultaneously to a group of students. Even when instruction is individually paced, a common or similar form of the written test is administered to each student. Sometimes written tests are adapted to individuals, such as tests administered by computer. Such adaptive tests, however, usually involve different subsets of test items common to all students.

Portfolios can be totally individualized. Each portfolio can be responsive to unique instructional goals established for the particular student. Individualizing portfolios usually pertains more to how rather than to what instructional goals are being assessed. For example, students who are learning writing skills typically share common instructional goals, although the specific level of performance each student is expected to achieve and the writings each student creates may vary widely. Portfolios can easily accommodate these differences, whereas other assessments, particularly objectively scored tests, often cannot.

Focus on Assessment of Products

A portfolio consists primarily of products representing samples of the student's work. Obviously, products are relevant to instructional goals. In writing, for example, instructional goals include being able to write essays, poems, letters, and other forms of communication. Products similarly are important outcomes in science, math, social studies, speech, art—virtually all academic disciplines.

The process by which a product is achieved, however, is also important. Sometimes the process is more important than the product. The teacher and student, when they review the products contained in a portfolio, usually cannot directly view the procedures that were used to produce the products; the process must be inferred. Even when a portfolio includes earlier drafts or versions of a product, someone reviewing the materials must infer the processes that joined each stage in the development of the final product. Changes in the process that led to changes in the product are usually not directly observed from the samples of work included in the portfolio. Portfolios provide a more direct assessment of student products than of the processes leading up to the product.

A student's process can be assessed by a variety of alternative techniques. Informal observations and questions are particularly useful, although, as noted in Chapter 11, informal assessments also have significant limitations. For example, they usually lack documentation and overestimate student achievement. Performance assessments represent a useful formal assessment technique for observing a student's process. Written tests can also measure aspects of the process a student is using. If portfolios are the only formal technique used to assess students' work, the teacher must remember that most judgments concerning the process a student is using are based on inferences rather than on direct observations.

Identify Students' Strengths Rather Than Weaknesses

Many formal assessments focus on students' mistakes rather than on their accomplishments. For example, marks made by a teacher on a written test usually identify errors. When a teacher hands back a multiple-choice test, most of the discussion concerns the incorrect answers. Perhaps one reason students do not look forward to taking tests is that the focus of results is on bad news—it is natural to avoid punishment.

Standardized tests also emphasize negatives. When criterion-referenced interpretations are used, standardized tests tend to focus on identifying skills in which students are deficient. With norm-referenced interpretations, scoring below average is perceived as more significant than is scoring above average, even though half the students taking the test would be expected to perform below the middle or average score.

Portfolios, on the other hand, emphasize student strengths rather than weaknesses. Students are encouraged to submit examples of their best work. Within this context, discussion easily focuses on what has been accomplished. A student's deficiencies are addressed in terms of new goals rather than in terms of inadequacies in current performance. Students usually enjoy producing portfolios more than taking tests, and this form of assessment tends to be a positive and constructive aspect of learning.

Two additional points are relevant here. First, portfolios do not necessarily have a monopoly on positive experiences within assessments. Although it is natural to emphasize the positive when using portfolios, a teacher has and can take advantage of the numerous opportunities within all formal and informal assessments to emphasize what students have achieved. As with portfolios, this encouragement must be specific and sincere. The student must perceive that the encouragement is relevant to her or his performance. Important errors need to be addressed; however, their relevance can be demonstrated by using them to plan instruction rather than presenting them merely as deficiencies in students' performance.

The second point pertains to the need for portfolios to be sensitive to errors. When students present their best work, they will avoid products that demonstrate problems. For example, a student will avoid using sentence structures or discussing an aspect of history that he or she does not understand. Carefully constructed written tests and performance assessments require a student to demonstrate proficiency with important skills. The content of a portfolio has to be similarly structured so that problems that a student is experiencing become apparent.

Actively Involve Students in the Evaluation Process

In professions that use portfolios, it is common for a teacher or mentor to help the student develop the portfolio. For example, the mentor of an aspiring artist, collaboratively with the student, will identify what the portfolio must contain and provide advice in selecting specific samples of work. Ultimately, however, the portfolio belongs to the student. It is evidence for prospective clients and employers of what the student—and not the mentor—can do. The aspiring artist must therefore be actively involved in the evaluation of products included in the portfolio.

A parallel situation exists when portfolios are used within the classroom. Student ownership is important to the process. The teacher provides guidelines and, in collaboration with the student, identifies goals to be met and the types of samples the portfolio will contain. The student is responsible for actually selecting the materials for inclusion. The teacher then helps the student evaluate the materials that are included.

Since the student owns the portfolio, the student as well as the teacher has continuous access to it, although the portfolio typically remains in the classroom. The student can show the portfolio to other students or to whomever he or she chooses. This approach to documenting student achievement contrasts noticeably with that of a teacher's maintaining a private grade book. The assessment process is more student centered and less teacher centered.

Communicate Student Achievement to Others

The purpose of professional portfolios is to communicate to others what a person can do. It is natural for prospective clients or employers to ask an individual for her or his portfolio, that is, for examples of previous work.

In a similar manner, student portfolios provide teachers with a useful framework for discussing students' progress with parents, counselors, and administrators. A student's portfolio contains examples of what the student is able to do. A portfolio is generally a more effective reference for discussing the student's progress than are examples of written quizzes and exams or scores on standardized tests.

As discussed later in this chapter, a student portfolio also contains a list of goals toward which the student is working, captions, such as notes provided by the student explaining the reason for including particular work in the portfolio, and evaluative comments by the student and teacher. All these elements can facilitate communication of the student's achievement to others.

The student can also use a portfolio to show others what he or she has achieved. Hebert (1992), principal of the Crow Island Elementary School in Winnetka, Illinois, describes how this is done each spring through a Portfolio Evening, when students discuss their portfolios with their parents. Prior to the evening, students review their portfolios, guided by questions such as

How has your writing changed since last September?

What do you know about numbers that you did not know in September?

What do you want to tell your parents about your portfolio?

How should you organize your portfolio to show your parents these things?

On the given evening, for about an hour, students sit individually with their parents and use the portfolio to describe what they have learned. The teacher circulates and highlights particularly important information for the parents.

Time Intensive

The preparation of a portfolio generally does not involve much additional time, since most of the material included in a portfolio would be prepared anyway. The periodic review of the portfolio is what can make the use of portfolios time intensive.

At scheduled intervals, the teacher and student review the portfolio. Typically, the teacher first examines a portfolio alone, then meets with the student to discuss the portfolio. Although time estimates vary, a common practice is to take about 30 minutes for the initial review and an additional 30 minutes to meet with the student. Therefore, approximately an hour per student is required each time portfolios are reviewed.

There are different views concerning the significant amount of time involved in this type of assessment. For example, in their book about the use of portfolio assessment in the teaching of reading and writing, Tierney, Carter, and Desal (1991) suggest that after a transitional period, the use of portfolios requires no additional time. According to these authors, the use of portfolios "involves a refocusing. Instead of doing a lot of group things or working out of a particular textbook or workbook, time can be allotted differently so that teachers are using that time to work with individuals, conferencing with individuals; maybe working with some small groups. It's a question of setting priorities differently and using the classroom time differently, more than it is taking more time" (pp. 7–8).

Moss and colleagues (1992) suggest that the use of portfolios "will clearly add to teachers' workloads. . . . Schools and districts interested in fostering the professionalization of teaching in this and other ways must seriously rethink the way teachers' workloads are structured. Disciplined inquiry and collaboration, both of which are essential to professional practice, require time" (pp. 19–20).

The amount of time associated with the use of portfolios depends largely on how often the teacher formally reviews portfolios with each student. At the elementary school level, it is reasonable to expect a total of 20 to 30 hours for each of these reviews. The amount of time would typically be greater at the secondary school level because of the nature of the content and the larger number of students. Teachers generally review portfolios individually with students every four to six weeks.

Frequent reviews of portfolios are preferable. A primary role of student portfolios—that is not a role of professional portfolios—is to determine what, in terms of instruction, should occur next. If this formative role is to be emphasized, four to six weeks between reviews represents an excessive time interval. If portfolios constitute the only formal assessment a teacher is using, reviews need to occur much more frequently, although that may be impractical. If, on the other hand, portfolios are used for general planning and other assessments are used for more detailed planning, a four- to six-week interval between portfolio reviews may be appropriate.

Reliability

As with any educational measure, reliability is important to portfolio assessments. Judgments of student achievement should be reasonably consistent where different teachers assess a student's work, or should different examples of work be included in the portfolio.

When portfolios are used to assess a student's writing skills, the student is usually responsible for selecting the samples of writing to be included in the portfolio and typically selects from among a number of papers. The teacher's judgment of that student's writing skills should not be affected by the particular sample of papers the student happened to select; otherwise, the teacher's judgment is being influenced by characteristics of the specific writing sample rather than by the student's proficiency with writing skills. Similarly, if two teachers agree on the criteria for scoring writing skills, they should assign the same scores to an individual student's portfolio; if they do not, it would suggest that characteristics of the teachers, separate from the student's writing skills, are influencing the judgment of each student's achievement. Similar illustrations can be drawn from any content area.

Little is known about how well judgments derived from portfolios generalize, perhaps because portfolios are a relatively new approach to assessing students. Other formal assessments, including written tests and even performance assessments, have a longer history within both classroom assessments and standardized testing programs.

The Rand Corporation (Koretz, McCaffrey, Klein, Bell, & Stecher, 1992) studied the reliability of portfolios used in a large assessment program. Their study involved a statewide program in Vermont that used portfolios to assess writing and math skills at the fourth- and eighth-grade levels. Results of the study raised some important concerns. Average reliability coefficients ranged from 0.33 to 0.43. In contrast, standardized performance assessments involving writing samples tend to have reliabilities greater than 0.70. Conventional standardized achievement tests usually have reliabilities near 0.90. These low portfolio reliabilities are of concern because, if the reliability coefficient is below 0.50, the performance of an individual student cannot be differentiated from the overall average performance of students (Kane, 1986). If the proficiency of a student cannot be distinguished from the average of the class, instruction cannot be meaningfully individualized.

The reliability of scores on a classroom assessment tends to be lower than that of scores on standardized assessments, largely because of the high amount of effort associated with developing and scoring standardized assessments. For example, in the Vermont assessment program, scoring criteria were established through extended discussions and teachers involved with scoring the portfolios were given special training. This level of preparation generally does not occur with classroom-level assessments.

Moss and other researchers (1992) examined the writing portfolios of ten high school students, which were being used for classroom assessments. As with the Vermont study, inter-rater reliabilities were very low. In their discussion of these low reliabilities, however, they pointed out that the use of independent raters to establish the reliability of portfolio scores might be inappropriate. With classroom assessments, the teacher, who generally has extensive knowledge about each student, scores portfolios. Unlike independent scorers, the teacher can use this knowledge to augment the scoring process. This, in turn, may improve consistency of ratings across different samples of work, or conceivably across ratings by different teachers, assuming these other teachers were similarly familiar with each student.

At this point, knowledge about the consistency of portfolio ratings is very limited. Current evidence indicates that the reliability of ratings may be low. Therefore, we need to be cautious when using portfolios to assess the achievement of individual students, particularly if the portfolios serve as the teacher's only formal assessment of student achievement.

DESIGNING STUDENT PORTFOLIOS

To some extent, the content of portfolios can be thought of as a series of performance assessments. To this extent the procedures for producing a performance assessment apply to designing portfolios; thus the design of student portfolios can build on procedures already discussed. Portfolios, however, allow students to choose the products upon which they will be evaluated. Portfolios also go beyond assessing students. They represent an instructional system and integrate student assessment into student learning. Because of their broader role, the design of portfolios depends heavily on how they are to be used.

Establish How the Portfolio Will Be Used

Because of the popularity of portfolios, it is fairly common to start placing student work into folders with the intent of implementing a portfolio system, but without really knowing what is to be done with all the material. This practice plays into one of the major weaknesses of portfolios; the substantial amount of time required for teachers to review portfolio contents. By first establishing how the portfolio will be used, one can restrict its contents to what is relevant and design its structure to facilitate its intended use.

A student's portfolio is potentially used for any of a variety of purposes. The more common purposes include the following:

■ Growth monitoring, in which portfolio content is used to document student progress toward goals or improvements in proficiency

■ Skill certification, in which the portfolio is used to establish which instructional goals the student has adequately accomplished

■ Evidence of best work, in which the portfolio contains a student's exemplary work and presents the highest level of proficiency the student has achieved with each goal

■ External assessment, in which the portfolio is used to establish student proficiency by agencies outside the classroom, such as the school, school district, or a state agency

■ Communication with parents, in which a portfolio may be taken home or even maintained at home to convey how the child is performing at school

The purpose of a portfolio should significantly affect its contents. For example, a portfolio used to monitor growth requires examples of work over time that substantiate growth toward various goals. A portfolio used for skill certification, in contrast, requires only work samples that establish the status with each goal. Prior work can be located elsewhere. A portfolio used to illustrate a student's best work also will contain only samples of work related to each goal.

When the purpose is clear, the content of a portfolio largely establishes itself. Designing a portfolio is much like planning for a meeting. When scheduling a meeting with another person, the purpose of that meeting dictates your preparation, including the supporting materials you bring along. You will be less effective in meetings when their purpose is unclear and you consequently come unprepared. The contents of a portfolio are supporting materials that will be used in your meeting or interaction with the student. Those materials will not be useful unless their content is driven by how they will be used in that meeting.

The purpose and content of portfolios used for external assessments is largely driven by the agency dictating their use. Particularly when the agency is the school or even the school district, the characteristics of the portfolio can be designed with local teacher input or negotiation. The content of portfolios used with external assessments has to be limited; however, a clear understanding of how the portfolios will be used is central to establishing the usefulness of their contents.

The content of portfolios used to communicate with parents also must be limited. Parents are not involved in the day-to-day happenings in the classroom and will be overwhelmed unless portfolio content is restricted. Again, the purpose must drive the content. Generally the purpose is to show the student's progress with particularly important skills. The portfolio may also guide parents into actions that help the child achieve particular goals. Parents' ability to understand the relevance of the student's work to a particular instructional goal strongly influences how parents will use the portfolio.

The portfolio is not simply a place to put students' work. It is an integral part of instruction that is used to facilitate assessment. The portfolio is most commonly used to prepare for meetings of student and teacher. A clear understanding of how the portfolio is to be used should drive its design and contents. A separate binder, or working portfolio, might be used for collecting all work, with appropriate samples of that work placed in the portfolio reviewed by the teacher, parent, or others. Some samples of work may be moved from one portfolio to another, as needs dictate. However, the clear understanding of each portfolio's use must control its content.

Center the Content of Portfolios on Instructional Goals

The instructional goals to be assessed constitute the second major factor driving portfolio design. The list of goals provides the framework for selecting and evaluating work samples. This list of goals specifies what the student is striving to achieve and indicates which skills the student should try to document through the portfolio. Similarly, the list of goals guides the teacher's and student's evaluation of the portfolio.

As discussed in previous chapters, goals are broader than performance objectives. A performance objective specifies the specific behavior that indicates that the student has obtained the capability being assessed. For instance, here is a performance objective:

Rule: Given the relative location of adjacent centers of low and high pressure in Earth's atmosphere, indicate the direction of the wind between these two centers.

Goals are stated more generally than objectives. An example of a goal would be

Understand the relation between atmospheric pressure and airflow.

Valencia (1990) names the following as examples of goals in reading:

Understanding the author's message

Learning new information from expository texts

Summarizing the plot of a story

Using word identification skills flexibly to construct meaning

Reading fluently

Exhibiting an interest and desire to read

A goal is often the equivalent of several objectives. Inferences are required to assess whether a student has achieved a goal. As with performance assessments, instructional goals rather than performance objectives are normally used with portfolios, in part because of the complexity of skills being assessed. Goals also are used with portfolios and performance assessments because they often provide a simpler and more manageable framework.

Within a portfolio, the list of goals should be placed in a prominent place, usually at the front, so that the student and teacher see them each time the portfolio is opened. *The goals must provide the basis for including each entry and all assessments.* To help focus attention, the list of goals can also be used as a log. Students can be asked to document in a space next to the relevant goal each sample of work they insert into the portfolio.

Translate Instructional Goals into Student Performance

As with written tests and performance assessments, portfolios do not directly measure student knowledge, but use student behaviors as an indication of what students know. Throughout this book, *capability* pertains to the knowledge we are trying to assess. We cannot see this capability because we cannot see what another person knows or is thinking. Therefore, we depend on a student's performance to provide an indication of the student's capability.

We also realize that there are different types of capabilities. Depending on the type of capability involved, different types of performance are particularly effective for assessing student knowledge. Psychologists organize knowledge into two basic types: declarative knowledge and procedural knowledge. In this book we have referred to declarative knowledge as information, and subdivide procedural knowledge into concepts, rules, and complex skills. Table 14.1 summarizes the types of performance we typically use to provide an indication of each type of knowledge.

Table 14.1
Types of performance used to assess the different capability categories

Category	Example of Goals	Performance Used to Assess Capability
Information	Recall the purpose of a science experiment	Ask students to state what they know
Concept	Recognize verbs within a sentence	Ask students to classify diverse and previously unused illustrations as examples versus nonexamples of the concept
Rule	Use the Internet to find the address and phone number of a business	Provide students a relevant but previously unused example and ask them to apply the rule
Complex Skill	Write an expository essay	Ask students to generate solutions to a previously unused problem that requires use of the complex skill

Although effectively used portfolios are an integral part of instruction and go beyond strictly assessing knowledge, the assessment components of portfolios can typically be thought of as a series of performance assessments. Our discussion concerning the design of performance assessments thus has direct relevance to the design of portfolios. In that discussion, the creation of a performance assessment was divided into three basic steps:

1. Establishing the capability to be assessed
2. Establishing the performance to be observed
3. Establishing procedures for scoring the performance

With portfolios and performance assessments, instructional goals must be examined in terms of the capabilities they represent. The nature of the capability must drive the type of performance used to assess students' knowledge. The products included in a portfolio are the outcomes of that performance. A scoring procedure must be established for each product. A checklist, rating scales, or a scoring rubric is commonly used to guide the scoring process.

Figure 14.1 illustrates a checklist used in a portfolio to score expository writing. This checklist is part of a cover sheet that accompanies each student's paper. Because expository writing is a complex skill, it is measured by asking students to generate solutions to a problem that requires use of the complex skill. In this case, students are asked to generate an expository essay. As with the assessment of all complex skills, students must be given flexibility in how they create this essay. As illustrated in Figure 14.1, the scoring plan references the characteristics that should be present within the essay, or whatever product students are expected to produce. As with performance assessments, portfolios can assess students' knowledge of information, concepts, and rules as well as complex skills.

Plan the Student into the Assessment Process

A major advantage of portfolios is that they actively involve students in the assessment process. Portfolios should be designed with this in mind.

The checklist within Figure 14.1 includes a place for students to assess their own performance. As with performance assessments, students are typically given the scoring plan prior to the assessment. With portfolios, the scoring plan helps guide the learning process and also allows students to assess their own knowledge. A problem with self-assessment is that some students do not have a basis for evaluating qualities included in the scoring plan. At the very least, though, the scoring plan structures learning. A more advanced student can assist another student, often to the benefit of both.

With portfolios, students can be planned into the assessment process in a variety of other ways. For instance, the cover sheet illustrated in Figure 14.1 includes a place for students to indicate strengths and problems experienced with writing the paper. The teacher's comments can be written after the teacher and student jointly establish the strengths of the paper and the appropriate focus for subsequent work.

Students also are actively involved with portfolios when they select products to be included. Although the criteria for including a product are established by the

Name _____ Date_____

Title of this paper: _____

_____

Expository Writing

	Self-Assessment	Teacher Assessment
Focus stays on the topic	Y ? N	Y ? N
Organization proceeds logically	Y ? N	Y ? N
Supporting ideas or examples are used	Y ? N	Y ? N
Sentences are complete except for deliberate fragments	Y ? N	Y ? N
Sentences have subject/verb agreement	Y ? N	Y ? N
Words with appropriate meaning are used	Y ? N	Y ? N
Words are correctly spelled	Y ? N	Y ? N

What I like best about this paper: _____

_____

_____

My greatest problem when writing this paper: _____

_____

_____

My teacher's comments on strengths of this paper: _____

_____

_____

My teacher's comments on where to place focus: _____

_____

Figure 14.1
Cover page for expository writing

teacher or by the teacher and student together, it is the student who applies the criteria. In addition, the student owns the portfolio, which is typically kept in the classroom, and has ready access to its contents. The student can and is encouraged to share the contents of the portfolio with others.

Students are actively involved when they provide annotations to support these products. They can use annotations to describe the process used to produce a product. For example, students can describe the process used to devise the main idea of a reading or they can explain how hypotheses were formed and conclusions drawn when performing a science experiment. The use of annotations can broaden the scope of portfolios, which are generally limited to product rather than process assessments—a significant limitation when importance is placed on the procedure or process students use to arrive at the product. Annotations can be written in the margins of papers, integrated within the body of text, or attached, like endnotes. As with any self-report, students, and older students in particular, may be influenced by what they think the teacher wants to hear. The quality of annotations also varies widely across students.

Figure 14.2 illustrates another way to involve students. These rating scales allow students to score the adequacy with which they implement good learning and work strategies. Specific behaviors included in the rating scales can change from day to day. The teacher and student together can establish the action that becomes the focus for the next day. The teacher can also convey agreement or disagreement with the student's ratings.

Take Steps to Make Review of Portfolios More Efficient

A major disadvantage of portfolios is that considerable time is required to review them and update students' records. This is particularly true in high school and often in middle schools, where subject matter and assessments are more complex and teachers work with a greater number of students. Often, changing classroom routines, for example, having students spend more time working individually or in small groups, can provide time to discuss evaluations with students. Such changes do not work equally well with all subject areas, nor with all students or all teachers. The bottom line is that portfolio assessments are generally time intensive. Whenever possible, steps should be taken to make the review of portfolios more efficient.

One strategy is to design portfolios and their review with efficiency in mind. Here are some techniques that can help. Place goal statements that guide the review at the front of each portfolio. If all portfolio content is not being included in a particular review, direct students to move products that are to be reviewed to the front. Alternatively, have students temporarily move material to be scored into an "active review" folder. A preprinted checklist, such as the one shown in Figure 14.1, or other scoring aid should be stapled by students to the front of each product so that it is immediately accessible. Similar products should be reviewed together, much as all students' responses to the same item are scored together when grading essay tests. (This strategy increases scoring reliability while reducing reading time.)

A second strategy to increase efficiency is to plan for success. When a student fails to meet standards, an additional review will be required unless the student's failure

Name _____ Date _____

What is most important for me to improve today?

Here Is How I Did Today

	Always	Usually	Sometimes	Never	Teacher Agrees
Follow directions without being reminded	★	☺	😐	☹	Y ? N

Today's best example:

	Always	Usually	Sometimes	Never	Teacher Agrees
Ask for help when needed	★	☺	😐	☹	Y ? N

Today's best example:

	Always	Usually	Sometimes	Never	Teacher Agrees
Keep working until finished with task	★	☺	😐	☹	Y ? N

Today's best example:

	Always	Usually	Sometimes	Never	Teacher Agrees
Do something nice for others	★	☺	😐	☹	Y ? N

Today's best example:

Here is what I am most proud I did today:

What is most important for me to improve tomorrow?

Figure 14.2
Behavior rating scales

is to be ignored. Also, portfolios with high-quality products require less time to review. Anything that will enhance the quality of products contained in portfolios will significantly increase the efficiency of their review. Techniques that will help include clearly communicating expectations to students by prominently displaying examples of good work that can serve as models, sharing with students the carefully constructed checklists or rating scales that will be used to score their work, and verbally stressing the importance and efficiency of good work. Another way to enhance the quality of work is to have advanced students monitor less advanced students and help them preview their portfolios.

Another strategy for reducing scoring time is to limit the number of goals that are assessed using portfolios. Portfolios can be used to assess almost any capability involving cognitive skills. Skills involving information, concepts, and rules, however, can often be assessed with conventional written tests. These tests are not authentic in the sense of being direct measures of targeted performance outcomes, but keep in mind that no test directly measures knowledge. All assessments are limited to being indicators of what students know. If portfolios were direct assessments of knowledge taught in schools, we would not be concerned with whether observed performance generalized to unobserved performance. Yet we need to be very concerned about the generalizability of portfolio assessments and performance assessments, as well as any educational measure. By depending in part on traditional written assessments and using portfolios or performance assessments with complex skills and other skills that can be assessed in no other way, we can improve the overall efficiency of assessment.

Commercial computer software is available to help manage portfolios. The features and cost of such software have to be evaluated in the context of local needs and resources. For more information you may look under Education using an Internet search engine such as Yahoo! or look through the CRESST or ERIC Assessment and Evaluation web sites.

In a college-level course that I teach concerned with classroom assessment, we depend heavily on portfolio assessments. Partly to increase efficiency, the portfolios are maintained on a computer and accessed through the Internet. Portfolios are established for projects rather than for students. That is, all students place in one portfolio their work related to one project. Approximately 25 portfolios are maintained for the same number of projects. All portfolios, including my reviews, are open to all members of the class. Personal information is sent directly to individual students using e-mail or face-to-face contacts. Software such as WebBoard or the forum feature within BlackBoard can be used to support electronic portfolios.

Use Multiple Observations to Increase Reliability

With portfolios, as with many classroom assessments, a teacher generally does not formally establish the reliability of scores. Doing so is usually impractical. On the other hand, a teacher can follow procedures that facilitate consistent observations. Two procedures are particularly appropriate with portfolios. The first, addressed earlier, involves carefully specifying the characteristics within students' work samples that are to be judged. This can be accomplished by developing a scoring plan for each goal, usually by devising a checklist, rating scales, or a scoring rubric. The second procedure involves applying this scoring procedure to multiple observations of student work.

The number of observations can be increased in a variety of ways. Students can be asked to include more samples of work or to submit diverse samples that demonstrate proficiency with an instructional goal. For instance, in reading, students can be asked to show that they can determine the message the author is trying to convey, not only in short stories, but also in a newspaper article or a poem. In science, students can be asked to demonstrate that pollution harms organisms by finding multiple news articles that describe the effects of pollution on diverse animals and plants. The number of observations can also be increased by having more than one person judge each student's work sample. The additional reviewer can be another teacher or even another student.

Each of these techniques increases the number of observations and, therefore, tends to improve the consistency with which portfolios are scored. Using all the techniques improves consistency more than using just one of the techniques. However, the single best technique is to base judgments of performance on diverse samples of work. Using diverse samples substantially improves the degree to which observations will generalize to other settings.

Because consistency improves when the number of observations is increased, judgments regarding a group of students are much more reliable than are judgments about individual students. Even though the reliability of judgments made about individual students can be quite low, portfolios can provide highly reliable judgments concerning the achievement of the class as a whole.

GUIDING STUDENTS' USE OF PORTFOLIOS

The validity of assessments, in part, depends on what a student includes in the portfolio. Students may vary in terms of the quality of work samples they include. Quality can vary both on whether it truly represents the student's best work and whether it allows assessment of the specific skills the teacher is trying to evaluate.

Moss, with others (1992), closely examined the work of ten students enrolled in a high school writing class, for which the teacher used portfolios to assess student achievement. The researchers examined the contents of both the students' portfolios and their comprehensive writing folders. The comprehensive folders contained all the writing that the students completed during the year. The researchers found that the work samples included in portfolios sometimes provided in-depth information concerning some qualities of the writing being assessed, but inadequate information about other qualities. In other cases, work samples provided a broader demonstration of the characteristics being assessed, but insufficient detail to detect changes in student performance with respect to individual characteristics. And in some cases, students failed to include samples of writing that the researchers judged to be their best work.

Professionals and students alike must be taught how to prepare a portfolio. Professionals such as architects, artists, and models are usually guided early on in the selection of materials to be included, learning to recognize the types of capabilities sought by prospective clients and employers, and how to select the best work to illustrate each of these capabilities. Students must be similarly guided. Otherwise, judgments of the student's achievement are influenced by the ability to develop the portfolio rather than by the degree to which the instructional goals have been achieved. For portfolios to be effective, the student must clearly understand the goals of instruction. The student must also understand the criteria that are to be used to score the portfolio. When the teacher reviews the portfolio with the student, the teacher should score the quality with which the portfolio is constructed as well as the quality of the work samples. Separate scores should be provided for the quality of the portfolio and for the quality of the work samples.

SUMMARY

Portfolios have become a widely used alternative for assessing student achievement. The concept of portfolios comes from professions in which portfolios are used to show examples of work to prospective clients and employers.

Student portfolios share some characteristics with their professional counterparts. For example, they are individualized, emphasize one's best work, and focus on products rather than on the process leading up to the products. Student and professional portfolios also have fundamental differences. Professional portfolios play a summative role, whereas student portfolios generally are used in formative evaluations. Others ultimately judge the content of professional portfolios, whereas the student and teacher judge student portfolios.

The use of portfolios to assess student achievement is time consuming. No additional time is associated with producing products to be included in the portfolio if producing these products is already part of the students' activities. The increased time involves regularly discussing portfolios with each student. Unless smaller samples of work are involved, portfolios are very time-consuming in the higher grades. Because of the amount of time involved, teachers generally review a portfolio with a student once every four to six weeks. This represents a particularly long interval when portfolios provide the basis for formative evaluations. It is best to supplement portfolio assessments with other formal and informal assessments.

The first step in designing portfolios is clearly establishing how they will be used. The content of portfolios is then based on the instructional goals they will be used to assess. As with performance assessments, these goals must be translated into student performance, that is, establishing the performance to be observed. Establishing the scoring procedures is also part of the portfolio's design. For portfolios to be effective, students must be designed into the assessment process as active partners. Generalizability of observations is a major concern with portfolio assessments. To minimize this problem, multiple and diverse products should be used to assess each instructional goal.

SOMETHING TO TRY

- ■ Many teachers, especially in early elementary grades, are using portfolios extensively, and often effectively. If the class includes practicing teachers, identify teachers who are currently using portfolios. Ask them to describe and, preferably, to show examples of their portfolios. Discuss with these teachers some of the issues presented in this chapter regarding advantages and limitations of portfolios. (Particularly because of the recent popularity of portfolios, there is a tendency for enthusiastic teachers to describe portfolios in positive but very general terms. Keep the discussion responsive to specific characteristics of portfolios.)

- ■ Individually (or with a small group) prepare a plan for scoring a portfolio in your academic area. The scoring plan should list the instructional goals that the portfolio is designed to assess. For each goal, a list of characteristics that would be used to judge each student's samples of work should be established. These characteristics could be developed as a checklist, rating scales, or a scoring rubric. This scoring plan should facilitate consistent scoring. That is, the checklist, rating scales, or scoring rubric should specify student characteristics that can be observed directly or involve only minimal inference. The scoring plan should involve judgments of multiple work samples. To facilitate generalizability, diverse samples of each student's work should be judged.

- ■ When portfolios are used, a teacher discusses each portfolio with the student approximately every four to six weeks. This represents a long interval if portfolios are being used in a formative as opposed to a summative role. For a class you might teach, list some specific ways to supplement these discussions with feedback from other formal and informal assessments.

ADDITIONAL READING

National Center for Research on Evaluation, Standards, and Student Testing. (1992). Portfolio assessment and high-technology videotape. Los Angeles. This 10-minute video illustrates the setup and use of classroom portfolios. The video and companion Guidebook for the Video Program are available from the CRESST web site or can be purchased from CRESST on CD-ROM. The Guidebook includes an annotated list of references concerned with alternative assessment.

Paris, S. G., & Ayres, L. R. (1994). *Becoming reflective students and teachers with portfolios and authentic assessment*. Washington, DC: American Psychological Association. This book describes advantages typically sought when portfolios are used in the classroom. It includes a number of illustrations of the types of forms students and teachers can use when assessing portfolio work.

Tierney, R. J., Carter, M. A., & Desal, L. E. (1991). *Portfolio assessment in the reading-writing classroom.* Norwood, MA: Christopher-Gordon. This book deals exclusively with the philosophy, development, and use of portfolios. The focus is on assessment of reading and writing, although ideas discussed in the book generalize fairly well to other content areas. The authors' illustrations throughout the book are particularly useful. An annotated bibliography concerning portfolios is included.

PART FOUR

Special Topics Related to the Assessment Process

CHAPTER 15

Questions for Guiding Student Assessments

The next three chapters address some special issues related to the assessment process in the classroom. Chapter 16 describes test-taking skills you can teach your students. Chapter 17 describes some ways that computers can be used to facilitate assessment. The present chapter poses four questions to guide the development and use of classroom assessments.

It may be helpful to identify what the present chapter does and does not do. What it *does not do* is introduce new material. What the present chapter *does do* is bring focus to four issues that are absolutely fundamental to any classroom assessment. Expressed as questions, these four issues are as follows:

- How will I interpret and use the assessment?
- What will I ask students to do in order to assess their knowledge?
- How will I know I measured the right thing?
- Will the student performance I observed generalize to that which I did not observe?

These four issues were introduced in the first part of the book. We presently reintroduce these issues because to do otherwise would make it easy to sideline these fundamental topics. Because these four issues are so critical to effective assessment, we will review their key points and also apply these points to material discussed in the more recent chapters. Discussion in the present chapter will be brief and to the point, with emphasis on application of what you have learned.

As you go through this chapter, try to clearly establish in your mind the four questions identified above. Failing to address these four questions substantially reduces and quite possibly renders useless the enormous amount of time you will spend on assessing your students. In contrast, being familiar with these key issues goes a long way toward helping you determine what your students know and what they do not know.

HOW WILL I INTERPRET AND USE THE ASSESSMENT?

As just noted, assessment consumes an enormous amount of time. Estimates suggest that typically more than 25% of a teacher's time is associated with planning, producing, administering, and finally using student assessments. For any effort consuming such a large portion of your time, you want to clearly establish early on in the process why you are doing it and how you are going to use the results.

We have learned that the basic use of assessment is to *evaluate* students. Recall that evaluation combines our measures of student performance with other information to establish the desirability and importance of what we have observed. Different types of evaluation commonly occur in the classroom. The choice of evaluation, that is, how we will use the results, is an important issue to be addressed prior to and during an assessment. Here are the four common types of evaluation we have identified, along with their purpose, when they occur, and the assessment techniques they typically used:

Preliminary evaluations

Purpose: To provide a quick but temporary determination of students' characteristics

When they occur: During the first ten days of school

Techniques used: Mostly informal observations and questions

Formative evaluations

Purpose: Determine what students have learned in order to plan instruction

When they occur: Continuously, during instruction

Techniques used: Mostly informal observations and questions; also, written and oral quizzes, classroom activities and performance assessments, homework, and portfolios

Diagnostic evaluations

Purpose: Identify problems that will prevent or are preventing a student from learning

When they occur: When difficulties in learning new knowledge are anticipated; or more typically, after difficulties in learning have been observed

Techniques used: Typically informal observations and questions; sometimes formal assessments such as a teacher's written test or a standardized test

Summative evaluations

Purpose: Certify what students have learned in order to assign grades, promote students, and refine instruction for next year

When they occur: At the conclusion of a unit of instruction

Techniques used: Mostly formal assessments, including written tests, performance assessments, projects, and portfolios

Let us focus on formative and summative evaluations; these occur most often. Because formative evaluations are used to decide what instruction should occur next, the assessments must be scored immediately in order to be useful. Assessments used for summative evaluations, however, do not have to be scored as quickly. They also can involve only a sampling of skills, since summative evaluations tend to provide overall judgments rather than decisions about every skill. Formative evaluations, in contrast, must be based on an assessment of every skill for which you are planning instruction.

Box 15.1 *Apply What You Are Learning*

The proposed outcomes for three different assessments are described here. If each of these assessments is to be used for a formative (rather than a summative) evaluation, which option, A or B, represents the better strategy for obtaining the assessment?

1. To determine whether chemistry students know the difference between an element and compound,

    A. use a quickly graded short quiz that asks students to classify examples of elements or compounds.

    B. include examples in a unit exam that students must classify as elements or compounds.

2. To determine whether computer-science students know how to enter a hyperlink in a web page,

    A. when reviewing their portfolios at two-week intervals, look for examples of hyperlinks.

    B. when informally observing web sites they are currently constructing, look for examples of hyperlinks.

3. To determine whether students are learning to spell important words,

    A. give the students a spelling test that you can score overnight.

    B. check whether these words are correctly spelled in a paper they turn in after the weekend.

Answers can be found at the end of the chapter.

The interpretation of an assessment influences how an assessment can be used. We learned that interpretation of student performance requires some kind of reference. In classroom assessments, we typically use these four references:

Ability-referenced   Answers how students are performing relative to what they are capable of doing. (Requires good measures of what students are capable of doing; their maximum possible performance.)

Growth-referenced	Answers how much students have changed or improved relative to what they were doing earlier. (Requires pre- and post-measures of performance that are highly reliable.)
Norm-referenced	Answers how well students are doing with respect to what is typical or reasonable. (To whom students are being compared must be clearly understood.)
Criterion-referenced	Answers what students can and cannot do. (Content domain that was assessed must be well defined)

Among these options, ability-referenced interpretations are definitely the weakest. The problem with an ability reference is that we seldom have a good measure of a student's maximum performance. (We may be aware of a student's "best observed" performance, but this usually does not establish that student's maximum possible performance.) Although it is common to make statements such as "If Tina would just try harder she would do better" or "Brian is doing about as well as he can," these statements represent ability-referenced interpretations of performance that are weak because they are hard to substantiate. Ability-referenced interpretations should always be avoided when the use of results has significant consequences.

Growth-, norm-, and criterion-referenced interpretations of a student's performance are all potentially useful. Each, however, requires a supporting condition, which is stated parenthetically in the list. For instance, a growth-referenced interpretation of student's performance requires pre- and post-measures of performance, both of which must be highly reliable.

Many people who interpret student performance have difficulty understanding what is meant by criterion-referenced interpretations. As noted earlier, to obtain a criterion-referenced interpretation the content domain "must be well defined." In essence, this means that the context in which a student's performance is described must establish what specifically it is the student can or cannot do. For instance, stating that a student can correctly apply spelling rules that involve words with *ie* and *ei* is criterion-referenced; it establishes what the student can do with respect to this well-defined content domain. On the other hand, stating that a student "is a good speller" or that the student "passed the spelling test" does not establish what the student can (or cannot) do. Therefore, those interpretations are not criterion-referenced. They also are not ability-, growth-, or norm-referenced; without a reference they are really not interpretable.

Box 15.2 *Apply What You Are Learning*

Here are seven interpretations. Using the options A through D, see if you can classify each interpretation as ability, growth, norm, or criterion-referenced. (*Hint:* Two of the seven interpretations involve two references and two other interpretations unfortunately involve no reference.)

    A. ability-referenced

    B. growth-referenced

C. norm-reference

D. criterion-referenced

1. In earlier papers placed in his portfolio, Jordan wrote paragraphs without clear topical sentences. Paragraphs within papers he recently placed in the portfolio almost always contain a clear topical sentence.

2. As I reviewed their portfolios, Denise is the most creative of the students in all of my art classes.

3. Andrea is very good in geography.

4. On the essay test, Craig correctly described the procedure a researcher must follow if employing the scientific method.

5. Based on the performance assessment, Stephanie demonstrated that she can make a hotel reservation using conversational French. To date, she is one of only six in the French class who has achieved this skill.

6. Based on a true–false test, Joshua demonstrated he can distinguish between imaginary versus non-imaginary numbers.

7. Cara has finally passed the statistics exam.

Answers can be found at the end of the chapter.

When an assessment is to be used for formative evaluations, criterion-referenced interpretations are generally best. That is because, from the teacher's perspective, it is easiest to determine what to do next when you know what students can or cannot do. Although of secondary importance, it is also useful to compare a student's performance to that of others to help establish what is typical and what is reasonable for that student. It is also helpful to have an idea of how much students are improving. Criterion-reference, however, will be the dominant interpretation with formative evaluations, but other references play a supportive role.

With summative evaluations, a norm-referenced interpretation usually is dominant. Summative evaluations tend to involve many skills, with few items used to measure performance on any one skill. Unlike criterion-referenced interpretations, norm-referenced interpretations can involve fairly broad, less well-defined content domains. However, with norm-referenced interpretations you need a good sense of to whom it is that you are comparing students' performance.

WHAT WILL I ASK STUDENTS TO DO IN ORDER TO ASSESS THEIR KNOWLEDGE?

What you will ask students to do obviously is a very important question. It is particularly important given that in almost all cases a student's performance is only an indication of what the student knows or is thinking. We cannot see students' knowledge.

Instead, we use the student's performance as just an indication of what students know.

We also understand that there are different types of knowledge. As a result, different types of performance serve as preferred indicators of these different types of knowledge.

The most basic categories of knowledge appear to be what psychologists call declarative and procedural knowledge. In this book we refer to declarative knowledge as *information*. Procedural knowledge is subdivided into what we are calling *discrimination, concepts, rules,* and *complex skills*. When you create an assessment, it is important to first identify the *type of knowledge* you are going to assess. Then you select the type of student performance that is appropriate for assessing that knowledge. Here are the types of performance that are good indicators for each of the various types of knowledge

Type of Knowledge	*Type of Performance Used in Assessment*
Information	Ask students to state what they know.
Discrimination	Ask students to identify the object that is different in some way.
Concept	Ask students to classify diverse and previously unused illustrations as examples versus nonexamples of the concept.
Rule	Provide students a relevant but previously unused example and ask them to apply the rule.
Complex skill	Ask students to generate solutions to a previously unused problem that requires use of the complex skill.

A common error is to ask students to state what they know when trying to assess their knowledge of a concept, rule, or even complex skill. Having students state what they know is appropriate for assessing declarative knowledge. It is ineffective at assessing the various types of procedural knowledge. The proper way to test students' knowledge of the *concept* of a bird, for instance, is to have the students distinguish between examples and nonexamples of birds. *The examples must be provided to the students rather than having the students provide the examples.* The examples need to be diverse and previously unused. Therefore, asking students to place in a portfolio examples of birds does *not* provide a good indication of whether students know this concept. A much better strategy is to provide pictures of diverse birds and also diverse animals that share obvious characteristics with birds. The examples of birds might be diverse in size (a hummingbird and eagle), diverse in color (a brightly colored parrot and a blue heron), and diverse in flying ability (a hawk and a penguin). The nonexamples should involve animals that share obvious characteristics with birds, such as animals that fly (bats and butterflies).

Declarative knowledge or information also represents important knowledge that must be assessed. For instance, it is appropriate to establish whether students can also describe what birds are. If both declarative and procedural knowledge are important in a given content area, and they generally are, then students' knowledge of both must be assessed.

Box 15.3 *Apply What You Are Learning*

Described here are some examples of knowledge that a teacher might try to assess. With each example are two proposals for assessing that knowledge, only one of which is appropriate given the type of knowledge involved. See if you can determine which performance is appropriate for each example.

1. Concept of a *preposition*
   A. Ask students to circle words in printed sentences you provide that are prepositions
   B. Ask students to define what a preposition is and provide examples
2. Concept of *advertisement*.
   A. Ask students to place diverse examples of magazine advertisements in their portfolios
   B. Ask students to indicate whether or not each magazine clipping you provide is an advertisement
3. Making change for $1 for a purchase of less than one dollar (this being procedural knowledge, specifically a rule)
   A. Ask the student to explain the procedure for making correct change
   B. Ask the student to provide the correct change for a less than $1 purchase paid for with a dollar bill
4. Knowing the URL address of the school's web site (this being declarative knowledge, or information)
   A. Ask the student to go to a computer and access the school's web site
   B. Ask the student to write on paper the school's web site URL address

Answers can be found at the end of the chapter.

HOW WILL I KNOW I MEASURED THE RIGHT THING?

Because we cannot directly see a student's knowledge, we must establish evidence of what it is we are measuring. This need to gather evidence is common to many disciplines, again because what is being studied cannot be observed directly. For example, much of what archaeologists do is use characteristics of artifacts to establish evidence of what took place in extinct cultures. Much of we what do in science, medicine, and engineering, and in the study of history and of the arts involves the assessment of things that cannot be seen. In each case, supporting evidence is important to establishing the validity of inferences drawn from that which we do see.

Earlier in this book, we learned that with student assessments it is convenient to organize validity evidence into these three categories:

Category	Type of Evidence
Construct-related	Evidence that the student behavior to be observed is appropriate for measuring the knowledge being assessed
Content-related	Evidence that the content or tasks included in the test corresponds closely to this appropriate behavior
Criterion-related	Evidence that performance on the test correlates with other indications of student knowledge

Construct-related evidence depends heavily on what we just discussed: establishing the type of knowledge we are trying to assess and then selecting a type of student behavior that provides a good indication of that type of knowledge. If declarative knowledge is being assessed, are students being asked to state what they know? If procedural knowledge such as a concept is involved, are students being asked to distinguish between examples and nonexamples provided by the test?

Content-related evidence involves doing something to appropriately control the content of the test. With formal assessments such as performance assessments, written tests, and portfolios, the content of a test is controlled by creating a content outline, such as a test blueprint or a list of performance objectives. With informal assessments such as casual observations and oral questions, the content of a test is controlled by including in the lesson plan an outline of what you will look for or what you will ask students.

With classroom assessments, criterion-related evidence simply involves deliberate watching for anything outside the test that substantiates or refutes what you learned from the test.

Box 15.4 *Apply What You Are Learning*

Here are some common techniques for gathering evidence about the validity of a test. See if you can correctly classify each example as being

    A. construct-related evidence

    B. content-related evidence

    C. criterion-related evidence

1. The teacher wants to determine whether students know the concept of an animal. Because the type of knowledge is a concept, the teacher is aware that students should classify illustrations she provides as examples versus nonexamples of an animal.

2. This teacher is going to use an informal assessment to determine whether students have learned the concept of an animal. To help make sure she asks appropriate questions, she includes in her lesson plan some examples and nonexamples of animals she will include in this assessment. Her examples of animals include cat, elephant, mosquito, fish, and eagle. Her nonexamples of animals included tree, rock, cloud, flower, and watermelon.

3. The results of the assessment suggest that students know the concept of an animal. This was substantiated the following week when students correctly used the terms *plant* and *animal* in class discussion.

4. The teacher wants to determine whether students can express the English equivalent of words spoken in Spanish. Since this represents declarative knowledge, the teacher is aware that students should simply state what they know, in this case, write the English equivalents of the Spanish words.

5. While producing the test, this teacher selects categories of words for which students must write English equivalents. The teacher did this to ensure that representative words are included in the test.

6. This teacher concluded students know their Spanish words quite well because they performed well on the test. However, during informal observations the following week, the teacher questioned the appropriateness of this conclusion because students appear to be having problems with similar vocabulary words.

7. The class is learning how to write letters that convey a point of view. The teacher is using portfolios to facilitate assessment of this skill. To control what students will place in their portfolios, the teacher provides students a coversheet for their portfolio entries that clearly states the goal being assessed and outlines the criteria to be used to judge the quality of students' letters.

8. A teacher wants to know whether students understand the idea of mechanical advantage. Specifically, the teacher wants to know whether students can calculate, for different placements of the fulcrum, the amount of force that will occur on one end of the lever when a specified force is applied to the other. Given that knowledge of a rule is being assessed, this teacher realizes that students should be tested with previously unused placements of the fulcrum.

Answers can be found at the end of the chapter.

WILL THE STUDENT PERFORMANCE I OBSERVED GENERALIZE TO THAT WHICH I DID NOT OBSERVE?

Intuitively we know that our observations of students may not generalize. For instance, had a student been asked different questions or had a different teacher reviewed the student's portfolio, somewhat and possibly dramatically different conclusions about the student may result.

Several sources of inconsistency potentially prevent us from being able to generalize beyond that which we observed. These inconsistencies are to be avoided when possible because they reduce the usefulness of our assessments. Assessments are much more useful when we can generalize beyond that which we observe. If we can generalize, then a relatively small number of assessments can tell us what we would have observed had a much larger number of assessments been used.

Again, *inconsistencies* within assessments reduce our ability to generalize beyond that which we observed. This makes it advantageous to identify sources of inconsistency and to take steps to reduce these inconsistencies in our assessments. Earlier in the book, five sources of inconsistencies were identified:

- Inconsistencies between earlier and later measures
- Inconsistencies between test items that supposedly measure the same skill
- Inconsistencies between alternate skills in the same content domain
- Inconsistencies from measuring unrelated qualities within one test
- Inconsistencies between different raters in the scoring of student responses

Not all five sources of inconsistency are of concern in a particular situation. For instance, teachers usually do not make generalizations about student achievement over time. Teachers know and actually hope that student knowledge changes. However, teachers often subconsciously assume a student's attitudes and motivation remain fairly consistent, even though intuitively we know this often is not the case. Inconsistency over time cannot be controlled. It is a reality that must be recognized.

At least some inconsistency between test items that supposedly measure the same thing is present. This is true even with skills as narrowly focused as multiplying single-digit numbers; for instance, multiplications involving zero or five are usually answered correctly more often than multiplications involving seven or eight. An effective way to reduce this and most other inconsistencies is to include more observations within the assessment, for instance, increasing the number of items.

Inconsistencies often occur between alternate skills within a content domain because of the complexities of many domains. The broader the content domain, the more inconsistency there tends to be between alternate skills. Therefore, more inconsistencies between alternate skills occur when broad goals rather than more narrowly focused performance objectives are used to control the content of tests. Performance assessments and portfolios, which use broader goals, are less likely to generalize than are written tests constructed from objectives. The generalizability of performance assessments and portfolios is improved substantially by including diverse tasks within the assessment rather than using only a narrow subpart of the instructional goal.

Including unrelated qualities within a test reduces generalizability. Qualities are unrelated if students' performance on one quality seems unrelated to their performance on the other. For instance, the neatness of a portfolio containing writing samples often has a low correlation with students' writing proficiency. Generalizability is improved by separately scoring and reporting performance on unrelated qualities within assessments.

Inconsistencies between different raters are more of a problem with performance assessments, portfolios, and essay tests than with multiple-choice and other objectively scored tests. Typically, only one teacher scores a classroom assessment but this does not reduce the problems associated with inconsistencies between raters. Having just one person score assessments only hides the problem. The score a student receives on a test should be a function of the quality of the student's work, not a function of whoever happens to be scoring the work. Developing and using a concise scoring plan significantly improves the generalizability of performance assessments, portfolios, and essay tests.

Box 15.5 *Apply What You Are Learning*

Described here are several assessments, each of which likely contains inconsistencies that inhibit a teacher's ability to generalize beyond that which was observed. Following each description are two possible sources of inconsistency, one of the two being much more likely to be a source of inconsistency for that particular assessment. For each assessment, identify which of the two sources of inconsistency represents the more likely problem.

1. A written test where students are asked to spell the names of large cities within the country. Which source of inconsistencies is more likely to be a problem?

   A. Inconsistencies between test items that supposedly measure the same skill; that is, the city names that happen to be included in the spelling test.

   B. Inconsistencies between different raters in the scoring of student responses; that is, differences between teachers with respect to what constitutes a correct spelling.

2. A handwritten paper placed in the portfolio where students demonstrate they can provide directions for driving from a nearby town to the school. The paper will be scored with respect to accuracy of directions, spelling, and penmanship. A concise scoring plan was developed. Which source of inconsistencies is more likely to be a problem?

   A. Inconsistencies between different raters in scoring each attribute; for instance, differences between scores assigned by teachers with respect to accuracy of directions.

   B. Inconsistencies between alternate skills in the content domain; for instance, low correlation between accuracy of students' directions and their penmanship.

3. A performance assessment is used to determine whether students appropriately load paper into the paper supply drawer of a computer laser printer. In the assessment, a student performs all aspects of loading the paper. The teacher is simply to judge whether the student's performance was adequate or inadequate. Which source of inconsistencies is more likely to be a problem?

   A. Inconsistencies between different raters in the scoring of student responses; that is, judging the adequacy versus inadequacy of a student's loading paper in the printer.

   B. Inconsistencies between alternate skills in the same content domain; that is, different aspects of loading paper being included in the performance assessment.

4. An informal oral question to determine whether students can point to the location on a world map where significant geological features are located, for instance, Victoria Falls. Each student is asked one question. Which source of inconsistencies is more likely to be a problem?

   A. Inconsistencies between different raters in the scoring of student responses, for instance, differences between teachers with respect to location of the geological feature.

   B. Inconsistencies between test items that supposedly measure the same skill; for instance, the location of other significant geological features.

Answers can be found at the end of the chapter.

SUMMARY

The fundamentals of the assessment process involve four issues. These issues are critical and must be addressed whenever assessments are produced, administered, and interpreted. The first pertains to establishing at the outset how the assessment is to be used. The typical use of assessments is to evaluate students, that is, to establish the desirability and importance of what is observed. This evaluation tends to be one of four types, these being preliminary, formative, diagnostic, and summative.

The second issue is concerned with determining what students should be asked to do in order to assess what they know. In part, this is a fundamental issue because knowledge cannot be seen. Instead, an observable performance must be identified that will provide a good *indication* of what students know. However, different types of knowledge are involved, with different types of performance serving as good indicators of each. Declarative knowledge or *information* is the first of the two basic types. Declarative knowledge is assessed by having students state what they know. The other basic type is procedural knowledge, which includes *discriminations, concepts, rules,* and *complex skills.*

The third issue pertains to establishing evidence of an assessment's validity. The need for this evidence again comes from the fact that one cannot directly observe knowledge. Evidence as to the interpretation of what was observed is essential. Evidence is grouped into three categories. Construct-related evidence goes back to identifying the type of knowledge involved and establishing an appropriate performance to indicate whether students have achieved this knowledge. Content-related evidence is concerned with establishing that the content of the test actually requires students to demonstrate the targeted performance. Criterion-related evidence involves looking for anything outside the test that substantiates or refutes what was learned from the test.

The fourth fundamental issue is concerned with whether student performance that was observed generalizes to that which was not observed. Performance that does generalize is more useful because a small number of assessments can then tell what would have been observed had a much larger number of assessments been used. Inconsistencies in observations reduce generalizability. Being aware of sources of inconsistency and where possible taking steps to reduce this inconsistency can improve the generalizability of assessments.

ANSWERS: APPLY WHAT YOU ARE LEARNING

15.1 1. A; 2. B; 3. A. Both assessments in each pair, in the right circumstance, represent a good assessment. However, a formative assessment requires prompt use of assessment results, because the results will immediately be used to determine how instruction will proceed. If you incorrectly answered any of these three items, look back at each pair of assessments and note which allows for a more immediate use of results.

15.2 1. B and D; 2. C; 3. no reference; 4. D; 5. C and D; 6. D; 7. no reference.

15.3 1. A; 2. B; 3. B; 4. B. *Item 1:* Because a concept is involved, students should be asked to classify words in sentences as examples versus nonexamples of prepositions. Circling words used as prepositions would accomplish this. The sentences should be ones not previously used to assess knowledge of prepositions. *Item 2:* Again, since knowledge of a concept is to be assessed, students should be asked to classify clippings not previously seen as examples versus nonexamples of advertisements. *Item 3:* Given that knowledge of a rule is being assessed, students should be asked to apply the rule they have learned for making change (a rule may involve more than a single step). *Item 4:* Given that declarative knowledge (information) is involved, students are assessed by asking them to state the school's web site address.

15.4 1. A; 2. B; 3. C; 4. A; 5. B; 6. C; 7. B; 8. A

15.5 1. A; 2. B; 3. A; 4. B. *Item 1:* Knowledgeable teachers will agree on the spelling of city names, however, students who can correctly spell the name of one city often incorrectly spell the name of another city. *Item 2:* Establishing a concise scoring plan will significantly reduce inconsistencies between raters. However, performance on the qualities being scored on this paper (accuracy of direction, spelling, and penmanship) is quite unrelated. *Item 3:* This is a tricky item if you are unaware that laser printers that use a paper tray are very similar with respect to how paper is loaded. However, the judgments teachers are to make (adequate versus inadequate) are vague; two teachers can easily disagree as to whether paper has been loaded adequately. For instance, does the paper have to be stacked perfectly even? A scoring plan will help here. *Item 4:* Knowledgeable teachers will likely agree on whether students have correctly pointed to the correct location on the map. However, students who can correctly locate one geological feature often cannot locate a different feature.

ADDITIONAL READING

Shepard, L.. A. (2000). *The role of classroom assessment in teaching and learning* (CSE Technical Report 517). Los Angeles: University of California, National Center for Research on Evaluation, Standards, and Student Testing/Center for the Study of Evaluation (available online at *http://www.cse.ucla.edu/CRESST/Reports/TECH517.pdf*). This paper describes an approach for integrating assessment into teaching and learning. Incorporating ideas from competing theories, the paper describes how classroom assessment can become a collaborative effort where students together with teachers actively use assessments to identify conceptual problems and improve understanding. Implications to research and professional development of teachers are discussed.

CHAPTER 16

Teaching Students How to Take Tests

A variety of factors influence students' scores on tests. Ideally, the only thing affecting scores should be students' proficiency with the skill the test is supposed to measure. The effects of all other factors decrease the test's validity. This chapter describes how to reduce the effect of one extraneous factor, specifically student ability to take a test. Three aspects of this factor are addressed. The first is student familiarity with the testing medium. The second part of the chapter suggests ways students can prepare for a test. This includes concerns regarding anxiety and the effects of coaching. The third section of this chapter discusses test-wiseness. Some students score higher on a test simply because they are familiar with procedures that optimize test performance.

Teachers sometimes underestimate the importance of training students to take tests. Possibly this is because teachers are among the most experienced and proficient test takers. Although this chapter is primarily designed to help you help others take tests, you probably will also find some new strategies that improve your own performance on future tests.

This chapter helps you achieve three skills:

- Identify the effects of familiarity with the testing medium on student performance.
- Identify procedures students should follow when preparing for a test.
- Recognize basic components of test-wiseness.

FAMILIARITY WITH THE TESTING MEDIUM

Two aspects of the testing medium are addressed here. The first is the effect of computer tests versus paper-and-pencil tests. The second pertains to the use of separate answer sheets with elementary school students.

Administering Tests by Computer versus Paper and Pencil

It is becoming increasingly popular to have students use computers to take tests. This procedure has definite advantages, including the ability to administer tests efficiently to individual students or to use adaptive testing where the specific items administered are adjusted based on how the student is performing.

Numerous studies, however, suggest that student performance may be somewhat different, usually lower, when the test is administered by a computer. However, results are not consistent. For example, Lee, Moreno, and Sympson (1986) compared the scores obtained by about 600 military recruits when administered computerized versus paper-and-pencil versions of an arithmetic reasoning placement test. Performance dropped 5% when a computer was used to administer the test. Replication of the experiment with another version of the test, however, resulted in no effect from using the computer.

Heppner, Anderson, Farstrup, and Weiderman (1985) studied the effect of computer administration on reading ability. They administered the Nelson–Denny Reading Test to 85 college students and staff using both paper-and-pencil and computerized modes. This test involves reading a series of short stories and answering several questions after each story. They found that examinees took about 30% more time to read the stories when they were displayed on a computer screen. Overall, when the test was administered by computer, performance dropped 10% on the items following the stories. Rather interestingly, examinees who were regular computer users showed a greater drop in performance between the computerized versus printed administrations. The lower performance associated with using computers might be a result of the lower resolution of computer monitors as opposed to material printed on paper. This problem may be diminished as the resolution of monitors improves, although high-resolution monitors were used in the Heppner study.

When the test administered by computer is identical in all ways with the paper and pencil version, scores tend to be more comparable. This is what was observed by Zandvliet and Farragher (1997), when they administered a paper-and-pencil test by computer to adult basic education students. This is also the finding by Bugbee (1996). However, computer-administered tests tend not to be fully equivalent. For instance, when taking advantage of options the computer provides, computerized tests often are adaptive. That is, a student's performance on previous items determines which items are administered subsequently. Inconsistent results have been observed with respect to characteristics of identical items administered within computer-adaptive versus conventional paper-and-pencil tests (Divgi & Stoloff, 1986; Hetter, Segall, & Bloxom, 1994; Spray, Ackerman, Reckase, & Carlson, 1989).

Wise, Boettcher, Harvey, and Plake (1987) studied the effects of computer anxiety and computer experience on printed versus computer-administered tests. Both modes were used to administer a math test to approximately 100 undergraduate and graduate students. They found that neither anxiety toward the computer nor lack of experience with computers affected test performance. Research by Shermis and Lombard (1998) suggests that anxiety experienced during a computer administration of a test may be a manifestation of test anxiety rather than computer anxiety.

The preceding studies are meant to be illustrative. They indicate that the mode in which a test is presented may affect resulting scores. Furthermore, more time apparently is required to read text displayed on a computer monitor rather than that printed on paper. Reasons for these findings, however, are not clear at this time. If a test will be interpreted by norm-referenced criteria, differences between modes might be adjusted by establishing separate norms for print and computerized administrations. This kind of adjustment will be more difficult for criterion-referenced interpretations.

Use of Separate Answer Sheets

A second concern is the effect of detached answer sheets on test performance. Gaffney and Maguire (1971) investigated this issue using groups of students enrolled in the second through ninth grades. Students in each grade recorded answers on a separate answer sheet. Each test included seven embedded questions that measured what was common knowledge to these students. Because students would be expected to answer these questions perfectly, wrong answers were assumed to indicate difficulty in using a separate answer sheet. Students were divided into three groups that were given the following types of training with use of detached answer sheets: (1) minimal instruction with no practice, (2) maximum instruction with no practice, and (3) maximum instruction with practice. The authors concluded that separate answer sheets should not be used before the fourth grade regardless of the amount of instruction and practice. In the fourth and fifth grades, detached answer sheets may be used *if* significant training and practice are provided. After the fifth grade, students do not require training or practice to use detached answer sheets.

Lassiter (1987) questions whether these findings are realistic because standardized tests (and certainly many classroom tests) do not use questions that all students are expected to answer perfectly. She compared the scores of third grade students when they were administered the Stanford Achievement Test. Consistent with the Gaffney and Maguire (1971) study, she found that students at this grade level performed worse when answers were recorded on a detached answer sheet. On the mathematics and reading subtests, scores dropped between 4% and 6%. This drop in scores was about the same for higher and lower ability students in the third grade.

PREPARING FOR A TEST

The most obvious way to prepare for a test is to study the content it is expected to measure. For classroom tests, this is probably the single most important aspect of preparation. This section addresses three other topics that affect student preparation for a test. These include the effect of coaching, conditions that depress test performance, and anxiety.

The Effect of Coaching

Coaching is generally associated with the preparation for a specific standardized test. Usually, a person, or "coach," familiarizes prospective examinees with the type of items to be expected on the test and teaches test-taking strategies (i.e., test-wiseness). Sometimes, coaching includes instruction about the type of content to be tested and simulates the administration of tests about that content. Coaching has become quite prevalent with various college admissions tests such as the SAT, GRE, or LSAT. Many private agencies and even colleges offer courses to help individuals prepare for these exams. Coaching is common at all grade levels, however.

The issue of coaching is controversial. For instance, developers of college admissions tests appropriately characterized their exams as measures of general ability that must be learned over an extended period of time. Historically, these test developers have taken issue with coaching programs, stating that short-term training has a negligible effect on test scores. Agencies that provide coaching countered by claiming that it substantially increased test scores.

More recently, a number of studies (e.g., Messick & Jungeblut, 1981) have demonstrated that coaching for admissions tests does increase scores somewhat. A highly systematic study involving the Graduate Record Exam was conducted by Powers and Swinton (1984). They mailed self-study preparation materials to approximately 7000 individuals who had registered to take the GRE. In addition, a strongly worded letter encouraging use of these materials was sent to half the participants. These materials were directed at only the analytical portion of this exam.

Powers and Swinton (1984) found that individuals who used the materials made significant but not phenomenal gains in scores. Interestingly, the greatest difference was observed between individuals who did versus did not receive the strongly worded letter of encouragement. Also, gains occurred only in the portion of the test to which coaching was directed (scores on the verbal and quantitative sections of the GRE were unaffected).

Bangert-Downs, Kulik, and Kulik (1983) reviewed 30 research studies concerned with the effect of coaching on standardized achievement tests. Their review included studies conducted at the elementary through college grade levels. Coaching appears to increase test scores about equally at all grade levels. The typical improvement was enough to change a student's score from the 50th to 60th percentile. (Percentile indicates the percentage of scores below a particular student's performance.) As will be shown in Chapter 22, this improvement represents a small gain, although the amount of gain is favorable in terms of the amount of time required for coaching.

Conditions That Depress Test Performance

Students have at least limited control over a variety of conditions that interfere with performance on both standardized and classroom tests. The first of these is lack of sleep. The ability to reason, work quickly, and concentrate are important to the completion of a test but are impaired by lack of sleep. An effective study procedure, albeit not the most common, is to prepare for a test over a period of time and get a good rest the night before an important test.

Eating can make one drowsy. Therefore, one should avoid a large meal before a test. Starches such as bread or french fries are particularly bad. So are alcoholic beverages. Salads and fruits in moderation are the best bet.

Significant personal and social experiences can also affect concentration and likewise performance on a test. Teachers should be sensitive to this and not plan testing activities just before or after a major social event or just before or after holiday vacations. Particularly in secondary school, students should be encouraged to schedule activities away from major tests that are expected to affect their concentration.

The Effects of Anxiety

Research indicates that a low-to-moderate negative correlation exists between anxiety and test performance. That is, as anxiety increases, scores on a test are depressed somewhat. Rocklin and Thompson (1985) conducted a study involving 90 college undergraduates to determine if the difficulty of a test alters the effect anxiety has on scores. Students were first administered an instrument that measures test anxiety. Then they were categorized into high-, medium-, and low-anxiety groups. All students were administered a difficult and an easy verbal aptitude test. Students correctly answered 41% of items on the difficult test and 83% on the easy test.

The least anxious students did best on the difficult test. For them, the average item difficulty was 45%, whereas it was approximately 35% for other students. The moderately anxious students, however, scored highest on the easier test. Their average score was about 90%, whereas the most and least anxious students averaged approximately 80%.

Anxiety is generally not regarded as desirable, although at moderate levels, it may actually facilitate performance on exams with difficulties comparable to typical classroom tests. High anxiety is undesirable, particularly in the extreme. Frequent administration of classroom tests should moderate anxiety for two reasons. First, it increases students' familiarity with the examination experience. Second, it reduces the significance of scores on any single exam.

TEST-WISENESS

Millman, Bishop, and Ebel (1965) defined *test-wiseness* as an examinee's ability to use characteristics of either a test or the test-taking situation to obtain a high score. Test-wiseness is distinct from skills the test is intended to measure. Therefore, differences in test scores caused by variability in students' test-wiseness threaten validity. Removing test-wiseness skills from those who have it is impossible. Variability in test-wiseness therefore is reduced by training students who have yet to achieve it.

The test-wiseness skills discussed here are grouped into the six categories proposed by Millman et al. (1965). The first four include using time effectively, avoiding errors, eliminating incorrect alternatives, and knowing when to guess. In contrast to these first four, the remaining two categories capitalize on the habits of the teacher who developed the test. They include being responsive to the teacher's intention and taking into account idiosyncrasies the teacher builds into test items.

Sometimes teachers resist teaching test-wiseness because it tends to increase scores without improving comprehension of the knowledge being assessed. For at least most aspects of test-wiseness, this concern is misdirected. Teaching students to use time efficiently and to proof their work carefully is desirable because these skills are useful in a variety of settings, including testing. A subset of test-wiseness skills, however, may appear less noble because they encourage students to profit from inadequacies teachers build into tests. Examples might include writing long responses to essay questions when the student knows that the teacher favorably grades long answers or avoiding option D on multiple-choice items because the teacher seldom uses that option for the correct answer. One can argue that teachers who build inadequacies into a test do a greater disservice than students who consider unintentional cues when trying to do well on a test. Nevertheless, as stated previously, test-wiseness threatens validity because it represents a skill a test is not designed to measure, and, unless all students are test-wise, the teacher cannot determine whether variation in students' scores is due to differences in their level of achievement or degree of sophistication at taking a test.

Use Time Effectively

Work Quickly and Pace Oneself.   Most tests have time limits, and, unfortunately, many teachers administer tests that are too long for the time allotted. Many of the standardized tests administered to older students have time limits that do not allow all examinees to complete every item. To maximize scores in these situations, students should customarily work as quickly as possible without making significant errors. They should determine how much time remains at the start of each test and estimate the average amount of time available for each item. Establishing a point in the test that should be reached when a third or half the time has elapsed may be useful. Of course, increasing the pace beyond reasonable levels when time is running out should be avoided. Students should be taught that in these situations it is important to maintain a quick but sensible pace and that it is crucial to stay on task for the remainder of the test.

Answer Time-Consuming Items Last.   When items are weighted equally, items that cannot be answered readily should be marked and answered later. This includes difficult items for which more thought is required to derive an answer and items involving extended computations. If there is any possibility that time will expire before the test is completed, the student should make sure that he or she has answered all easy items.

Answer High-Point Questions First.   If time is limited, items that will result in the maximum number of points at the end of the time period should be answered first. If a test includes both essay and objectively scored items, more points per unit of time usually can be obtained by answering the objectively scored items first. This technique is not useful on most standardized tests because items representing high- and low-point gainers are usually grouped and timed separately.

Answer the Specific Question Posed by Short-Answer and Essay Items.   Especially with essay items, students have a tendency to write everything they know. This consumes time that might be used to answer or proof other items. Also, if the teacher is using a carefully developed scoring plan, points are not gained by including information superfluous to the question. Unfortunately, many teachers do not establish a clear scoring plan for essay items and deduct points for erroneous statements regardless of whether they are pertinent to the test item. This increases the importance of answering only the questions addressed by the test item.

Mark Items for Later Review and Changing of Answers.   Students should be taught to mark items for which the correct answer is uncertain. Often, later items will give insights into how to solve some of the preceding difficult items. Marking difficult items saves time by making them easier to find when insights occur.

Often, students hesitate to change responses when they review previously answered multiple-choice items. Research consistently indicates that students average two points gained for each point lost from changing answers (see, for example, Davis, 1975; Fabrey & Case, 1985; and Matthews, 1929). McMorris and Weideman (1986) hypothesized that if students are encouraged to go with their second opinion, they may tend to lose points by changing answers they previously would have avoided changing. However, the results of their research showed that students, after being encouraged to go with the second opinion, still typically gain points by changing answers. The total number of points gained from changing answers is usually small.

Avoid Errors

Follow Directions Carefully.   Test directions on standardized tests are generally more involved than those for classroom tests. Also, the administrator has less flexibility in clarifying instructions on standardized tests. Particularly at the elementary level, students will be more able to follow directions on standardized tests if similar directions are used and reviewed on several classroom tests.

Students should be taught to scan quickly directions on all tests and mark anything that may affect the score. This includes time limits, how items are to be answered and recorded, what work is to be shown, and whether there is a choice as to which items are to be answered.

Directions for individual items should also be noted. Students have particular problems with directions to essay items. They often lose points simply by not answering the question. Look for key words and phrases such as "list," "define," "give two examples," and "compare and contrast." As noted earlier, critical time is frequently lost by writing answers for questions that were not asked.

Estimate Answers.   If computations are involved, when possible, the answer should first be approximated and then computed exactly. The correctness of the exact answer can be judged against the approximation. If approximating an answer is impossible or too time-consuming, a likely range of values should be anticipated. For example, if on a test you were asked to compute a Kuder–Richardson reliability coefficient, you know the answer should be between .00 and 1.00. Unfortunately, many students who derive an answer outside the likely range of values simply stay with their answer. At the very least, the item should be marked for review if time remains when the test is completed.

Proof Work.   As you undoubtedly know, points are often lost on a test through careless errors. Any time remaining at the end of a test should be used to proof answers. Sitting idly at the conclusion of an exam often amounts to giving away some easily earned points.

If a separate answer sheet is being used, the accuracy of markings should be verified. This can be facilitated if the intended answer is marked in the test booklet as well as on the answer sheet.

Mark Answers Carefully.   Answers must be marked carefully when a separate answer sheet is used. Ink should never be used, both because it prevents the changing of answers and because marks made in ink are not detected by many scoring machines.

The large scoring machines that score standardized tests and those used by centralized testing services in school districts and at colleges are very accurate. They are becoming increasingly able to sense even very poorly marked answers.

Relatively inexpensive desktop scanners are becoming very popular. These scanners are very accurate when marks are made clearly. They are also quite good at distinguishing between poor erasures and new markings. Desktop scanners often have problems detecting lightly made marks. If you can easily read the printed letter inside a bubble after the answer sheet is marked, this mark may be too light. Many desktop scanners read through the center of each bubble space. If you use doughnut-like marks with a hole in the middle, the scanner may not see the mark.

It was noted in an earlier section that elementary students require significant training when first using a separate answer sheet. Hills (1981) has recommended the use of games to facilitate this training. He proposes distributing answer sheets to students and then calling out a series of item numbers and answer spaces to be marked. When finished, the marks form the outline of an object such as a tree or person's face. Marks are called out in a random order. A contest might be created by seeing who will first name the object being drawn. Special points can be awarded for overall accuracy and adequacy of marks.

Eliminate Incorrect Alternatives

When answering multiple-choice items, test-wise students eliminate distracters that are clearly wrong. If a guess must be made, this procedure increases the probability of selecting the correct response. This strategy seems quite obvious; however, it represents a learned skill. Research, such as that by Millman and Setijadi (1966) and Lo and Slakter (1973), indicated that international students obtain lower scores on multiple-choice items. In part, this is because they do not deductively isolate the correct response. Many elementary students will also lack this skill until they become experienced with the multiple-choice format.

A similar problem occurs with students inexperienced with the multiple-choice format. Students often read through the options until one is found that answers the stem. A better response that appears later in the list may then be missed. When answering multiple-choice items, the student should read all options for each item.

When reviewing a previously completed test, the teacher should help the class reason through multiple-choice options illustrating how distracters can be eliminated. Information contained in an item analysis report can help identify options that need a more careful explanation (see Chapter 12).

Know When to Guess

Chapter 9 discourages "formula scoring" when scoring multiple-choice items within classroom tests. Formula scoring adjusts each student's test score by subtracting points proportional to the number of items answered incorrectly. This procedure encourages students to omit an answer rather than guess when they have no idea what the answer is. When teachers appropriately tell students to answer all items even if guessing is required, then the best strategy is obvious: A student should always guess when necessary.

Formula scoring, however, is used by some teachers and with certain standardized tests. Research such as that by Cross and Frary (1977) and Rowley and Traub (1977) indicated that under these circumstances, guessing still increases students' scores. Of course, if a student can eliminate one or more of the multiple-choice distracters, guessing among the remaining alternatives is advised. Directions to most standardized tests explicitly give such advice, but research suggests that students underestimate what they know. When students cannot consciously eliminate even one distracter, guessing increases their scores more than can be explained by chance (Cross & Frary, 1977; Rowley & Traub, 1977).

More recent research by Angoff and Schrader (1984) disputed these findings. Using two college admissions tests (SAT and GMAT), they found examinees' scores on a formula-scored test did not vary as a function of instructions. When tests were formula scored, students did no better when told to always guess than when told to guess only when one or more distracters could be eliminated. On the other hand, students who were told to always guess did no worse than those given more restrictive directions. So from the students' perspective, probably the best advice is still to always guess when necessary.

Be Responsive to the Teacher's Intentions

Respond to Teacher's Intended Sophistication.   Particularly with essay questions, students must anticipate the degree of sophistication the teacher is seeking in an answer. For example, a thorough response to "Explain the Cause of the American Civil War" would require several volumes. Depending on the class, a teacher who asked this question more likely would look for a brief response that focused on the slavery controversy, Lincoln's election as president, and the resulting secession of Southern states from the Union, or possibly events associated with the battle at Fort Sumter. Yet a brief response such as "Slavery caused the Civil War" may lack the sophistication the teacher is seeking.

The need for students to read into the teacher's intentions can be reduced if the essay item concisely describes the task students are to complete. When students' responses depart significantly from the intended answer, however, a teacher can improve test-wiseness by explaining why, within the context of the class, the intended answer was the expected response.

Respond to the Teacher's Scoring Criteria.   Teachers should use a deliberately constructed scoring plan when evaluating answers to essay items. When a careful scoring plan is not developed, however, students often can increase test scores by writing longer responses, using good penmanship, presenting a response that is highly organized, and avoiding spelling errors and faulty grammar.

Account for Idiosyncrasies Built Into Test Items

Teachers unintentionally build a number of idiosyncrasies into tests. Students can often increase scores by being aware of these habits. Some examples follow.

Selecting "C" as the Correct Multiple-Choice Option.   Carter (1986) conducted an experiment to determine whether seventh-grade students are aware of clues often embedded in multiple-choice items. One clue pertains to the frequent use of option C as the correct answer. In her experiment, Carter (1986, p. 21) administered the following item to students:

> Debbie is probably _____ years old.
>
> A. 5
> B. 8
> C. 12
> D. 16

Although students were provided no information suggesting which option was correct, approximately 70% selected option C. When asked to elaborate on the choice, a student explained:

> My teachers never put the right answer on A. Sometimes it's on B, but most often it lands there (pointing to answer C on test). And the last choice D is usually dumb, especially in Ms. _____'s class. (Carter, 1986, p. 21)

Selecting the Longest Multiple-Choice Option.   Carter (1986, p. 21) also studied the tendency for the correct multiple-choice option to be longer than the distracters. The following item was administered to seventh-grade students:

The main theme of the story is based on a conflict concerning Debbie's desire

A. for rain.
B. to believe that supernatural powers do not influence people and her fear that curses may be impossible.
C. to watch television.
D. to be grown.

Half the students selected option B, although a third of the students selected option D. A typical reason given by students for selecting the longest response was "Look, I figure my teacher doesn't have time to write all that unless it's the right one" (p. 21).

Carter (1986) was interested in why a large percentage of students selected option D, particularly given that students generally avoid this choice. Apparently, students had recently read numerous stories about "growing up" and therefore assumed this would be reflected in the correct answer.

Selecting the Multiple-Choice Option That Is Cued by the Stem. Teachers often give unintentional clues to the correct option through the stem. To illustrate, try to determine the correct answers to the following two items:

1. All but one of the following are parts of a sailboat. The exception is an

   A. halyard.
   B. mainsheet.
   C. outrigger.
   D. shroud.

2. The captain of a ship entering a controlled harbor should contact the

   A. auditor.
   B. harbormaster.
   C. inspector.
   D. monitor.

In the first item, option C is grammatically consistent with the stem. In the second item, option B is similar to a key word contained in the stem. Therefore, both represent the probable (and in these examples, the correct) response.

Quite often, students can pick out the correct answer simply because it "sounds right." Carter's (1986) review of classroom tests indicated that teachers frequently give cues to the correct response in the stem content and grammar.

Assuming That Options Containing Absolutes Are False. Most concepts taught in schools include exceptions or qualifiers and therefore do not exist as absolutes. In fact, special attention is often and appropriately given to exceptions. Therefore, testwise students correctly anticipate that multiple-choice options and true-false items that contain words such as *always* and *never* represent incorrect statements.

Overview of Test-Wiseness

Some test-wiseness skills simply consist of student ability to recognize weaknesses teachers build into tests. Using the checklists discussed in Part 2 of this book will help one avoid these deficiencies within written tests. The majority of test-wiseness skills concern how to work productively when taking a test such as using time wisely and avoiding errors. Many, but definitely not all, students learn these skills on their own without deliberate training by teachers. Numerous students, particularly those in earlier grades or from different cultures, will likely benefit from deliberate training in test-wiseness.

As with other skills, students probably differ in their ability to learn how to be test-wise. This, coupled with the fact that many students learn such skills on their own, led Scruggs and Lifson (1985) to caution educators not to overemphasize the influence of test-wiseness on test validity. Nevertheless, teachers should be alert and responsive to differences in the test-wiseness of students.

SUMMARY

Three factors that affect student performance on a test have been addressed: familiarity with the testing medium, preparation for the test, and test-wiseness.

Familiarity with the testing medium includes the mode used to present the test and the procedure that students use to record responses. Tests increasingly are being displayed on computer monitors instead of printed on paper. Research indicates that students require more time to read text displayed on even high-resolution monitors and, to a lesser degree, have difficulty comprehending what they read (Heppner, Anderson, Farstrup, & Weiderman, 1985; Lee, Moreno, & Sympson, 1986; Wise, Boettcher, Harvey, & Plake, 1987). The reason for this is unclear. Preliminary research suggests that lack of experience with computers and anxiety associated with using computers are not the cause (Heppner, Anderson, Farstrup, & Weiderman, 1985).

Research regarding detached answer sheets indicates they should not be used before the fourth grade. Students in the fourth and fifth grades benefit from training and experience with detached answer sheets (Gaffney & Maguire, 1971; Lassiter, 1987).

Recent studies have shown that examinees at all grade levels benefit somewhat from coaching (Bangert-Downs, Kulik, & Kulik, 1983; Messick & Jungeblut, 1981; Powers & Swinton, 1984). A variety of other conditions depress test performance, including lack of sleep, eating a heavy meal, and conflicting personal and social events. Test anxiety also affects test performance. Usually, anxiety depresses scores, although moderate anxiety may actually increase scores on easier tests.

Test-wiseness is the ability to improve scores by taking into account the nature of a test and conditions under which it is administered. Skills associated with being test-wise were grouped into six categories: using time effectively, avoiding errors, eliminating incorrect alternatives, knowing when to guess, being responsive to the teacher's intentions, and taking into account idiosyncrasies built into a test. The latter two categories pertain to deficiencies that teachers often, although needlessly, build into a test.

ADDITIONAL READING

Putka, G. (1992, April 14). Cat and mouse: SAT cram schools intensity battle with the College Board over coaching of students. *The Wall Street Journal,* pp. A1, A4. This article describes a number of tricks taught by SAT coaching schools and the countermoves used by the test developers.

Smith, M. L. (1991). Meanings of test preparation. *American Educational Research Journal, 28,* 521–542. This article describes techniques teachers have been found to use to help their students perform well on a standardized test. Techniques range from teaching test-taking skills to teaching content known to be on the test.

CHAPTER 17

Using Computers to Facilitate Assessment

Computers have undergone phenomenal development. The idea of a digital computer originated with Blaise Pascal, a 17-century mathematician. At age 18, he invented the adding machine to help his father, who was a tax collector. In the 1940s, the first electronic computer was developed at the University of Pennsylvania, and in the 1950s the first commercially sold electronic computer was produced. The cost of hardware and personnel needed to support the first electronic computers was so high that it was believed that only a dozen of the world's largest corporations would ever be able to afford computers.

Today, computers are so prevalent in our lives that one can, without interacting with another person, use an existing computer and the Internet to order a new custom-configured computer that will be home delivered within the week. That new computer will have many times the power of a machine that would be shared by the entire faculty at a typical major research university just 30 years ago. Now it is common for teachers to purchase a personal computer for use at home. In the classroom, teachers use computers for activities as diverse as fostering student creativity, illustrating concepts, individualizing instruction, administering tests, maintaining records, and assigning course grades.

As you are aware, *applications* of computers are also undergoing phenomenal development. Many current applications were not even at a conceptual stage a few years earlier. Popular applications such as word processing, digitally recorded music purchased or played over the Internet, speech recognition, and computer-generated special effects for movies and television were unforeseen by early computer engineers.

This chapter discusses the application of computers to educational testing, particularly classroom testing. Although the role of computers in testing is significant, it is also constrained by three basic conditions. First, there is a larger market for other applications such as word processing and data management than for classroom assessment. In fact, some of the more successful applications of computers in testing are adaptations of data management and word processing software. This condition is changing, however, in part because of developments related to interactive distance learning.

A second constraining factor is the inconsistent nature of classroom activities and computers. Computers, in a dynamic sense, are very simple machines, whereas classrooms represent highly complex environments. However, because computers do what they do very quickly and consistently, their capabilities can be adapted to many classroom needs. For example, computers can very rapidly compare pairs of values. This allows computers to compare the spelling of each word within a student's paper to the words within a dictionary or to convert words spoken into a microphone to a written document.

Because of the speed and consistency of computers, they can emulate complex rules by chaining together large numbers of simple actions. This, for instance, allows computers to check the subject–verb agreement of sentences as well as more complex grammatical rules. Likewise, computers can be programmed with "artificial intelligence," which involves a framework of rules for creating new rules and solving unanticipated problems, but such applications require effective chaining of simple steps by insightful humans. Although an analogy is sometimes drawn between a computer and the human mind, the computer cannot intelligently respond to truly unanticipated events. Unfortunately and fortunately, the assessment of students and other classroom activities are full of such events. Developers of computer software are at a real disadvantage when addressing the complex needs inherent in the interactions between teachers and students.

A third factor limiting the use of computers is that many activities associated with classroom testing not only are unanticipated, but also are not well understood. Take for instance the widely adopted mastery learning strategy. It is not known whether the improved achievement associated with mastery learning strategies is the result of integrating assessment and instruction, or simply caused by spending additional time on instruction. It is not even entirely clear what conditions are unique and critical to realizing benefits from the use of mastery learning. An instructional technique works one time but not another for no apparent reason. Programming a computer for classroom application is somewhere between difficult and impossible because so much is unknown regarding what specifically must be done.

These three factors constrain the application of computers to assessment and other aspects of education. (These factors also restrict computer applications in other professions such as medicine and law). Nevertheless, computers do provide important benefits to a variety of professions including education. This chapter reviews both the constraints and benefits of computers as they pertain to classroom assessment. The following four interrelated applications of computers are addressed:

- Development of test items
- Production of tests

- Administration and scoring of tests
- Management of student progress records

These applications are often not distinct. In fact, some applications such as management of student records invariably accompany other applications such as scoring of tests or assignment of course grades.

Because of the rapid developments in computer technology, this chapter generally does not discuss capabilities of specific machines or computer software. Information of that nature is better obtained through more frequently updated sources such as the Internet, periodicals, workshops, and literature distributed by vendors of computer hardware and software. The present chapter does include numerous examples to illustrate present and anticipated roles of computers in classroom testing. Information obtained through this chapter should facilitate your review of current developments concerned with computer applications to classroom assessment.

USING COMPUTERS TO DEVELOP TEST ITEMS

Computers can facilitate the creation and also the improvement of test items. The computer's ability to develop new items is more restricted than its ability to help improve existing items.

Developing New Items

A computer can create test items that measure factual skills such as associating names and dates with historical events and identifying elements in the periodical table. To write such items, a computer must be provided the same type of information a teacher would use. For instance, to generate items that determine whether students can correctly associate composers of Western classical music to historical musical periods, a computer would need to know how the equations are to be phrased and formatted as well as names of composers and associated eras. Figure 17.1 illustrates how this information might be structured for a computer.

Of course, a teacher can similarly construct items regarding composers, and can probably do so in less time than required to program the computer. But in some respects, the computer has an advantage. Once it is programmed, students can request a set of items from the computer without involving the teacher, or, as discussed later, the computer can quickly create items and assemble them into the parallel forms of a test.

The computer is also effective at creating items requiring computations. For example, the computer can be provided an item form that specifies the mathematical operations to be involved, how the numbers are to be displayed, and the range of numbers to be used. The computer might similarly generate items requiring students

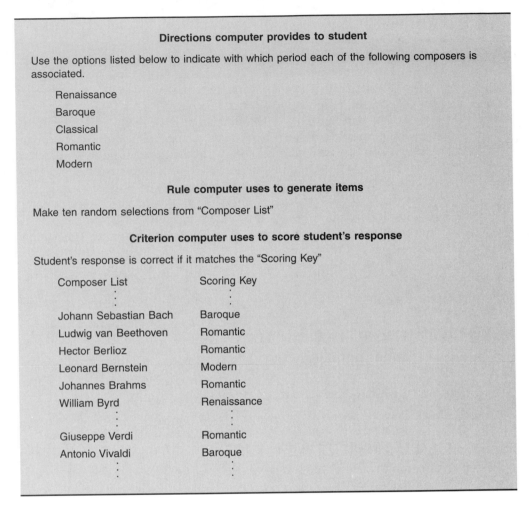

Figure 17.1
An item form for computer-generated items to test student knowledge of composers associated with Western musical periods

to solve quadratic equations. Figure 17.2 illustrates how such a math item might be structured for a computer. A computer can similarly be programmed to create items related to sentence structure, as long as concise rules can be established. When procedural rather than declarative knowledge is involved, further rules have to be programmed into the computer if nonsensical items are to be avoided, such as meaningless but grammatically correct sentences.

A computer can use text from various sources and then determine whether students can identify words it deliberately misspells using prescribed spelling rules, or, using text, a computer could test student ability to recognize parts of speech; students could be asked to classify the words that the computer can unequivocally identify as being a noun, verb, adjective, and so on.

Directions computer provides to student: Use factoring to solve for x in the following quadratic equation . . .

Rule computer uses to generate items

Present equation $x^2 + bx + c = 0$.

Set values of b and c to random integers between 1 and 9.

The value $b^2 - 4$ must be positive.

Criterion computer uses to score student's response

The student must give two answers (order not important) . . .

1. $x = \dfrac{-b + \sqrt{b^2 - 4c}}{2}$

2. $x = \dfrac{-b - \sqrt{b^2 - 4c}}{2}$

Figure 17.2

An item form for computer-generated items to test student ability to solve quadratic equations

As the capabilities of computers and their programming techniques evolve, the sophistication of computer-generated items is likely to expand. For example, if a computer could be instructed in vocabulary and rules for generating a coherent series of sentences, it might be able to generate reading tests or tests that examine student ability to translate between languages. Or if a computer could be programmed with rules of logic, the computer might be able to generate logical and illogical propositions for the student to evaluate. In the foreseeable future, the question remains as to whether it is more efficient to program a computer to create items or to create the items without involving a computer. At present, however, it is generally much easier to write new items than program a computer to create items. The developer of curriculum materials is more likely to develop programs that create items than is the individual teacher.

Revising Existing Items

A computer can greatly facilitate the review of items. This capability is very useful because improving an existing item requires less time than creating a totally new item. Also, new items tend to be more ambiguous than items that have been previously used and revised.

For instance, when multiple-choice items are involved, a computer can perform the computations associated with item analysis techniques such as those described in Chapter 10. When short-answer or completion items are involved, the computer can administer and score students' responses, as long as response options are limited. The computer can then distinguish between wrong answers that the item developer had anticipated, such as common misconceptions, and wrong answers that were unanticipated, which can be used to help identify ambiguities within the item.

USING COMPUTERS TO PRODUCE TESTS

Computers can significantly help with test production. This section examines two rather distinct roles of computers in test production. In the first, a computer is used to assemble the words and graphics of a test into a functional and attractive document. This procedure you will recognize as *word processing*. In the second role, a computer is used both to manage a potentially large set of test items and to produce tests by selecting samples of these items that match certain specifications. This procedure is called *item banking*.

Word Processing

Word processing has become the single most popular application of personal computers. A word-processing program can obviously be used to create and revise documents efficiently, including tests printed on paper or those displayed using a computer. Word processors can also easily insert objects such as pictures and diagrams, including those copied from electronic sources such as the Internet and supplements that come with curriculum materials.

Here are some of the common word-processing features that are particularly useful when producing tests. Some of these features may be unanticipated.

1. *Spelling and grammar checkers:* The computer quickly spots misspelled words and often lists the correct spelling of words you may have intended to use. The computer can spot many grammatical errors or words used inappropriately, and can suggest ways to state ideas more directly, such as changing a sentence from the passive to active voice.

2. *Automatic numbering:* The test items can be numbered automatically. This feature helps make sure items are numbered correctly. It prevents two items being assigned the same number or getting the numbering out of sequence. Also, to improve test security, you can quickly create a second form of a test by moving the second half of the test ahead of the first; the automatic numbering quickly renumbers the items.

3. *Style templates:* A word-processing program comes with a large set of preprogrammed styles. You also can easily create your own. These styles are one of the most underutilized major features of a word processor. A *style* is a preprogrammed format that you can apply to a word, sentence, or paragraph. Invoking a style immediately sets, for instance, all characteristics of a paragraph that one can control through formatting, such as size and type of font, indentations, tab settings, and spacing above and below the paragraph. For example, when producing a multiple-choice test, you might create one style for item stems and another for the options that follow a stem. The style associated with the item stems could automatically number the test items. The style associated with the item options could automatically label each option with the appropriate letter and indent the options under the stem. Collectively, the stem and option styles could establish appropriate spacing between adjacent items and ensure that an item stem and its options are not split between two pages within the test. Different styles can be created for other item formats.

4. *Page layout:* A word processor can format text into multiple columns, as in newspapers. Using two or more columns per page decreases the width of each line, which often makes test items easier to read. Also, using multiple columns usually increases the number of test items included on each page and reduces reproduction costs.

5. *Print preview:* You can see on the screen exactly what each page will look like when printed. If, for instance you dislike the appearance of a page or find a page break unacceptable, you can quickly remedy the problem before printing the test.

6. *Macros:* These allow you to record and later play back a series of keystrokes. For example, a macro can be recorded that alphabetically sorts the options to each multiple-choice item, places the appropriate letter in front of each option, correctly formats each stem and options, and sequentially numbers the test items, all with a single keystroke.

7. *Graphics features:* You can insert special characters and illustrations. Special characters are particularly useful in foreign language and math tests. Most word processors also include a formula editor that helps create typed formulas. Photographs, artwork, and graphs are also easily included.

ITEM BANKING

Estes and Arter (undated) define an item bank as a "large collection of distinguishable test items" (p. 5). *Large* means the bank includes more items than one would include in a single test. *Collection* implies that the items are grouped together. This grouping may be accomplished by recording items in a computer file or even by writing them on index cards and keeping them in a box. *Distinguishable* implies that the bank includes descriptions for each item such as its difficulty or the skill it measures. This description provides the basis for selecting items for inclusion in a particular test.

Item banks are becoming increasingly popular. In part, this is because items are time-consuming to develop. If items are added to the bank as they are developed, the expense of developing new items for every test can be reduced. When appropriate, teachers can further reduce the cost of item development by sharing items between banks. The popularity of item banking is also increasing because of the growing availability of computers.

Item banks have typically been developed by state departments of education, research institutes, and private companies. Some are sold or distributed free, whereas others are for the private use of the agency. Most item banks are designed for use at state or district levels. This emphasis is somewhat unfortunate because the majority of testing and therefore test development occurs at the classroom level. The popularity of item banking at the classroom level is increasing as item-banking software becomes more visible to classroom teachers, such as through computer disks and web sites developed by publishers of curriculum materials.

Aside from developing the items, a major cost associated with establishing a computerized item bank is inputting the items into a computer. Some item-banking programs facilitate this process by incorporating word-processing features. For instance, the program may help format test items in such the same way as a word-processing macro. Some publishers provide electronic copies of test items on CD-ROM or other medium, which greatly facilitates their entry into a computerized item bank.

Item-banking software is generally much less adept at working with graphics than most word-processing programs. It also is less adept at handling material that is common to a group of items, such as a reading passage that precedes a series of items. With item banking, all content related to an item usually must be maintained with individual items.

Item-banking software can generate single or multiple forms of a test, even up to a separate form for each student. Many item-banking programs retain within the computer the answer key to each form it generates. These answer keys are later used to score the tests. Some item-banking programs automatically update statistical information for each item when the tests is scored, such as how often the item has been used and its difficulty.

Millman and Arter (1984) pointed out that when an item-banking program produces a test, the difficulty of that test depends on which items happened to be sampled. This in turn affects how students will perform on the test. (A similar issue occurs with computer adaptive testing, which is discussed later in this chapter.) Some item-banking programs control the difficulty of the items that are selected. Of course, a teacher assembling a test without the aid of a computer has these same problems.

Monitoring the quality of items within banks is important. Computers cannot evaluate item quality or the adequacy of procedures for categorizing items. This concern is particularly significant when items are imported from external sources such as textbook publishers and other teachers. If you use an item bank, you should review the appropriateness and quality of items. The item bank should also be reviewed periodically to identify and delete test items that are no longer relevant.

USING COMPUTERS TO ADMINISTER AND SCORE TESTS

Previous sections have described the use of computers to construct test items and facilitate test production. The present section examines the use of computers to administer and score tests.

Computers are sometimes used to administer tests in such a limited manner that they really provide no advantage over pencil-and-paper tests. This would be the case if the computer presented the same set of items to every student. A number of years ago, Roid (1986) warned that "computer applications are ill-fated unless they provide a new dimension to testing not possible with non-automated techniques" (p. 37). Page-turning tasks can be accomplished at less cost without the computer, and a computer often adds some of its own handicaps to testing. For instance, compared to a printed test, computer-administered tests tend to be administered in a noisier environment, provide less visual resolution for text and graphics, and reduce a student's ease and sometimes flexibility in moving between items. Students usually cannot write on computer screens as readily as they can on paper, which may affect the way students respond to items such as those involving computations. Administering a test by computer appears to change students' scores, affect the rate at which responses to items are omitted, and alter the number of items that can be answered within a given amount of time. These characteristics affect the interpretation of computer-administered tests. With norm-referenced tests, for example, separate norms usually have to be established for computer-administered and paper-and-pencil versions of a test.

Computers have several advantages over conventionally administered tests. One is the computer's flexibility in presenting stimuli. As many of the electronic games clearly illustrate, computers have the potential to produce complex and quite realistic simulations, and likewise assess students' abilities to solve problems that printed tests must measure indirectly. Computers can also adapt the test to the ability of the student taking the test; for instance, administering more difficult items to more proficient individuals. Another advantage is the computer's ability to provide immediate feedback at the conclusion of each test and automatically maintain student records.

Computer Adaptive Tests

Computer adaptive testing is one of the more significant innovations within computer administered tests. With computer adaptive testing, the computer selects subsequent items based on each examinee's performance on previous items. Examinees who correctly answer previous items tend to subsequently get more difficult items. Likewise, examinees who incorrectly answer items tend to get easier items. By adjusting items as the test progresses, it is possible to establish the examinee's level of performance using fewer items and likewise less time. Demonstrations of computer adaptive testing can be found on the Internet. Locations include the ERIC Assessment and Evaluation site (*http://ericae.net*) and the Educational Testing Service site (*http://www.ets.org*).

An important consideration with computer adaptive testing is that the same scale must be used to report results from the test even though different examinees answer different items. With large-scale testing such as the Professional Assessments for Beginning Teachers (The Praxis Series), this is accomplished using a procedure available within what is called item response theory (IRT).

With item response theory, an item characteristic curve is established for each item. Two item characteristic curves are illustrated in Figure 17.3. Using a common scale across all items (and all examinees), each curve establishes the probability that examinees of different ability levels will correctly answer the item. As you would anticipate and as both curves in Figure 17.3 illustrate, the probability of correctly answering an item increases as the ability of examinees increases. Obviously, the curves in Figure 17.3 are not straight lines. That means that at some ability level, examinees' probability of correctly answering the item improves rapidity. The ability level at which this happens varies from item to item. The best item to administer to an examinee is the one whose curve has the steepest slope for that examinee's ability level. This is because, the higher the slope of the curve, the more the item is able to distinguish a student's ability from somewhat lower or higher ability levels.

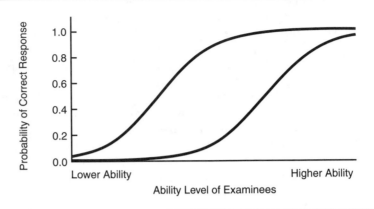

Figure 17.3
Item characteristic curves for two test items

Box 17.1 *Apply What You Are Learning*

Figure 17.3 shows item characteristic curves for two items. Using information from the preceding paragraph, is Item A or Item B more appropriate for students with higher ability? Why?

Answer can be found at the end of the chapter.

Based on whether or not the examinee correctly answers an item, the estimate of the examinee's ability is increased or decreased. The next item administered by the computer is the item with the curve having the steepest slope for the new estimate of the examinee's ability. The computer continues administering items until the estimates of the examinee's ability level stabilize.

Computer adaptive testing is used with large-scale testing programs such as the Professional Assessments for Beginning Teachers and the Graduate Record Examination. An increasing number of the standardized achievement tests administered by school districts will use computer adaptive techniques. Computer adaptive testing is usually limited to these large testing programs. The reason for this is that the responses from a large number of examinees are required in order to establish the item characteristic curve for each test item.

Nonadaptive Computer Administered Tests

Computer administered tests that are not adaptive are also commonly used in schools. Although different items may be administered to each student, the items administered to a particular student are selected randomly from an item pool rather than based on that student's performance on previous items within the test. These computer-administered tests may be integrated into special instruction delivered by computer, such as within math or reading modules. Teachers in many content areas also use computer software to administer classroom quizzes or tests, thus allowing students to be assessed individually when they are ready.

With these nonadaptive tests, however, an item characteristic curve has not been established for each test item, so there is no ability scale that is common across items. You want to be alert to this phenomenon. When different items are being administered to each student, but items are selected randomly rather than adaptively selected based on performance with earlier items, differences in the performance of students may be nothing other than the result of these students being administered different items. Always use your personal observations and other sources of information to supplement estimates of student performance obtained from these tests.

Sometimes, tests administered by computer use the same items for all students. When students take the tests at different times, the use of common items may reduce test security. On the other hand, when the same items are administered to all students, it is easier to interpret scores on the test, since the scores are not confounded by students having completed different test items.

Computer Scoring of Constructed Responses

Computers or other electronic devices have been scoring multiple-choice and other objectively scored tests for over 40 years. The efficiency of electronic scoring is largely responsible for the extensive use of objectively scored formats. Over 30 years ago, but on a much smaller scale, computers were also used to score students' responses to completion and even essay items. These initial applications were quite basic when compared to capabilities available today. They were nevertheless very insightful applications of the early computers. Computers scored completion items by matching answers students entered through a keyboard to word lists entered into the computer's memory. Computers scored essays by using variables that had been found to correlate well with scores given by expert human raters (Page, 1968), such as total number of words within the essay, average number of words within each sentence, and other characteristics not explicitly used to score essays. The scores assigned by the computer, however, correlated with human raters as well as the human raters' scores correlated with each other.

Computer scoring of constructed responses has become more common and more sophisticated. Completion items are still scored by matching students' keyboard entries to word lists stored in the computer, although software now can detect and override misspellings, and accommodate alternate phrasings and extraneous words or spacing included in a response.

Computer scoring of essays is still mostly experimental, although the scoring algorithms are much more sophisticated. Grammar, sentence structure, and style can be evaluated much as they presently are by current word-processing programs. In large-scale testing programs involving essays, computers are being used to reduce the cost of scoring papers. With some tests, instead of using multiple readers, one reader and a computer evaluate each response. Additional readers are used when the first reader and computer disagree. In the foreseeable future, software will be available that can provide a basic review of essay papers written for classroom assignments.

Approaches to computer scoring of constructed responses are quite varied. Braun, Bennett, Frye, and Soloway (1990) describe the use of a computer to score students' ability to correct a faulty computer program. To accomplish this, the computer has to evaluate the logic a student is applying as well as determine names being used for variables. In this research, the computer was generally able to assign the appropriate score to a student's solution, but was less able to diagnose specific errors that caused incorrect solutions.

Davey, Godwin, and Mittelholtz (1997) described a computer-based test where examinees proof a writing passage presented on the computer screen. Using a mouse, the examinee points to a location within the passage where a change is to be made with respect to grammar, organization, or style. Clicking on the passage causes a menu of possible edits of the passage to appear. The examinee selects among these options. A given option may correct an error within the written passage, replace the error with another error, or create an error where none existed. When applied to postsecondary students, this technique along with its scoring procedures was found to be at least as good as alternative techniques used to place students in appropriate-level writing classes.

USING COMPUTERS TO MANAGE STUDENT PROGRESS RECORDS

Computers are extremely proficient at maintaining, managing, and reporting data. In fact, general-purpose spreadsheet and database management software are among the most popular applications of personal computers. Within education, computer management of records makes it practical to track students, to determine quickly what each student has achieved, and to formulate plans for future instruction. The data management capabilities of computers can facilitate the integration of testing and instruction and thus help personalize learning. A computer can also become a means of collecting and reviewing student work, becoming in essence an electronic portfolio.

Software used to manage student progress is not easy to classify because computer programs placed in a particular category tend to share, with considerable variability, capabilities of programs in other categories. For our purposes, we will use three categories to discuss management software: electronic portfolios, web-based management systems, and electronic gradebooks.

Electronic Portfolios

Tuttle (1997) describes an electronic portfolio as a concise, annotated collection of student work that reflects educational standards, which is essentially the same description one might give their nonelectronic counterparts. Because they utilize a computer, electronic portfolios provide some additional features. For instance, in addition to print and graphics, they can contain multimedia material that involves sound, motion, and hyperlinks. They can easily be updated and revised. Depending on the software, the portfolio can be accessed over the Internet, allowing students and teachers to work with its contents while in the classroom or at home. If other teachers use comparable software, electronic portfolios can easily follow students into other classrooms or potentially other schools. However, unless material is created in electronic form, it must be scanned or converted through some other means. Also, electronic representation sometimes loses qualities, such as texture within artwork or the structural strength of a constructed object.

As with any portfolio that is used for assessment, instructional goals must guide its use. The software must also provide students a means to include annotations that establish how submitted products demonstrate proficiency with respective goals. The software must also provide a means for teachers to provide feedback and for students to respond. The software should also alert the student and teacher to new entries that have been made, and should provide the teacher a means of recording and monitoring student progress with each goal.

Several electronic software programs have been developed, such as the Grady Portfolio Assessment and Scholastic's Electronic Portfolio. An alternative is to use a multimedia program such as HyperStudio. Still another option is to use a web-based program such as WebBoard (*http://webboard.oreilly.com*), which allows students to post categorized material including computer files. Teachers and other students can subsequently respond to that material. Tuttle (1997) lists several electronic portfolio computer programs as well as multimedia software that is useful for electronic portfolios.

Web-Based Management Systems

A web-based management system such as BlackBoard (*http://www.blackboard.com*) consists of a ready-made web site into which a teacher can place a variety of course materials and student records. Because it is on the Internet, the teacher and students can access the system while at school or at home. Course materials maintained in the system might include announcements, a class schedule, descriptions of assignments, student work, tests, and class records.

A management system can administer tests over the Internet. Multiple-choice and completion items are scored by the computer, and the student records are updated automatically. Brief-response essay items can also be administered, with the teacher later scoring responses and recording scores. Various options can be used with these assessments. For instance, students can be allowed single or multiple attempts on each test. At the end of each test, students can be allowed to review the items and their answers, and even view feedback comments provided for each item by the teacher. Passwords can be employed, but because students are able to access the class web site from anywhere, conditions under which a test is administered usually cannot be monitored. This lack of security may cause teachers to minimize the weights assigned to online tests or quizzes, or to use the system to administer practice tests.

A web-based management system allows students to electronically submit assigned work. The teacher can make assignment work and feedback a private interaction between the student and teacher. Alternatively a discussion-board format can be used where students' work and the teacher's feedback are public to all students in the class. E-mail is then used when feedback or comments should be made privately to a student. Students can work jointly on assignments within groups. Assignment work can be posted to the web site either as text or as attached files, which allows submission of multimedia material. The web site can serve as an electronic portfolio for each student. A teacher can allow students to access through the web site their own scores on tests and other records.

The company that creates the web-based software may allow a teacher to use without cost the management system on a server supported by the company. Alternatively a school or school district can purchase a license to use the software on a locally operated server.

Electronic Gradebooks

A task many teachers learn quickly not to enjoy is maintaining student records and later assigning end-of-term grades. The worst part of this chore is the weighting and totaling of each student's scores.

A variety of computer programs are available to help with this task. The programming task is straightforward, and many teachers write their own grading programs. Typically, a grading program allows the teacher to enter each student's scores and then totals these scores using weights specified by the teacher. Most programs then assign grades using the criteria provided by the teacher.

The better grading programs also identify students for whom scores are missing. Some programs allow the teacher to insert notes for future reference or to display on the computer screen the scores for a single student. These latter two options help the teacher discuss course grades with a student. Various grading programs provide options for handling missing scores such as setting a student's omitted score to zero or excluding the score when computing grades.

Assigning grades usually involves inputting a substantial number of scores. The ease with which this is accomplished should be considered when selecting a grading program. Programs that require scores to be entered alphabetically by student name are less efficient than those that make it easy to enter scores in whatever order student work is evaluated. Some programs automatically enter scores from tests when the computer administers the tests or when the tests are scored by a desktop scanner.

Knowing how a grading program assigns weights to scores and how it handles missing scores is important. For example, some grading programs automatically assign a zero to any test or assignment that a student has not completed. That procedure is equivalent to a weather observer recording the day's high temperature as zero whenever a measure of the temperature is missing. Chapter 18 describes how to combine scores into an overall grade.

The Tucows web site (*http://tukids.tucows.com*) lists and rates computer educational programs, particularly those used by children. This web site includes a section for parents and teachers that evaluates gradebook software among other programs. The web site uses the number of "cows" rather than the more familiar "stars" to convey its ratings, with five cows designating software judged most superior. The Tucows web site uses computer servers located at a number of regional sites. To access their ratings, first select a site near you and then click on the software link.

Evaluating Management Software

Several factors influence the effectiveness of data-management programs. Key factors include the following:

1. *The data management system must retain and be able to retrieve useful information.* This represents the single most important quality of data management systems. In the classroom as in most settings, this is a vague quality. Usefulness of information depends largely on what a user such as the teacher will do with it. Normally, a classroom record management system contains achievement information, possibly as detailed as each student's status on individual skills. The management system might also record scores on standardized tests, anecdotal notes, procedures for contacting parents, and medical information. Data management systems can also retain information such as class schedules, extracurricular activities, and payment of activity fees. The list is endless. The needs of the individual teacher must determine what is relevant and useful.

2. *A data management system must be able to summarize information.* Usually, a teacher will want to detect trends across students before analyzing details. For instance, the teacher will try to determine which skills cause the greatest difficulty and then identify specific students experiencing problems with these skills. Unfortunately, developers of some record management programs favor reports that list all available information for each student. The magnitude of information then makes reports difficult to use. Reports can summarize data by computing averages, by categorizing and indicating the number of students in each category, and by graphing distributions or patterns.

3. *A data management system should anticipate the needs of teachers.* This is very difficult to accomplish unless the developer is extremely familiar with what teachers do in the classroom. Also, many potential applications of a data management program simply are not anticipated. One way to anticipate needs is to design a flexible program. That is, the teacher should be provided a large number of options for inputting student records and generating reports. Ideally, data management systems should provide a shell from which the teacher can easily modify and develop a sophisticated personalized management program. This is the strategy used by general-purpose data management programs such as Access.

4. *A data management system should be easy to learn.* It has been suggested that the time saved by using computers is replaced with the time required to select and learn new computer software. This will always be true to some degree. However, the efficiencies associated with using a computer to manage student data are improved if the system is easy to learn. The easiest programs to learn are those with limited capability. One quickly outgrows such programs, and the time spent learning the system is lost. A preferred strategy is for a sophisticated program to include several basic procedures that are both useful and easy to learn. The teacher can then build on knowledge of these basic procedures as familiarity with the data management system expands.

5. *A data management system must be easy and efficient to use.* A variety of techniques make some data management systems easier to use than others. Logical words or keys on the keyboard should be used to execute commands. Allowing the teacher to decide the names or keys associated with commands often helps. A minimal number of steps should be required to proceed from one operation to another. A mouse or other device can be used to display and point at the desired command on the computer screen and thus quickly execute actions. Some data management programs remember which options the teacher previously selected and make these choices the defaults for later operations. Data management systems often have built-in, context-sensitive help messages that on request explain what should be done next or list available options. This saves frequent references to the user manual and is very handy for less commonly used procedures.

6. *A data management system must provide valid information.* Data management systems are usually very accurate in that they correctly reproduce data that have been entered into the computer. As obvious as the need may seem, the validity of those data often is not questioned. Within classrooms, the most frequently used data are student achievement of individual skills. The tests and other observations used to generate those data most accurately measure those skills. Decisions as to whether a student has sufficiently mastered each skill must be based on a sufficient number of valid items.

7. *When possible, the data management system should automate the management of students.* Many decisions about students' actions can be automated by a data management system. If a computer controls test administration, the management system can allow retesting if it meets specified conditions such as an appropriate lapsed time since the initial test or a sufficiently limited number of attempted retests. A management system can also prevent students from taking subsequent tests (or proceeding) if critical prerequisite skills have not been achieved. When instruction is individualized, the system can verify whether students are pacing themselves appropriately. By allowing the computer to automate selected aspects of student management, more time is available to the teacher for tasks a machine cannot perform.

SUMMARY

Dramatic changes in computer technology have occurred within a period of a few years, but radical changes in education, including educational measurement, have not resulted from the use of computers. Basic reasons for this include the relatively small market for computer applications within testing, the complexities of the classroom environment, and the lack of full understanding regarding optimal strategies for using measurement within instruction.

Four applications of computers to testing were addressed: development of test items, production of tests, administration and scoring of tests, and management of student progress records. Often, several of these applications are combined into a single system.

The future of computer applications in testing is difficult to predict. Situations such as a critical teacher shortage or the development of a highly efficient and easy-to-use language for programming artificial intelligence could dramatically change both the interest in and capabilities of computer applications. Emerging popular trends can also affect future applications. In discussing evolving changes in communication technology, Duncanson and Chew (1988) pointed out that "revolution requires demand as well as capacity" (p. 286). Computers represent a significant tool within educational measurement. Their use should be approached openly, enthusiastically, and cautiously.

ANSWERS: APPLY WHAT YOU ARE LEARNING

17.1 Item B is more appropriate for students of higher ability. Within Figure 17.3, the horizontal axis represents a range of students' abilities, with lower abilities at the left. For students at a given ability level, one wants to use the item whose item characteristic curve is the steepest at that ability level. The item characteristic curve for Item B has the steeper slope at higher ability levels.

CHAPTER 18

Reporting Student Performance
to Parents and Others

S chools use a variety of systems to report student progress. The most common are conferences, narrative systems, such as letters to parents, checklists, and letter grades. These systems are often used in combination to supplement one another. For instance, parent conferences may be used in combination with letter grades.

Particularly with older students, letter grades are the most widely used system for reporting performance. Letter grades are vaguely defined; therefore, important considerations include determining on what to base grades and the levels of proficiency to be associated with each grade.

Achievement of course objectives is usually listed as the major consideration when assigning grades. Other factors often include student motivation, attitude, and effort. Grades sometimes also reflect discipline, such as when they are adjusted because a student handed an assignment in late or cheated on a test. Incorporating achievement, motivation, attitude, effort, and discipline into a single grade may broaden the meaning of grades, but it also complicates their interpretation.

In addition to determining what should be included in grades, a teacher must establish criteria for each grade and weights to associate with individual assessments.

This chapter helps you achieve three skills:

- Recognize advantages and limitations of alternative systems for reporting student performance outside the classroom
- Establish criteria when assigning letter grades
- Determine the role of grades in motivating and disciplining students

ALTERNATIVE REPORTING SYSTEMS

Schools use a variety of systems to report student performance. The individual teacher typically does not have control over which system is used. However, by briefly describing each system and identifying its major advantages and limitations, this chapter will help you recognize the capabilities of whatever system you are expected to use. The systems discussed here are percentage grades, letter and number grades, pass–fail marks, checklists, written descriptions, portfolios, and conferences with parents.

Percentage Grades

Percentage grades assign each student a number between 0 and 100. In the United States at the beginning of the twentieth century, this system was the most popular grading system. Most schools no longer assign percentage grades; however, many teachers use percentage grades to report students' performance on individual tests and assignments. Also, school districts often use percentage grades to communicate standards that teachers are to use when assigning letter grades. The term *percentage* is used because these grades are assumed to represent the percentage of content a student has mastered.

Advantages.   The major advantage of percentage grades is that they provide a convenient summary of student performance. They can be recorded and processed quickly. If the distribution of grades for a given class is known, percentage grades provide a quick overview for a counselor or other audiences of student performance relative to others in the class.

Limitations.   One limitation of this reporting system is that the name itself is misleading. A student who receives a 100 probably has not mastered 100% of course content in the sense that further improvement is impossible. Nor is it correct to state that a person who receives a 75 has learned three fourths of the content. Simply changing the difficulty of the tests or class assignments will significantly alter students' percentage scores.

A second limitation of percentage grades is that they imply a degree of precision that cannot be justified given the reliability of grades. Although percentage scores outside the range of 50% to 100% are rarely assigned, teachers cannot distinguish among levels of student achievement as accurately as the scores suggest.

A third limitation is that percentage grades do not indicate the combination of skills that a student has achieved. Instead, the percentage grade provides an overall indication of student achievement.

Letter Grades

Letter grades consist of a series of letters; typically, five letters are used. Sometimes letters are selected that correspond to certain adjectives (e.g., Excellent, Good, Average, Poor, Unacceptable). The most common series is A, B, C, D, and F. The vast majority of elementary and secondary schools and postsecondary institutions use letter grades.

Some teachers and many school systems relate letter grades to percentage grades. For instance, the range of 90% to 100% might be equated to an A. As indicated previously, percentage grades really do not represent percentage of mastery. Therefore, associating a range of scores with each grade poorly defines letter grades. Unfortunately, this point is often ignored. A teacher or school district may be thought to have higher grading standards than another if higher percentages are associated with respective grades. Because the difficulty of tests and assignments significantly affects the percentage of maximum points that students receive, letter grades cannot be meaningfully associated with percentage scores.

Advantages.   As with percentage grades, the major advantage of letter grades is that they provide a convenient summary of student performance. A second advantage is that they approach the optimal number of categories for reporting student progress. If a grading system has too many categories, such as with percentage grades, the system implies precision that does not exist. A grading system with too few categories has reduced reliability and fails to report meaningful distinctions among students.

Mitchelmore (1981) proposes using a number of categories that result in assigning grades within one value of their true grade to at least 90% of students. (A true grade is the grade each student would receive if grades were perfectly reliable.) For individual tests and assignments the maximum acceptable number of grades would vary from three to nine. The number of grades in letter-grading systems fits within this range.

A third advantage of using the letter grades A to F is their prevalence and hence familiarity in the United States and some other countries. However, this familiarity can lead to making claims for grades that are unfounded. Letter grades derive much of their meaning from their relative positions on a scale or from what we have come to expect of students who have received a particular grade. This also is how values on other scales, such as temperature and weight, derive much of their meaning. The principal meaning of the grade B is derived from it being below an A and above a C. With experience, teachers and students learn to anticipate the specific level of performance associated with a given grade, much as we learn to anticipate how comfortable the outside air will be when we are simply told the temperature. Unlike grades, however, a temperature scale is tied to absolute events, such as the freezing and boiling points of water. As we note later, letter grades more adequately communicate student performance when teachers strive to use common grading standards.

Limitations.   As with percentage grades, one limitation of letter grades is that they do not indicate the combination of skills that a student has achieved. They provide only a general indication of performance.

A second limitation is that a letter grade by itself does not provide sufficient information to determine whether a student should be promoted to the next grade level in school. Nevertheless, schools typically identify a specific letter grade, which, if assigned, prevents the student from advancing. F is often used for that purpose. If a minimally acceptable level of performance that was educationally meaningful were established, teachers could reserve the F grade for students who achieved below that standard.

A variety of procedures have been proposed for setting minimum standards (Berk, 1986; Shepard, 1984). For our purposes, a minimum standard is defined as the point below which students have been shown to be unable to learn subsequent material effectively. If a grade such as F is used to indicate that a student is performing below the minimum standard, that grade should be reserved for identifying such students. Because of its meaning, an F grade should not be assigned to some predetermined percentage of students.

A related problem arises when grades are averaged. In college, for example, an F usually indicates that a student has not gained sufficient proficiency to be given credit for a course. However, a C average is usually required to graduate or advance past a particular year in school. A similar procedure is used in high schools, but with different cutoff requirements. This approach assumes that low achievement in one area can be counterbalanced by high achievement elsewhere. Little attention is given to the issue of in which areas, specifically, the low and high achievement appears and whether this combination indicates that the student would benefit more from retention or promotion. This issue is particularly relevant given that the benefits of retaining students have not been established. For example, Holmes and Matthews (1984) reviewed 44 students concerned with the effects of repeating a grade in school on elementary and junior high students. They concluded that the negative effects of retention in grade consistently outweigh the positive outcomes.

Pass–Fail Marks

A pass–fail marking system collapses all letter grades into two categories. For example, the F grade could represent failing status, with all other letter grades considered a pass. Sometimes a D, or a C in graduate school, is assumed to represent failing status. A variation of pass–fail is pass–no pass, where grades are recorded in a transcript only when a student has demonstrated sufficient mastery of course content. Beginning in the 1960s, pass–fail marks gained considerable popularity. Their intent was to encourage students to explore academic subjects they would otherwise avoid because of anticipated low grades (Weller, 1983). Pass–fail grades are used almost exclusively at the postsecondary level. Usually, pass–fail is offered as an optional grade, although some institutions use this marking system exclusively. A variation of pass–fail is a pass/no-pass policy in which a student's record lists only the courses that a student has passed.

Advantages.   The proposed advantages of pass–fail grades have been that students will broaden their program of studies and take more challenging courses if provided a pass–fail option. However, studies indicate that students do not vary the courses they select when allowed to take a course pass–fail (Stallings & Smock, 1971).

Limitations.   Pass–fail grades have a number of significant disadvantages not shared by other marking systems. One general limitation of pass–fail marks is that they reduce the utility of grades. Advisors are less able to determine how students are achieving in courses when the pass–fail option is used. Colleges are less able to estimate how well an admissions applicant will succeed when a transcript contains a substantial number of pass–fail grades. Students tend to use the pass–fail option to avoid low grades in courses they would take regardless of the grading options. Research suggests that students achieve less when a pass–fail system is used (Karlins, Kaplan, & Stuart, 1969).

A second limitation is that pass–fail grades tend to have low reliability. Ebel (1965) estimated that if the reliability of grades using a five-category system were 0.85, reducing the number of categories to two would reduce the reliability to 0.63. This lower reliability of pass–fail grades was also observed in research by Millman, Slovacek, Kulick, and Mitchell (1983).

Checklists

A checklist allows a teacher to indicate which of a variety of statements describes a given student. Statements on the checklist may pertain to specific academic skills, behavioral and attitudinal traits, or some combination of these. A distinct checklist can be established for each course to reflect the content of the subject area. Checklists are often used to report student attitude and work habits in addition to academic skills. The use of checklists is normally limited to elementary and some secondary schools.

Advantages.   The major advantage of checklists is that they more adequately communicate student performance. Lack of specific information is a significant limitation of the preceding systems. A second advantage is that checklists allow the teacher to report separately a variety of traits relevant to instruction. With letter grades, teachers are tempted to combined multiple, unrelated qualities into a single grade, which substantially increases the difficulty parents and others have with interpreting what they mean. Checklists circumvent this problem.

Limitations.   Checklists are time-consuming to prepare and process. Computers can alleviate this problem, particularly when handheld computers are used for recording observations and other assessments of student performance. Incorporating a summary grade into checklists enables school personnel and staff at other institutions to process them more efficiently.

Another concern is that great care must be taken to construct a checklist with statements that clearly describe pertinent behaviors. Statements should express behaviors and traits that are directly observable. Inference by teachers, parents, and others should not be required when interpreting what statements mean. For example, "The student uses appropriate punctuation when writing sentences" is more useful than "The student writes well." Guidelines discussed in Chapter 12 for constructing a checklist generally apply in this present content. Because checklists are primarily used to provide information to parents, parents should assist in the development and revision of checklists used for grading.

Particularly in elementary and middle schools, checklists are increasingly being used as a substitute for letter grades. This change often is initiated by teachers who, with at least some justification, are concerned about the negative effects that letter grades have, particularly on less proficient students. When parents are not heavily involved in the development and ongoing evaluation of the checklists, little or nothing is gained by giving parents the detailed information that a checklist can provide. Often, parents cannot effectively use the detailed information unless a teacher narrative accompanies it. Checklists can also be misleading, because they sometimes appear to present inconsistent information. For example, early in the year, a checklist might indicate that a student is using correct punctuation when writing sentences. Later in the year, when more complex punctuation skills are taught, the same checklist might indicate that the same student is not using punctuation correctly. The parents will likely conclude that the child is losing rather than gaining proficiency.

Typically, parents are unable to use highly detailed information about a child's achievement. They do not observe the day-to-day details of classroom work and often are unaware of the pedagogy critical to effective learning. Usually, parents want to know whether everything is all right in general and what they can do to facilitate the child's achievement in school. This information may best be conveyed through a general rating of performance within each academic area, accompanied by brief written descriptions that help the parents interpret and use these ratings.

Written Descriptions

An alternative or supplement to assigning grades is to write a narrative description of each student's work. The narrative can describe traits that facilitate or restrict learning, in addition to the student's accomplishments. As with a checklist, the primary audience for written descriptions is parents.

Advantages.   The major advantage of written descriptions is their flexibility. They can include whatever is relevant. They can focus the reader's attention on the most significant issues.

Limitations.   The flexibility of written descriptions is also their greatest limitation. Considerable care must be taken to write clearly and to provide a comprehensive description of each student. Both what is and what is not included in the description can be misconstrued. For example, when an ongoing trait has not been mentioned in previous narratives or by prior teachers, this trait may be assumed by the reader to be a new or developing quality when it is first reported. Similarly, a previous description that is absent from a present report can be assumed to represent a change in the student's performance. This limitation can be reduced by reading previous written descriptions, a time-consuming process.

The consistency of written descriptions can be improved by following an outline agreed to by all teachers. As with checklists, it is best if the outline is developed jointly with parents. By following the outline, the reader knows what is being rated. This approach avoids misinterpretations from the omission of information.

Another limitation of written descriptions is that they are time-consuming to prepare and read. For this reason, they are generally impractical for teachers at secondary schools and for others who evaluate a large number of students. Written descriptions also pose problems for counselors and others who review a large number of student progress reports; the volume of reading can be substantial, and reports from different teachers are usually written without a common framework.

Parent Conferences

Many schools supplement written grade reports with conferences between teachers and parents. These conferences are most successful when ideas expressed are supported by concrete illustrations, such as portfolios or other examples of work. Particularly when examples of work are involved, students can be effectively involved as participants in these conferences with parents.

A portfolio usually changes its role when used within a parent conference. With student assessments, a portfolio presents evidence of whether a student has achieved the various instructional goals. These goals drive the content and use of the portfolio. Within parent conferences, the portfolio helps the teacher communicate important findings to a parent. Although instructional goals remain relevant, it is the communication of findings that now drives portfolio content and use. For this reason, a fraction of material from an assessment portfolio is used during the conference. Because material is being selected to communicate particular findings, it may be unrepresentative. When that happens, it is important to make sure the parent understands the unrepresentative nature of selected content.

Advantages.   The major advantage of parent conferences is direct communication with the teacher. As opposed to writing a letter, a conference allows the teacher to use feedback from the parent to assure that ideas are being communicated accurately and with appropriate emphasis. A conference can also increase parents' involvement in the child's schooling, both directly and psychologically, resulting in benefits to the instructional process.

Limitations.   Parent conferences share two important limitations with written descriptions. First, because they often are unstructured, care must be taken to provide a representative description of the student. This problem is minimal, however, because conferences usually play a supplementary role in reporting student progress. Also, the direct communication with parents allows the teacher to sense inadequate communication.

A second limitation common to written descriptions is that parent conferences are time-consuming. Conferences require considerable planning time on the part of teachers, in addition to the time needed for the conference itself. It is often difficult for parents to attend conferences at times that are convenient for teachers.

A limitation unique to conferences is that they usually provide no permanent documentation of what was communicated. The supplemental role of parent conferences minimizes this concern.

Box 16.1 *Apply What You Are Learning*

Indicate (A or B) which reporting system is superior with respect to the characteristics being questioned.

Which reporting system provides a record that is easier to average across subject areas?

1. A. Letter grades
   B. Written descriptions
2. A. Percentage grades
   B. Parent conferences

Which reporting system provides precision more consistent with classroom measures of student achievement?

3. A. Letter grades
   B. Percentage grades
4. A. Letter grades
   B. Pass–fail marks

Which reporting system best indicates the specific skills a student has learned?

5. A. Checklists
   B. Percentage grades
6. A. Letter grades
   B. Parent conferences

When each student has several teachers, which reporting system is more likely to identify the subject in which a particular student is having the greatest difficulty?

7. A. Letter grades
   B. Pass–fail marks

Which reporting system is most likely to help a counselor recommend the colleges to which a student should apply for admission?

8. A. Checklists
   B. Letter grades

Answers can be found at the end of the chapter.

ESTABLISHING GRADING CRITERIA

Most schools use letter grades to report student performance. The meaning of letter grades is often vague, since a single letter is used to communicate very complex information. Teachers can offset this vagueness by carefully establishing grading criteria. Doing so involves (1) determining the nature and number of assessments on which to base grades, (2) selecting the weight to be given each assessment, and (3) setting the performance standard for each grade.

Nature and Number of Assessments

In most elementary and secondary schools, the content of the curriculum is set by others, typically both the local school district and a state agency. Teachers are usually responsible for determining how to teach and assess this content and for assigning grades.

If the primary function of these grades is to communicate students' academic proficiency, assessments on which grades are based must be measures of what students have learned. These assessments may involve diverse measures obtained throughout the school term. However, only a content expert, typically the teacher, can determine the nature and number of assessments that should be used to establish student proficiency. Here are some factors a teacher should consider.

1. As a whole, items included in grades should provide a representative sampling of all the instructional objectives covered during the term. Thus, a variety of measures, such as written tests, performance assessments, and assignments, can be included.

2. A grade should be based on multiple observations of achievement. The reliability of scores on one project or one written test is usually no better than moderate. Increasing the number of observations is one of the most effective techniques for increasing reliability of grades or of any assessment.

3. A grade need not include all items for which student scores have been retained. Most seatwork, homework, and quizzes are used for formative rather than summative roles. When their role is formative, these assessments generally should not be considered when assigning grades.

4. Items that are unrelated to instructional objectives should be excluded from grades. For instance, unless promptness and participation are specifically identified as instructional objectives, they should be excluded from grades, or at least their influence should be minimized when weights are determined for each assessment.

Determining the Weight to Be Given Each Assessment

The weight given each assessment is also based on the professional judgment of the teacher. Quite obviously, more significant assessments are weighted more heavily. Weights should correspond to the relative importance of the instructional objectives being assessed. Weights should not be based on amount of student effort, class time, or time required to assess student work unless these variables are important to the instructional objectives being assessed. Taken as a whole, the weights assigned to various assessments should make logical sense in terms of overall instructional objectives.

In addition to influencing the grade each student receives, giving additional weight to a test, project, or other measure affects the reliability and validity of the grade. If additional weight is given to a measure that has low reliability or validity, the reliability and validity of the overall grade are reduced. Therefore, if you heavily weigh an assessment when assigning grades, take particular care to ensure that this assessment is reliable and valid.

When less than 10% of the overall grade is based on a particular assessment, that assessment has a minimal and usually negligible effect on the overall grade. For this reason, variables not directly related to instructional objectives, such as participation and promptness, can be included within the grading scheme without actually affecting the grades that are assigned. I am not encouraging inclusion of such variables— simply acknowledging that, to an extent, one can get away with it. (Authors also walk fine lines!) Watch out for cumulative effects. If, for example, participation and promptness are each given 10%, their cumulative effect becomes more substantial. If they are included, minimal weight should be assigned to variables indirectly related to instructional objectives.

Establishing Performance Standards

Establishing performance standards for grades requires selection of a reference to which student performance will be compared. Four references are often considered:

1. A student's ability to learn
2. A student's prior performance
3. The performance of other students
4. Predefined levels of performance

Teachers often try to combine references (Nava & Loyd, 1991). For example, a teacher might use predefined levels of performance, such as 90% for an A, 80% for a B, and so on, but then adjust each student's grade based on an estimate of how much the student has improved. This procedure results in a grade that lacks meaning. With the two references combined, the grade can no longer be interpreted in light of either reference: It no longer describes student performance in terms of the predefined levels, and it no longer describes how much the student has improved. The simultaneous use of two or more references usually makes it impossible to interpret the grade. When assigning grades, select and use one reference exclusively.

Ability to Learn.   Using student ability as a reference for setting performance standards is intuitively appealing, but it has some serious problems. It is appealing because all students have an equal chance of receiving a high grade. However, here are the problems:

1. A teacher does not typically have reliable and valid measures of students' ability to learn skills within each content area.

2. When reasonable measures of ability do exist, they predict how well students will perform *relative* to others. That is, they predict which students are likely to achieve the lower versus higher performance. Aptitude measures usually do not indicate the maximum achievement of a student of a particular ability level. A teacher cannot use these measures to determine the fraction of potential a student has achieved.

3. Parents and others who interpret a student's grades generally are not provided measures of student potential. Without such information it is not possible to interpret grades referenced to student potential.

Prior Performance.   How much a student has improved over prior performance also provides an appealing reference for setting performance standards. Using this reference, a student who begins with less achievement does not have to learn more in order to receive the same grade as a student who began with a higher level of achievement. However, basing grades on how much students have improved results in grades being largely controlled by the error that is inherent in every teacher's assessments. Here is why.

Because of their less than perfect reliability, the scores on even the best assessments have some error. This error is then transferred to student grades that are based on these assessments. Although we hope that the differences in the grades students receive reflect real differences that exist among students, some of the differences in grades will always be caused by errors within the assessments. If a teacher adjusts grades based on students' prior performance, this in effect removes differences in grades associated with real differences that exist among students. This adjustment does not remove errors inherent in each assessment. Consequently, by removing real differences among students, a much larger portion of differences in grades becomes associated with errors in the assessments. This serious problem becomes even worse when a teacher's measurement of students' prior performance is based on a recollection of earlier performance rather than on a formal assessment of student achievement prior to instruction. Grades should not be based on the improvement of each student's performance because of the substantial effect errors in assessment have on these grades.

Performance of Other Students.   Using the performance of others as the standard of performance involves presetting the distribution of letter grades. For example, a teacher might assign an A to the top 15% of the students, B to the next 25%, and so on. This is sometimes called grading on the curve, but that is a misnomer because no particular curve is involved. Three concerns are often associated with basing standards on the performance of other students:

1. Standards may vary depending on which students are enrolled in the class. This is particularly true for small classes but can be reduced as a problem if several sections of a class can be combined for grading purposes.

2. The performance of other students provides a vague and often hard-to-defend performance standard. Simply telling a student or parent that a lower grade was assigned because others performed better lacks clarity.

3. Using the performance of others as a reference encourages competitive rather than cooperative learning. Competitive learning is sometimes supported on the basis that it is more like the real world. Teachers, however, usually favor cooperative learning, believing that cooperative learning improves achievement.

Predefined Levels of Performance.   Assigning grades based on predefined levels of performance associates each grade with a fixed performance regardless of the distribution of grades ultimately assigned in the class.

School districts, as well as colleges, use different techniques to establish performance levels for each grade. Often percentages are associated with each grade. For instance, 90% to 100% might correspond to an A, 80% to 90% a B, and so on. Recall that grades historically were reported as percentages rather than as letters. As we noted, these percentages do not refer to percentage of mastery. Simply using easier or more difficult assignments or tests significantly changes students' percentage scores. Therefore, teachers who associate the same percentages with each grade are likely not using the same grading standards. Teachers who are teaching similar classes and whose students end up with approximately the same distribution of grades are more likely to be using similar grading standards.

Although the distribution of grades is not the reference when grades are based on predefined levels of performance, the resulting distribution of grades can help teachers determine whether they are using equivalent levels of performance for assigning grades. If grade distributions vary dramatically among teachers, this information can be used to help evaluate grading standards for the next term.

A second approach to defining performance standards is to associate adjectives with each letter grade. Common associations are A = outstanding, B = very good, C = satisfactory, D = weak, and F = unsatisfactory. Schools often use these or similar descriptions on grade reports. Certainly, these words are limited by their vagueness, but so are percentage scores, although less obviously so. (For instance, the interpretation of 90% is heavily influenced by the difficulty of the task that students are asked to complete, just as the interpretation of "outstanding" is heavily influenced by the meaning a teacher attaches to this adjective.)

A third and superior approach to defining preset performance standards is to describe the characteristics of students associated with each letter grade. This is similar to establishing the descriptions associated with a scoring rubric (see Chapter 12).

One technique for establishing these descriptions is first to identify which students were assigned each letter grade during the previous comparable term or year. Then, the subset of students who scored within the middle of each grade range is selected. Approximately the middle 50% of students within each grade range is appropriate. Finally, the performance of each of these subsets of students is described in terms of the broad instructional goals of the content being taught. As with a scoring rubric, it is best to use the same variables when describing performance within each of these subsets of students. These descriptions become the preset performance standards for assigning grades to subsequent students.

Letter grades assigned using preset standards will communicate student performance to parents and others only if these preset standards are meaningfully communicated along with the dissemination of the letter grades. This is most effectively done by establishing and distributing descriptions of standards such as we have just discussed. Although such descriptions can be readily distributed to parents and made available to school personnel, they cannot generally be distributed to other audiences who have to interpret grades. For those audiences, grades must be interpreted through reference to more vague standards, such as how students with a particular average of grades tend to perform.

ROLE OF GRADES IN MOTIVATING AND DISCIPLINING STUDENTS

Grades can strongly motivate students. (To illustrate, how alert are you when the instructor explains grading procedures?) The motivational role of grades comes quite naturally. High grades are continually associated with desirable qualities, such as good work. Low grades are related to less desirable outcomes, such as low performance.

Sometimes low grades are used to punish students, for instance, to show disapproval of students' turning in assignments late or cheating on tests. The motivating potential of grades, however, is not universal. Particularly among students who have had limited success in school, the promise of a high grade or the threat of a low grade has negligible effect.

Use of Grades to Motivate Students

Deutsch (1979) describes grades as "the basic currency of our educational system." Not unlike monetary outcomes, the positive associations with high grades can result in grades' being perceived as an end unto themselves. Educators generally resist excessive emphasis on grades. Some recommend that they be abolished. Nonetheless, grades in some form are likely to continue. Accountability has always been regarded as a necessary part of education at all levels. Assessment of student learning will always be a significant aspect of accountability. Students will learn to associate values with any index of achievement, no matter what form it takes or how abstract it becomes. Grades, or their substitute, will always elicit some motivational qualities.

We can debate whether teachers should use grades to motivate students. Obtaining a high grade should be synonymous with achieving a high degree of course objectives. We can argue that motivating students to obtain high grades is equivalent to encouraging high achievement. On the other hand, grades have no intrinsic value. The extrinsic value they obtain is conveyed, in part, by teachers who themselves typically completed a baccalaureate degree or beyond. Teachers have had an above-average success with grades and are likely to reinforce motivational attributes they themselves have associated with grades.

Use of Grades to Discipline Students

Grades serve as a convenient and often effective disciplinary tool. Cullen, Cullen, Hayhow, and Plouffe (1975) found that students were more likely to avoid a low grade than work for a high grade. This facilitates teachers' use of grades as punishment. Particularly at the secondary and postsecondary levels, grades have been used to discipline students for a variety of actions, including delinquent homework, truancy, and cheating.

In spite of their convenience, grades should not be used to discipline students. Previous discussion has indicated the need for grades or any scores to measure a single trait. The internal consistency or reliability of grades is reduced when used to communicate multiple characteristics that are unrelated. Individuals who later interpret grades without direct knowledge of the student typically assume that the grades indicate degree of academic competence. Disciplining students through grades, therefore, invalidates their later interpretation.

Two disciplinary actions involving grades have a particularly significant negative impact on the usefulness of grades: assigning zero credit for incomplete work, and lowering grades in response to cheating.

Zero Credit for Incomplete Work.   Teachers often reduce the credit that students receive on an assignment when the work is turned in late. As indicated previously, the practice of incorporating unrelated qualities into a grade reduces the usefulness of grades when interpreted by others. This effect is particularly profound when the teacher assigns a score of zero to missing or incomplete work. A teacher may perceive the assignment of a zero to be an appropriate punishment for not completing a task. The teacher might also assign a zero score simply as a nonpunitive response to the student's failure to earn any points on the test or assignment. However, the fact that a student is missing a score is not synonymous with the student's having zero achievement with the competency represented by the score. (An analogy that comes to mind is the weather service's recording today's maximum temperature as zero whenever the maximum reading is missing.) A zero score has a very potent effect on a student's grade because its numerical value deviates considerably from other scores assigned the student. The effect is so strong that using a zero to indicate a missing score in essence may override all other assessments you have obtained for that student. If the zero is being given for disciplinary purposes, the assigned grade may have little relation to the student's achievement of instructional goals.

Obviously, the best resolution of a missing score is to have the student complete the missing assignment. If this is not possible, an alternative is to obtain some indirect estimate of that student's proficiency. A substitute score may be established by reviewing the student's performance with similar skills and substituting this performance for the missing score. If the missing score represents a heavily weighted component of course grades, a grade of "incomplete" might be assigned until the student has completed the missing activity, if the school provides this option. To reiterate, a major reason for not assigning a score of zero when a score is missing is that the zero probably does not represent a best estimate of the student's achievement with the skills represented by that score.

A student's failure to compete work is not to be ignored. Punishment for inexcusable failure to complete work may be necessary. Encouraging and rewarding good work habits is desirable. Using grades to punish or reward students for behavior that is not a direct indication of student achievement significantly lowers the ability of others to interpret grades. Alternative reactions that are more closely related in time and relevance than end-of-term grades should be used to shape students' promptness in completing work.

Lowering Grades in Response to Cheating.   Cheating on tests or other class activities is usually viewed as a serious offense, and rightfully so. Disciplinary action is appropriate. However, lowering grades is an inappropriate response to cheating, again because of the negative impact of such action on the interpretation of grades.

Assigning an F grade is a common response to cheating on a test. Honor codes established at some schools even support this reaction. In the few legal cases that have been presented, courts interpret cheating as a disciplinary, not an academic, matter and do not support a disciplinary role for grades.

From a measurement perspective, grades should reflect the teacher's best assessment of each student's achievement. If a test score is invalid because a student cheated, the student should be reexamined, using a test of similar difficulty. Unless instruction is individually paced, the student may be asked to complete the same or a parallel test without further preparation.

SUMMARY

Schools use a variety of systems to communicate students' performance to parents and others. These systems include conferences, narrative reports, checklists, percentage grades, letter grades, and pass–fail marks. The most commonly used system is letter grades. A number of school systems use checklists to augment or replace letter grades, particularly at the early elementary levels. Most schools use conferences, usually between a teacher and parent. The use of checklists and conferences was addressed in earlier chapters.

When interpreted by others, letter grades generally are assumed to report a student's achievement of instructional goals. Including other factors in grades, such as disciplinary actions, makes grades more difficult or impossible to interpret. Grades should rely on a number of assessments, which collectively represent a broad cross section of instructional objectives covered during the term. Particular attention should be given to the reliability and validity of assessments assigned the heavier weights.

A single reference should be used when assigning grades. One reference might be students' ability to learn; however, it may not be possible to obtain an appropriate measure of ability to learn. Improvement over prior performance represents another reference, but grades based on improvement often are influenced entirely by errors in the assessments. The performance of other students can be used as a reference for grading, although many teachers prefer not to use this approach. Also, unless large numbers of students are involved, the performance of the class may vary widely from one year to another. Assigning grades based on predefined levels of performance is generally the most preferred option. These levels of performance might be established using percentages, although it is better to establish descriptions of performance associated with each letter grade, much like a scoring rubric.

Grades motivate many students. The consequences of depending heavily on grades to motivate students are unknown, but strong dependence on grades to motivate students is generally regarded as undesirable. Grades should not be used to discipline students.

ANSWERS: APPLY WHAT YOU ARE LEARNING

18.1 1. A;   2. A;   3. A;   4. A;   5. A;   6. B;   7. A;   8. B.

SOMETHING TO TRY

■ How would you determine what you should discuss during a conference with parents? Name specific ways in which planning for a parent conference is similar to planning portfolios.

- Design a checklist that could be used to report student performance in a class you might teach. Use guidelines for constructing a checklist discussed in Chapter 12.

- List some specific techniques sometimes used by teachers to assign grades that make it difficult for parents and others to interpret the grades. Relate these techniques to points addressed in this chapter.

- Should letter grades be eliminated? If yes, what should replace them? If no, what specific changes should be made to how letter grades are assigned and used?

- A common procedure for establishing minimum scores for each grade is to look for breaks in the distributions of students' scores. Do you see any significant problems with using this procedure to assign grades?

- Design a plan for assigning end-of-term grades for a class you might teach. Your plan should identify specific assessments on which grades would be based.

ADDITIONAL READING

Brookhart, S. M. (1991). Grading practices and validity [Letter to the editor]. *Educational Measurement: Issues and Practice, 10(1)*, 35–36. For numerous reasons, the various audiences to which grades are directed interpret grades in somewhat different ways. The dilemma this creates for teachers is clearly described in this letter.

Christiansen, J., & Vogel, J. R. (1998). A decision model for grading students with disabilities. *Teaching Exceptional Children 31(2)*, 30–35. This article discusses issues and presents a decision model related to determining grading practices for students with disabilities.

Cross, L. H., & Frary, R. B. (1999). Hodgepodge grading: Endorsed by students and teachers alike. *Applied Measurement in Education, 12,* 53–72. Based on surveys of teachers and students, this article discusses the common practice of incorporating factors other than achievement in grades assigned students.

Friedman, S. J. (1996). Who needs to know that Andy got a D? *Clearing House, 70(1)*, 10–12. This article discusses from a legal and psychological perspective the practice of having students report their scores aloud in class.

Geisinger, K. F. (1982). Marking systems. In H. E. Mitzel (Ed.), *Encyclopedia of educational research* (5th ed., pp. 1139–1145). New York: Free Press. This selection reviews research pertaining to grading and focuses on the purpose of grades, discussion of alternative marking systems, and psychometric qualities of grades.

Hills, J. R. (1981). *Measurement and evaluation in the classroom* (2nd ed.). Columbus, OH: Merrill. Pages 345–357 discuss legal aspects of grading.

PART FIVE

Standardized Tests

CHAPTER 19

Characteristics of Standardized Tests

In this chapter, we explore basic characteristics of standardized tests. In Chapters 20 and 21, we describe the types of scores used most often to report performance on standardized tests. In Chapter 22 this information becomes the basis for evaluating uses of standardized tests that directly affect teachers and their classrooms. A number of these uses are beneficial. However, some common uses of standardized tests are of little or no benefit to education, and some are detrimental to the classroom environment.

A standardized test is a test designed to be administered consistently, even when proctored by different examiners at separate locations. Most commercially published tests are standardized. So are the tests used by various state governments and school districts to measure student competencies. These exams would have limited value unless they were administered consistently at each site.

Most standardized tests are *group administered,* with the exam administered concurrently to a number of students. To ensure a common administration, group-administered standardized tests use highly specific instructions that the examiner must follow precisely. Many group-administered tests use exact time limits to help ensure the same administration to all students.

Some tests are designed to be *individually administered.* Such tests are more flexible regarding instructions given to students and the amount of time allocated to completing the test. People who administer these tests, however, must be specially trained so that consistent criteria are used to determine whether a student satisfactorily performed a task, and to decide whether the student should proceed to more advanced tasks contained in the test.

Standardized tests can be categorized as measures of aptitude, achievement, interest, attitude, and personality. Aptitude tests are used to estimate what a student *will be able to do,* whereas achievement tests are intended to measure what a student *has accomplished.* Interest, attitude, and personality instruments often are not considered "tests," because they measure a person's typical rather than maximum behavior. This chapter focuses on aptitude and achievement measures because teachers use these kinds of tests more often.

A standardized test is designed as either a criterion-referenced or norm-referenced measure. Some instruments are appropriately interpreted in both contexts. A criterion-referenced measure must be directly interpretable in terms of the tasks the student can and cannot perform. The adequacy of this interpretation depends on how well defined the domain of tasks is and how relevant these tasks are to the student's instructional program. A norm-referenced measure is interpreted in terms of the performance of other examinees. A description of how others have performed on a particular test is referred to as a *norm.* Publishers of norm-referenced standardized instruments provide norms for the test. The adequacy of these norms depends in part on how recently they were established and the representativeness of individuals included in the norm group.

Often one thinks of standardized tests as being limited to conventional item formats such as multiple-choice. In fact, some believe that "standardized test" refers to a multiple-choice test that is simultaneously administered to a lot of people, probably because these traits are common to many standardized tests. However, the term *standardized* pertains to controls placed on its administration and actually has nothing to do with the types of items included on the test. Increasingly, standardized tests are including items that require constructed responses or are including performance assessment components. A standardized test can be made up entirely of performance assessments or likewise can involve portfolios.

Individual teachers are typically more involved in the administration and interpretation of standardized tests than in their selection. The selection process usually involves committees that include teachers. This chapter therefore identifies some resources that facilitate the selection of standardized tests.

Standardized tests play a variety of roles within schools. This chapter provides the background for addressing these roles, whereas the later chapters help you evaluate specific applications of standardized tests. The present chapter is concerned with helping you achieve the following four skills:

- Distinguish between aptitude and achievement tests.
- Identify common types of aptitude and achievement tests.
- Evaluate the adequacy of domain and norm specifications of a standardized test.
- Identify resources for selecting and evaluating standardized tests.

DISTINCTION BETWEEN APTITUDE AND ACHIEVEMENT TESTS

It is useful to compare achievement and aptitude tests in terms of their purpose, the types of skills they measure, and the procedures used for establishing their validity and reliability.

Purpose of Aptitude and Achievement Tests

The fundamental distinction between aptitude and achievement tests is their intended use. The overall purpose of aptitude tests is to estimate how well students will learn. Such estimates facilitate a variety of decisions such as grouping students or identifying students who will benefit from special types of instruction. Aptitude tests help select students for admission to academically competitive schools. They also help students formulate realistic educational and vocational goals.

Achievement tests measure students' present status with a set of skills. When scores are compared to norms, achievement tests indicate strengths and weaknesses of a student or group of students as compared to those in the norm group. When used in conjunction with aptitude measures, achievement tests are used to evaluate the effectiveness of instructional programs and to identify students with learning disabilities. Standardized achievement tests are used to ensure that students are taught critical skills and also to establish a minimum academic standard for promotion and graduation. Not without controversy, standardized achievement tests are sometimes used to motivate and raise student and teacher expectations, or even control the curriculum. Achievement tests are used to exempt students from instruction in skills they have already learned or to group students based on what they have yet to learn. Some achievement tests are designed to diagnose problems handicapping a student in math and reading.

Skills Measured by Achievement and Aptitude Tests

Although the uses of achievement and aptitude tests are generally different, both types of tests measure previously learned skills. In fact, tests have no choice but to measure learned skills. Even though we often try to make inferences to underlying or even innate capabilities, we are always limited to measuring student behaviors that we can see. *All behaviors that are measurable are learned.*

Achievement and aptitude tests do tend to measure different behaviors. Achievement tests typically measure more specific and recently acquired skills, whereas aptitude tests tend to measure more general abilities that are learned over an extended period of time. Achievement tests measure skills taught in school such as mathematics, reading, and writing. Aptitude tests tend to measure skills learned informally, such as knowledge of vocabulary and ability to solve problems involving spatial relations between objects. Figures 19.1, 19.2, and 19.3 are examples of items contained in standardized achievement tests. Figures 19.4 and 19.5 illustrate items contained in aptitude tests.

Sometimes people are surprised that aptitude tests do not measure innate abilities but rather measure what a student has learned. It is important to recognize that all psychological and educational tests must measure observable behaviors. How well a student has learned skills in the past often provides a good estimate of skills the student will learn in the future. Given that the purpose of aptitude tests is to estimate a student's ability to learn new material, using measures of prior learning is a reasonable strategy for predicting subsequent learning.

Any achievement test conceivably can be used as an aptitude test in the sense that it will predict future achievement. However, as the skills tested by the achievement test become a smaller subset of skills essential to learning later skills, the ability of

Amanda plans to make a wooden rack for holding test tubes. As shown below, the rack is to contain four drilled holes. Each hole is to be ³/₄ inch in diameter. The shape between adjacent holes and also the space beyond the holes at each end is to be 1¹/₂ inch.

What is the overall length (x) of this wooden rack? Show your work, or explain in words how to determine the answer.

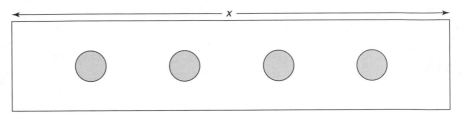

Figure 19.1
Example item from a mathematics test

Figure 19.2

Example item from a reading comprehension test

Read the paragraph, and then select the main idea.

> During the storm, the electric power went out. Dinner was in the oven and stopped cooking. The refrigerator stopped working. It was dark because the lights would not work. We could not watch television. We could not listen to the stereo. We could not read a book.

What is the main idea?

A. All the lights went out.

B. Lightning struck the power line.

C. Storms can be dangerous.

D. We depend on electric power.

an achievement test to predict the later achievement will decrease. For example, an achievement test measuring multiplication skills will more accurately predict a student's ability to learn exponents than solve quadratic equations, even though multiplication is an integral part of both skills. An appropriate achievement test provides the better short-range prediction of students' ability to learn a specific skill. An aptitude test provides the better longer range prediction of students' ability to learn material in a variety of school subjects.

By measuring broad skills, aptitude tests are less affected by experiences specific to a particular classroom or year in school, but aptitude measures do reflect learning that occurs informally, particularly in the home and community. Consequently, scores on aptitude tests are influenced by a variety of cultural factors. Physical impairments, particularly those of sight and hearing, also affect scores on aptitude tests. A number of instruments such as "culture-fair" tests have been developed to better measure latent aptitude. These instruments typically minimize language-dependent skills by

Figure 19.3
Example item from a writing test

A committee within the state legislature is debating a proposed law that would require middle and high school students to maintain a C average in order to participate in extracurricular activities such as school sports and clubs.

Think about whether or not this proposed law is a good idea. Now write to convince the committee to support your point of view.

Figure 19.4
Example item from a vocabulary test

Directions: Select from the list the word whose meaning is most similar to the underlined word.

<u>audacious</u> friend   A. bold

                              B. loud

                              C. nervous

                              D. pleasant

Directions: Point to the object on the right that would complete the series on the left.

Figure 19.5
Example item from a sequential series test

using pictures or diagrams such as those illustrated in Figure 19.5. As a rule, non-verbal aptitude tests are less able to predict how well students will learn in a school setting simply because academic tasks are highly verbal. Nonverbal aptitude tests may identify students who have a high potential to learn and presently are less proficient with verbal skills.

These nonverbal tests still measure prior learning. It is possible to construct tests such that average differences in performance across identifiable cultural groups are minimized. However, scores will always vary as a function of differences in what individuals have learned. When interpreting aptitude tests, it is important to remember that scores on all tests are affected by prior learning and do not represent direct measures of innate ability.

Although aptitude tests measure skills that are learned gradually, a student's score on any aptitude measure can change considerably over time. An aptitude test can under- or overpredict a student's ability to learn as a result of the test not measuring skills relevant to a particular subject, varying levels of student motivation, or other sources of measurement error inherent in tests.

Validity and Reliability of Achievement and Aptitude Tests

Because aptitude and achievement instruments have distinct roles, different procedures are used to establish both their validity and reliability. The purpose of an achievement test is to determine status with a particular set of skills. Therefore, the match between the content the test is designed to assess and the skills measured by the test is fundamental. In contrast, the role of an aptitude test is to predict a future performance. Consequently, the degree to which scores on the test correlate with the future performance is particularly relevant. The following discussion contrasts procedures used for validating and establishing the reliability of achievement and aptitude tests.

Validity of Standardized Tests.   The purpose of both classroom and standardized achievement tests is to determine students' status with a particular set of skills. Likewise, as with classroom tests, content-related evidence of validity is emphasized. The content that a standardized achievement test is expected to measure must closely match the skills that its items actually measure. As with classroom tests, this involves establishing a list of performance objectives to be measured by the test or specifying this content through a table of specifications. Because of the comprehensiveness of standardized achievement tests, fairly elaborate procedures are often used to establish content to be measured. This may include analyzing the content of relevant textbooks, syllabi, and other instructional materials used by a variety of schools throughout the country. The appropriateness of the test, however, ultimately must be judged by those anticipating use of the test, such as content experts in a school district. The usefulness of a standardized achievement test depends largely on how adequately it samples the skills judged relevant by its users and how effectively the developer of the test communicates this sampling plan to potential users. The technical manuals that accompany standardized tests typically used by school districts normally provide considerable detail explaining how content included in the test was established.

As with classroom tests, the validity of standardized achievement tests must not depend exclusively on content-related evidence. Construct-related evidence is also critical. Those who develop a standardized achievement test should establish the nature of the knowledge to be assessed and show that the performance inherent in the test items is appropriate for the type of capabilities the test is trying to measure. In fact, it was largely a concern about the construct being measured that caused a number of test publishers and state testing programs to include performance assessments in these standardized tests.

The major standardized achievement tests often report criterion-related validity evidence. Scores on the test are correlated with variables such as scores on other tests, grades assigned by teachers, and other measures of student achievement.

Aptitude tests are primarily used to predict future achievement. Consequently, the degree to which scores on the test correlate with future performance is relevant. This, again, is referred to as criterion-related validity evidence. Because scores on the aptitude tests are correlated with later measures of achievement, this type of validity is referred to as predictive validity. Aptitude tests at least nominally represent a measure of an underlying psychological construct. For example, many of the aptitude tests used in schools have been described as intelligence tests, although terms such as *school ability* or *learning ability* rather than *intelligence* have become more common. Consequently, their construct-related evidence of validity should establish the nature of intelligence or learning ability, and provide evidence that student behaviors observed through these tests are appropriate indicators of the construct.

Earlier we noted that both achievement and aptitude tests measure prior learning. Achievement tests measure recently learned skills typically taught in school settings, whereas aptitude tests tend to measure skills learned informally outside of school. The nature of skills measured by achievement versus aptitude tests, however, represents a continuum rather than two distinct groups of skills. Both standardized achievement and aptitude tests often measure skills representing points somewhere between the two extremes of this continuum. Similarly, some standardized tests play both a certification and predictive role. Reading readiness tests illustrate this point. For such tests, both content and predictive validities should be used to help demonstrate that the test measures what it is intended to measure. Reading readiness tests are validated by demonstrating that they measure the skills prerequisite to learning reading (content validity) and that they correlate with students' later achievement in reading (predictive validity).

Messick (1989b) describes how the validation of a test must consider not only how test scores are interpreted, but also how they are used. Validation must further consider consequences resulting from the interpretation and use of these tests. Chapter 22 helps you evaluate common uses of standardized tests and discusses some of their important consequences to students and teachers.

Reliability of Standardized Tests.   Aptitude and achievement tests should have internal consistency. That is, each test (or subtest) should measure a single entity so that student performance legitimately can be represented by a single score. The Kuder–Richardson (KR-20) formula is the most commonly used procedure for estimating internal consistency reliability.

The KR-20 formula may underestimate the internal consistency of tests designed to provide criterion-referenced interpretations. This problem occurs when scores on criterion-referenced tests have limited variability. Some authors propose that consistency in classification (mastery versus nonmastery) is a more appropriate measure of reliability for criterion-referenced tests. However, interpreting scores in a criterion-referenced context does not presume the existence of a passing score (Nitko, 1984). Commercially published criterion-referenced tests usually report the Kuder–Richardson reliability coefficient. This seems appropriate because students typically obtain a range of scores on both criterion-referenced and norm-referenced standardized tests.

There is potential subjectivity in the scoring of performance assessments and other item formats where students construct responses. For these, consistency between raters should be demonstrated. Because of costs and time constraints, when performance assessments are used with standardized tests, only a very limited number of assessments can be included. For instance, students might be limited to writing in response to one or two prompts. Evidence should be reported that indicates the degree to which students would perform the same had a different prompt been used.

Aptitude tests estimate a student's ability to learn new skills. Because aptitude tests are designed to predict future learning, their scores should remain consistent across time. Test–retest reliability is the procedure for estimating this consistency. Computing test–retest reliability actually is redundant to determining predictive validity. This is because the predictive validity of a test can be satisfactory *only if* the test has adequate reliability over the length of the prediction. If an aptitude test is judged to have adequate predictive validity, it can be assumed to have sufficient reliability.

When alternative forms of an aptitude or achievement test are available, the publisher should demonstrate that these forms can be used interchangeably. This is established in part through alternate-form reliability, in which the correlation between scores on the two forms is determined.

APTITUDE TESTS

In the previous section, standardized tests were classified as measures of aptitude or achievement. This section discusses three types of aptitude tests commonly used in education: readiness tests, scholastic aptitude tests, and college admission tests. When used, readiness tests are typically administered prior beginning of the first grade. Scholastic aptitude tests are often administered about every fourth year, generally beginning in the third or fourth grade. College admissions tests are predominantly taken by students applying to colleges, although some schools encourage a broader use of these tests.

Readiness Tests

Most readiness tests are concerned with reading skills. They typically include a series of subtests. Most or all subtests are administered orally. Here are some of the types of subtests included in these readiness tests:

- **Auditory discrimination:** Distinguishing between similar-sounding words
- **Visual discrimination:** Identifying differences between letters, numbers, words, or pictures
- **Vocabulary:** Identifying the meaning of words, or selecting words that describe pictures
- **Comprehension:** Interpreting words, sentences, or directions
- **Memory:** Following a series of directions or repeating a story read earlier
- **Copying and drawing:** Reproducing letters, numbers, and other objects, or completing other tasks requiring motor coordination

A reading readiness test can be classified as either an achievement or aptitude measure. On the one hand, these tests are used to help determine whether a student has achieved skills prerequisite to learning how to read. On the other hand, readiness tests can provide *short-term* predictions of students' reading performance. The latter quality may be useful for grouping students during the first one or two years in school.

When used as an achievement test, validity should be established by showing that a particular test measures skills prerequisite to learning to read. The names given subtests such as those listed previously usually provide only vague descriptions of what is assessed by a given test. Specific items within a test should therefore be reviewed to help select the test most consistent with the way reading is taught locally.

If the readiness test will be used to predict students' ability to learn reading, its manual should indicate the correlation between the readiness test and reading achievement one or two years later. Correlations between scores on reading readiness tests and standardized reading achievement tests tend to be .40 to .75 over a one-year period. Therefore, when reading readiness tests are used to group students, the teacher should expect considerable overlap in performance among students placed in different reading groups. Because these tests have low correlations with achievement one year later, teachers should anticipate shortly regrouping students. Again because of their low correlations with even short-term achievement, these tests should not serve as the basis for determining when students are to enroll in school.

Academic Aptitude Tests

A variety of academic aptitude tests are used in schools. These tests are often referred to as intelligence tests, learning ability tests, and school ability tests. Academic aptitude tests differ among themselves with regard to the specific tasks examinees are asked to perform. Sections of a particular test may contain verbal, quantitative, and nonverbal components. Verbal sections depend heavily on the examinee's proficiency with spoken or written language, such as identifying correct meanings of words. Quantitative sections require the solution of exercises involving numbers. Nonverbal sections involve problems that exclude reading and computations such as the items illustrated in Figure 19.5.

Scores on scholastic aptitude tests are often reported in several formats such as percentiles, stanines, and deviation IQs. A given test may provide separate verbal, nonverbal, and quantitative scores, or an overall score may be used. Because the skills being measured vary across tests, scores on separate intelligence tests are not interchangeable, even when they use the same type of scale such as IQs. This is true even if the two tests use the same name for a particular score such as *nonverbal IQ*. On the other hand, correlation between scores across scholastic aptitude tests is fairly high. Therefore, although scores on one test should not be substituted for scores on another, how students score on one test is a rough indication of how they would score on another aptitude test.

Academic aptitude as a construct is not well defined. There is considerable discussion in research literature as to the nature of the intellect, which conceivably could suggest what scholastic aptitude tests should measure. In their review of the research, Wagner and Sternberg (1984) described how intelligence is viewed by some psychometricians as involving a basic general factor (e.g., Spearman), and by others as including a number of distinct factors (e.g., Thurstone, Guilford). Mental ability has been conceptualized as a developmental phenomenon (e.g., Piaget), and also as how individuals process intellectual information (e.g., Newell and Simon). Developers of academic aptitude tests unfortunately tend not to establish the construct they propose to measure.

Regardless of how adequately one establishes a construct, any academic ability test is limited to measuring observable behaviors that are *learned*. Scores on all aptitude tests must therefore be recognized as measures of learned skills as opposed to direct measures of some innate capacity. Scores on an academic ability test are affected by the individual's ability *and* opportunity to learn the skills measured by the test. These abilities and opportunities are not static qualities.

Most academic ability tests used in schools are group-administered and are used primarily to estimate future success in school. Examples include the *Cognitive Abilities Test,* the *Otis–Lennon School Ability Test,* and the *Test of Cognitive Skills.* Excluding "intelligence" from their names helps reduce the perception that these tests measure innate and static abilities. Most group-administered scholastic aptitude tests are developed as a series. Separate versions of the tests are designed for various age groups, ranging from early elementary through high school grades. These tests are often administered or proctored by teachers, but are usually selected by the school district's testing office.

Validity evidence tends to focus on correlations of test scores with subsequent measures of student achievement. The correlation between scores on these tests and scores on standardized achievement tests administered three to four years later is about .80. Correlations with course grades are approximately .60.

Individually administered aptitude tests have several advantages over group-administered tests. Their greatest asset is that the examiner can more readily observe the specific nature of the student's responses. If the student does not complete a task because he or she misunderstood directions, the examiner can give redirection within prescribed limits. The examiner also has greater freedom in motivating the student to do well and, through observation, can be sensitive to circumstances that affect test performance. Individually administered tests also require less autonomous work by the student and are less dependent on reading skills.

Individually administered tests are costly to use. In addition to the expense of requiring one-on-one administrations, the examiner must be highly trained in the use of these tests. The examiner also prepares a report that summarizes clinical observations and discusses the student's test performance. Because of their cost, individually administered aptitude tests are given in response to referrals. Most states require students to be evaluated through an individually administered test before being placed in special education.

The individually administered tests most commonly used are the *Stanford–Binet Intelligence Scale, Fourth Edition,* and the Wechsler scales. The Stanford–Binet consists of a single instrument designed for use with preschool through high school ages. The Wechsler scales consist of three instruments: the *Wechsler Preschool and Primary Scale of Intelligence* (ages 3 to 7), the *Wechsler Intelligence Scale for Children—Third Edition* (ages 6 to 16), and the *Wechsler Adult Intelligence Scale—Third Edition* (ages 16 to adult). These instruments typically consist of a series of subtests or tasks with items ordered by difficulty. The examiner begins with items that the student can confidently answer correctly and progresses until it is established the student cannot answer more difficult items. Scores are usually reported as deviation IQs.

College Admissions Tests

The two major college admissions test programs are administered by the College Entrance Examination Board and the American College Testing (ACT) Program. Both the College Board and the ACT Program are organizations that provide a variety of services in addition to their testing programs.

The College Board through Educational Testing Services (ETS) administers the *Scholastic Assessment Test* (SAT). This three-hour SAT-I exam produces verbal and math scores expressed as percentile ranks and standard scores. The standard scores range from 200 to 800, with an average score of 500. The percentile ranks are based on individuals administered the exam during a particular year; however, the standard scores are equated to high school students graduating in 1990. Therefore, the percentile and standard score scales are not equivalent.

A series of one-hour achievement tests is administered as supplements to the SAT. These achievement tests referred to as the SAT-II are available in a variety of topics including English composition, mathematics, foreign languages, and various physical sciences. Individuals may take one or more of these exams subsequent to the SAT-I administration. Scores on the achievement tests are also reported as percentile ranks and standard scores.

The College Board also administers the Preliminary Scholastic Assessment Test/ National Merit Scholarship Qualifying Test. This two-hour exam is taken in the junior year of high school. It is useful for counseling students concerning college enrollment and is used for screening applicants to National Merit Scholarship Awards. Verbal, math, and writing skills scores are reported on a 20-to-80 scale.

The American College Testing program was established more recently than the College Board. The ACT Assessment covers four skill areas: English, mathematics, reading, and science reasoning. Scores in each of the areas are reported using a scale that ranges from 1 to 35, along with a composite score that is an average of the four scores.

Both the SAT and the ACT tests are intended to help predict performance in college. Predictive validity is established by correlating test scores with freshman grade-point average in college. These correlations are generally between 0.4 and 0.6. Although the predictive validity is only moderate, using a college admissions test in conjunction with other factors such as high school grades provides a better prediction of performance in college than is obtained without using scores from the admissions tests.

An issue that has become associated with admissions tests is what is called "truth in testing" legislation. The name parallels consumer-protection laws such as "truth in advertising" and "truth in lending." Generally, truth in testing legislation requires that test publishers (1) inform examinees about the purpose of the test, (2) describe procedures used to develop the exam, (3) describe the validity and reliability of the test, and (4) provide examinees the option of reviewing copies of their scored test. Programs that are involved with admissions tests, such as the College Board and ACT, support the first three of these requirements but oppose public disclosure of scored tests. Disclosure restricts the reuse of test items and consequently increases the number of new items that must be developed for each administration. This increases the cost and potentially lowers the quality of the items, since the next test would contain a higher percentage of new items. Legislated disclosures of scored exams have found occasional errors within the tests, although the frequency of errors has been small.

ACHIEVEMENT TESTS

Most standardized tests administered in schools are achievement tests. We will look at three groups of these tests: diagnostic tests, achievement batteries, and the National Assessment of Educational Progress. Diagnostic tests are used primarily in reading and arithmetic and are designed to detect underlying problems that prevent learning in these areas. Diagnostic tests are administered to students experiencing difficulty in reading or arithmetic.

An achievement battery consists of a series of subtests, each measuring an academic area such as math, science, or reading. Many school districts administer an achievement battery each year to every student. Achievement batteries are used to monitor the performance of individual students, schools, and even teachers. They are also used to compare the performance of students and school districts to national norms.

The National Assessment of Educational Progress, like achievement batteries, measures student achievement in several academic areas. However, only a sample of students throughout the nation are tested in a given year, and the academic area being assessed varies from year to year. The purpose of the National Assessment is to evaluate overall performance of students throughout the country and within states, rather than assess the performance of individual students. In essence, it is a national census of educational achievement.

Diagnostic Tests

A number of achievement tests have been developed to diagnose problems causing students difficulty in arithmetic and particularly reading. Diagnostic tests are not administered to all students, but to a subset of students having particular problems in arithmetic or reading. The diagnostic test is expected to indicate specific skills in which the student is deficient. To accomplish this, a diagnostic test must have the following characteristics:

1. The test must provide a series of scores, each representing performance in a specific skill.
2. The specific skills must each be critical to learning reading or arithmetic.
3. The scores on specific skills must each have high reliability.
4. The correlation between these scores should be low.

In essence, a diagnostic test is a series of achievement tests, each designed to measure a behavior that is critical to reading or arithmetic. These tests provide independent measures of the respective skills, and thus the validity and reliability must be established separately for each scale. If the correlations among subtests are high, this would indicate the subtests are measuring a common ability rather than a series of distinct skills. Similarly, *patterns* among scores will have low reliability unless the reliability of each subtest is high *and* the correlations among the subtests are low.

Diagnostic tests tend to be deficient in most of the qualities listed. All diagnostic tests provide a series of scores. However, manuals to these tests often fail to establish that the skills being measured are critical to learning reading or arithmetic. The reliability of diagnostic subtests ranges between .50 and .90, with the lower two thirds of this range being below that of the better standardized achievement tests. The correlations among subtests, when reported, are moderately high. This, coupled with the often only moderate reliabilities, means the subtests generally lack sufficient reliability to distinguish between levels of achievement and are too highly correlated to establish specific skills that are causing a student difficulty.

From a measurement perspective, diagnostic tests have significant limitations. Consequently, their scores must be interpreted conservatively. Many diagnostic tests are administered to one student at a time. The test therefore provides a structured setting through which the examiner can try to gain insights into the student's difficulty. The observations that the examiner documents become as important as, and usually more important than, the scores obtained on the test. Diagnostic tests are particularly useful to individuals such as reading specialists who are trained in identifying specific learning problems.

Achievement Batteries

In schools, the most widely used type of standardized achievement test is the achievement battery. An achievement battery is a series of single-subject tests designed and packaged so that they can be administered and interpreted together. A typical achievement battery includes subtests in reading, vocabulary, language usage, math, science, and social studies. Students' scores are reported for each subtest and often for each skill measured by a subtest.

Each achievement battery is produced as a series. Different levels of the test are produced for various grade levels, collectively covering elementary or secondary grades, or both. Two parallel forms of each grade level may be produced that can be used interchangeably. Items are dominated by the multiple-choice format, although increasing numbers of constructed-response items are being used. Performance assessments, where students provide a writing sample in response to a prompt or work through a science problem, are also becoming more commonplace. Performance assessments understandably add considerably to the amount of time required to administer an achievement battery, and even then can include only a very limited number of assessments. Usually the performance assessment component is offered as a standalone and optional supplement to the basic achievement battery. Web sites for publishers of several widely used achievement batteries are listed in Table 19.1. Brief descriptions of each of these and other tests are available within the ETS/ERIC Test File, which can be accessed by going to the *Test Locator* within the ERIC Assessment and Evaluation web site (*http://ericae.net*). Some

Table 19.1
Publishers of Achievement Test Batteries

CTB/McGraw-Hill (*http://www.ctb.com*)

California Achievement Tests
Comprehensive Tests of Basic Skills
TerraNova

Harcourt Brace Educational Measurement (*http://www.hbem.com*)

Metropolitan Achievement Tests
Stanford Achievement Test Series

Riverside Publishing (*http://www.riverpub.com*)

Iowa Tests of Basic Skills
Iowa Tests of Educational Development
Tests of Achievement and Proficiency

achievement batteries and score reports can be customized to match state or district standards.

When a school system uses an aptitude test and achievement battery from the same publisher, each student's report often lists the average scores on each subtest earned by other students with the same aptitude score. This facilitates the interpretation of scores and helps identify students whose achievement in a particular area is significantly discrepant from other students of equal general ability.

The most important advantage of an achievement battery over a combination of separate single-subject tests is that norms for all the subtests are based on the same examinees who were administered the subtests at the same point in time. This allows one to compare the performance of a student or school across subject areas. A secondary advantage of using test batteries is that they are efficient. Less time and cost are required to administer an achievement battery than to administer a group of single-subject tests measuring similar content.

Test batteries do have disadvantages. Because they are designed to measure skills in several content areas within a reasonable amount of time, fewer items are used to measure each content area than are included in many commercially available single-subject tests. This sometimes results in lower reliability for subtests within a battery (typically .75 to .90) and also decreases the battery's ability to determine a student's strengths and weaknesses within each content area. A second disadvantage of using test batteries is that a school system cannot select the test in each content area that most closely matches local objectives. Although a school district typically uses the series of tests from one achievement battery, it is quite possible that separate achievement batteries better match the content taught at different grade levels.

Although the general content measured by various achievement batteries is quite consistent, each battery measures reasonably distinct skills. This is to be expected because the content measured by each battery is developed by an independent group of curriculum and measurement specialists. Also, given the breadth of content measured by an achievement battery, the specific skills sampled by each battery will vary just by chance.

Some individually administered test batteries have been developed. Many items on these tests are read orally, and students typically respond verbally or by pointing. These batteries are often used in special education settings. Individually administered batteries include the *Peabody Individual Achievement Test* and the *Wide Range Achievement Test*. Particular care must be taken in the interpretation of scores on these tests. Each measures broad content areas with relatively few test items. Therefore, these tests are more useful for indicating overall achievement than for determining which skills a student has mastered. Likewise, the reliability of scores tends to be lower than for the group-administered tests. In some cases, the validity and reliability of these tests are not carefully documented. Content measured by these tests is not updated as frequently as that of the group-administered achievement batteries.

Many states have also developed specialized achievement batteries that are administered instead of or in addition to the commercial achievement batteries. These tests often include performance assessments, particularly in writing, and sometimes are built around a portfolio format. They are specifically constructed to measure state performance standards but cannot provide national norms. Many states administer versions of the tests at selected grades, such as third, fifth, eighth, and tenth, and then require students to pass the high school version of the test before graduating.

More so than most achievement batteries, tests developed by states are designed for criterion-referenced interpretations. The fact that they measure narrowly defined instructional objectives facilitates this quality. Commercially published achievement batteries have traditionally been interpreted within a norm-referenced context. The trend in recent years has been for publishers to facilitate the criterion-referenced interpretation of their achievement batteries by clarifying the objectives or domains measured by the test and by increasing the number of items used to assess each skill.

National Assessment of Educational Progress

The National Assessment of Educational Progress (NAEP) was established in 1969 to provide a national census of academic achievement. Originally, samples of students at four ages (9, 13, 17, and adults from 26 to 35) were assessed over skills within ten content areas: art, career and occupational development, citizenship, literature, mathematics, music, reading, science, social studies, and writing.

The NAEP does not provide measures of individual student achievement. Scores are reported only in summary form, with performance broken down by student age, sex, socioeconomic status, community characteristics, and geographic region. The proportion of students correctly answering items associated with each skill is reported. A subset of the test items is released with reports. Other items remain secured and are used in later tests to detect trends in student performance.

The NAEP has undergone several significant changes (for example, see Messick, Beaton, & Lord, 1983). Beginning in 1990, its sampling design was altered to allow state-by-state comparisons. Prior to that time, legislation prohibited such analysis. Beginning in 1994, the NAEP also involved nonpublic schools. The emphasis has shifted from simply reporting performance to trying to identify conditions causing observed patterns of scores. Consequently, the NAEP now collects additional contextual information from students and educators concerning curriculum and instructional procedures. The performance of students with functional handicaps and those with limited knowledge of English are also being evaluated.

The NAEP provides important measures that are unavailable through other assessment programs. For example, a problem often associated with standardized achievement batteries is that scores within a school district tend to improve after a particular test is used for several years and then drop when the test is replaced with an alternative instrument. The NAEP uses different but representative samples of schools for each assessment; therefore, changes in scores can more readily be associated with actual trends in student achievement. Another measure the NAEP provides is comparison of educational achievement among regions of the country. Governmental agencies and the press have used national college admissions tests for such comparisons. A problem associated with such comparisons is that the content of admissions tests is selected to maximize prediction of college achievement rather than provide a representative sampling of content taught in schools. Another problem is that students taking these tests are not always representative. In some states, almost all high school students take these exams, whereas in other states only students applying to competitive colleges take the admissions tests. Because the NAEP uses a representative sampling from all regions of the country, comparisons are more meaningful.

The NAEP web site (*http://nces.ed.gov/nationsreportcard/site/home.asp*) includes a wealth of information related to the National Assessment, including descriptions of the assessment programs in each content area and discussions of recent results.

EVALUATING DOMAIN AND NORM SPECIFICATIONS OF STANDARDIZED TESTS

With criterion-referenced interpretations, stating that a student correctly answered 45 of 50, or 90% of the test items, is of no use without a clear description of the skill being measured. Likewise, with norm-referenced interpretations, stating that the student's score of 45 is at the 80th percentile provides no information without knowing with whom this student is being compared. The usefulness of a reference, whether it is criterion-referenced or norm-referenced, depends on how clearly the reference is specified and how relevant that specification is to the students being assessed.

Criterion-Referenced Interpretations: Need for Clarity and Relevance of the Domain Specification

As with classroom tests, criterion-referenced interpretations of standardized tests require a clear description of the domain being measured. With criterion-referenced tests, the developers of standardized achievement tests have a more difficult task of concisely defining the domain being assessed than does the classroom teacher. To a large part, this is because the domain being measured by a standardized test is much broader than that of a teacher's classroom test. Nevertheless, if any test is to be criterion-referenced, the domain must be sufficiently defined so that, from performance on the test, one is able to state what a student can and cannot do. This description should not require reference to the performance of other students, which in fact is the basis for a norm-referenced interpretation. This description also should not require reference to a passing score for interpretation, even though such a reference may be advantageous to instructional planning.

In addition to being well defined, the content domain must be relevant. Relevance involves two considerations. First, does the domain correspond to the skills being taught in the local schools? Second, if the test measures a *sample* of behaviors, can one generalize from the sampled tasks in a manner that is instructionally meaningful? This is often a problem for standardized tests because a single achievement test is designed to sample material covering more than a year of instruction.

Determining whether one can generalize adequately from the sampled tasks depends in part on how precisely the domain being measured is defined and how representative test items are of that domain. For example, knowledge related to the location of countries within Central America represents a more precise domain than the location of countries within the Western Hemisphere. Based on students' performance on a question pertaining to the location of Costa Rica, one can more adequately judge whether further instruction is needed regarding the location of other Central American countries than one can concerning the location of countries such as Brazil and Canada. It is easier to generalize from a student's performance on a sample of test items when (1) the skills included in the domain become more specific or focused and (2) the number of test items used to measure the domain increases. That is, one can more adequately give a criterion-referenced interpretation to test scores if the test uses a substantial number of items to measure a highly focused domain. This in part is why it is easier for classroom tests than for standardized achievement tests to be criterion-referenced.

Norm-Referenced Interpretations: Need for Clarity and Relevance of the Norm Group

Norms are a summary of how others have performed on a particular test. With standardized tests, norms are usually based on several thousand students. This norm group is often intended to be representative of a larger population, such as all students in the United States attending the eighth grade.

Norms may be presented in a variety of formats. One way is to indicate how many examinees in the norm group obtained each score. A student's raw score on the test is then interpreted by comparing it to the scores obtained by students in the norm group. This is how students and teachers give norm-referenced interpretations to classroom tests.

More typically, norms for standardized tests are presented in a table similar to Table 19.2. This table shows that a student who correctly answered 15 items (a

Table 19.2
Illustration of the type of table used with a standardized test for converting raw scores to various derived scores

Raw Score	Percentile Rank	Stanine	Grade Equivalent
26	99	9	10.1
25	99	9	9.7
24	99	9	9.3
23	98	9	8.8
22	96	8	8.3
21	91	8	7.8
20	86	7	7.4
19	77	6	7.0
18	65	6	6.7
17	52	5	6.4
16	39	4	6.1
15	27	4	5.7
14	17	3	5.3
13	10	2	4.9
12	5	2	4.5
11	3	1	4.0
10	2	1	3.6
9	1	1	3.1
8	1	1	2.7
7	1	1	2.3
6	1	1	1.9

raw-score of 15) performed at the 27th percentile, which is at stanine 4, or at the 5.7 grade equivalent. The interpretation of a student's performance requires knowing the characteristics of standard scores, percentiles, and grade-equivalent scales. These norm-referenced scores are discussed in the next two chapters. However, even after one has learned the characteristics of these scores, they cannot be interpreted without having a clear description of who students are being compared to. For example, knowing that a student scored higher than 27% of those taking the test is of little use unless one has a clear understanding of who the test was administered to.

The publisher of a standardized test should clearly describe and a teacher interpreting the results must understand the students on whom the norms are based. The publisher should provide norms for each group to whom examinees are likely to be compared. The publisher should also describe how individuals included in the norm group were sampled and the date on which the norms were established.

Norms for major aptitude tests and achievement batteries are based on extensive samples. The sampling plan is usually stratified so that the norm group includes proportional numbers of students from each region of the country, socioeconomic level, sex, and race. The sampling procedures are generally well documented in the manuals to these tests, and separate norms are often provided for various subgroupings such as regions of the country and sex.

Baglin (1981) found that a substantial proportion of schools decline to participate in the development of norms. Schools involved in the norming tend to be those that currently use or plan to use the particular test. This may bias norms by including a high percentage of students from schools whose curriculum matches the test as opposed to a nationally representative sample of students. More recently, test publishers have more adequately reported participation rates. National norms are difficult and expensive to develop properly. If a test manual is vague about how norms were established, one should question their adequacy.

Norms need not always be based on a national sample. Norms for tests developed by individual states or school systems are usually based on whoever completes the test, such as all eighth graders attending public schools in the state. If the nature of individuals included in the norm group is carefully described, the user of the test can judge the appropriateness of comparing students' scores to the norms.

Both the year and time of the year in which norms were developed should be stated in the manual. Over a period of years, norms become dated because the emphasis and effectiveness of instruction and the characteristics of students change. The time of year that norms were established is relevant because students' abilities progress during the school year. This is particularly true with skills measured by achievement tests. To improve accuracy of comparisons, standardized tests should be administered at the same time of year that norms were established. Manuals to some standardized tests provide norms derived at two or three points during the school year, which in turn provides flexibility with regard to when the test may be administered locally.

The relevance of norms depends on the group to which students taking the test are to be compared. Scores on commercially published aptitude tests and achievement batteries are generally compared to overall national norms. Quite often, comparisons to more than one group are useful. For instance, one may wish to compare a student's score in reading to students from the same region of the country, sex, or socioeconomic background, as well as to overall national norms.

RESOURCES FOR EVALUATING AND SELECTING STANDARDIZED TESTS

A variety of reference sources are available to assist in the identification, evaluation, and selection of standardized tests. These references complement each other. For instance, the *Mental Measurements Yearbook* contains critical reviews of a large number of standardized tests, but much like an encyclopedia, it is out of date before it can be published. Catalogs provided by test publishers contain current information about standardized tests but do not provide critical analyses of these instruments. The first reference to be described here, the *Standards for Educational and Psychological Testing,* does not discuss specific instruments but provides specific criteria for evaluating standardized tests.

Standards for Educational and Psychological Testing

The purpose of the *Standards for Educational and Psychological Testing* (1999) is to provide criteria for evaluating tests, testing practices, and the effects of test use. The *Standards* is a paperback book containing 15 chapters on topics such as validity, reliability, norms, fairness, and the responsibilities of test users.

Each chapter provides a background description of the issue being discussed and then lists a series of specific standards relevant to that issue. Each set of standards is well thought out and establishes reasonable expectations. This book provides an excellent framework not only for evaluating and selecting tests, but also interpreting and using results. The 1999 *Standards* replaces an earlier edition that was published in 1985.

Mental Measurements Yearbooks

The *Mental Measurements Yearbooks* are a series of reference works, each providing a description and critiques of a substantial number of published tests. The *Yearbook* is published every other year. A typical entry includes the test title, the purpose of the test, publication date, name of publisher, time required to administer, available forms, cost, and a list of journal articles and other publications that discuss the test. Most entries include two critiques of the test written by specialists familiar with the test. Only tests developed or revised since the publication of the last *Yearbook* are included. The *Yearbook* is available in the reference section of college libraries, and at the testing offices of school districts and colleges. The volume of *Mental Measurements Yearbooks* containing the review of a particular test can be found by going to the Test Locator at the ERIC Assessment and Evaluation web site (*http://ericae.net*).

An electronic version of *Mental Measurements Yearbook* is available on CD-ROM through SilverPlatter (*http://www.silverplatter.com/catalog/mmyb.htm*). This service provides a full listing of the published reviews, but is updated with new reviews every six months. Many libraries have the SilverPlatter version of the *Mental Measurements Yearbook* in their reference section.

Professional Journals

A number of professional journals review recently developed or revised tests, or contain research articles in which qualities of a particular test are being investigated. Libraries have online and other electronic reference tools such as *FirstSearch* and *SliverPlatter* that can locate articles within these journals.

Publishers' Catalogs and Specimen Sets

Many test publishers provide catalogs listing current information about their tests. Catalogs typically provide a brief description of the purpose and features of each test, the age or grade range for which it is intended, administration time, and costs. Publishers' catalogs do not and are not designed to provide evaluative reviews of tests.

Publishers will usually sell a sample of materials associated with a particular test. This specimen set typically includes a copy of the test booklet, its manual, and example answer sheets and score reports. A specimen set is invaluable for determining the specific skills measured by a test, the adequacy of manuals, and the quality of printing. Procedures for ordering test-related materials are described in each publisher's catalog. Website addresses for publishers of widely used achievement batteries are included in Table 19.1. The Test Locator feature of the ERIC Assessment and Evaluation web site (*http://ericae.net*) provides an extensive list of web site and mail addresses for test publishers.

Web Sites Related to State Assessments

State agencies and some school districts maintain web sites for many of the state-level testing programs. These sites often list instructionals goals or standards a test intends to cover, score results from recent tests, and instructional resources. These sites can be located using the major Internet search engines such as Excite (*http://excite.com*), NorthernLight (*http://northernlight.com*), and Yahoo! (*http://yahoo.com*). Using the acronym for a test sometimes facilitates the search for information.

SUMMARY

A standardized test is a test designed to be administered consistently across a variety of settings. Various standardized tests are designed to provide criterion-referenced or norm-referenced interpretations. Most standardized tests are group administered, although a number of tests must be administered to one student at a time.

This chapter focused on standardized aptitude and achievement tests. An aptitude test is designed to predict future achievement, whereas an achievement test is used to measure current performance. Consequently, predictive validity tends to be more prominent in the validation of aptitude tests and content-related evidence more dominant with achievement tests. Both aptitude and achievement tests measure skills that students have learned. Aptitude tests tend to measure more general skills that are learned informally, whereas achievement tests measure more specific skills such as those taught in a particular grade in school. Both aptitude and achievement tests should demonstrate internal consistency. If alternative forms of a test are intended to be used interchangeably, alternative-form reliability should be established. Inter-rater reliability should be established for performance and other assessments involving subjective scoring.

Types of aptitude tests discussed include reading readiness tests, scholastic aptitude tests, and college admissions tests. Types of achievement tests discussed include diagnostic tests, achievement batteries, and the National Assessment of Educational Progress. The purpose and characteristics of these tests were addressed.

All scores must be given a frame of reference to be interpreted. Criterion and particularly norm references are used with aptitude and achievement tests. The value of each reference depends on how clearly the domain specification or norm group is described and how relevant that description is to the students being assessed.

Different sources are available to help identify, evaluate, and select standardized tests. Those described include the *Standards for Educational and Psychological Testing, The Mental Measurements Yearbooks,* professional journals, and publishers' catalogs. Internet resources facilitate finding detailed information about individual tests.

SOMETHING TO TRY

■ Obtain a copy of *Standards for Educational and Psychological Testing.* Read the *primary* standards listed within one of the chapters of Part 1, such as those associated with validity, reliability, or norms. Using the technical manual provided with an achievement battery used by local schools, identify which standards are meaningfully addressed in the technical manual.

■ Obtain a copy of the test booklet for a current or recently outdated achievement battery, and similarly the booklet for a group-administered aptitude test. Compare the abilities that items in these two tests measure. For the two tests, contrast where students tend to learn the abilities measured by these respective tests.

■ Using a test booklet, look at the skills measured by the version of an achievement battery designed for the grade level for which you teach. Does the test fail to cover any critical skills that are taught at your grade level, and does the test cover skills predominantly taught at an earlier or later grade level? What implications does this have to the interpretation and use of the test?

ADDITIONAL READING

Linn, R. L. (1999). *Assessments and accountability.* (CSE Technical Report 490). Los Angeles: University of California, National Center for Research on Evaluation, Standards, and Student Testing/Center for the Study of Evaluation. (Available at *http://www.cse.ucla.edu/ CRESST/Reports/TECH490.pdf*). Reviews the role of tests in several educational reform movements during the past 50 years.

Pellegrino, J. (1992). Intelligence and aptitude testing. In M. C. Alkin (Ed.), *Encyclopedia of educational research* (6th ed., Vol. II). New York: Macmillan. Discusses issues related to intelligence and aptitude testing.

Shepard, L. A. (1997). The Centrality of Test Use and Consequences for Test Validity. *Educational Measurement: Issues and Practice. 16*(2), 5–8. Describes how the consequences of test use are an important part of test evaluation.

Wagner, R. K., & Sternberg, R. J. (1984). Alternative conceptions of intelligence and their implications for education. *Review of Educational Research, 54,* 179–223. This article provides a good overview of how intelligence has been conceptualized and discusses implications these views have in teaching verbal information and intellectual skills.

CHAPTER 20

Using Standard Deviation to Interpret Scores

Average air temperatures in Chicago and San Francisco are surprisingly similar. The annual average temperature in Chicago is approximately 50 degrees Fahrenheit, and in San Francisco it is 55 degrees, but it would be incorrect to conclude from this information that the pattern of temperatures is the same in these two cities. The temperature in San Francisco is very constant. In January, the temperature typically reaches a nighttime low of 45 degrees and in August a daytime high of 65 degrees. A jacket or a warm sweater is sufficient to stay comfortable much of the year. In Chicago, the temperature is quite variable. The nighttime low in January is around 15 degrees, and the daytime high in August is typically 85 degrees. Swimsuits on the beach are popular in the summer, but even the warmest sweater will not prepare you for the beach in winter.

Knowing simply the average temperature is not sufficient. The variability of temperatures is equally important. In fact, whenever measurements are taken, you need to know the average and variability of the numbers regardless of whether they represent measures of temperature, precipitation, height of people, or student achievement.

For our purposes, the most useful index of variability is standard deviation. Knowing both the average and standard deviation of scores will help us interpret student performance on classroom and standardized tests.

Scores on tests are often easier to interpret if the scores are converted to a new scale where the average and standard deviation of the converted scores have preset values. These converted scores are called standard scores. We will look at the standard scores most commonly used with educational tests and describe characteristics of these scores that are important to their interpretation.

Standard deviation helps interpret scores in another context. As you are well aware, measurement error affects scores on educational tests. Knowing how much variability in scores is associated with measurement error is important to interpreting changes in a student's scores over time or for interpreting differences in scores between students. Standard deviation is used to indicate how much scores vary as a result of measurement error.

This and the next chapter describe the scores most often used with standardized tests. In Chapter 22, we use this and other information to evaluate uses of standardized tests that directly affect teachers and their classrooms.

The present chapter helps you achieve three skills:

- ■ Use of standard deviation to describe student performance
- ■ Interpretation of commonly used standard scores
- ■ Use of standard deviation to interpret errors in measurement

USE OF STANDARD DEVIATION TO FACILITATE INTERPRETATION OF SCORES

This section describes how standard deviation can be quickly estimated. Next, procedures for using standard deviation to interpret test scores are demonstrated. Then, the limitations of standard deviation units when interpreting students' scores are discussed.

Estimation of Standard Deviation

Standard deviation is calculated by determining how far scores deviate from the average score. The specific average being referenced is the *arithmetic mean,* referred to here simply as the *mean (M).* The mean of scores is calculated by adding the scores and dividing this sum by the number of scores. If three students had test scores of 9, 5, and 7, the mean of their scores would be

$$\frac{9 + 5 + 7}{3} = \frac{21}{3} = 7.0$$

The standard deviation (SD) indicates how far scores deviate from the mean. Appendix A gives the formula for standard deviation and provides an example of its computation. The standard deviation can be estimated quickly by dividing the range of scores (difference between the highest and lowest scores) by an appropriate value. Table 20.1 lists the values to be used for different numbers of students. For example, if the scores of 3 students were involved, Table 20.1 indicates the standard deviation of the 3 scores would be estimated by dividing the range of those scores by 2. For the three scores 9, 5, and 7, the range of the scores is 9 to 5, or 4 points. To estimate the standard deviation, this range would be divided by 2, giving us $4/2 = 2.0$.

Table 20.1
Divisors for estimating standard deviation

Number of Students	Value of Divisor
3 (a small group of students)	2
10 (a small-size class)	3
25 (a medium-size class)	4
100 (a large class, or several classes combined)	5

Note: The divisors used for estimating standard deviation are approximation of values from *Biometrika Tables for Statisticians* (Vol. 1, 3rd ed., p. 189) by E. S. Pearson and N. O. Hartley, 1966, London: Cambridge University Press

---

Box 20.1 *Apply What You Are Learning*

Use Table 20.1 to estimate the standard deviation on a test if a range of 25 students' scores is as follows:

1.   16 points

2.   18 points

3.   20 points

Use Table 20.1 to estimate the standard deviation of scores on a test if the range of 100 students' scores is as follows:

4.   20 points

Using the patterns you see in Table 20.1, estimate the standard deviation of scores on a test if the range of 60 students' scores is as follows:

5.   20 points

Answers can be found at the end of the chapter.

Note that the estimated value of the standard deviation will become larger if the range of scores increases. The standard deviation increases as scores increasingly diverge from the mean (and from each other). On the other hand, if all scores were equal, the range of scores would equal zero. That is, if all students obtain the same score, the standard deviation of the scores is equal to zero.

Remember that Table 20.1 is used to estimate standard deviations. The procedure described in Appendix A is used to calculate the actual value of the standard deviation. A disadvantage of using the range of scores to estimate standard deviation is that this range can be unstable. That is, if the score for the student obtaining either the highest or lowest score changes significantly, the estimate of standard deviation also changes significantly. Appendix A shows that the actual computation of standard deviation takes into account how far each score deviates from the mean, not just the highest and lowest pair of scores. In most cases, estimating the standard deviation of scores is sufficient. When it is not, the standard deviation of the scores is usually provided for you.

Using Standard Deviation to Interpret Test Scores

Characteristics of Standard Deviation.   Describing some of the characteristics of standard deviation will facilitate its use for interpreting test scores. The numerical value of standard deviation describes how far scores deviate from the mean. Therefore, as scores spread out further from the mean, the standard deviation increases proportionally. To illustrate this, here are the scores six students obtained on an initial test:

8   12   14   14   16   20

Using the formula in Appendix A, the standard deviation of these six scores is 4.0. These six students later obtained the following scores on a second test:

14   16   17   17   18   20

Using the same formula, the standard deviation of these six scores is 2.0. Notice that the scores on the second test are closer together, spread out half as much as the scores on the first test. Because they spread out half as much, the standard deviation of scores on the second test is half that of the scores on the first test.

Box 20.2 *Apply What You Are Learning*

Listed here are the scores on six tests. The standard deviation of the scores on the first two tests is given. What is the standard deviation of scores on the remaining tests?

Scores	Standard Deviation
Test 1: 8, 12, 14, 14, 16, 20	4.0
Test 2: 14, 16, 17, 17, 18, 20	2.0
Test 3: 20, 18, 17, 17, 16, 14	?
Test 4: 22, 20, 19, 19, 18, 16	?
Test 5: 44, 40, 38, 38, 36, 32	?

Answers can be found at the end of the chapter.

In these examples, the standard deviation of scores on Test 1 is 4.0 and the mean of the scores 14.0. On that test, if someone had obtained a score of 18, that score would be 4 points higher than the mean score, which is 14. One would therefore say 18.0 is above the mean by a distance of 1 standard deviation. Similarly, 10.0 is 1 standard deviation below the mean. Notice that most but not all students on Test 1 obtained scores within 1 standard deviation of the mean (higher than 10, but lower than 18).

The proportion of students who will achieve scores within 1 standard deviation of the mean is quite predictable. As illustrated in Figure 20.1, if the pattern of test scores matches the theoretical normal curve, 68% or approximately two-thirds of the scores will fall within the interval that is 1 standard deviation above and below the mean. Extending this interval to 2 standard deviations above and below the mean captures 96% of the scores. Three standard deviations above and below the mean capture almost 100% of the test scores. You should memorize these percentages because they will become very useful to interpreting test scores.

Box 20.3 *Apply What You Are Learning*

If normally distributed test scores have a mean equal to 70 and a standard deviation equal to 10, what percentage of their scores will be between

1.   60 and 80?

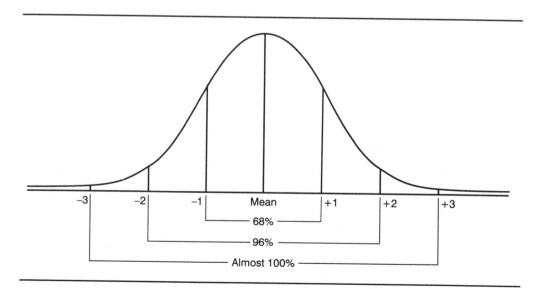

Figure 20.1
Percentage of scores within a normal distribution falling within 1, 2, and 3 standard deviations of the mean

2. 50 and 90?

3. 40 and 100?

If normally distributed test scores have a mean equal to 40 and a standard deviation equal to 5, what percentage of these scores will be between

4. 35 and 45?

5. 25 and 55?

If normally distributed test scores have a mean equal to 90 and a standard deviation equal to 2, what percentage of these scores will be between

6. 86 and 94?

7. 84 and 96?

Answers can be found at the end of the chapter.

Scores on most tests are not normally distributed, so the percentages in Figure 20.1 represent approximations. These percentages, however, are quite close to what you will observe on most tests.

Expressing Scores in Standard Deviation Units.   Knowing the percentages associated with standard deviation intervals within a normal curve helps describe students' relative performance. For instance, simply knowing that two students achieved scores of 24 and 32 on a test is not sufficient to interpret their scores, but if one also knows that the mean and standard deviation on that test are 20.0 and 4.0, then 24 and 32 represent scores that are 1 and 3 standard deviations above the mean. Recalling the percentages associated with standard deviation units, the score of 24 can then be interpreted as being above the majority of other scores and the score of 32 as being above virtually all other scores on the test.

Box 20.4 *Apply What You Are Learning*

Assuming the mean and standard deviation on a test are 20.0 and 4.0, how many standard deviations are each of the following scores above or below the mean?

   28 22 26 16 8

Answers can be found at the end of the chapter.

Comparing a Student's Performance on Two Exams.   Here is a question one *cannot* answer using just the information provided:

A student earned 12 out of 20 points on a first test and 15 out of 20 points on a second exam. Relative to other students taking these tests, on which test did this student do best?

This question can be answered if the means and standard deviations of scores on both tests are provided. The means and standard deviations are as follows:

	Mean	Standard Deviation	
Test 1	10.0	2.0	Score of 12 is 1 standard deviation above the mean.
Test 2	14.0	2.0	Score of 15 is 0.5 standard deviations above the mean.

From this information, this student scored higher than others on the first test. Knowing how many standard deviations a student's scores are from respective score means is very useful information when a student's performance is to be compared to that of other students.

Box 20.5 *Apply What You Are Learning*

Here is information concerning test scores in reading, mathematics, and science:

	Reading	Math	Science
Number of test items	90	60	80
Mean of scores	60	40	40
Standard deviation of scores	10	5	10

Use this information to determine whether each of the following statements is true or false.

1. Jenni scored 70 in reading and 60 in science. Relative to other students, she did better in reading than science.

2. Paul scored 50 in both reading and math. Relative to other students, he did about the same in reading and math.

3. Murray scored 40 in both math and science. Relative to other students, he did about the same in math and science.

4. Terri scored 35 in both math and science. Relative to other students, she did about the same in math and science.

5. Patrick scored 50 in reading and 30 in math. Relative to other students, he did better in reading than math.

Answers can be found at the end of the chapter.

Limitation of Standard Deviation Units When Interpreting Scores

The major limitation of standard deviation units is that they describe student scores in relative and not absolute terms. For example, most students will score higher than 2 standard deviations below the mean, but that information by itself does not indicate whether a score that is 2 standard deviations below the mean represents inadequate or adequate performance, or even a desirable versus undesirable score.

Unfortunately, this limitation of standard deviation units is commonly ignored. A below-average score on a test is often described as undesirable or even unacceptable. Such reasoning is just as much in error as assuming persons whose age is below the average age are too young or those older than average are too old. Similarly, the adequacy of a student's performance on a test cannot be judged by knowing how many standard deviations the performance is above or below the mean test score.

The usefulness of relative interpretations of test scores, on the other hand, should not be minimized. Many day-to-day observations and decisions, including the following, are based at least in part on relative interpretations of measures:

Is it warm outside?

Are these vegetables fresh?

Is this a prestigious university?

Am I so sick that I should go to the hospital?

Based on our experiences, we can give meaningful answers to these questions and take appropriate actions. In fact, experience provides a basis on which to make absolute decisions when our measures represent scores on a relative scale. In the same manner, scores on many educational tests are expressed using standard deviations. By learning what to expect from students scoring a certain distance below (or above) average, we can interpret their scores.

Transforming Scores to a Standard Scale

Knowing how many standard deviations a score is from the average score provides a fairly clear indication of a student's relative performance on a test. However, the standard deviation and mean of test scores will be easier to interpret if convenient values can be used. Notice how the values of the mean and standard deviation in Problem 1 are more convenient to work with than those in Problem 2:

Problem 1: If the mean of scores on a test is 50 and the standard deviation of these scores is 10, how many standard deviations above the mean is a score of 60?

Problem 2: If the mean of scores on a test is 37.3 and the standard deviation of these scores is 4.7, how many standard deviations above the mean is a score of 42?

The answer to both of these problems is 1.0.

The mean and standard deviation of raw scores cannot be determined in advance of administering a test. (A raw score is the number of points a student obtained on a test, for instance, the number of items answered correctly.) Their values, however, typically resemble those of Problem 2 in the sense that they are awkward to use. Fortunately, students' raw scores can be transformed to a new scale without changing their meaning. The new scale can be designed to have convenient predetermined values for its mean and standard deviation. When test scores are transformed to a scale that has a predetermined mean and standard deviation, the transformed scores are called standard scores.[1]

INTERPRETATION OF COMMONLY USED STANDARD SCORE SCALES

Three common standard score scales are discussed in this chapter: T-scores, deviation IQ scores, and stanines. (A fourth scale, NCE scores, is described in the next chapter.) Standard scores have several advantages and limitations that affect their interpretation. These characteristics are discussed following the initial descriptions of these standard scores.

T-Scores

The T-score is a standard score with a mean equal to 50 and standard deviation equal to 10. A student whose raw score is equal to the test mean will obtain a T-score of 50. Likewise, a student whose score is 1 standard deviation *below* the mean will obtain a T-score of 40. A student who scored 2 standard deviations *above* the mean will have a T-score of 70. T-scores are rounded off to whole numbers and are computed using either linear or normalized transformations.

Box 20.6 *Apply What You Are Learning*

Here is how each of several students performed on a standardized test. What *T-score* did each of these students obtain?

1. Michael scored 1 standard deviation *above* the mean.
2. Stephen scored 2 standard deviations *below* the mean.
3. Seth scored 0.5 standard deviation *above* the mean.
4. Lisa scored 1.5 standard deviations *above* the mean.
5. Randall scored 2.5 standard deviations *below* the mean.

Answers can be found at the end of the chapter.

---

[1]Two quite different techniques are used to convert raw scores to a standard score scale. The first technique for converting raw scores is called a linear transformation. The desired values for the mean and standard deviation are obtained by adding, subtracting, multiplying, and/or dividing each raw score by numerical constants. The procedure is equivalent to that used to convert temperatures from one scale to another, such as from Fahrenheit to Celsius.

The second technique assumes that the ability being measured by a test is normally distributed. To convert raw scores, the percentage of students that score below each raw score on the test is first determined. With this percentage, a statistical table (or the formula for the normal curve) is then used to obtain the appropriate standard score. Because of its association with the normal curve, this technique is called a normalized transformation.

Although linear and normalized transformations use different techniques, approximately the same standard scores are usually obtained with either technique. For classroom applications, it is not necessary to know which transformation is being used.

Deviation IQ Scores

Earlier intelligence tests derived a mental age score for a child and compared that score to the individual's chronological age. The ratio of mental age to chronological age, when multiplied by 100, became the child's *intelligence quotient* or IQ. The concept of an intelligence quotient was not useful for older adolescents or adults because a person's intellectual capabilities were believed to cease development before the age of 20 years.

Analysis of scores of the then-dominant intelligence test indicated that the mean and standard deviation of IQs were approximately 100 and 16, respectively. Therefore, to get around the problem of comparing mental age to chronological age, performance on intelligence tests was expressed using a standard score with mean and standard deviation preset at 100 and 16. This standard score was referred to as a deviation IQ score. A person whose performance on the intelligence test was at the mean was assigned a deviation IQ score of 100. Likewise, an individual whose performance was 1 standard deviation above the mean was assigned a score of 116.

Box 20.7 *Apply What You Are Learning*

Here is how several individuals performed on an intelligence test. What is each person's deviation IQ score if the mean of these scores is 100 and the standard deviation is 16?

1. Theodore scored 1 standard deviation *above* the mean.
2. George scored 2 standard deviations *below* the mean.
3. Tina scored 0.5 standard deviation *above* the mean.
4. Barbara scored 1.5 standard deviations *above* the mean.
5. Laura scored 2.5 standard deviations *below* the mean.

Answers can be found at the end of the chapter.

Any values can be used for the mean and standard deviation of a standard score scale. Publishers of intelligence tests quite consistently use a mean of 100; however, standard deviation values other than 16 are commonly used. Knowing the standard deviation being used with a particular intelligence test is of course important to the interpretation of its scores. Also, different intelligence tests measure different abilities. Therefore, knowing what an intelligence test measures is also highly relevant to its interpretation.

Stanine Scores

The term *stanine* is an abbreviation of the words *Standard NINE,* and its value is limited to the range of 1 to 9. Stanine is a standard score with a mean equal to 5 and standard deviation equal to 2. A student whose raw score equals the test mean will obtain a stanine score of 5. A score that is 1 standard deviation below the mean equals a stanine of 3. Students who score 2 or more standard deviations below and above the mean are assigned stanines of 1 and 9, respectively. Stanines are derived using a normalized transformation.

Because only nine numbers are associated with stanine scores, more than one raw score often ends up being assigned the same stanine. Each stanine score potentially refers to a small group of raw scores.

A score that is 3 standard deviations above the mean is assigned a stanine of 9, not 11, because stanines are limited to a range of 1 to 9. A stanine of 9 refers to a wider range of scores because it includes all scores from the highest score to a score approximately 2 standard deviations above the mean. A stanine of 1 represents a similarly wide range of scores.

Box 20.8 *Apply What You Are Learning*

Here is how each of several students performed on a standardized test. What stanine did each of these students obtain?

1. Miles scored 1 standard deviation *above* the mean.
2. Janie scored 2 standard deviations *below* the mean.
3. Chris scored 0.5 standard deviation *above* the mean.
4. Greg scored 1.5 standard deviations *above* the mean.
5. Mindy scored 2.5 standard deviations *below* the mean.

Answers can be found at the end of the chapter.

Normal Curve Equivalent Scores

One additional standard score that is commonly used is called the *normal curve equivalent score,* and is usually referred to as the NCE score. NCE scores have a preset mean of 50 and a rather unusual standard deviation of 21.06. This standard deviation value resulted from the association of NCE scores and percentiles. The NCE score is described in the next chapter, along with the discussion of percentile ranks.

Considerations When Interpreting Standard Scores

A standard score indicates how many standard deviations a student's score is below or above the mean. The interpretation of a standard score can be helped by visualizing it as a point on one of the scales in Figure 20.2. Knowing the mean and standard deviation of a standard score locates the score on its scale. For example, because *T*-scores have a mean and standard deviation of 50 and 10, a *T*-score of 35 is 1.5 standard deviations below the mean.

Converting from raw scores to standard scores does not change the meaning of students' performance on that test. The conversion simply changes the reporting of performance from one scale to another. The conversion is very similar to converting temperatures from Fahrenheit to Celsius. Temperature measurements on one scale have the same meaning as on the other, even though the numerical values change. (On one cold winter morning, a television announcer stated, "The temperature outside is 10 degrees below zero, and if you think that's bad, it's more than 20 degrees below zero Celsius." Be careful not to make this kind of incorrect inference when you work with test scores that have been converted to standard scores. Standard scores facilitate but do not alter the interpretation of scores on tests.)

As noted earlier, the interpretation of standard scores depends in part on the nature of the norm group. For instance, even if a high school achievement test and a college achievement test both use *T*-scores to report results, their scores are not interchangeable. Although a *T*-score of 50 would represent the mean on both tests, average high school and college students are not equivalent.

When comparing standard scores from different tests, one must also recognize that the abilities measured by the respective instruments are different. Therefore it is not surprising if a student obtains different scores in math and reading even if the tests use the same standard scores. It is similarly not surprising if a student obtains different deviation IQs on two intelligence tests. Chapter 19 noted that various intelligence tests measure different skills. A variety of tests share generic names such as achievement, aptitude, and intelligence. Use of a common name does not automatically mean that the tests measure the same skills. Scores on tests must be interpreted in light of the specific skills measured by the instrument.

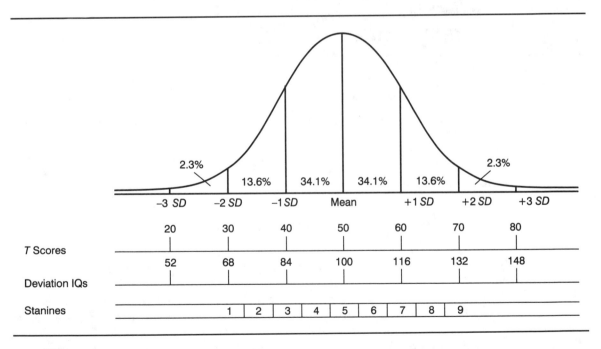

Figure 20.2
Corrected standard scores on a scale that is 3 standard deviations below to 3 standard deviations above the mean

Box 20.9 *Apply What You Are Learning*

Listed here are a variety of standard scores. Indicate whether each score is

A. high (*more than* 1.5 standard deviations above the mean)
B. somewhat above the mean
C. at the mean
D. somewhat below the mean
E. low (*more than* 1.5 standard deviations below the mean)

1. *T*-score of 50
2. *T*-score of 80
3. *T*-score of 25
4. *T*-score of 45
5. Deviation IQ of 145
6. Deviation IQ of 70

7. Deviation IQ of 85
8. Deviation IQ of 110
9. Stanine of 5
10. Stanine of 7
11. Stanine of 9
12. Stanine of 4

Answers can be found at the end of the chapter.

Advantages of Standard Scores

Three advantages of standard scores are identified here. First, standard scores divide differences in performance into equal intervals. For instance, performances represented by *T*-scores of 40 to 45 to 50 to 55 represent approximately equal differences in whatever ability the test is measuring. This is an attribute that people tend to assume of any scale, such as scales used in measures of temperature, weight, and height. People often fail to understand, however, that some scales used with standardized tests, including the percentile and grade-equivalent scales discussed in the next chapter, do not share this attribute of equal intervals.

A second advantage of standard scores is that they can be added and subtracted, and also averaged across students. Both percentile ranks and grade-equivalent scores should be converted to an equal-interval scale before they can be added, subtracted, or averaged.

A third advantage is that standard scores can be used to compare a student's performance across tests. Particularly when using a test battery consisting of several subtests, one is interested in determining relative strengths and weaknesses by comparing a student's ability across skill areas. Standard scores (and percentile ranks) permit such comparisons. For example, if a student's stanine scores in math and verbal skills are 4 and 2, respectively, one can conclude that the student has performed better in math. The next chapter shows why a student's performance across content areas can be compared using percentiles but cannot be compared using grade equivalents.

Limitations of Standard Scores

Two limitations of standard scores are described here. First, many standard-score scales imply a degree of precision that does not exist with educational tests. Horst, Tallmadge, and Wood (1975) suggested using one third of a standard deviation as the minimum difference of educational significance. Differences of less than one-third standard deviation are usually not measurable. This means that differences less than 3 points on the T-score scale and 5 points in deviation IQs are not meaningful. Both of these scales are too precise.

Stanines do not share this problem. Personally, I prefer the simplicity of stanine scores when communicating norm-referenced test results to students and parents. By describing stanine scores as ranging from 1 to 9, with 5 representing the middle score, people seem to interpret the scores correctly. They assume the scores represent equal intervals along a scale, they correctly interpret the relative position of a score in terms of the midpoint and extremes of the scale, and they do not infer that the scores have precision beyond that which the test can deliver.

A second limitation of standard scores is that they represent measures of relative standing as opposed to measures of growth. A student who progresses through school in step with peers remains at the same number of standard deviations from the mean. The constant standard score may suggest (incorrectly) that growth is not occurring. Hoover (1984) identified this as an advantage of grade-equivalent scores. The effectiveness with which growth can be described by grade-equivalent scores is discussed in the next chapter.

USING STANDARD DEVIATION TO INTERPRET ERRORS IN MEASUREMENT

Standard deviation has been shown to be an index of how far test scores vary from the mean. Knowing the mean and standard deviation of test scores provides a fairly clear idea about how scores on the test are distributed.

Standard deviation also can be used to indicate the error in students' scores—the difference between scores they are observed to get on a test and students' true scores. A true score is the score a student would receive if the test were perfectly reliable. Because of measurement error, the score a student receives on a test usually differs from that individuals's true score. By calculating the standard deviation of these measurement errors, we can describe the magnitude of this error for a given test. As with other measurements such as those of temperature, height, and time, and scores on a test cannot be meaningfully interpreted unless the amount of measurement error is known.

Nature of Measurement Error

Measurement error results in students obtaining scores on tests that differ from their true scores. The magnitude of this error can be determined for groups of students

Table 20.2
Illustration of measurement error and standard error of measurement

	True Score	Measurement Error	Observed Score
Richard	30	0	30
Ellen	27	3	30
Catherine	25	−1	24
Elizabeth	24	2	26
Michael	23	−3	20
Mark	23	2	25
Anita	23	0	23
Erin	22	−2	20
Thomas	21	−3	18
Charlene	19	−2	17
David	16	4	20
Mean	23.00	0.00	23.00
Standard deviation	3.74	2.45	4.47

but not for individual students. This point is illustrated by a hypothetical example in Table 20.2. (This example is hypothetical because it lists each student's true score. Typically one would not know a student's true score. Instead, one would know only the score each student obtained on the test, that is, the student's "observed score.") The first column of numbers in the table shows the true score for each student. The second column indicates the measurement error resulting from less than perfect reliability. These errors resulted in students obtaining the observed test scores listed in the third column. Measurement error randomly alters each student's test score. As illustrated in the second column, this error did not affect Richard's score, added 3 points to Ellen's score, and subtracted 1 point from Catherine's score.

This measurement error is random and its effect varies unpredictably among students. For this reason, you will know a student's "observed" score, but not the measurement error for that student and, more important, not the student's true score. This means each student's true score is above or below his or her observed test score by an indeterminable amount.

Fortunately, the variability of this measurement error, for a group of students, can be estimated for a given test. That is, the standard deviation of measurement errors can be estimated for scores on a test, even though the measurement error for individual students is not determined. We call this standard deviation of errors the standard error of measurement.

The formula illustrated in Appendix A is often used to estimate standard error of measurement. The standard error of measurement is usually computed for you. With standardized tests, it is provided in the test manual and sometimes in reports. If your classroom tests are computer scored, standard error of measurement is often provided as part of the item analysis reports.

Interpreting Standard Error of Estimate

Standard error of measurement is interpreted much as we have previously interpreted standard deviations. This can be illustrated using the hypothetical example in Table 20.2. In this example, the center column of numbers lists the measurement error for each of the students. These errors are larger for some students than for others. Although some errors have negative signs, indicating the score observed on the test is lower than the student's true score, the negative sign does not influence the magnitude of the error. For instance, the scores that both Catherine and Michael obtained on the test (observed scores) are three points in error from their respective true scores, albeit in different directions.

In Table 20.2, the standard deviation of the measurement errors, shown at the bottom of the column, is 2.45. This is the standard error of measurement. Just as with other standard deviations, approximately two thirds of the numbers (measurement errors) are therefore expected to be within 2.45. Notice within our example that when you include the negative errors, 7 of 11 or 68% of the measurement errors are within 2.45 points of zero error. That is, these students' observed scores are within 2.45 points of their true scores 68% of the time.

Let us generalize from our example. If you are provided the standard error of measurement for scores on a test, you can make statements about the precision of students' test scores:

1. Approximately 68% of the time, you will be correct if you say a student's true score is within 1 standard error of measurement of that student's observed score.

2. Approximately 96% of the time, you will be correct if you say a student's true score is within 2 standard errors of measurement of the observed score.

3. Almost 100% of the time, you will be correct if you say a student's true score is within 3 standard errors of measurement of the observed score.

Box 20.10   *Apply What You Are Learning*

Assume the standard error of measurement for a test was calculated to be 3.0. Based on this information, indicate whether the following statements are true or false:

1. If a student scored 18 on the test, one can be 68% confident that the student's true score is between 15 and 21.

2. If a student scored 24 on the test, one can be 96% confident that the student's true score is between 18 and 30.

3. If a student scored 20 on the test, the student's true score is definitely between 17 and 23.

4. If a student scored 30 on the test, one can be 96% confident that the student's true score is between 27 and 33.

Answers can be found at the end of the chapter.

SUMMARY

Standard deviation is an index of variability. As scores become more diverse from their arithmetic mean, the standard deviation of these scores increases. If scores are normally distributed, an interval that is 1 standard deviation on either side of the mean captures 68% of the scores. Two standard deviations within the mean capture 96%, and 3 standard deviations include almost 100% of the scores. Even when test scores are not normally distributed, percentages close to these values usually occur.

Scores on a test can be described in terms of how many standard deviations they are away from the mean score. Doing so helps describe a student's score relative to the performance of others. Similarly, by expressing scores in terms of standard deviations, one can determine a student's relative performance on two different tests.

Standard deviations are limited to describing a student's relative performance. Because they do not indicate a student's absolute score, they cannot indicate whether an acceptable level of performance was achieved. Useful interpretations, however, can be derived from knowledge of a student's relative performance.

Standard scores describe a student's performance in terms of standard deviation units. The more commonly used standard scores include *T*-scores, deviation IQs, stanines, and NCEs. With the exception of NCE scores, these standard scores set both the mean and standard deviation at values that are easy to use. A linear or normalized transformation may be used to establish standard scores, although the interpretation of resulting standard scores is basically the same.

When interpreting standard scores, one must know the nature of the norm group on which they are based. One must also recognize that the skills measured by two different tests may be distinct even if the tests use the same standard score to report results.

Most standard scores imply that a test is more precise than it really is. Stanines are an exception. Standard scores indicate student status, but they do not indicate student growth.

In addition to indicating students' relative performance, standard deviation also can be used to express the reliability of test scores. The standard deviation of measurement errors is referred to as standard error of measurement. With standard error of measurement, one can specify the confidence that a student's true score is within a given interval of the score that this student obtained on a test.

ANSWERS: APPLY WHAT YOU ARE LEARNING

20.1 1. $16/4 = 4.0$; 2. $18/4 = 4.5$; 3. $20/4 = 5.0$; 4. $20/5 = 4.0$; 5. approximately 4.5. (*Hint:* Table 20.1 does not give a divisor for 60 students. Therefore, estimating standard deviation using divisors of 4 and then 5, and splitting the difference, is close enough.)

20.2 For Tests 3 through 5, the standard deviations are 2, 0, 2.0, and 4.0. Note that for Tests 3 and 4, the dispersion of scores is the same as the scores on Test

2; as a result, the standard deviations are the same. If the ordering of the scores changes but the overall dispersion of the scores is unchanged, the standard deviation remains the same. Note that although the scores for Test 4 are higher, the dispersion is the same as the scores on Tests 2 and 3. The scores on Test 5 are twice the corresponding scores on Test 4. Since the dispersion of scores on Test 5 is twice that of those on Test 4, the standard deviation is twice as large.

20.3 1. 68%; 2. 96%; 3. almost 100%; 4. 68%; 5. almost 100%; 6. 96%; almost 100%. Look closely. Notice that Items 1 and 4 represent intervals of 1 standard deviation above and below their respective means, Items 2 and 6 represent intervals of 2 standard deviations, and Items 3, 5, and 7 represent intervals of 3 standard deviations. That information alone is the basis for determining the percentage of scores contained in the specified intervals.

20.4 The first three scores are 2, 0.5, and 1.5 standard deviations above the mean. The next two scores are 1 and 3 standard deviations below the mean. Note that you must use decimal points when scores fall between standard deviation units.

20.5 *Statement 1:* False. Jenni scored 1 standard deviation above the mean in reading and 2 standard deviations above the mean in science. She did better in science. *Statement 2:* False. Paul scored 1 standard deviation below the mean in reading and 2 standard deviations above the mean in math. He did better in math. *Statement 3:* True. Murray scored at the mean in both math and science. He did equally well in both. *Statement 4:* False. Terri scored 1 standard deviation below the mean in math and 0.5 standard deviation below the mean in science. She did better in science. *Statement 5:* True. Patrick scored 1 standard deviation below the mean in reading and 2 standard deviations below the mean in math. He did better in reading.

20.6 1. 60; 2. 30; 3. 55; 4. 65; 5. 25.

20.7 1. 116; 2. 68; 3. 108; 4. 124; 5. 60.

20.8 1. 7; 2. 1; 3. 6; 4. 8; 5. 1.

20.9 1. C; 2. A; 3. E; 4. D; 5. A; 6. E; 7. D; 8. B; 9. C; 10. B; 11. A; 12. D. To determine the answers, convert each score to standard deviation units. For example, a *T*-score of 80 (Item 2) is 3 standard deviations above the mean. Therefore, the correct answer to Item 2 is A because this *T*-score is "high" (more than 1.5 standard deviations above the mean).

20.10 *Item 1:* True. An interval that is 1 standard error of measurement above and below the observed score has a 68% chance of capturing the true score. *Item 2:* True. An interval that is 2 standard errors of measurement above and below the observed score allows 96% confidence. *Item 3:* False. An interval that is 1 standard error of measurement above and below allows 68% confidence. One cannot be definite that this interval includes the true score. *Item 4:* False. One is 68% confident, not 96%, that an interval that is 1 standard error of measurement above and below the observed score captures the true score.

ADDITIONAL READING

Hills, J. R. (1986). *All of Hills' handy hints*. Washington, DC: National Council on Measurement in Education. This booklet is a compilation of articles previously written by Hills regarding the interpretation of selected standard scores, percentile ranks, and grade equivalents. Each article presents a series of true–false items followed by an explanation of their answers.

CHAPTER 21

Interpreting Percentile Ranks and Grade-Equivalent Scores

S tudent performance on standardized tests is often expressed as a percentile rank. The *percentile rank* of a score is the percentage of scores falling below that score. If a student who correctly answered 40 items is at the 78th percentile rank, then 78% of individuals in the norm group correctly answered fewer than 40 items. Percentile rank is often used to help interpret scores because its meaning is easy to conceptualize.

Percentile ranks are expressed as whole numbers ranging from 1 through 99. An important consideration when interpreting percentile ranks is recognizing that they do not represent equal intervals. For example, the difference between percentile ranks of 5 and 10 will be shown to be much more significant than a difference between 45 and 50. Therefore, this chapter pays particular attention to interpreting percentile ranks in light of these unequal intervals.

Percentile rank is sometimes confused with percentage scores. For example, one might erroneously conclude that a student scoring at the 60th percentile rank correctly answered most of the test items. In this chapter, the distinction between percentile ranks and percentage scores is clarified.

This chapter then discusses grade-equivalent scores. Grade-equivalent scores are intuitively appealing because they relate performance on a test to a familiar variable: grade in school. Grade-equivalent scores reflect growth because their numerical value increases as a student progresses through school. Percentiles and standard scores do not share this attribute because a student's test score is compared with peer performance. If a student's progress is consistent relative to these peers, the student's percentile rank and standard score do not change over time.

Grade-equivalent scores are easily misinterpreted. This concern is so significant that many measurement specialists discourage their use. Nevertheless, grade equivalents are commonly used to describe performance on standardized tests.

Therefore, it is important that you know the characteristics of grade-equivalent scores to ensure their appropriate interpretation.

This chapter helps you achieve four skills:

- Recognize the characteristics of percentile ranks
- Distinguish between interpretations of percentile ranks and percentage scores
- Describe how grade-equivalent scores are determined
- Recognize the characteristics of grade-equivalent scores

CHARACTERISTICS OF PERCENTILE RANKS

Computation of Percentile Ranks

Table 21.1 illustrates how percentile ranks are computed. The first two columns indicate the number of students obtaining various raw scores on a 50-item test. (A raw score is the number of points a student obtained on a test, for instance, the number of items answered correctly.) Column 3 lists the percentage of students scoring below each score. For instance, because 30 is the lowest score obtained on the test, 0% of the students scored below this score.

Column 3 illustrates one approach to computing percentile ranks. More typically, percentiles are computed by assuming that each score represents a midpoint within a score interval, with half the scores within the interval below this midpoint and half above. This approach is illustrated in column 4. Note that the exact percentile rank of the raw score 30 is 0.5. This occurs because no scores are below the score of 30, and half of the one score at 30 is assumed to be below the midpoint. The half of one score out of 100 scores produces the exact percentile rank of 0.5.

The exact percentile rank is similarly computed for each raw score. For instance, the exact percentile rank of the score 35 is 8.0. The sum of the six scores below 35 and half of the four scores at 35 total 8.0 out of the 100 scores. Percentile ranks are rounded to the nearest whole number. The minimum and maximum percentile ranks are 1 and 99. Column 5 within the table illustrates this rounding.

The process of using midpoints may needlessly complicate the computation of percentile ranks. Comparison of columns 3 and 5 shows that this alternative procedure resulted in approximately the same percentile ranks except for scores near the middle of the distribution.

Percentile ranks of standardized test scores are often based on several thousand examinees. To facilitate discussion, the illustration in Table 21.1 is computed using only 100 examinees.

Unequal Intervals of Percentile Ranks

Table 21.1 illustrates an important property of percentile ranks:

The numerical value of percentile ranks changes more rapidly near the center than near the lower or upper ends of a distribution of raw scores.

Table 21.1
Percentile ranks of raw scores normed on 100 students

(1) Raw Score	(2) Frequency	(3) Percentage Below	(4) Exact Percentile Rank	(5) Percentile Rank
50	0	100	100.0	99
49	1	99	99.5	99
48	0	99	99.0	99
47	2	97	98.0	98
46	2	95	96.0	96
45	6	89	92.0	92
44	4	85	87.0	87
43	9	76	80.5	81
42	10	66	71.0	71
41	10	56	61.0	61
40	12	44	50.0	50
39	13	31	37.5	38
38	8	23	27.0	27
37	6	17	20.0	20
36	7	10	13.5	14
35	4	6	8.0	8
34	3	3	4.5	5
33	1	2	2.5	3
32	1	1	1.5	2
31	0	1	1.0	1
30	1	0	.5	1
29	0	0	0.0	1

Mean and standard deviation of the raw scores are 40.0 and 3.5, respectively.

Notice how the two students who answered 30 and 32 items correctly obtained similar percentile ranks. Likewise, similar percentile ranks are associated with the raw scores 47 and 49. However, the percentile ranks of students scoring two points apart near the center of the distribution are more discrepant. For instance, the raw scores 40 and 42 correspond to percentile ranks 50 and 71, a difference of 21 points!

Percentile ranks change *inconsistently* because more students tend to achieve middle versus low or high test scores. In Table 21.1, the student who obtained a raw score of 30 would have to answer five additional items correctly to surpass the score of five other students. The student who scored 49 could have missed four more items on the test before being surpassed by four students. In contrast, every additional test item answered correctly by a student scoring 40 results in that student surpassing an additional 12, 10, and 10 students. Very little change in performance by students near the average score results in substantial changes in their percentile rank. Equal changes in test performance by low- and high-scoring students has little impact on their percentile ranks. This important characteristic must be taken into account when interpreting percentile ranks.

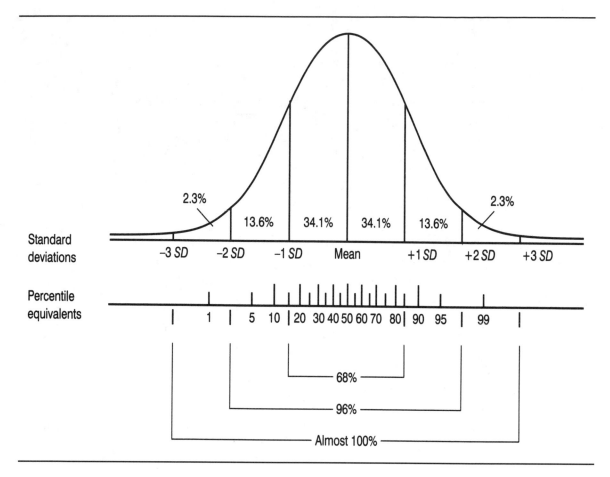

Figure 21.1
Percentile rank equivalents of selected points within a normal distribution

Standard deviation units can facilitate interpretation of percentile ranks. Recall that if scores are normally distributed, 68% of the scores will fall within 1 standard deviation of the mean. As illustrated in Figure 21.1, the symmetrical nature of the normal distribution will split this percentage into 34% above and below the mean. If the mean is at the 50th percentile, 1 standard deviation surpasses an additional 34% of the scores. Therefore, a score that is 1 standard deviation above the mean is at the 84th percentile. Similarly, 1 standard deviation below the mean drops below 34% of the scores, placing that point at the 16th percentile.

The interval from 2 standard deviations below to 2 standard deviations above the mean would capture approximately 96% of the scores. The remaining extremes of the distribution contain approximately 4% of the scores (2% in each extreme). Therefore, as illustrated in Figure 21.1, scores that are 2 standard deviations below and above the mean would be at the 2nd and 98th percentiles. Because the numerical value of percentile ranks does not exceed 1 and 99, points that are 3 standard deviations below and above the mean correspond to the 1st and 99th percentiles.

If standard deviation units represent equal intervals (this usually is assumed to be true) and test scores are distributed normally, then percentile ranks of 1, 2, 16, 50, 84, 98, and 99 all represent equal changes in test scores. These percentile benchmarks represent useful numbers to remember.

Box 21.1 *Apply What You Are Learning*

If test scores are distributed normally, indicate whether each of the following statements is true or false:

1. The difference between test scores at the 50th and 84th percentiles is about equal to the difference between test scores at the 84th and 98th percentiles.

2. The difference between scores at the 50th and 70th percentiles represent a *greater* difference than between scores at the 84th and 98th percentiles.

3. The difference between scores at the 1st and 16th percentiles is about equal to differences between scores at the 16th and 50th percentiles.

Answers can be found at the end of the chapter.

Look back at Table 21.1. Note how the percentiles that are used as benchmarks (1, 2, 16, 50, 84, 98, 99) relate to the scores in that table. The mean and standard deviation of the raw scores are 40.0 and 3.5, respectively. The students who obtained a raw score of 40 on this therefore scored at the mean and are at the 50th percentile rank. (The mean is not always exactly but is usually close to the 50th percentile.) A point that is 1 standard deviation below the mean (between raw scores 36 and 37) is approximately at the 16th percentile rank. Similarly, the point that is 1 standard deviation above the mean (between raw scores 43 and 44) is near the 84th percentile rank. Scores that are 2 standard deviations below and above the mean (33 and 47) are at or near the 2nd and 98th percentile ranks.

Remember, changes in percentile of 1, 2, 16, 50, 84, 98, and 99 represent approximately equal changes in student performance on a test. It is tempting to assume that equal numerical changes in percentile ranks correspond to equal changes in performance on a test, but that is not the way percentiles function. For instance, a change in percentile rank from 2 to 16 represents about the same change in performance on a test as a change in percentile rank from 16 to 50. Remember those percentile benchmarks; they will help you later!

Inappropriateness of Adding, Subtracting, or Averaging Percentile Ranks

One might be tempted to find the difference between two percentile ranks or average the percentile scores of individuals to determine the overall performance of a student on several tests. *When computing an arithmetic mean, one must assume that a series of numbers represents equal intervals.* This causes a problem with percentile scores.

This problem can be illustrated with the ranking of athletic teams. If nine athletic teams in a collegiate conference are ranked, the average rank will always be five, but the performance of the team ranked five might not represent the mean for the conference. If the five highest ranked teams are fairly similar but the remaining teams are quite different in their performance, this fifth-ranked team will actually be more like the highly ranked teams than the average performance for the conference. The average rank will not identify the athletic team of average ability.

Percentiles rank test scores into 99 divisions. As previously discussed, these divisions do not represent equal differences in student ability. The difference in performance represented by percentile ranks of 1 and 2 or 98 and 99 is many times the difference represented by percentile ranks of 50 and 51. Percentile ranks therefore should not be averaged with the arithmetic mean, and they should not be added or subtracted. Doing so gives considerable weight to differences between near-average scores and virtually no weight to differences among low or high scores.

Normal Curve Equivalent Scores versus Percentile Ranks

Normal curve equivalent (NCE) scores were introduced in the previous chapter. NCE scores are a standard score with a preset mean of 50 and standard deviation of 21.06. This somewhat unusual value for standard deviation is used so that NCE scores will match percentile ranks at three points: 1, 50, and 99. As with percentiles, test publishers who use NCE scores limit their range from 1 to 99.

Although percentile and NCE scores look similar, they have an important difference, which is illustrated in Table 21.2. In this table, raw scores, NCE scores, and percentile ranks are listed for a 50-item test. The frequencies show the number of students who obtained each score. Notice the following comparison of NCE scores to percentiles that are illustrated in Table 21.2:

Similarities of NCE Scores and Percentile Ranks

■ When the NCE score is 50, the percentile rank is also 50. Likewise, when the NCE score is 1 or 99, the percentile rank is also 1 and 99.

■ Both NCE scores and percentile ranks range from 1 to 99.

Difference Between NCE Scores and Percentile Ranks

■ Equal changes in student raw scores result in equal changes in NCE scores but not in percentile ranks. In our illustration, for each 1-point change in raw score, the NCE score changes by 6 points. This proportional change is true for any NCE score until the limiting score of 1 or 99 is reached. In contrast, for each 1-point change in raw score, unequal changes occur in percentile ranks. In our illustration, for example, if a student correctly answered 41 rather than 40 items, the student's percentile rank would change from 61 from 50, a change of 11 points. But if a student correctly answered 47 rather than 46 items, the student's percentile rank would change to 98 from 96, just 2 points. Notice that this results in

Table 21.2
NCE scores and equivalent percentile ranks

	(1) Raw Score	Frequency	(2) NCE Score	(3) Percentile Rank
	50	0	99	99
	49	1	99	99
	48	0	98	99
	47	2	92	98
	46	2	86	96
	45	6	80	92
	44	4	74	87
	43	9	68	81
	42	10	62	71
	41	10	56	61
	40	12	50	50
	39	13	44	38
	38	8	38	27
	37	6	32	20
	36	7	26	14
	35	4	20	8
	34	3	14	5
	33	1	8	3
	32	1	2	2
	31	0	1	1
	30	1	1	1
Mean	40.0		50	
Standard deviation	3.5		21.06	

NCE scores and percentile ranks being quite different for most raw scores. For this reason, always think of NCE scores and percentile ranks as being different types of scores. They cannot be interchanged.

NCE scores are often used in research settings and by program evaluators in school districts. Because of their unusual standard deviation, NCE scores are not practical to use when discussing test scores with parents. Interestingly, NCE scores are becoming more common on reports for parents on standardized tests. Percentile ranks, however, may also be confusing to parents (and many teachers) because they represent uneven intervals.

DISTINCTION BETWEEN PERCENTILE RANKS AND PERCENTAGE SCORES

Because percentile ranks and percentage scores are both based on percentages, they are sometimes confused with each other. The distinction between these two types of scores is important. A student's percentile and percentage scores on a test are usually quite different. Also, percentile scores are used in a norm-referenced context whereas percentage scores are applicable to criterion-referenced interpretations.

As stated previously, percentile rank is the percentage of scores falling below a given score. A student scores at the 20th percentile by outperforming 20% of other individuals in the comparison group. But the students scoring at the 20th percentile probably answered other than 20% of the test items correctly. If the test consisted of easy items, the lowest scoring 20% of examinees conceivably could have correctly answered more than 90% of the items. Or if the test items were difficult, students scoring at the 95th percentile could have incorrectly answered many or even most of the items.

Box 21.2 *Apply What You Are Learning*

Indicate whether each of the following statements is true or not necessary true:

1. A student scoring at the 80th percentile correctly answered the majority of items on the test.

2. A student scoring at the 80th percentile correctly answered more items than a student scoring at the 60th percentile.

3. A student who correctly answered 80% of the items scored somewhere above the 20th percentile.

4. If students scoring at the 70th percentile correctly answered 70% of the items, then students scoring at the 80th percentile correctly answered 80% of the items.

Answers can be found at the end of the chapter.

DETERMINATION OF GRADE EQUIVALENTS

Understanding how grade-equivalent scores are computed provides a basis for discussing their interpretation. Let us assume that a 30-item mathematics test has been developed to measure content typically taught in the fourth grade. To establish grade equivalents, this test is administered to students in selected grades, and the average score for each grade is determined. This process is illustrated in Table 21.3.[1] In this illustration, 300 students from the third, fourth, and fifth grades are administered the math test at the beginning of their school year. The numbers of students from each grade obtaining each raw score are listed. For example, 8 students in the fourth grade obtained a raw score of 20.

Table 21.3 indicates that the raw score 18 is at the median for fourth graders. (The median is the middle score, that is, the score at the 50th percentile.) Conse-

---

[1]Several different approaches are used to compute grade equivalents. The technique discussed here is illustrative only and is somewhat simplified. However, the characteristics described here using the present illustration are consistent with those of grade-equivalent scores used with achievement batteries.

Table 21.3

Computation of grade-equivalent scores using median scores observed for third, fourth, and fifth graders

Raw Score	3rd Graders	4th Graders	5th Graders	Grade Equivalent	
		Number of Students			
30			2	6.4	
29		1	2	6.2	
28		1	3	6.0	
27		2	6	5.8	
26		3	7	5.6	
25		3	9	5.4	
24		3	10	5.2	
23		4	10	5.0	observed
22		4	9	4.8	
21		5	8	4.6	
20	1	8	7	4.4	
19	2	10	4	4.2	
18	2	12	3	4.0	observed
17	6	9	2	3.8	
16	7	9	2	3.6	
15	10	5	2	3.4	
14	14	4	1	3.2	
13	16	4	1	3.0	observed
12	13	3	1	2.8	
11	11	3		2.6	
10	8	3		2.4	
9	4	3		2.2	
8	2	2		2.0	
7	2			1.8	
6	1			1.6	
5	1			1.4	
4				1.2	
3				1.0	
2				K.8	
1				K.6	
0				K.4	
Totals	100	100	100		

quently, a score of 18 represents the 4.0 grade equivalent. The medians for students in the third and fifth grades are similarly determined. In Table 21.3, these medians place the raw scores of 13 and 23 at grade equivalents of 3.0 and 5.0.

Grade equivalents are then interpolated for scores falling between observed medians. Within Table 21.3, the grade equivalents of the scores 14 through 17 become grade equivalents 3.2, 3.4, 3.6, and 3.8, respectively. Grade equivalents are similarly extrapolated for scores falling outside the range of the medians. For example, the raw score of 30 is assigned a grade equivalent of 6.4. Depending on the possible range of scores, grade equivalents might be extrapolated into kindergarten (K), as illustrated in the table, or even into preschool.

Grade equivalents are computed to one place beyond the decimal point. By convention, this last digit is often interpreted as months of the school year. A .9 refers to the end of the ninth, or last, month of the academic year. A .1 refers to the end of the first month, and .0 alludes to the beginning of the school year. Within Table 21.3, a distance of 5 raw score points separates medians at the third, fourth, and fifth grades. As a result, grade equivalents are interpolated at intervals of .2, or 2 months. With standardized tests, it is common for a 1-point difference in raw score to represent a .2- to .6-point (2- to 6-month) difference in grade equivalents.

Box 21.3 *Apply What You Are Learning*

Answer the following questions using Table 21.3:

1. What are the grade equivalents associated with raw scores 28, 10, and 2?
2. What percentage of fourth graders scored above the median score of fifth graders? (*Hint:* There are a total of 100 fourth graders.) What percentage of fourth graders scored below the median score of third graders?
3. At what grade are the skills taught that are measured by this particular test?
4. Was this test administered to first, second, or sixth graders?

Answers can be found at the end of the chapter.

Table 21.3 illustrates the technique used to compute grade equivalents. Depending on the test, somewhat different procedures may be used. For example, the test may be normed partway through instead of at the beginning of the school year. If the test were normed in November, the median raw score of fourth graders would become the 4.2 grade equivalent. Sometimes more "observed" grade equivalents are obtained by norming the test at more than a single time of the year. Nevertheless, most grade equivalents represent interpolated or extrapolated values.

Often, test content is a compilation of material taught in more than a single grade. To establish equivalents for all possible raw scores, however, the range of grade-equivalent scores usually extends well beyond the grades for which the test content is appropriate. To facilitate the illustration, Table 21.3 is based on a total of 300 examinees. Typically, norms are based on substantially more students.

CHARACTERISTICS OF GRADE-EQUIVALENT SCORES

Grade-equivalent scores encourage direct interpretations. A fourth-grade student who obtains a grade-equivalent score of 6.2 is said to have performed equivalent to a sixth-grade student in the second month of school. Similarly, a fourth-grade student who obtains a grade-equivalent score of 2.0 is said to have performed approximately two years below grade level. These will be shown to be erroneous interpretations of grade-equivalent scores. School personnel often favor grade-equivalent scores because of their apparent ease of interpretation, but many publishers of standardized tests discourage the use of grade-equivalent scores because of their frequent misinterpretation. Discussing the characteristics of grade-equivalent scores will help clarify this issue.

Grade Equivalents Identify Median Scores

A grade equivalent represents the median test score for that particular grade. Fifty percent of the students in a typical fourth grade are expected to score below the fourth-grade equivalent, 50% of seventh graders are expected to score below the seventh-grade equivalent, and so on. Therefore, large portions of students in a typical school invariably will be above and below these median values.

Negative connotations are often associated with scores below the median grade level. A fourth-grade student whose grade-equivalent score is 2.0 might be considered to be two years below grade level. A common inference would be that this student is two years behind a reasonable expectation for 4th graders. However,

> grade-equivalent scores do not represent standards that students should be expected to achieve. Because grade equivalents are median scores, they represent points below which half the scores occur.

If the overall performance of students improves, half the students will again score below grade level when grade-equivalent scores are recalibrated. Therefore, as long as norms are appropriate, half the students in a typical school will score below grade level and half above grade level. It is quite common with grade-equivalent scores for a fourth grader to score below the second-grade level or above the sixth-grade level.

Many people improperly associate *undesirable* with the label *below average*. When used to express grades and test scores, *average* often implies a minimally acceptable standard. In contrast, dictionaries define average as *typical, representative,* or *midpoint.* Perhaps the expression *midscore* should be used to express average performance.

Grade Equivalents Do Not Convey Months of the Year

As illustrated in Table 21.3, grade equivalents are anchored using the median scores from selected grades. Grade-equivalent scores between these medians are obtained from interpolation, and those outside these medians through extrapolation. Test manuals often propose that the number to the right of the decimal be treated as months. For example, a grade equivalent of 7.1 would refer to the average seventh-grade performance in October. A grade equivalent of 7.9 would refer to June in the seventh grade, and 8.0 identifies average performance at the beginning of the eighth grade. During the school year, however, students do not learn at the constant rate that is suggested by these numbers. Also, achievement probably decreases rather than increases over the summer. Because student growth in the course of a year is not linear, equating grade-equivalent scores to specific months of the year should be avoided.

Grade Equivalents Exceed Grade Levels at Which Skills Are Taught

The grade-equivalent scores in Table 21.3 vary from K.4 to 6.4. This basically is the full range of grades in elementary school. The test illustrated here, however, was designed to measure math skills taught in the fourth grade. The grade-equivalent scores extend well beyond the level at which the content of this test is taught. It would be incorrect, for example, to say that K.4 represents the typical math proficiency of kindergarten students, or that 6.4 represents the typical proficiency of sixth graders with sixth-grade material. Students in kindergarten and sixth grade are learning different math skills than fourth graders.

The characteristic of grade equivalents exceeding the range of grades at which skills are taught is particularly a problem at the middle and high school levels. The content of instruction varies considerably at these grade levels. Given that the typical range of grade-equivalent scores on standardized tests is six to eight grades, grade equivalents on high school tests commonly extend into postsecondary grades when the content being measured is only taught within a couple of grades at the secondary level.

The reciprocal of this problem is that a grade-equivalent score has different meanings when students from two grades obtain the same score. For example, separate achievement tests designed for the fifth and ninth grades both would have scores representing the 7.0-grade equivalent. These two scores would not have equivalent interpretations, however, because they refer to the typical performance of a seventh grader with fifth-grade and ninth-grade materials, respectively.

Berk (1981) warned against the still fairly common practice of using a grade-equivalent score of two or more years below current placement as a procedure for identifying learning disabled students. Grade-equivalent scores *do not* identify the grade level at which a student is performing. Discrepancy between a grade-equivalent score and placement simply indicates a student is scoring below (or above) the midpoint of scores obtained by peers.

Grade-equivalent scores *are able* to indicate a student's *relative* performance. The score of 6.5 on a given test is higher than that of 5.5 and lower than that of 7.5. This of course is a characteristic shared by all other types of scores including percentile ranks and standard scores. For a given test, the correlation between rankings of students on any of these scales will be very high. After evidence is established that students below (or above) a particular test performance will benefit from special instruction, a percentile rank, standard score, or grade-equivalent score can be used to represent this level of performance.

Standard Deviations of Grade-Equivalent Scores Are Inconsistent

Test manuals do not provide the standard deviation of grade-equivalent scores because the grade equivalent is intended to serve as a developmental scale rather than to indicate a student's performance relative to other members of a single group.

However, lack of a standard deviation limits the interpretation one can give grade equivalents because it prevents the determination of whether a score is unusually low or high.

Hills (1983) pointed out that because standard deviations differ between content areas for students in a given grade, it is not possible to use grade equivalents to compare a student's performance in two skill areas. For example, in early elementary grades, students' language skills are more varied than their arithmetic skills. The implication this has to grade equivalents is illustrated in Table 21.4. These grade equivalents are based on the second-grade administration of an achievement battery in the fourth month of the school term (January). Students' grade equivalents on the spelling and computation subtests are listed for selected percentile ranks. Although the 2.4-grade equivalent is at the 50th percentile on both tests, the grade equivalents differ considerably at other percentile points. Because students are more similar in math skills in elementary grades, the range of grade-equivalent scores is less on the computation test than the spelling test. One cannot assume that a student scoring at the 84th percentile would benefit more from advanced placement in spelling than computations simply because there is a one-year difference in these grade equivalents (3.8 versus 2.9). Without any special instruction, differences in grade equivalents between language and math skills diminish proportionally in later grades.

The standard deviation of grade equivalents is also uneven over time. The range of grade-equivalent scores is smaller for younger students than for older students. Because of this characteristic, most above-average students gain more than one grade equivalent each year, average students tend to gain one grade equivalent, and most below-average students gain less than one grade equivalent per year. Many educators are alarmed when they incorrectly perceive that students in the lower half learn less than one year's worth of material each year. This pattern is simply a characteristic caused by the unequal standard deviations of grade-equivalent scores.

It is important to remember that grade equivalents *do not represent standards*. Like standard scores and percentiles, grade equivalents are unable to indicate whether

Table 21.4
Grade-equivalent scores in spelling and computation at selected percentile ranks

Percentile Ranks	Grade Equivalent	
	Spelling	Computation
99	5.5	3.8
98	4.7	3.4
84	3.8	2.9
50	2.4	2.4
16	1.6	1.8
2	1.1	1.5
1	K.8	1.2

a student knows as much as he or she should know. Grade equivalents *do represent norms.* Like standard scores and percentiles, they do indicate whether a student scored below, at, or above the middle performance of other students. Because the standard deviation units of grade equivalents are unknown, unlike with standard scores and percentiles, it is not possible with grade equivalents to determine how far a student scored below or above the middle performance of other students.

Box 21.4 *Apply What You Are Learning*

Here are the grade-equivalent scores of three fifth graders in language usage and social studies. The test was given at the beginning of the year.

	Language Usage	Social Studies
Byron	8.0	7.0
Anna	5.0	5.0
Jodi	3.5	3.5

Based on these scores, what are the answers to the following questions?

1. Can one tell whether Bryon is doing better in language usage or social studies? Why or why not?
2. Can one tell if Anna is doing the same in language usage and social studies? What about Jodi?
3. Three years from now, will Byron's grade equivalent in language usage most likely be below, at, or above 11.0? Three years from now, will Anna's grade equivalent in language usage most likely be below, at, or about 8.0? At that time, will Jodi's language usage most likely be below, at, or above 6.5?

Answers can be found at the end of the chapter.

SUMMARY

Percentile ranks indicate the percentage of examinees in the norm group who scored below each score. Percentile ranks represent unequal intervals. Changes of 1 percentile are significant for low and high scores, but differences of several percentiles are insignificant for average scores. Percentile ranks of 1, 2, 16, 50, 84, 98, and 99 represent approximately equal intervals.

Percentile rank and percentage scores should not be confused. In addition to being numerically different, percentile ranks are used in a norm-referenced context, whereas percentage scores are applicable to criterion-referenced settings.

Percentile rank and NCE scores should also not be confused. NCE scores are a standard score. The mean and standard deviation of 50 and (21.06) results in NCE scores obtaining the same numerical value as percentile ranks at 1, 50, and 99. At other points, NCE scores and percentiles do not share common values.

Grade-equivalent scores indicate the median performance of students from different grades on a single test. Most grade equivalents are derived through interpolation and extrapolation. With grade-equivalent scores, the digit to the right of the decimal point is often interpreted as months of the school year, although this practice is inappropriate.

Unlike percentile ranks and standard scores, grade-equivalent scores are designed to reflect student growth. In that a student's grade-equivalent scores increase across time, they achieve this intended characteristic.

However, by associating test scores with grade in school, grade-equivalent scores invite erroneous interpretations. Grade equivalents do not represent standards that students should achieve and do not identify the grade at which content is or should be taught. They simply identify median scores obtained by students in various grades. Actually, most grade-equivalent scores represent hypothetical medians in the sense that they are derived from interpolations and extrapolations from observed medians.

Grade equivalents often exceed the range of grades at which skills measured by the test are taught. Skills on a test designed for the fourth grade, for instance, are usually not taught in kindergarten or eighth grade, even though grade equivalents for one test usually have a range of this magnitude. Similarly, two distinct tests that measure third-grade and seventh-grade content will both contain grade-equivalent scores representing fifth-grade performance. These scores, however, are not compatible, because they represent median performance of fifth graders with third- and seventh-grade material. These problems with grade equivalents increase in secondary grades because the content taught is more diverse across grades.

The standard deviation of grade-equivalent scores is inconsistent across content areas. Therefore, grade-equivalent scores cannot be used to compare a student's achievement in two different content areas.

ANSWERS: APPLY WHAT YOU ARE LEARNING

21.1 *Item 1:* True. The difference between the mean and 1 standard deviation above the mean is the same as between 1 and 2 standard deviations above the mean. *Item 2:* False. The difference between the mean and a point less than 1 standard deviation above the mean is less than the difference between points 1 and 2 standard deviations above the mean. *Item 3:* False. The difference between approximately 1 and 3 standard deviations below the mean is greater than the difference between the mean and 1 standard deviation below the mean.

21.2 *Item 1:* Not necessarily true. If a test is difficult, an individual scoring higher than 80% of other examinees may have correctly answered less than half of the items. Conceivably, even a person scoring at the 99th percentile could have answered less than half the items. *Item 2:* True. The 80th percentile corresponds to a higher score than the 60th percentile. *Item 3:* Not necessarily true. If a test is easy, every examinee (including the lowest scoring students) could correctly answer more than 80% of the items. *Item 4:* Not necessarily true. The 80th percentile is definitely higher than the 70th. Therefore, in this example, individuals scoring at the 80th percentile correctly answered *more* than 70% of the items but not necessarily 80% of these items.

21.3 *Item 1:* 6.0 (beginning of the sixth grade), 2.4 (fourth month of the second grade), and K.8 (eighth month of kindergarten). *Item 2:* 13 of 100, or 13%, of the fourth graders scored above the raw score 23; 14% of the fourth graders scored below the raw score 13. *Item 3:* The test measures content taught in fourth-grade math classes. (If you correctly answered this item, you are a very careful reader.) *Item 4:* This test was administered only to students at the beginning of third, fourth, and fifth grades. It was not administered to first, second, or sixth graders; to students midway through these grades; or to students in kindergarten.

21.4 *Item 1:* Byron is above average in both areas. Because the standard deviations of the scores are unknown, we do not know in which area he is doing better. *Item 2:* Anna is at the 50th percentile in both areas and therefore is doing the same. Jodi is below average in both areas. Because the standard deviations of the scores are unknown, we do not know if he is doing the same in both areas. *Item 3:* Because grade-equivalent scores spread out more as students get older, in three years Byron will most likely score above 11.0, Anna will most likely score at 5.0, and Jodi will most likely score below 6.5.

SOMETHING TO TRY

- Obtain actual or simulated score reports on a standardized achievement battery for several students. Try to select reports that include at least one standard score, percentile ranks, and grade equivalents. State for each student what the scores do and do not tell you about the student. Your interpretation should be consistent with characteristics of each type of score. If you personally know the students, evaluate their scores, taking into account what you know about them through other sources of information.

- Obtain the norm tables for a standardized achievement battery. Compare percentile ranks to raw scores. Does correctly answering one more item on the test change percentile ranks more for average scores (those near the 50th percentile) or more for scores significantly above or below average? Why does this happen?

- Again using tables for a standardized achievement test, look at the grade-equivalent scores. How many more items does a student have to correctly answer in order to change one full year on the grade-equivalent scale? Try to find out what the standard error of measurement is for raw scores. Convert this standard error of measurement to the grade-equivalent scale for that test. What are the implications with respect to interpreting the grade equivalents? Do the same for the percentile ranks and standard score scales.

- How do parents and teachers interpret grade-equivalent scores? Or alternatively, how have you interpreted these scores? Using the characteristics of grade-equivalents described in this chapter, being as specific as possible, which of these interpretations are correct and which are in error?

CHAPTER 22

Evaluating Uses of Standardized Tests

S tandardized tests play a variety of roles in education. They help determine when early elementary students are ready to be taught reading. They help identify the students to be placed in special ability groupings. They are used to monitor student achievement and facilitate evaluation of instructional programs.

Standardized tests represent a positive resource in education. Unfortunately, their use can lead to erroneous conclusions and actions. In part, this is because users are unfamiliar with the characteristics of a particular type of score being used with the test, such as the special attributes of percentiles, or individuals fail to take into account errors associated with the less than perfect reliability and validity inherent to all tests. Sometimes, a particular application is simply not compatible with the test's capabilities.

This chapter is designed to help you identify appropriate uses of standardized tests. Discussion focuses on the following seven applications:

- Grouping students according to ability
- Identifying students to receive special education
- Evaluating schools and teachers
- Addressing the needs of individual students
- Using performance assessments in standardized tests
- Establishing performance standards
- Certifying potential and practicing teachers

Typically, a specific test is used in a variety of applications. For instance, an achievement battery is often used to establish what a student has learned, to help identify students who have learning disabilities, and to evaluate the effectiveness of instruction in a school district. The following discussion of various applications of standardized tests stresses the need to use a test whose characteristics are consistent with its intended role and limiting the use of test scores to the tests' capabilities.

GROUPING STUDENTS ACCORDING TO ABILITY

Teachers and administrators use aptitude and achievement tests to group students at all elementary and secondary grade levels. Aptitude tests are typically used for comprehensive groupings in which the same ability groups are maintained for instruction in several content areas. Standardized achievement tests are more likely used when groupings are formed for a specific subject such as reading or mathematics.

This section lists the advantages and disadvantages usually associated with ability grouping. The impact of grouping on subsequent achievement is then addressed. Finally, the important implications of statistical regression on student grouping are discussed.

Advantages and Disadvantages of Ability Grouping

Various advantages and disadvantages have been associated with grouping. One claimed advantage is that with reduced student diversity in a class, instruction can proceed at a more appropriate pace. Also, restricting the range of abilities is expected to allow a faster pace of instruction because fast learners are less distinct from slow learners within each group. Another typical advantage is that instructional techniques can be more adequately matched to student abilities and needs. The teacher also may more easily motivate more capable students to set higher goals. Also, the frustration of less able students may be reduced because they will not be competing with high-ability students.

Significant disadvantages are also associated with grouping. Instruction will be provided at a slower pace for students placed in lower ability groups, and teachers along with students in lower ability groups may have depressed aspirations. Students in lower ability groups may lack the stimulation provided by high-achieving students and may also be labeled as inferior. Placing students into ability groups might also be considered undemocratic in the sense that it promotes an elitist society.

Impact of Ability Grouping on Student Achievement

Ability grouping has been used extensively in education since the beginning of this century, yet research studies such as those reviewed by the National Education Association (1968) and by Esposito (1973) failed to identify overall gains in achievement resulting from placing students into ability groups. Slavin (1987) proposed that the reason prior research reviews did not find benefits is that these studies failed to distinguish between various approaches to grouping students.

In his review of research conducted within elementary schools, Slavin (1987) categorized studies according to the type of grouping being evaluated. He found that research consistently demonstrates no improvement from placing students into comprehensive groupings. That is, placing students into ability groups for instruction across several content areas does not improve student performance. However, maintaining heterogeneous classes and regrouping students when teaching mathematics and reading has been shown to improve achievement. These subjects are more hierarchical than science and social studies; consequently, deficiencies in early instruction are more likely to compound difficulties with later instruction.

Two approaches to regrouping students for instruction in mathematics and reading have been associated with improved achievement. One is to form subgroups within the classroom when teaching these subjects. Another is to teach these subjects simultaneously in several classrooms, with students leaving their homeroom class to join students of similar ability.

Slavin (1987) proposes that effective grouping of students in specific content areas requires the use of measures more specific than the general aptitude measures provided by intelligence tests. This suggests that standardized achievement tests will be better for grouping students for specialized instruction than will standardized aptitude tests. A teacher's own test may be superior to a standardized achievement test as long as the test is carefully constructed and measures knowledge critical to skills that students are about to learn. Slavin also points out that a grouping plan must allow students to be recategorized when errors in measurement or changes in student performance are detected. This important point is reinforced later in this section.

Slavin (1990) later extended his research to secondary schools. There he found no evidence in the research that indicates grouping benefits student achievement. Ability grouping appears equally ineffective in all subject areas. Assigning students to different levels of the same course had no effect on the achievement of low-, average-, or high-ability students. Slavin noted that the lack of affect due to grouping may be the result of *not* varying teaching methods. He states that "if teachers continue to use some form of lecture/discussion/seatwork/quiz, then it may matter very little in the aggregate which or how many students the teachers are facing" (p. 492). Slavin noted that, particularly at the high school level, placing students of higher versus lower ability on different tracks affected the nature and number of courses students took in a particular content area.

Lou and others (1996) focused on research that had been conducted when students were grouped *within* classes. This research is more common in elementary school settings, although their review of the research encompassed all grade levels. Their overall finding was that when grouping took place within classes, homogeneous ability groups achieved more than heterogeneous groups. However, this finding was not consistent across ability levels. Low-ability students learned significantly more in heterogeneous groups, whereas medium-ability students learned more in homogeneous ability groups. High-ability students learned equally well in homogeneous and heterogeneous groups. The size of the groups was important. The improved achievement took place when groups involved 3 or 4 members. Students in groups involving 6 to 10 members did not learn more than students from ungrouped classes. Their literature review showed that the use of within-class grouping was more beneficial in math and science than in reading, language arts, and other subjects. They found that the best results occurred when students worked within small groups *and* instruction methods and materials were adapted to small-group learning.

The widespread practice of placing students into comprehensive ability groups apparently does not improve student achievement. However, grouping students for instruction in selected content areas, often temporarily, along with making adjustments to how instruction is delivered, may result in significant achievement gains.

Using Aptitude Tests to Predict Achievement

Publishers of the more widely used achievement tests also produce aptitude tests. When a school district uses an aptitude test and achievement battery from the same publisher, the publisher often provides predictions from the aptitude test of each student's achievement on the achievement battery. That is, the publisher indicates the typical level of performance on the achievement battery for students obtaining a particular score on the aptitude test. This allows teachers and counselors to determine whether a student's *actual* performance on the achievement battery is above or below that of other students who obtained the same aptitude test score.

Although test publishers usually do not present these predictions in this manner, Figure 22.1 contains a scatterplot that shows what is happening in this prediction. Each point in this scatterplot represents one student's score on both the aptitude and achievement test. If you look closely, you will see a small arrow aimed at one of the points near the lower-left portion of the scatterplot. This point is above the score of 85 on the aptitude test scale and to the right of where the score of 36 would be on the achievement test scale. That is, this point represents a student who scored 85 on the aptitude test and then scored 36 on the achievement test. Of course, you can also see the elongated circle drawn around the 11 points representing the group of students who scored 85 on the aptitude test. Although these 11 students scored the same on the aptitude test, they obtained a range of scores on the achievement test, from 31 to 53.

A straight line, known as a *regression line,* is drawn diagonally through the scatterplot. This regression line provides the best fit to all the points within scatterplot and is the type of line test publishers use to predict scores on an achievement test based on students' scores on an aptitude test. With respect to the 11 students who scored 85 on the aptitude test, this regression line goes through their points near the level at which scores on the achievement test are 44 or 45. Therefore, the test publisher will estimate that students scoring 85 on the aptitude test will score 44 or 45 on the achievement test.

As is obvious in the scatterplot, any group of students who obtain the same score (such as 85) on the aptitude test do not obtain the same score on a corresponding achievement test. About the same number of students score above as below the achievement score predicted by the regression line. Underachievement is no more of a definitive explanation for a student scoring below predicted achievement than is overachievement the explanation why the same number of students score above predicted achievement. Various explanations, including measurement error on the aptitude and achievement tests, explain why students with the same aptitude test score

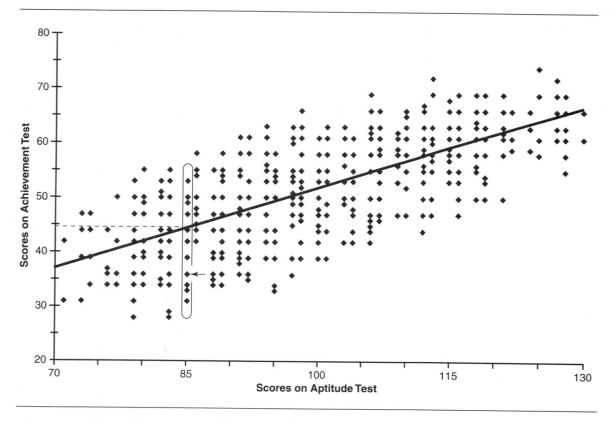

Figure 22.1
Scatter plot illustrating relation between aptitude and achievement scores

do not obtain the same achievement test score. Be careful to look for those explanations, and do not automatically conclude that a student who scores below "predicted" performance on an achievement battery is an underachieving student.

Implications of Statistical Regression

An important consideration when interpreting test scores is the expected change in student performance resulting from statistical regression:

> Whenever there is a less than perfect correlation between two sets of scores, a student's score on a subsequent performance is expected to be closer to the average score than that student's score on the initial test.

Students who score above average on a test tend to perform relatively lower on a subsequent measure. Likewise, students who score below average on a test tend to score relatively higher on a succeeding measure. This is true whenever correlations are involved such as the correlation between two forms of a test (alternate-form

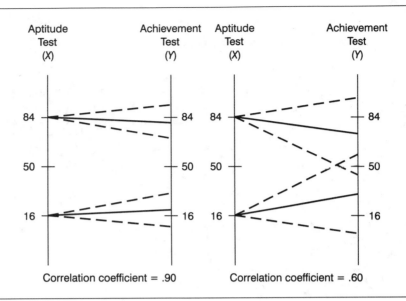

Figure 22.2
The effect of regression when scores on an aptitude test are used to predict later scores on an achievement test. Notice that the regression effect is more pronounced as the correlation decreases.

reliability) or the correlation between an aptitude test and later achievement (predictive validity).

The lower the correlation between two sets of scores, the more pronounced the regression effect. This is demonstrated in Figure 22.2 by using two different values of correlation. Within each example, percentile ranks are illustrated for an aptitude test (X) and a subsequent achievement test (Y).

In the left illustration, the correlation between the aptitude and achievement tests is 0.90. A student who scores 1 standard deviation above the mean (approximately the 84th percentile) on the aptitude test is expected to score 0.90 standard deviation above the mean on the achievement test (approximately the 82nd percentile). However, not all students starting at the 84th percentile will end at the 82nd percentile. It can be demonstrated that two thirds of students scoring at the 84th percentile on the aptitude test will be expected to score between approximately the 68th and 91st percentiles on the achievement test score. This is illustrated by the dotted lines within Figure 22.2.

The reverse effect occurs for students scoring below average on the initial test. When the correlation is 0.90, students scoring 1 standard deviation below the mean (approximately the 16th percentile) on the aptitude test are expected to score 0.90 standard deviation below the mean (approximately the 18th percentile) on the achievement test. As illustrated by the dotted lines, two thirds of these students will be expected to score between the 9th and 32nd percentiles on the achievement test.

This regression effect becomes more pronounced as the correlation decreases. Notice in Figure 22.2 that the expected change in scores (the solid line between each pair of dotted lines) angles closer to the average score on the achievement test as the correlation decreases from 0.90 to 0.60. For example, when the correlation is 0.60, a student scoring at the 16th percentile on the aptitude test is expected to score at the 27th percentile on the achievement test. The variability of scores on the achievement test for students with the same aptitude score also increases. For instance, when the correlation is 0.60, two thirds of students scoring at the 16th percentile on the aptitude test are expected to score approximately between the 8th and 58th percentiles on the achievement test.

The lesson here is that students tend to score closer to the average score on a subsequent measure than they do on an initial test. Differences observed between students on an initial test tend to wash out on the next measure. As the correlation decreases, differences observed on the initial test tend to disappear. For this reason, tests used to group students must have high predictive validity in order to minimize the regression effect. Similarly, tests with which multiple forms are used interchangeably must have high alternate-form reliability.

The regression effect becomes more pronounced for scores that begin further from the mean. For instance, if the correlation between an aptitude test and achievement test is 0.60, a student scoring 1 standard deviation below the mean on the aptitude test is expected to score 0.60 standard deviations below the mean on the achievement test, but if a student scores 2 standard deviations below the mean on the aptitude test, this student is expected to score 1.20 standard deviations below the mean on the achievement test. These expected changes amount to 0.4 standard deviation in the first instance but 0.8 standard deviation in the second.

Box 22.1 *Apply What You Are Learning*

Three students obtained deviation IQ scores of 115, 100, and 70 on an aptitude test (mean = 100; standard deviation = 15). The correlation of this test with a subsequent achievement test (predictive validity) is less than 1.00. Is it possible to estimate at what percentiles these three students will score on a subsequent achievement test?

Answers can be found at the end of the chapter.

Because the students who are placed in special education tend to obtain exceptional scores on tests, the regression effect is more significant with these students. Therefore, it is particularly important to use multiple high-quality tests when determining whether a student should be placed in special education.

It is important to recognize that the regression effect is not caused by a change in students' ability. Regression is simply a statistical phenomenon that is inherent in measurement error. Unless the correlation between a test and the criterion it is trying to predict is 1.00 (a highly unlikely event), the regression effect will be present. The regression effect becomes more pronounced as the correlation decreases.

For test–retest reliability, the regression effect means that one should expect any subset of students to score closer to the average score on the retest than on the initial test. For predictive validity, one should similarly expect any subset of students to score closer to the average score on whatever variable the test is intended to predict.

Whenever students are grouped on the basis of test scores or any other measure, changes in an individual student's performance should be expected over time. Teachers must expect and be alert to these changes. As a result of the regression effect, the most likely change in a given student's performance is toward the mean.

Box 22.2 *Apply What You Are Learning*

Classroom tests and other judgments by teachers of students' abilities usually have lower reliability than standardized aptitude tests. Will the regression effect be more significant with teachers' judgments or with standardized tests?

Answers can be found at the end of the chapter.

IDENTIFYING STUDENTS TO RECEIVE SPECIAL EDUCATION

When a student's abilities are sufficiently exceptional, using augmented or alternative instructional procedures is required. The classification of exceptionalities is complex and includes mental, physical, and emotional qualities. Mental exceptionalities are emphasized here because of the significant role of standardized aptitude and achievement tests in establishing students' needs in this area.

Salvia and Ysseldyke (1998) observed that different states assign different names to the same handicap, and different criteria are used to identify exceptional students. For instance, in Pennsylvania mentally handicapped students have a maximum IQ score of 80, whereas in Minnesota the maximum IQ score is 70. For purposes of this discussion, the following definitions of mental handicap and learning disability will be used:

- *Mentally retarded student:* A student whose general mental ability is sufficiently low for the student to experience serious difficulties with the normal curriculum. In terms of performance on a standardized aptitude test, a mentally handicapped student typically scores 2 or more standard deviations below the mean on an individually administered intelligence test.

- *Students with learning disabilities:* A student who obtains average or above-average scores on general aptitude measures but has significant difficulties with the normal curriculum. The student's difficulty with the curriculum might be specific to selected content areas or general to the total curriculum.

The action taken when a student is characterized as being mentally retarded or having a learning disability depends both on the severity of the student's condition and procedures followed by the state or school district. Actions vary from providing supplemental instruction to placing a student in special classrooms or schools.

A gifted student is often defined as one who scores more than 2 standard deviations above the mean on general aptitude measures; however, the corresponding achievement of gifted students is more vague. Although not discussed in this text, many of the measurement issues associated with identifying gifted students parallel those regarding the classification of other exceptional students.

The following discussion identifies the advantages and disadvantages of labeling students, bias in placement procedures, the technical adequacy of tests used to help place exceptional students, and the need to interpret test scores appropriately when placing students.

Advantages and Disadvantages of Labeling Students

The process of classifying students and the act of labeling students as a result of this classification are controversial. Ysseldyke and Algozzine (1982) stated that the major advantage of labeling students is their subsequent admission to a special service. Gallagher (1976) identified other advantages of labeling: (1) a means of initiating plans to counteract negative conditions, (2) a means of calling attention to a specific problem to obtain additional resources, and (3) a basis for conducting research into procedures that prevent or treat negative conditions.

Labeling students clearly has disadvantages. Algozzine and Mercer (1980) addressed two problems associated with labeling. First, labeling often does not result in differential treatment for individuals and therefore fails its most basic function. Second, when labels are perceived as negative, they affect the perceptions of the student and others in a way that may limit social, emotional, and academic growth. Certainly, not all labels are negative. For instance, the designation *gifted* is generally perceived as an asset. Certain labels for the same condition are often preferred over others. Salvia and Ysseldyke (1998) indicate for instance that parents may prefer *autistic* or *learning disabled* over *mentally retarded*.

Bias in Placement Procedures

Disproportionate numbers of minority students are in special education. On the one hand, this represents an advantage for minorities because of the increased expenditures per student in special education. Academic expectations, however, are often lower in special education curricula. This is a significant concern to affected minority groups because placement in special education may promote greater discrepancies in achievement rather than remediating present deficiencies.

Aptitude tests have become a logical target of this concern. In a legal case in California (*Larry P. v. Riles,* 1972), the court ruled that intelligence tests cannot serve as the basis for placing African-American students in classes for the mentally handicapped. In a contradictory case in Illinois (*Parents in Action on Special Education [PASE] v. Hannon,* 1980), after reviewing items on commonly used intelligence tests, the judge ruled that these tests could be used with African-Americans for placement

If two groups of individuals have overall equal ability, but scores on a test designed to measure that ability differ for these two groups, then the test is said to be *biased.* Typically, the two groups being contrasted differ with respect to their race, sex, native language, or physical handicap. Whichever groups might be contrasted, bias threatens the validity of a test in that the test is measuring something other than what it is supposed to measure. The potential for measurement bias must be treated as a serious concern.

For a variety of reasons, bias is difficult to detect. One reason is that usually other factors are present that could be causing differences in test scores. One should not automatically conclude that differences in scores between groups are due to bias within the test. Certainly, test bias should be evaluated. But if the test is detecting differences that have developed for other reasons, including biasing factors in instruction or background experiences, then taking steps to equate scores on the test would not be as productive as correcting or compensating for the factors actually causing the bias.

Several techniques have been developed to detect bias within tests. These techniques are usually classified as procedures for detecting either *item bias* or *test bias.* Item-bias procedures help evaluating individual items as opposed to the test as a whole. One common technique for detecting item bias in essence rank orders items on a given test according to their difficulty. This ranking is done separately for two groups such as Latino and non-Latino examinees. The items are assumed to be free of bias if this ranking orders items the same way for both groups. If these rankings for a particular item are discrepant, suspicion of bias is raised for that item.

All procedures for detecting item bias share some weaknesses. First, these procedures identify which items are behaving suspiciously but do not establish specific characteristics of the items that are probable cause for bias. A second weakness is that item-bias procedures assume the test as a whole is free of bias. This of course may not be true. A third problem is that there is usually only a moderate and sometimes low agreement among various item-bias procedures as to which test items are behaving suspiciously.

A second group of procedures is intended to detect *test* bias. Unlike item-bias techniques, these procedures do not assume that the test as a whole is free of bias. A disadvantage of test-bias procedures is that when they detect possible bias, they do not indicate which subset of items within the test is causing the bias.

Test-bias procedures are used exclusively with placement or selection tests. For example, they would help evaluate potential bias in college admissions tests. Test-bias procedures detect bias by contrasting groups with respect to performance on a criterion external to the test. For instance, test scores on a college admissions test might be contrasted for female and male students who succeeded in college to see if, based on the test, these two groups of students would have had an equal chance of being admitted to the college. Alternative procedures for detecting test bias give somewhat inconsistent results, much as do the item-bias procedures. Because test-bias procedures are used only with tests used to predict performance, they are more appropriate for aptitude than achievement tests.

Figure 22.3
Detection of item and test bias

purposes. He observed that the issue of bias cannot be analyzed without a detailed examination of items on the test and noted that the content of items with which African-Americans performed poorly did not contain material that favored other racial groups. In 1993, the *Larry P.* case was revisited. Parents of African-American students argued that not allowing school personnel to administer intelligence tests to African-American students had a discriminatory effect because students could not become eligible for services provided to students classified as learning disabled without

Of course, preventing bias from entering a test is preferred. Over the past two decades, considerable emphasis has been placed on evaluating items for potential bias as a part of the test development process. Items thought to contain bias are excluded or revised before the test is produced. Unlike the item- and test-bias procedures described earlier, evaluating items for bias before they are used depends on judgments of reviewers rather than statistical analyses. Typically, a review team is established to evaluate the items. The team consists of members who collectively are knowledgeable with characteristics of students from various backgrounds. In a book edited by Berk (1982), several authors provide detailed discussions of judgmental and other procedures for detecting item bias.

Recently, considerable attention has been generated by what has become known as the "Golden Rule" strategy for preventing test bias. The name does not come from the well-known biblical code but rather from an out-of-court settlement involving the Golden Rule Insurance Company, the Illinois Department of Insurance, and the Educational Testing Service (ETS). The insurance company claimed that an exam used by the State of Illinois and developed by ETS to license new insurance agents was discriminatory against African-Americans. That settlement has been used as a model for preventing bias in various educational and professional placement and certification exams; however, ETS and most measurement specialists now question its appropriateness.

The Golden Rule settlement stipulated that when new test items are field tested, they will be categorized into two groups. An item is placed in the first group if it meets two conditions: (1) at least 40% of each racial group correctly answers the item and (2) the difference in the rates that examinees from different racial groups correctly answer the item does not exceed 15%. All items not meeting these conditions are placed in the second group. When the actual exam is constructed, the number of items required to measure each content area is specified. Then, items that measure each content area are selected from the first group of test items. If insufficient items from the first group are available for a particular content area, only then are items in that content area selected from the second group. Values other than 40% and 15% might be used.

Measurement specialists who oppose using the Golden Rule strategy favor statistical procedures designed to more directly detect item bias (such as those alluded to earlier). They point out that differences in item difficulty do not necessarily imply item bias. Furthermore, they indicate that the subsets of test items this procedure places into the first group tend to measure a nonrepresentative set of skills within each broad content area that a test is designed to measure.

Advocates of the Golden Rule strategy observe that other procedures for preventing item bias are not fully adequate and that it is only reasonable to use the subset of content-valid items that are about equally difficult for minority and reference groups before selecting other items. A useful discussion of these issues is included in a series of six articles published in *Educational Measurement: Issues and Practice* (Haney & Reidy, 1987).

establishing a discrepancy between ability and achievement. Ability is established with an intelligence test. The judge ruled in favor of the parents, thus allowing again the administrations of intelligence tests to African-American students. (Figure 22.3 identifies some of the issues involved in detecting bias in tests.)

Even with the significant attention being given to the disproportionate placement of minorities in special education, their representation increased. For example, a study by Tucker (1980) indicated that during the previous eight years, the proportion of minority students in the Southwest United States had increased even though considerable effort had been given to reversing this trend. This was coupled with a 10% increase in the total number of students placed in special education. This disproportionate number of minorities placed in special education and the role of intelligence testing rightfully remains an important topic (see for example, de la Cruz 1996).

Concerns about placement of minorities in special education and potential bias in aptitude tests were instrumental in passing Public Law 94-142. Basically, this law stipulates the following:

1. All handicapped students are entitled to a publicly funded education.

2. Services to be provided and goals to be obtained must be established for each student.

3. Tests and other diagnostic procedures used to evaluate students must be free of cultural bias.

4. Each student must be regularly reevaluated.

5. Handicapped students must be taught in regular classes, or "mainstreamed," whenever possible.

It must be understood that tests are not the only potential source of bias when placing students. For example, Ross and Salvia (1975) provided teachers with reports describing the aptitude and achievement of anonymous third-grade children. Although the test data indicated each child was borderline mentally handicapped, simply attaching a photograph of a physically more or less attractive child to the report significantly affected the teachers' diagnosis of each child's mental capability.

Ysseldyke and Algozzine (1982) describe a study of 159 school psychologists and other educators who participated in meetings to determine the placement of students. Every participant read a case folder description of each child and was allowed to access other information such as aptitude and achievement scores, performance scores on adaptive behavior scales, and the results of behavioral observations and checklists. Although all data indicated each child was performing in a normal range, the study indicates that the *reasons for referral* significantly affected the participants' placement decisions. Children referred for behavior problems were more often diagnosed as emotionally disturbed than students referred for academic problems. In essence, the reason for referral was biasing decisions concerning the placement of the child.

Ysseldyke and Algozzine (1982) state, "No child can benefit from the intended advantages of special and remedial education without being identified as eligible. The negative effects, as well, will not accrue without identification" (pp. 121–122). Minimizing the role of tests in placing students is not likely to reduce errors in classifying students. For instance, Mehrens and Lehmann (1987), in their discussion of administrative uses of aptitude tests, refer to studies that indicate eliminating aptitude testing may actually increase bias in placement. Also, the earlier discussion in this chapter indicates that the regression phenomenon becomes a greater concern if scores from appropriate standardized tests are excluded from placement decisions.

Using Technically Adequate Tests When Placing Students

The *Standards for Educational and Psychological Testing* (1999) specify technical standards to be used in the construction and evaluation of tests. Salvia and Ysseldyke (1981) used a then-current edition of the *Standards* to evaluate the validity, reliability, and norms of approximately 100 standardized tests widely used for placing students in special education. They found that 27 of these tests use inadequately described norms, 11 had inadequate reliability or incomplete reliability data, and 16 had questionable validity. Tests found to be deficient included some of the instruments most widely used for evaluating and placing students in special education.

Thurlow and Ysseldyke (1979) evaluated the technical adequacy of tests used in 44 model programs for learning disabled children. Of the 30 tests that were used by 3 or more of these centers, only 5 of the tests were found to have adequate norms, 10 had adequate reliabilities, and 9 demonstrated appropriate validity. Given that this review was limited to model programs, one might be pessimistic about the adequacy of tests being used elsewhere.

Shepard (1983) states that inadequate tests are used when more appropriate instruments are available. This appears to be the result of specialists continuing to use tests they have traditionally used rather than evaluating the adequacy of alternative instruments. Shepard also observes that when a diagnosis is inconclusive, specialists tend to administer additional tests. Because of the limited number of quality instruments, the technical adequacy of the subsequently administered tests tends to be less than that of the initial test.

Using technically inadequate tests for placing students in special education is unjustifiable. Individuals who select and administer tests should be familiar with the current *Standards for Educational and Psychological Testing*. They should limit their selection of standardized tests to those instruments whose manuals establish the adequacy of the test with respect to these standards. Each test should be evaluated within the specific context in which is to be used.

Appropriately Interpreting Test Scores When Placing Students

Preceding chapters describe characteristics of percentiles, standard scores, and grade-equivalent scores. For instance, Chapter 22 describes how percentiles represent unequal units, with the 16th percentile presenting a point approximately 1 standard deviation below the mean. Chapter 22 also describes how procedures used for determining grade-equivalent scores result in half the students within a typical school falling below grade level. Because students' abilities become more heterogeneous as they progress through school, the normal range of grade-equivalent scores also increases in later grades.

Shepard (1983) referenced a survey of 2000 psychologists and learning disability teachers and found many of them unaware of these characteristics of percentile and grade-equivalent scores. For instance, half of these specialists did not expect an IQ of 90 (judged to be in the normal range) to be at the 25th percentile (thought to be a fairly low score). Both these scores are about two thirds of a standard deviation below the mean. They also did not expect half the students to obtain grade-equivalent scores below grade level. Because an IQ of 90 is judged as normal, comparable performance on an achievement test is expected to be near the 50th percentile or at grade level. Consequently, a student with an IQ of 90 who scores below grade level might be diagnosed with a learning disability because of the apparent discrepancy between aptitude and achievement.

The same would happen with grade-equivalent scores. Many educators who interpret tests are unaware that, because of how grade-equivalents are determined, half the students in a typical school will score below grade level. If a middle or high school student obtained a deviation IQ score of 90 (two thirds of one standard deviation below the mean), a *comparable* grade equivalent on a standardized achievement test would be 1.5 to 2.5 grade levels below the grade in which the student was presently enrolled. Taking into account measurement error present in both the aptitude and achievement tests would increase that apparent discrepancy some more. The inclination of educators unfamiliar with characteristics of grade-equivalent scores would be to judge these students as having a learning disability because the achievement (reported as grade equivalents) appears lower than their aptitude, when in fact that interpretation is wrong.

When grouping students, all educators should be familiar with characteristics of scores used with standardized tests. Information presented in Chapters 20 and 21 is a valuable foundation for interpreting standardized test scores. One should be able to identify equivalent scores across the various scales and to recognize the advantages and limitations of these scales.

EVALUATING SCHOOLS AND TEACHERS

Because student achievement is the single most important outcome of formal education, in one sense it is logical that achievement tests be used in the evaluation of schools and teachers. Standardized achievement tests in particular might be appropriate because they provide a common measure across school districts, schools, and classrooms. However, issues pertaining to the selection, administration, and interpretation of tests are critical to their usefulness in this role. Teacher and school evaluations are addressed separately here, although several significant issues related to standardized tests are common to both.

Evaluating Schools

Standardized achievement tests are often used to compare the performance of students within one school district to national or regional norms. Similarly, the relative achievement of schools within a district is often compared. For a standardized achievement test to assume this role, the test must measure content appropriate for the schools being evaluated, and the publisher must provide normative data based on a relevant sample of students.

Publishers are interested in widespread use of their tests. Therefore, achievement tests developed by each publisher tend to measure the subset of content common to the curriculums of a majority of schools. This contributes to the similarity in content across various achievement batteries. It also means that instructional goals that are unique to a particular school district are not likely to be reflected in a standardized test. Therefore, standardized tests are most useful in evaluating the subset of a district's curriculum that is common to schools throughout the country.

Various achievement tests, however, do not measure precisely the same skills. In part, this is because different publishers working independently are likely to include different samples of skills, even when they sample from the same general domain. Also, various tests are developed at different times by different persons and reflect variations in emphasis that occur over time and between individuals.

It is appropriate for a school district to use standardized achievement tests that most clearly reflect local values. School districts that are willing to participate in the establishment of norms will also tend to be districts that believe the particular test best reflects their values. Consequently, norms reflect this bias. The degree to which scores for a particular district would change if an alternative test were used is unknown, although the correlation of scores across tests would likely be fairly high because each test samples content common across a majority of schools.

School districts typically use alternative levels of one publisher's tests across several or all grades being evaluated. This is a good practice because the content measured at each level is coordinated and norms across levels of the test are generally based on the same school districts. Even though this facilitates a district using the test to compare the performance of students at different grade levels, the relative achievement of students at different grades may vary simply because of the time when instruction for various topics is introduced. Consequently, the relative performance of a given school district may appear to improve or worsen at a particular grade level simply as a function of when specific content is taught locally versus in the norm group.

When used to evaluate instructional programs at a district level, scores are generally interpreted within a norm-referenced context. Therefore, selection of a test that provides norms based on a well-defined and appropriate sample of students is important. Typically, publishers of major tests provide norms for various subgroups such as regions of the country and urban versus nonurban school districts. Alternative norms facilitate the interpretation of scores. They have also led to confusion. For example, if districts choose to use standardized test scores to "prove" that local students are being provided high-quality instruction, a district within a region of the country that scores high on standardized tests will compare students' performance to national norms, whereas a district within a lower scoring region will compare student performance to regional norms. Disseminating scores in terms of both the total and relevant subcategories of the norm group is generally more appropriate.

When interpreting tests, one must also know how recently the norms were established. Because of the expense of developing national norms, they are revised infrequently and therefore cannot reflect national or local changes in the content emphasized in instruction. The relevancy of norms is also reduced when teachers inadvertently or deliberately emphasize the specific sample of skills measured by a test. Student performance commonly will "improve" relative to the norms after a particular test has been used for several years and then drop when an alternative test is introduced. When a standardized achievement battery is used to evaluate instructional programs of districts rather than measure the achievement of individual students, an alternative is to administer the test to a sample of classrooms or schools rather than every student. This is practical within larger school districts, where using a sample of students still results in a substantial number of students being tested. Administering achievement batteries to only a sample of classrooms reduces the tendency to teach the specific content of these tests and also reduces costs and increases time available for instruction. Also, because student performance will not shift dramatically from year to year, it is appropriate to administer such tests less frequently than once per year if the purpose of testing is to evaluate programs.

Although standardized tests are often used to evaluate individual schools, the school building generally does *not* represent a meaningful unit of analysis when the achievement of students is being evaluated over time. Year-to-year variation in the characteristics of students and teachers can change significantly at a given school. For example, shifting school boundaries to adjust for uneven growth within a community can significantly change the characteristics of students attending a particular school.

Recall from Chapter 5 that Messick (1989b) described validity as not only an issue of test interpretation, but also as being concerned with how the test is used and the consequences of various interpretations and uses. Haladyna, Nolen, and Haas (1991) have pointed out serious concerns regarding the use of standardized tests and, in turn, illustrate the relevance of this broader view of test validity where consequences of testing are taken into account. They list a number of uses of test results that include not only the evaluation of instructional programs and personnel, but also the use by newspapers to rank schools and school districts and even by real estate agents to rate the quality of neighborhood schools. This places considerable pressure on teachers and administrators to do whatever is necessary to improve test scores, even if it does not benefit student achievement.

Haladyna, Nolen, and Haas (1991) describe techniques used to improve scores and categorize the techniques as ethical, unethical, and highly unethical. Within the ethical category, they included activities such as encouraging students to do well, checking answer sheets for bad erasures, and training students in test-wiseness skills. Within the unethical category, they include actions such as changing the curriculum to match the content of the standardized tests, teaching students how to answer items similar to those included in the test, and using commercially available materials that prepare students for content included in specific tests. These techniques will improve test performance and probably improve student achievement within the narrowly focused subset of skills sampled by the test; they also distort and possibly lower the overall achievement of students. Activities that they classify as highly unethical include teaching verbatim items that will be included in the test and dismissing low-achieving students on test days.

The term *test score pollution* has been coined to describe this condition. In essence, the validity of legitimate interpretations of test scores is contaminated by uses made of the scores and, more important, by the resulting consequences of these uses.

The contamination of test scores will continue as long as standardized tests are used as a sole dominant indicator of school quality. Standardized testing should be continued because it can provide indications of student achievement that are unavailable through other means. Procedures that will help reduce test score pollution include the significant use of other indicators of quality such as the adequacy with which proven instructional practices are applied, and by testing samples of schools and classrooms so that classroom and school-level comparisons are de-emphasized along with the motivation to boost performance artificially on standardized tests.

Evaluating Teachers

The use of standardized achievement tests to evaluate teachers is controversial. On the one hand, student achievement is an important outcome of effective instruction. However, student achievement is significantly affected by factors over which the teacher has little or no control, such as student characteristics. Furthermore, scores on a test can be affected by teaching directly to its content.

Millman (1981) identifies five conditions that should be met when student achievement data are used to evaluate the performance of teachers:

- The tests should be sensitive to classroom instruction. This means aptitude tests or tests that measure skills taught through a series of courses should not be used.

- The test should measure the skills taught by the teacher.

- The measures of student achievement should be reliable. As discussed earlier, reliability is improved by increasing the number of test items used to measure student achievement. This can be accomplished both by using longer tests and by combining scores from several tests.

- The testing procedure must be equitable in that all teachers must know specifically the skills to be tested.

- Scores must be comparable. This means that one must be able to compare legitimately the achievement of students taught by different teachers either by assigning equivalent students to each teacher or by statistically adjusting for differences among students.

Travers (1981) points out that the use of student achievement as a measure of effective teaching is a relatively recent phenomenon even though teacher effectiveness has been evaluated for some time. Until the twentieth century, the teacher was perceived as a manager. Travers indicates that the teacher was expected to provide students the opportunity to learn by giving assignments and listening to student recitations. Within the twentieth century, the responsibility for student achievement shifted to the teacher, with the teacher becoming responsible for producing an environment that resulted in learning. Consequently, the criterion of an effective teacher changed from being a capable manager to being accountable for students' achievement. Travers questions the appropriateness of these present criteria and points to the failure of the *board schools* in late-nineteenth-century England, where teachers were paid in proportion to the number of students whose achievement exceeded the national average; teachers overemphasized the subset of content sampled by the tests.

An alternative to the use of achievement tests to evaluate teachers is to evaluate teachers by establishing whether they use instructional methods that research unequivocally establishes as beneficial to learning (including the use of test results rather than the performance of students on standardized achievement tests). This approach holds teachers responsible for effectively managing instructional activities as opposed to increasing test scores. In that context, it would be in a teacher's best interest to obtain accurate achievement measures for students.

The controversy of how to evaluate instructional personnel will probably remain unresolved, and the perceived role for achievement testing will vary. If scores on achievement tests are the dominant component in evaluating teachers, then conditions such as those suggested by Millman (1981) should be met. Regardless, the significant consequences that evaluation procedures have on teaching strategies and outcomes must be considered when judging the validity of standardized achievement tests.

ADDRESSING THE NEEDS OF INDIVIDUAL STUDENTS

The major role of testing within schools should be to facilitate the instruction of students. Each application of standardized tests discussed in this chapter, such as grouping students and evaluating schools or teachers, is intended to facilitate instruction, albeit not always successfully. With the availability of computer-generated reports, teachers commonly receive detailed prescriptions for individual students based on student performance on a standardized achievement battery. Sometimes, the reports identify which skills each student has and has not mastered.

Cautions given previously regarding criterion-referenced interpretations are relevant here. For example, mastery of specific skills is often based on only one to four test items. This results in a large number of students being misclassified with respect to mastery status. Justification for the performance level associated with mastery is usually not clear. Also, skills measured by a standardized achievement test represent a subset of what is taught in school.

LeMahieu and Wallace (1986) contrasted the evaluative and diagnostic roles of testing to illustrate characteristics a standardized testing program must have in order to facilitate instruction of individual students. The role of *evaluative testing* is to provide information regarding the overall status of students such as those enrolled in a school district. This type of monitoring can occur infrequently and be based on a sample of students. The purpose of *diagnostic testing* is to determine the strengths and weaknesses of individual students.

LeMahieu and Wallace point out that the conditions prerequisite to diagnostic testing are unique. First, assessments must measure carefully articulated learning outcomes. This requires a more detailed coverage of content than is usually provided by test publishers. Second, test results must be provided to teachers within days following the test administration rather than the several weeks normally required to process standardized tests. Third, tests designed for diagnostic purposes should be administered at several points during the school year to monitor growth and identify students whose achievement patterns are changing. Standardized achievement tests tend to be ineffective in a diagnostic role. That is, their characteristics are not consistent with those essential to establishing the instructional needs of individual students.

USING PERFORMANCE ASSESSMENTS IN STANDARDIZED TESTS

Considerable attention is now being given to using performance assessments in standardized achievement tests. As is well known, until recently, most large-scale testing programs used the multiple-choice format exclusively, often giving the misimpression that "standardized test" refers to a multiple-choice test.

Including the performance assessment format in standardized achievement tests provides a major benefit. As we have noted throughout this book, although traditional formats such as multiple-choice can measure important knowledge involving *information, concepts,* and *rules,* they cannot measure the category of knowledge we call *complex skills.* Performance assessments, however, can measure this type of knowledge. Not all essential knowledge involves complex skills, but much of it does. Unless performance assessments are included in standardized achievement batteries, these skills go unevaluated, at least within the highly influential venue of standardized testing.

Not all changes in item format involve performance assessments. Many recent standardized achievement tests have included constructed-response items, for instance in math, where the student writes out the final answer rather than selecting the answer among multiple-choice options. In contrast, examples of performance assessments include providing a sample of writing in response to a prompt or combining prior knowledge with hands-on science observations to interpret results from the observations. These assessments require a student to bring together knowledge of information, concepts, and rules to solve a problem. An important characteristic of these performance assessments is that different students can solve the problem by using different sets of prior knowledge, and likewise can exhibit different behaviors in the process of solving the problem.

The content of standardized tests influences what is and is not learned within classrooms, particularly when test results are used to evaluate schools and teachers. Testing programs are often established with the primary intent of influencing instruction (Linn, 1993; Resnick & Resnick, 1992). When standardized tests are used in this role, including performance assessments within tests can be expected to increase emphasis on teaching complex skills.

As we have learned, performance assessments have a particular problem with generalizability. Through careful preparation of a scoring plan, even complicated performance assessments can be scored reliably. However, virtually every study of performance assessments indicates that performance observed when students complete one task does not generalize well to what is observed when they complete another task.

Um (1995), for example, when investigating a statewide writing assessment being piloted in Florida, found that the generalizability was too low for assessing the proficiency of individual students. To increase generalizability to acceptable levels, the assessment would have to involve more writing samples than would be practical. Shavelson with others (1998) found the same results. One set of performance assessments in science that they developed required students to solve a series of six problems involving shadows cast by towers of equal height located at different points on Earth. Each of the problems required students to use prior knowledge to draw conclusions from what they observed in experiments. Although scoring was found to be reliable, the students who performed well with one problem were different from the students who performed well on each of the other problems. A student's success depended on which problem was involved.

Generalizability can be improved to acceptable levels by increasing the number of observations. With respect to establishing the proficiency of individual students, teachers have this option but standardized tests do not. A teacher can over time administer many more performance assessments to each student than can a standardized test. Furthermore, a teacher can also use other classroom observations to substantiate evaluations obtained through these performance assessments. Standardized testing programs do not have this privilege.

The number of observations can also be increased by assessing *groups* of students rather than individual students. That is, the generalizability of performance assessments within standardized tests can become adequate by changing the purpose of an assessment to that of evaluating achievement at the school or district level. Sampling would be required. Different students would complete different tasks. This would *not* allow using the test to certify the knowledge of each student. That would remain the responsibility of teachers. In the foreseeable future, this is the only realistic option. In the context of standardized tests, performance assessments cannot obtain an acceptable level of generalizability for assessing the knowledge of individual students.

ESTABLISHING PERFORMANCE STANDARDS

State testing programs, whether or not performance assessments are involved, invariably end up having to set performance standards students must achieve to pass the test. A variety of procedures for setting a passing score have been proposed, although these approaches can be categorized into two groups. The more commonly used approach is to have raters review the content to be assessed. For example, Angoff (1971) asks raters to estimate the probability of minimally competent students correctly answering each item. Ebel (1972) requires raters to categorize items by difficulty and relevance, and then to estimate the probability of minimally competent students correctly answering items within each category. Nedelsky (1954) proposes that when multiple-choice items are involved, reviewers evaluate the options to each item and identify the options a minimally competent student would be expected to eliminate. From this information, a passing score is established for the test as a whole. An extension of these procedures is to administer the test to a sample of students, look at the resulting distribution of test scores, and evaluate the previously determined standards.

The second and less frequently used approach to setting passing scores consists of making judgments about student achievement. Zicky and Livingston (1977) propose that teachers or other judges categorize each student in a group as competent or not competent with the content to be assessed. The passing score on the test then becomes the point that best discriminates between these two categories.

A variety of studies have looked at the implications of using alternative procedures for setting passing scores. Poggio, Glasnapp, and Eros (1981), for example, contrasted standards obtained from the four methods referred to previously (Angoff, 1971; Ebel, 1972; Nedelsky, 1954; Zicky & Livingston, 1977) by using approximately 900 teachers from five elementary through secondary grades as judges. The Ebel approach consistently resulted in the highest passing score and the Nedelsky approach in the lowest. The passing scores derived through the four approaches were quite divergent. For example, on one 60-item test, passing scores of 28, 39, 43, and 48 were derived.

Alternative approaches to setting passing scores are equally defensible. Consequently, establishment of a passing score represents an arbitrary action. However, to make decisions concerning placement in remedial groups or awarding of a diploma, a passing score must be established. As with many decisions in measurement and education in general, the setting of passing scores depends on and is limited to an informed judgment. If a passing score is perceived as too stringent, society will find the cost of responding to the consequences to be unacceptable. Society will also judge the passing score to be unacceptable if it is perceived to be too low.

CERTIFYING POTENTIAL AND PRACTICING TEACHERS

Interest in the use of examinations to certify teachers increased substantially during the 1980s; however, this practice is not new. Kinney (1964) traced the practice in the United States back to colonial Virginia, where each county was expected to appoint an individual to examine and license schoolmasters. The practice of certifying new teachers was both widespread and disparate during the nineteenth century. Prospective teachers might simply be asked to read aloud a short passage, demonstrate handwriting, and complete a few easy arithmetic problems. On the other hand, Kinney described a rather classic 1860 case in San Francisco where *one portion* of the exam asked candidates to name all the rivers, bodies of water, cities, and countries in the world, as well as the boundaries to each state within the United States—all within 1 hour.

Near the beginning of the twentieth century, education reform resulted in the elimination of teacher certification tests. Instead, aspiring teachers were given formal training in pedagogy through the then newly formed colleges for teachers. The lack of uniform quality among graduates, however, resulted in renewed interest in examining prospective teachers. In 1940, the American Council on Education established the *National Teacher Examination* (NTE).

Many states now require prospective teachers to take the NTE or another certification exam. Some states also require practicing teachers to be tested if they wish to be promoted to a higher status such as "master teacher." Other states have required the passing of recertification exams as a condition of continued employment. Collectively, as in the nineteenth century, these exams are extremely diverse in their content, difficulty, and role.

Shepard and Kreitzer (1987) describe the impact of the *Texas Examination of Current Administrators and Teachers* (TECAT), an exam that represents one extreme with respect to these referenced qualities. The TECAT measured limited content (basic reading and writing skills), and was fairly easy (97% passed the exam on their first try); failing to eventually pass the exam had a profound consequence (termination of employment). The TECAT was administered in 1986 as a precondition to the state legislature's passing of a tax increase and pay raise for teachers. Legislators were unwilling to support the tax bill unless "illiterate" teachers were removed from the schools. Because of the consequences to individuals failing this exam, an immense effort ensued to help teachers prepare for the test. For example, the University of Texas at Austin and the Texas Classroom Teachers Association developed a review course and 300-page study book. They trained 130 presenters, who conducted workshops for 90,000 teachers. Along with the Austin Independent School District, the University of Texas developed and distributed 12 videotapes covering TECAT skills. The major teachers' organizations also developed materials or conducted workshops for members.

Shepard and Kreitzer (1987) point out that the consequences of failing the test (termination of employment) coupled with the easiness of the test negatively affected teacher morale and the public's perception of teachers. For example, they found teachers were humiliated by news reports in which stories of teachers and their organizations protesting the test were presented adjacent to examples of absurdly easy skills that the exam measured. In their subsequent interviews, Shepard and Kreitzer found that the vast majority of teachers felt that publicity surrounding the test damaged rather than improved public confidence in education.

Shanker (1985) proposes use of a distinct teacher exam to enhance the quality of education. He proposes that an exam should parallel professional exams such as the bar and medical boards by being comprehensive in content, difficult, and prerequisite to becoming certified to teach. Shanker proposed this test while serving as president of the American Federation of Teachers. He stipulated that this exam should be established from within the profession rather than through a governmental agency and argued that there is "no other way to make teaching a genuine profession, to convince the public to pay teachers what they're worth, to empower teachers to make the educational decisions, to attract the best and the brightest to our ranks, or to ensure high-quality education for the country's children" (p. 29).

History suggests that examinations will continually be used to certify teachers. Teaching is too highly visible in our society in terms of impact on the future of children, taxation, social values, and politics to expect otherwise. The impetus for certification exams will likely come from governments unless the teaching profession institutes tests representing higher standards.

Certification exams represent achievement as opposed to aptitude measures. They should not be expected to predict how successful a teacher will be. Instead, they should indicate whether prospective teachers have achieved knowledge understood to be prerequisite to effective teaching. Shanker (1985) argues for including an internship program as part of a certification exam. He notes that teaching is "the only profession in which a person begins the first day with the same responsibilities he or she will have on the last day" (p. 30).

As with other achievement tests, content-related evidence of validity is of prime importance to teacher certification tests, but this assumes that relevant content is obvious. Content validity of the NTE was established by reviewing the curriculum of teacher preparation programs. If curricula in general were deficient—for instance, with training in diagnosing learning disabilities or developing classroom tests—the test would not measure these important skills. Validation of certification exams needs also to address how results from the exams are to be used, as well as the consequences of their interpretation and use.

SUMMARY

This chapter has addressed seven issues related to standardized testing. The first of these was the use of standardized tests to place students in ability groups. Several advantages and disadvantages have been associated with this practice; however, in most circumstances the grouping of students has failed to improve student achievement. Ability grouping has improved achievement at the elementary level when students are grouped for instruction in selected topics but retained in heterogeneous groups for the remainder of instruction. Because of changes in students and inaccuracies in tests, one should expect to reclassify many students after establishing the initial grouping. Because of statistical regression, one should also expect students who scored above or below the mean on an initial test to, as a group, score closer to the mean on a subsequent test.

Standardized aptitude and achievement tests also help identify students with exceptionalities who will be provided special education. Exceptionalities include the mentally handicapped, those with learning disabilities, and the gifted. Advantages and disadvantages are associated with classifying or labeling students as exceptional. Concern exists regarding the disproportionate number of minorities identified as mentally handicapped. Legal cases that have addressed the potential bias in tests used to identify exceptional students have resulted in mixed conclusions. Sources of bias other than tests have been found to affect student placement. Many of the tests commonly used to identify exceptional students have been found to lack validity, reliability, and appropriate normative information even when more appropriate tests are available. In addition to evaluating the technical adequacy of tests, it is important that individuals who identify exceptional students be aware of the characteristics of percentile, standard, and grade-equivalent scores.

Scores on standardized achievement tests tend to be factors when evaluating teachers and particularly schools. These tests focus on common skills as opposed to skills unique to a district or region. Even though comparisons are made to appropriate norm groups, there is a tendency for the performance of students in a school district to "improve" after a particular achievement battery is used over a period of time.

Using standardized tests to evaluate teachers is controversial. When achievement tests are used for this purpose, a series of conditions must be maintained if the achievement scores are to be meaningful. Variables other than student achievement can also be used to evaluate teachers, including teachers' ability to apply sound instructional procedures.

Performance assessments are becoming more prominent in standardized tests. Without performance assessments, *complex skills* cannot be assessed. Performance on these assessments, however, does not generalize well. Particularly with performance assessments, standardized tests are more able to facilitate evaluation of groups of students rather than individual students. A variety of techniques are available for setting performance standards, all of which rely heavily on human judgment.

Exams have been used for some time to certify potential and practicing teachers. The nature and specific role of teacher certification tests varies considerably. Case studies suggest that their use can actually decrease public confidence in education. More demanding exams are generally expected to result in higher professional prestige. Certification exams actually are specialized achievement tests; they should not be expected to have predictive validity. Establishing the content validity of such exams is difficult in that the specific knowledge desired of teachers is not clearly established.

ANSWERS: APPLY WHAT YOU ARE LEARNING

22.1 It is not possible to determine precisely how these students will score on a subsequent achievement test. Here is what we can say: On the aptitude test, the three students scored 1 standard deviation above the mean, at the mean, and 2 standard deviations below the mean, respectively. These correspond approximately to the 84th, 50th, and 2nd percentiles. Although regression occurs over all scores, every student's score does not regress toward the mean. Therefore, we would expect, but do not know for sure, that each of these students will score closer to the mean on the subsequent achievement test than they did on the aptitude test. We would expect the student scoring 115 on the aptitude test to score lower than the 84th percentile on the achievement test. We would expect the student scoring 70 on the aptitude test to score higher than the 2nd percentile on the achievement test. Because the student who scored 100 on the aptitude test scored at the mean, regression toward the mean cannot occur. This student would be expected to score at the mean (generally the 50th percentile) on the achievement test.

22.2 The regression will be more pronounced with teachers' judgments. As reliability decreases, the regression toward the mean is greater. Consequently, the regression effect will be more pronounced if students are grouped solely on the basis of the judgment of teachers as opposed to also using scores on standardized tests.

SOMETHING TO TRY

■ One explanation as to why grouping students into ability groups does not improve achievement is that the same teaching techniques are used whether or not students are grouped. Is this true? Based on training you have received and your experience, how would you vary your teaching techniques for groups of different ability levels?

■ In Chapter 1, a distinction is drawn between *measurement* and *evaluation*. Standardized achievement tests are often used to *evaluate* school districts, schools, and individual teachers. Identify information that should be added to test scores in order to *evaluate* schools and teachers. Identify ways that this additional information can be disseminated when test scores are distributed to the media.

ADDITIONAL READING

Haney, W. (1981). Validity, vaudeville, and values: A short history of social concerns over standardized testing. *American Psychologist, 36,* 1021–1033. This article uses recent controversies in education to illustrate the impact of social issues on the use of tests.

APPENDIX A

Illustration of Selected Statistical Procedures

Computation of the Mean and Standard Deviation

The arithmetic mean and standard deviation are often used to provide an overall description of numeric scores. Their computation is illustrated using the scores from a reading readiness test for the following five students:

	Reading Readiness Scores (X)	Reading Achievement Scores (Y)
Vicki	8	21
Todd	14	27
Donna	17	25
Stuart	20	33
Joyce	26	29

As illustrated here, the mean (M) is an average calculated by first adding up the scores and then dividing this sum by the number of scores.

$$M = \frac{\Sigma X}{n} \qquad (A.1)$$

where M = mean score
ΣX = sum of the scores
n = the number of scores

$$M = \frac{8 + 14 + 17 + 20 + 26}{5} = \frac{85}{5} = 17.0$$

The standard deviation (SD) indicates how far scores deviate from the mean. The formula for standard deviation is

$$SD = \sqrt{\frac{\Sigma(X - M)^2}{n - 1}} \qquad (A.2)$$

where Σ = sum of
$(X - M)$ = difference between a student's score and the mean of the scores
n = the number of scores

Note from Formula A.2 that the value of the standard deviation will become larger if the difference between scores and the mean increases. In other words, the standard deviation increases as scores increasingly diverge from the mean (and from each other). On the other hand, if all scores were equal, they in turn would each equal the mean. Then the numerator of the formula would equal zero, making the value of standard deviation equal to zero.

The computation of standard deviation can be broken into five steps. These steps follow using the previous five students' scores on the reading readiness test.

Step 1. Find the difference between each student's score and the mean of the scores:

$$8 - 17.0 = -9$$
$$14 - 17.0 = -3$$
$$17 - 17.0 = 0$$
$$20 - 17.0 = 3$$
$$26 - 17.0 = 9$$

Step 2. Square each of these differences:

$$-9^2 = 81$$
$$-3^2 = 9$$
$$0^2 = 0$$
$$3^2 = 9$$
$$9^2 = 81$$

Step 3. Sum the squared differences:

$$81 + 9 + 0 + 9 + 81 = 180$$

Step 4. Divide this sum by $n - 1$ (the number of students less one):

$$\frac{180}{(5-1)} = \frac{180}{4} = 45.0$$

Step 5. Obtain the square root of this quotient.

$$\sqrt{45.0} = 6.71$$

Completing these five steps by hand is time-consuming, particularly when working with a large number of scores. Some inexpensive calculators have a built-in standard deviation function. With such a calculator, one simply enters the scores and then presses one button to calculate standard deviation. Also, many computer programs that are available for analyzing scores on classroom tests also compute standard deviations.

If you compute the mean and standard deviation for scores on the reading achievement test, you will find the mean equals 27.0 and the standard deviation equals approximately 4.47.

Computation of the Correlation Coefficient

A correlation coefficient indicates the degree of relationship between two or more variables. The correlation coefficient has a numerical range of 0 to 1 and can be positive or negative in value. The coefficient illustrated here is based on the Pearson product-moment correlation. The Pearson correlation coefficient is computed from pairs of scores for each of a number of individuals. We illustrate this computation using the previous five students' reading readiness and reading achievement scores.

The formula for the Pearson product-moment coefficient is

$$r_{XY} = \frac{n\Sigma XY - (\Sigma X)(\Sigma Y)}{\sqrt{[n\Sigma X^2 - (\Sigma X)^2][n\Sigma Y^2 - (\Sigma Y)^2]}} \quad (A.3)$$

where r_{XY} = the correlation coefficient
ΣX = the sum of all scores on the first variable
ΣX^2 = the sum of all the first variable scores after they are squared
ΣY = the sum of all scores on the second variable
ΣY^2 = the sum of all scores on the second variable after they are squared
ΣXY = the sum of the products of all pairs of scores
n = the number of pairs of scores

To compute the correlation coefficient, one first calculates the values for each of the components within Formula A.3:

$$\Sigma X = 8 + 14 + 17 + 20 + 26 = 85$$
$$\Sigma X^2 = 8^2 + 14^2 + 17^2 + 20^2 + 26^2$$
$$= 64 + 196 + 289 + 400 + 676 = 1625$$
$$\Sigma Y = 21 + 27 + 25 + 33 + 29 = 135$$
$$\Sigma Y^2 = 21^2 + 27^2 + 25^2 + 33^2 + 29^2$$
$$= 441 + 729 + 625 + 1089 + 841$$
$$= 3725$$
$$\Sigma XY = (8)(21) + (14)(27) + (17)(25)$$
$$+ (20)(33) + (26)(29)$$
$$= 168 + 378 + 425 + 660 + 754$$
$$= 2385$$
$$n = 5$$

Then these values are inserted in the formula:

$$r_{XY} = \frac{(5)(2385) - (85)(135)}{\sqrt{[(5)(1625) - (85)^2][(5)(3725) - (135)^2]}}$$

$$= \frac{11,925 - 11,475}{\sqrt{(8125 - 7225)(18,625 - 18,225)}}$$

$$= \frac{450}{\sqrt{(900)(400)}} = \frac{450}{600} = 0.75$$

The Pearson correlation coefficient is used in a variety of situations in which one needs an indication of the relationship between two variables. For example, the correlation coefficient can be used to help determine the predictive validity of a test. In the previous example, the two variables are reading readiness and reading achievement scores. If the achievement scores were obtained several months after the readiness scores, the correlation coefficient would indicate the predictive validity of the reading readiness test. In other words, the coefficient would describe how well scores on the reading readiness test are related to later scores on the reading achievement test.

The Pearson correlation can also be used to indicate the reliability of a test. For example, if each of the previous five students were later retested on the reading readiness test, we would then have two scores for each student: an initial score and a subsequent score. Using these pairs of scores for the X and Y variables in Formula A.3, we could compute the correlation between scores on the test and retest. This would be the test–retest reliability coefficient.

Likewise, if there were two forms of the reading readiness test and each of the previous five students was administered both forms, we would again have two scores for each student: the score on the first form of the test and the score on the second form. Using these pairs of scores in Formula A.3, we could compute the correlation between students' scores on the two forms of the test. This would be the alternate-form reliability coefficient.

Computation of Kuder–Richardson Formula 21 Reliability

When computing an index of internal-consistency reliability by hand, the Kuder–Richardson formula 21 (KR-21) reliability coefficient involves one of the easier computations. The formula for KR-21 is

$$KR\text{-}21 = \frac{k}{k-1}\left(1 - \frac{M - \frac{M^2}{k}}{SD^2}\right) \qquad (A.4)$$

where k = the number of items on the test
M = the mean of the scores on the test
SD = the standard deviation of scores on the test

For the previous five students, the mean on the reading readiness test was calculated to be 17.0 and the standard deviation to be approximately 6.7. If we were also told that this readiness test involved 30 items, we could then use Formula A.4 to compute the KR-21 reliability coefficient.

$$KR\text{-}21 = \frac{30}{30-1}\left(1 - \frac{17.0 - \frac{(17.0)^2}{30}}{6.7^2}\right)$$

$$= \frac{30}{29}\left(1 - \frac{17 - \frac{289}{30}}{44.89}\right)$$

$$= 1.03\left(1 - \frac{17 - 9.63}{44.89}\right) = 1.03\left(1 - \frac{7.87}{44.89}\right)$$

$$= 1.03(1 - 0.164) = (1.03)(0.836) = 0.861$$

Computation Using the Spearman–Brown Formula

As the number of items on a test is increased, the reliability of the test tends to improve. The Spearman–Brown formula estimates what the reliability coefficient will become after the number of items is changed.

$$r_{est} = \frac{nr}{1 + (n-1)r} \qquad (A.5)$$

where r_{est} = the estimated new reliability coefficient
r = the original reliability coefficient
n = the number of times the test is lengthened

For example, had the reliability of a 12-item test been found to be 0.50, the Spearman–Brown formula estimates that doubling the length of the test to 24 items will increase the reliability to

$$r_{est} = \frac{(2)(0.50)}{1 + (2-1)0.50} = \frac{1.00}{1.50} = 0.67$$

APPENDIX B

Professional Opportunities in Educational Measurement

An expanding number of career opportunities is available in educational measurement. You may wish to be aware of some of the options. Specialists work in a variety of areas such as identifying better techniques for measuring student performance, helping educators become familiar with capabilities and constraints of educational measurement, improving the accuracy of tests, researching statistical properties of tests, and investigating ways to use computers in measurements.

Individuals with masters and doctoral degrees in measurement are employed by schools, universities, research and development institutes, private industry, and state and federal governments.

Information concerning career opportunities, application procedures, and financial aid can be obtained directly from university departments offering degree programs in educational measurement. For addresses and other material, consult the graduate catalogs of universities. On the Internet, also check the Opportunities section of the National Council for Measurement in Education (http://ncme.org/). Graduate students in educational measurement typically have undergraduate majors or substantive work in mathematics, statistics, psychology, sociology, or education, although undergraduate majors in other areas are common.

REFERENCES

Airasian, P. W. (1997). *Classroom assessment* (3rd ed.). New York: McGraw-Hill.

Algozzine, B., & Mercer, C. D. (1980). Labels and expectancies for handicapped children and youth. In L. Mann and D. A. Sabatino (Eds.), *Fourth review of special education*. New York: Grune & Stratton.

American Psychological Association, Educational Research Association, & National Council on Measurement in Education. (1999). *Standards for educational and psychological testing*. Washington, DC: American Psychological Association.

Angoff, W. H. (1971). Scales, norms, and equivalent scales. In R. L. Thorndike (Ed.), *Educational measurement*. Washington, DC: American Council on Education.

Angoff, W. H., & Schrader, W. B. (1984). A study of hypotheses basic to the use of rights and formula scores. *Journal of Educational Measurement, 21,* 1–17.

Bangert-Downs, R. L., Kulik, J. A., & Kulik, C. C. (1983). Effects of coaching programs on achievement test performance. *Review of Educational Research, 53,* 571–585.

Berk, R. A. (1981). Focal point: What's wrong with using grade-equivalent scores to identify LD children? *Academic Therapy, 17,* 133–140.

Berk, R. A. (1982). *Handbook of methods for detecting test bias*. Baltimore, MD: Johns Hopkins University Press.

Berk, R. A. (1986). A consumer's guide to setting performance standards on criterion-referenced tests. *Review of Educational Research, 56,* 137–172.

Bliss, L. B. (1980). A test of Lord's assumption regarding examinee guessing behavior on multiple-choice tests using elementary school children. *Journal of Educational Measurement, 17,* 147–154.

Bloom, B. S. (Ed.). (1956). *Taxonomy of educational objectives: Handbook 1. Cognitive domain*. New York: McKay.

Bloom, B. S., Madaus, G. F., & Hastings, J. T. (1981). *Evaluation to improve learning*. New York: McGraw-Hill.

Braun, H. I., Bennett, R. E., Frye, D., & Soloway, E. (1990). Scoring constructed responses using expert systems. *Journal of Educational Measurement, 27,* 93–108.

Brown, F. G. (1983). *Principles of educational and psychological testing* (3rd ed.) New York: Holt, Rinehart & Winston.

Budescu, D., & Nevo, B. (1985). Optimal number of options: An investigation of the assumption of proportionality. *Journal of Educational Measurement, 22,* 183–196.

Bugbee, A. (1996). The equivalence of paper-and-pencil and computer-based testing. *Journal of Research on Computing in Education, 28,* 282–299.

Carter, K. (1986, Winter). Test-wiseness for teachers and students. *Educational Measurement: Issues and Practice, 5,* 20–23.

Cartwright, C. A., & Cartwright, G. P. (1984). *Developing observation skills.* New York: McGraw-Hill.

Chase, C. I. (1979). Impact of achievement expectations and handwriting quality on scoring essay tests. *Journal of Educational Measurement, 16,* 39–42.

Chase, C. I. (1986). Essay test scoring: Interaction of relevant variables. *Journal of Educational Measurement, 23,* 33–41.

Clauser, B. E., & Mazor, K. M. (1998). Using statistical procedures to identify differentially functioning test items. *Educational Measurement: Issues and Practice, 17(1),* 31–44.

Coffman, W. E. (1971). Essay examinations. In R. L. Thorndike (Ed.), *Educational measurement* (2nd ed.). Washington, DC: American Council on Education.

Cross, L. H., & Frary, R. B. (1977). An empirical test of Lord's theoretical results regarding formula scoring of multiple-choice tests. *Journal of Educational Measurement, 14,* 313–321.

Cullen, F. T., Cullen, J. B., Hayhow, V. L., & Plouffe, J. T. (1975). The effects of the use of grades as an incentive. *Journal of Educational Research, 68,* 277–279.

Daly, J. A., & Dickson-Markman, F. (1982). Contrast effects in evaluating essays. *Journal of Educational Measurement, 19,* 309–316.

Davey, T., Godwin, J., & Mittelholtz, D. (1997). Developing and scoring an innovative computerized writing assessment. *Journal of Educational Measurement, 34,* 21–41.

Davis, R. E. (1975). Changing examination answers: An educational myth? *Journal of Medical Education, 50,* 685–687.

Debra P. v. Turlington, 644 F.2d 397 (Atlanta Cir. 1981)

Deutsch, M. (1979). Education and distributive justice. *American Psychologist, 34,* 391–401.

Diamond, J. J., & Evans, W. J. (1973). The correction for guessing. *Review of Educational Research, 43,* 181–192.

Diederich, P. A. (1973). *Short-cut statistics for teacher-made tests.* Princeton, NJ: Educational Testing Service.

Divgi, D. R., & Stoloff, P. H. (1986). *Effect of the medium of administration on ASVAB item response curves* (Report No. 86-24). Alexandria, VA: Center for Naval Analyses.

Duchastel, P. C., & Merrill, P. F. (1973). The effects of behavioral objectives on learning: A review of empirical studies. *Review of Educational Research, 43,* 53–70.

Duncanson, J., & Chew, J. (1988, July). The ultimate link? *Byte,* 278–286.

Ebel, R. L. (1965). *Measuring educational achievement.* Englewood Cliffs, NJ: Prentice Hall.

Ebel, R. L. (1972). *Essentials of educational measurement.* Englewood Cliffs, NJ: Prentice Hall.

Ebel, R. L. (1982). Proposed solutions to two problems of test construction. *Journal of Educational Measurement, 19,* 267–278.

Ebel, R. L., & Frisbie, D. A. (1986). Essentials of educational measurement (4th ed.). Upper Saddle River, NJ: Prentice Hall.

Esposito, D. (1973). Homogeneous and heterogeneous ability grouping: Principal findings and implications for evaluating and designing more effective educational environments. *Review of Educational Research, 43,* 163–179.

Fabrey, L. J., & Case, S. M. (1985). Further support for changing multiple-choice answers. *Journal of Medical Education, 60,* 488–490.

Fisher, T. H. (1983). Implementing an instructional validity study of the Florida high school graduation test. *Educational Measurement: Issues and Practice, 2(4),* 8–9.

Fitzpatrick, R., & Morrison, E. J. (1971). Performance and product evaluation. In R. L. Thorndike (Ed.), *Educational measurement* (2nd ed., pp. 237–270). Washington, DC: American Council on Education.

Frary, R. B. (1989). The effect of inappropriate omissions on formula scores: A simulation study. *Journal of Educational Measurement, 26,* 41–53.

Frisbie, D. A. (1973). Multiple-choice vs. true-false: A comparison of reliabilities and concurrent validities. *Journal of Educational Measurement, 10,* 297–304.

Gaffney, R. F., & Maguire, T. O. (1971). Use of optically scored test answer sheets with young children. *Journal of Educational Measurement, 8,* 103–106.

Gagné, R. M. (1985). *The conditions of learning and theory of instruction.* New York: Holt, Rinehart & Winston.

Gallagher, J. J. (1976). The sacred and profane uses of labeling. *Mental Retardation, 14,* 3–7.

Haladyna, T. M., & Roid, G. H. (1983). Reviewing criterion-referenced test items. *Educational Technology, 23(8),* 35–38.

Haladyna, T. M., Nolen, S. B., & Haas, N. S. (1991). Raising standardized achievement test scores and the origins of test score pollution. *Educational Researcher, 20(5),* 2–7.

Hambleton, R. K., Mills, C. N., & Simon, R. (1983). Determining the lengths of criterion-referenced tests. *Journal of Educational Measurement, 20,* 27–38.

Haney, W. M., & Reidy, E. F. (Eds.) (1987). Golden rule or ruse? [Special edition]. *Educational Measurement: Issues and Practice, 6(2),* 4–25.

Hebert, E. A. (1992). Portfolios invite reflection—from students and staff. *Educational Leadership, 49,* 58–61.

Heppner, F. H., Anderson, J. G. T., Farstrup, A. E., & Weiderman, N. H. (1985). Reading performance on a standardized test is better from print than from computer display. *Journal of Reading, 28,* 321–325.

Hetter, R. D., Segall, D. O., & Bloxom, B. M. (1994). A comparison of item calibration media in computerized adaptive testing. *Applied Psychological Measurement, 18,* 197–204.

Hills, J. R. (1981). *Measurement and evaluation in the classroom* (2nd ed.). Columbus, OH: Merrill.

Hills, J. R. (1983). Interpreting grade-equivalent scores. *Educational Measurement: Issues and Practice, 2(1),* 15.

Holmes, C. T., & Matthews, K. M. (1984). The effects of nonpromotion on elementary and junior high school pupils: A meta-analysis. *Review of Educational Research, 54,* 225–236.

Horst, D. P., Tallmadge, G. K., & Wood, C. T. (1975). *A practical guide to measuring project impact on student achievement.* Washington, DC: U.S. Department of Health, Education, and Welfare, Office of Education.

Hoover, H. D. (1984). The most appropriate scores for measuring educational development in the elementary schools: GE's. *Educational Measurement: Issues and Practice, 3(4),* 8–14.

Hughes, D. C., & Keeling, B. (1984). The use of model essays to reduce context effects in essay scoring. *Journal of Educational Measurement, 21,* 277–281.

Hughes, D. C., Keeling, B., & Tuck, B. F. (1980). The influence of context position and scoring method on essay scoring. *Journal of Educational Measurement, 17,* 131–135.

Huynh, H. (1976). On the reliability of decisions in domain-referenced testing. *Journal of Educational Measurement, 13,* 253–264.

Kane, M. T. (1986). The role of reliability in criterion-referenced tests. *Journal of Educational Measurement, 23,* 221–224.

Karlins, J. K., Kaplan, M., & Stuart, W. (1969). Academic attitudes and performance as a function of a differential grading system: An evaluation of Princeton's pass-fail system. *Journal of Experimental Education, 37,* 38–50.

Kinney, L. (1964). *Certification in education.* Englewood Cliffs, NJ: Prentice Hall.

Kirst, M. (1991). Interview on assessment issues with Lorrie Shepard. *Educational Researcher, 20(2),* 21–23.

Kissock, C., & Iyortsuun, P. (1982). *A guide to questioning: Classroom procedures for teachers.* London: Macmillan Press.

Koretz, D., McCaffrey, D., Klein, S., Bell, R., & Stecher, B. (1992). *The reliability of scores from the 1992 Vermont portfolio assessment program: Interim report.* RAND Institute on Education and Training, National Center for Research on Evaluation, Standards, and Student Testing. (ERIC Document Reproduction Service No. ED 355 284)

Kuder, G. F., & Richardson, M. W. (1937). The theory of estimation of test reliability. *Psychometrika, 2,* 151–160.

Larry P v. Riles, 343 F. Supp. 1396 (N.D. Calif. 1972).

Lassiter, K. (1987, April) *An examination of performance differences of third graders using two types of answer media.* Paper presented at the annual meeting of the National Council on Measurement in Education, Washington, DC.

Leary, L. F., & Dorans, N. J. (1985). Implications for altering the context in which test items appear: A historical perspective on an immediate concern. *Review of Educational Research, 55,* 387–413.

Lee, J. A., Moreno, K. E., & Sympson, J. B. (1986). The effects of mode of test administration on test performance. *Educational and Psychological Measurement, 46,* 467–474.

LeMahieu, P. G., & Wallace, R. C., Jr. (1986). Up against the wall: Psychometrics meets praxis. *Educational Measurement: Issues and Practice, 5(1),* 12–16.

Linn, R. L. (1993). *Educational assessment: Expanded expectations and challenges.* (CSE Report 351). Los Angeles: University of California, National Center for Research on Evaluation, Standards, and Student Testing/Center for the Study of Evaluation.

Linn, R. L., Baker, E. L., & Dunbar, B. D. (1991). Complex, performance-based assessment: Expectations and validation criteria. *Educational Researcher, 20(8),* 15–21.

Linn, R. L., & Gronlund, N. E. (1995). Measurement and assessment in teaching (7th ed.). Upper Saddle River, NJ: Merrill/Prentice Hall.

Lo, M. Y., & Slakter, M. J. (1973). Risk taking and test-wiseness of Chinese students. *Journal of Experimental Education, 42,* 56–59.

Lord, F. M. (1952). The relationship of the reliability of multiple-choice tests to the distribution of item difficulties. *Psychometrika, 18,* 181–194.

Lord, F. M. (1977). Optimal number of choices per item: A comparison of four approaches. *Journal of Educational Measurement, 14,* 33–38.

Lou, Y., Abrami, P. C., Spence, J. C., Poulsen, C., Chambers, B., d'Apollonia, S. 1996). Within-class grouping: A meta-analysis. *Review of Educational Research, 66,* 423–458.

Mager, R. (1984). Preparing instructional objectives (2nd ed.). Belmont, CA: David S. Lake.

Marso, R. N. (1970). Test item arrangement, testing time, and performance. *Journal of Educational Measurement, 7,* 113–118.

Matthews, C. O. (1929). Erroneous first impressions on objective tests. *Journal of Educational Psychology, 20,* 280–286.

McMorris, R. F., & Weideman, A. H. (1986). Answer changing after instruction on answer changing. *Measurement and Evaluation in Counseling and Development, 19,* 93–101.

Mehrens, W. A., & Lehman, I. J. (1987). *Using standardized tests in education* (4th edition). New York: Longman.

Melton, R. F. (1978). Resolution of conflicting claims concerning the effect of behavioral objectives on student learning. *Review of Educational Research, 48,* 291–302.

Messick, S. (1989a). Meaning and values in test validation: The science and ethics of assessment. *Educational Researcher, 18(2),* 5–11.

Messick, S. (1989b). Validity. In R. L. Linn (Ed.), *Educational measurement* (3rd ed., pp. 13–103). New York: American Council on Education.

Messick, S., Beaton, A., & Lord, F. M. (1983). *National assessment of educational progress reconsidered: A new design for a new era.* (NAEP Report 83-1). Princeton, NJ: Educational Testing Service.

Messick, S., & Jungeblut, A. (1981). Time and method in coaching for the SAT. *Psychological Bulletin, 89,* 191–216.

Millman, J. (1973). Passing scores and test lengths for domain-referenced measures. *Review of Educational Research, 43,* 205–216.

Millman, J. (1981). Student achievement as a measure of teacher competence. In J. Millman (Ed.) *Handbook of teacher evaluation.* Beverly Hills, CA: Sage.

Millman, J., & Arter, J. A. (1984). Issues in item banking. *Journal of Educational Measurement, 21,* 315–330.

Millman, J., Bishop, C. H., & Ebel, R. L. (1965). An analysis of test-wiseness. *Educational and Psychological Measurement, 25,* 707–726.

Millman J., & Setijadi. (1966). A comparison of the performance of American and Indonesian students on three types of test items. *Journal of Educational Research, 59,* 315–319.

Millman, J., Slovacek, S. P., Kulick, E., & Mitchell, K. J. (1983). Does grade inflation affect the reliability of grades? *Research in Higher Education, 19,* 423–429.

Mitchelmore, M. C. (1981). Reporting student achievement: How many grades? *British Journal of Educational Psychology, 51,* 218–227.

Moss, P. A., Beck, J. S., Ebbs, C., Matson, B., Muchmore, J., Steele, D., Taylor, C., & Herter, R. (1992). Portfolios, accountability, and an interpretive approach to validity. *Educational Measurement: Issues and Practice, 11(3),* 12–21.

National Education Association. (1968). *Ability grouping research summary.* Washington, DC.

Nava, F. J. G., & Loyd, B. H. (1991). *The effect of student characteristics on the grading process.* Paper presented at the annual meeting of the National Council on Measurement in Education, San Francisco.

Nedelsky, L. (1954). Absolute grading standards for objective tests. *Educational and Psychological Measurement, 14,* 3–19.

Nitko, A. J. (1984). Defining "criterion-referenced test." In R. A. Berk (Ed.), *A guide to criterion-referenced test construction* (pp. 8–23). Baltimore, MD: Johns Hopkins University Press.

Oosterhof, A. C., & Coats, P. K. (1984). Comparison of difficulties and reliabilities of quantitative word problems in completion and multiple-choice item formats. *Applied Psychological Measurement, 8,* 287–294.

Oosterhof, A. C., & Glasnapp, D. R. (1974). Comparative reliabilities and difficulties of the multiple-choice and true-false formats. *Journal of Experimental Education, 42,* 62–64.

Oosterhof, A. C., & Salisbury, D. F. (1985). Some measurement and instruction related considerations regarding computer-assisted testing. *Educational Measurement: Issues and Practice, 4,* 19–23.

Page, E. (1968). *The analysis of essays by computer.* Final report submitted to Office of Education, Washington, D.C. Bureau of Research (ERIC Document No. ED028633)

Parents in Action on Special Education (PASE) v. Hannon, 74C3586, (N.D. Ill. 1980).

Poggio, J. P., Glasnapp, D. R., & Eros, D. S. (1981). *An empirical investigation of the Angoff, Ebel, and Nedelsky standard setting methods.* Paper presented at the annual meeting of the American Educational Research Association, Los Angeles.

Posey, C. (1932). Luck and examination grades. *Journal of Engineering Education, 23,* 292–296.

Powers, D. E., & Swinton, S. S. (1984). Effects of self-study for coachable test item types. *Journal of Educational Psychology, 76,* 266–278.

Rafoth, B. A., & Rubin, D. L. (1984). The impact of content and mechanics on judgments of writing quality. *Written Communications, 1,* 446–458.

Resnick, L. B., & Resnick, D. P. (1992). Assessing the thinking curriculum: New tools for educational reform. In B. R. Gifford & M. C. O'Connor (Eds.), *Changing assessments: Alternative views of aptitude, achievement and instructions* (pp. 9–35). Boston: Kluwer Academic Publishers.

Rocklin, T., & Thompson, J. M. (1985). Interactive effects of test anxiety, test difficulty, and feedback. *Journal of Educational Psychology, 77,* 368–372.

Roid, G. H. (1986). Computer technology in testing. In B. S. Plake & J. C. Witt (Eds.). *The future of testing* (pp. 29–69). Hillsdale, NJ: Lawrence Erlbaum Associates.

Ross, M. B., & Salvia, J. (1975). Attractiveness as a biasing factor in teacher judgments. *American Journal of Mental Deficiency, 80,* 96–98.

Rowley, G. L., & Traub, R. E. (1977). Formula scoring, number-right scoring, and test-taking strategy. *Journal of Educational Measurement, 14,* 15–22.

Salvia, J., & Ysseldyke, J. E. (1981). *Assessment in special and remedial education* (2nd ed.). Boston: Houghton Mifflin.

Salvia, J., & Ysseldyke, J. E. (1998). *Assessment* (7th ed.). Boston: Houghton Mifflin. A substantial part of the book is devoted to the review of tests widely used in special education.

Scruggs, T. E., & Lifson, S. A. (1985). Current conceptions of test-wiseness: Myths and realities. *School Psychology Review, 14,* 339–350.

Shanker, A. (1985). A national teacher exam. *Educational Measurement: Issues and Practice, 4(3),* 28–30.

Shavelson, R. J., Baxter, G. P., & Pine, J. (1992). Performance assessments: Political rhetoric and measurement reality. *Educational Researcher, 21(4)*, 22–27. Los Angeles: University of California, National Center for Research on Evaluation, Standards and Student Testing/Center for the Study of Evaluation.

Shavelson, R. J., Ruiz-Primo, M. A., Schultz, S. E., & Wiley, E. W. (1998). *On the development and scoring of classification and observation science performance assessments* (CSE Report 458). Los Angeles: University of California, National Center for Research on Evaluation, Standards, and Student Testing/Center for the Study of Evaluation.

Shepard, L. A. (1983). The role of measurement in educational policy: Lessons from the identification of learning disabilities. *Educational Measurement: Issues and Practice, 2(3)*, 4–8.

Shepard, L. A. (1984). Setting performance standards. In R. A. Berk (Ed.), *A guide to criterion-referenced test construction* (pp. 169–198). Baltimore, MD: Johns Hopkins University Press.

Shepard, L. A., & Kreitzer, A. E. (1987). The Texas teacher test. *Educational Researcher, 16(6)*, 22–31.

Shermis, M. D., & Lombard, D. (1998). Effects of computer-based test administrations on test anxiety and performance. *Computers in Human Behavior, 14*, 111–123.

Slavin, R. E. (1987). Ability grouping and student achievement in elementary schools: A best-evidence synthesis. *Review of Educational Research, 57*, 293–336.

Slavin, R. E. (1990). Achievement effects of ability grouping in secondary schools: A best-evidence synthesis. *Review of Educational Research, 60*, 471–499.

Spray, J. A., Ackerman, T. A., Reckase, M. D., & Carlson, J. E. (1989). Effect of the medium of item presentation on examinee performance and item characteristics. *Journal of Educational Measurement, 26*, 261–271.

Stallings, W. M., & Smock, H. R. (1971). The pass-fail grading option at a state university: A five-semester evaluation. *Journal of Educational Measurement, 8*, 153–160.

Subkoviak, M. J. (1976). Estimating reliability from a single administration of a mastery test. *Journal of Educational Measurement, 13*, 265–276.

Subkoviak, M. J. (1988). A practitioner's guide to computation and interpretation of reliability indices for mastery tests. *Journal of Educational Measurement, 25*, 47–55.

Swaminathan, H., Hambleton, R. K., & Algina, J. (1974). Reliability of criterion-referenced tests: A decision-theoretic formulation. *Journal of Educational Measurement, 11*, 263–267.

Taylor, W. L. (1953). Cloze procedure: A new tool for measuring readability. *Journalism Quarterly, 30*, 415–433.

Thurlow, M. L., & Ysseldyke, J. E. (1979). Current assessment and decision-making practices in model LD programs. *Learning Disability Quarterly, 2(4)*, 15–24.

Tierney, R. J., Carter, M. A., & Desal, L. E. (1991). *Portfolio assessment in the reading-writing classroom*. Norwood, MA: Christopher-Gordon.

Travers, R. (1981). Criteria of good teaching. In J. Millman (Ed.), *Handbook of teacher evaluation*. Beverly Hills, CA: Sage.

Tucker, J. A. (1980). Ethnic proportions in classes for the learning disabled: Issues in nonbiased assessment. *Journal of Special Education, 14*, 93–105.

Tuttle, H. G. (1997). Electronic portfolios tell a personal story. *Multimedia Schools, 4(1)*, 32–37. (Also available at *http://www.infotoday.com/MMSchools/jan97mms/portfol.htm*)

Um, K. R. (1995). Sampling effects of writing topics and discourse modes on generalizability of individual student and school writing performance on a standardized fourth grade writing assessment. Unpublished doctoral dissertation, Florida State University, Tallahassee.

Valencia, S. (1990). A portfolio approach to classroom reading assessment: The whys, whats, and hows. *The Reading Teacher, 43*, 338–340.

Wagner, R. K., & Sternberg, R. J. (1984). Alternative conceptions of intelligence and their implications for education. *Review of Educational Research, 54*, 179–223.

Weller, L. D. (1983). The grading nemesis: An historical overview and a current look at pass-fail grading. *Journal of Research and Development in Education, 17,* 39–45.

Wesman, A. G. (1971). Writing the test item. In R. L. Thorndike (Ed.), *Educational measurement* (2nd ed.). Washington, DC: American Council on Education.

Wilcox, R. R. (1976). A note on the length and passing score of a mastery test. *Journal of Educational Statistics, 1,* 359–364.

Wise, S. L., Boettcher, L. L., Harvey, A. L., & Plake, B. S. (1987, April). *Computer-based testing versus paper-and-pencil testing: Effects of computer anxiety and computer experience.* Paper presented at the annual meeting of the American Educational Research Association, Washington, DC.

Yalow, E. S., & Popham, W. J. (1983). Content validity at the crossroads. *Educational Researcher, 12(8),* 10–14.

Yen, W. M. (1997). The technical quality of performance assessments: Standard errors of percents of pupils reaching standards. *Educational Measurement: Issues and Practice, 16(3),* 5–15.

Ysseldyke, J. E., & Algozzine, B. (1982). *Critical issues in special and remedial education.* Boston: Houghton Mifflin.

Zandvliet, D., & Farragher, P. (1997). A comparison of computer-administered and written tests. *Journal of Research on Computing in Education, 29,* 423–438.

Zicky, M. L., & Livingston, S. A. (1977). *Manual for setting standards on the basic skills assessment tests.* Princeton, NJ: Educational Testing Service.

Name Index

Subject Index

D

Debra P. v. *Turlington*, 55
Decision making and mastery tests, 162–166
Declarative knowledge. *See* Knowledge, types of
Derived scores. *See* Grade-equivalent, Percentile rank, and Standard scores
Deviation IQ, 368, 407–408
Diagnostic evaluation, 8, 9, 10, 21–22, 274
Diagnostic tests, 348
Difference scores, reliability, 16
Difficulty of items. *See* Item difficulty
Directions. *See* Instructions for tests
Discrimination and cultural bias. *See* Bias, cultural
Discrimination knowledge. *See* Knowledge, types of
Discrimination of items. *See* Item discrimination
Distracters, multiple-choice, 115, 116, 122–124
Distracter analysis, 178–181. *See also* Item analysis
Distribution, normal, 363, 367
Domain-referenced. *See* Criterion-referenced tests
Domains and criterion-referenced tests
    adequacy of, 352–353
    ordered and unordered, 18–19

E

Eating before test, 291
Educational Resources Information Center (ERIC), 309, 357
Embedded alternate-choice items, 141–142
ERIC, 309, 357
Error in measurement, 372–374
Essay items
    advantages and limitations, 98–100
    analytical versus holistic scoring, 110–111
    assigning number of points, 103, 161–162
    brief-response versus extended response, 100–101
    checklist for, 107
    computer scoring of, 311–312
    qualities desired in, 100–106
    scoring plan, 102–106, 110–112
Estimating answers, 293–294
Evaluation
    versus assessment and measurement, 5–7
    defined, 5
    diagnostic, 8, 9, 10, 21–22
    formative, 8, 9, 10, 22
    preliminary, 8, 9, 10, 21
    of schools, 408–411
    of standardized tests, 355–357, 395–418
    summative, 8, 9, 10, 22

    of teachers, 408, 411–412
    types of, 8–9, 10, 274
Exceptional children, assessment of, 402–408
Extrapolated scores, 387–388, 390

F

Face validity, 54
Failing grades, 321–322
Focused alternate-choice items, 144
Formal assessments
    versus informal, 7–8, 191
    classroom roles, 8–9
    validity, 51–52, 56
Formative evaluation, 8, 9, 10, 22, 274–275
Formula scoring and guessing, 174–175, 295
Framework for assessment, 273–284

G

Gagné's categories of learning outcomes, 28, 29
Generalizability
    performance assessments, 218–219, 413–414
    types of, 78–79, 281–283
Gifted students, 403
Goals, 42, 227, 259–261. *See also* Performance objectives
"Golden Rule" strategy, 405
Gradebooks, electronic, 314–315
Grade-equivalent scores
    determining, 386–388
    interpreting, 388–392, 407–408
Grades, end of term
    basis for assigning, 326–330
    and cheating, 332
    checklists, 323–324
    and computers, 314–315
    difficulty of tests, 167–168, 320, 321
    disciplining students, 331,332
    failing students, 321–322, 332
    incomplete work, 331–332
    letter grades, 320–322
    motivating students, 327, 328, 331
    pass-fail, 322–323
    percentage, 320, 321, 385–386
    purposes of, 319, 327
    reliability of, 323
    setting standards for, 322, 328–330
    types of, 320–325
    weighting scores, 327–328
Group versus individual performance, 78